THE

WRITINGS AND SPEECHES

OF

GROVER CLEVELAND

From photograph by Pach Bros., N.Y.

THE

WRITINGS AND SPEECHES

OF

GROVER CLEVELAND

SELECTED AND EDITED, WITH AN INTRODUCTION,

BY

GEORGE F. PARKER

NEW YORK

CASSELL PUBLISHING COMPANY

104 & 106 FOURTH AVENUE

PREFACE.

WITH Mr. Cleveland's consent, I have gathered into this volume a representative collection of the speeches, public papers, and letters of a man who has been for many years the most prominent figure in his country. It gives, I think, under a fair classification, his opinion on all the topics upon which he has spoken. I am sure that, by means of it, the reader will be able to form a complete estimate of his character as it is shown in his public utterances.

The matter has been classified under twenty-five chapter headings. No reader, however critical, can know better than myself how difficult it is to make such a classification strictly accurate ; but, when it is considered that Mr. Cleveland has freely expressed his opinions, during the past ten years, upon every topic that interested his neighbors or his countrymen, and in every form common to public discussion, the result will, I am inclined to believe, be fairly satisfactory.

An attempt has been made, in the index, to indicate everything so plainly that no reader can have trouble in tracing what Mr. Cleveland has said upon any topic. Everything on the tariff question could not be placed in the chapter entitled "Taxation and Revenue." In his first message to the Common Council of Buffalo, and in speeches and letters accepting nominations, there are paragraphs giving his idea of the principles of taxation, which must be sought in them. The same is true of pensions, labor, and other questions. It is believed, however, that a clew to all these will be supplied by this completeness of the index.

The selections have been arranged under each chapter heading in chronological order. This, I am confident, will commend itself to readers, most of whom will, naturally, be attracted first to some particular part of the work, in the expectation of finding at once what may have been said upon a question in which they themselves are most interested. Under the plan adopted this will be easy.

Parts of messages have been separated and classified under their appropriate headings. Those familiar with the annual messages of an Executive know them to be composed of paragraphs treating of various questions. Such a document is subjected to no wrench when it is separated, and the various sections are incorporated under their proper headings. Except in two or three instances, each is complete, and when purely formal or local matter has been omitted, the fact is indicated in the usual way. Every speech is published in full.

The earlier speeches and letters have presented some difficulties. Most of them have been collected from the newspapers in which they were originally published; some after transmission by telegraph. I have had, however, some advantages in collating such documents and letters. As neither Mr. Cleveland nor anyone for him had had an opportunity to see them or correct errors in copying or transmission, when first published, he kindly consented to go over them with me, in order to correct misprints and to suggest the proper reading in a document which has puzzled by a text hopelessly mixed by some printer. I have also compared the documents, as carefully as possible, with official copies, and have been enabled, by these precautions, to correct a good many errors. In some cases I have done this by reference to manuscript documents in my possession. Most of the later speeches have presented no serious difficulty, because the proofs were carefully read when they were first published.

Before Mr. Cleveland's retirement from the Presidency, neither he nor anybody for him had kept his speeches with anything like system. I have found it necessary to make a careful search in order to discover some of the earlier speeches, some of which I found, upon inquiry, Mr. Cleveland himself had forgotten. Since March, 1889, I have carefully preserved copies of speeches and letters with the purpose, now carried out, of issuing them in book form.

So, if there are faults in editing or arrangement, they are mine. Mr. Cleveland has done no more than I have said. He merely gave me absolute authority to make the collection in such way as I chose, and I have done the best I could in both gathering and arranging it in such a way as to make it effective to students of our political history.

G. F. P.

INTRODUCTION.

The present generation of readers, studious of the history of our earlier days, and curious as to the lives and ideas of the men who made that history, has demanded new and complete collections of the works of the fathers of the republic. Two new editions of the writings of Washington compete for favor ; and when, in 1885, a change in party supremacy brought to the Presidency the representative of opinions long excluded from our national policy, an increased demand at once arose for the works of Thomas Jefferson. When the agitation of a great fiscal problem was begun in earnest in 1887, the advocates of the protective policy could find nothing better to illustrate their theories than by a recurrence to the report on Manufactures made by Alexander Hamilton, while Secretary of the Treasury in the administration of our first President. Interest in the opinions of men in our later history has also been revived until the works even of those within very recent times—always less accurately known than those more remote—have been added to the list. This impulse has adorned our political literature with many studies of great value to the future historian, and has enabled the reader of to-day to estimate, with some approach to accuracy, the character and achievements of the leaders of thought and action who have preceded him in the arena of politics.

No apology, then, is necessary for bringing together the

writings and speeches of a man who, during the past ten years, has so profoundly influenced the thought and action of his countrymen, and who has held, with the highest acceptance, the greatest official place in the gift of his fellow-men. Nor can it be deemed inappropriate if such a work is accompanied by a modest attempt to analyze in some degree the character of the man, as shown by his public utterances, or to measure the elements that gave him, within so brief a time, a unique position in the affections of his countrymen, and made him a power in a great nation.

In the rise and development of our public men, the legislative body has been so conspicuous in their training that it might not unfairly be termed the fitting school for the Presidency. Of the twenty-three men who have filled that august place, all but four saw service—most of them comparatively early in life—in Continental Congresses, in Constitutional Conventions, in one or the other House of Congress, or in State Legislatures. Many of them were conspicuous figures in such bodies, and the result in some instances was that their aspirations were early directed toward the lofty place which they were finally called to fill.

Some were thus brought prominently before their countrymen, in important positions, during a long term of years. Thus, Washington did not reach the Presidency until fourteen years after he had become the most conspicuous soldier of the New World ; nor Jefferson until a quarter of a century after he had made his name immortal by writing the Declaration of Independence. It was not until twenty-one years after he did his great work of collaboration in the writing of the " Federalist" that Madison became President. John Quincy Adams did notable diplomatic work thirty-one years prior to his election as President ; and his rival and successor, Jackson, did not finally reach the goal of his ambition until thirty-two years after he had entered public life, as the first representative of the then new State of Tennessee, in the lower house of Congress. In later times, James Buchanan's legislative career in Pennsylvania began forty-three years before his inauguration as President, while the like service of Abraham Lincoln, in Illinois, preceded his culminating success by twenty-seven years.

Without multiplying examples, it is plain that the public man who reaches this high office after such training must, of necessity, leave behind him, upon his retirement, a great body of writings and speeches. The genius of our institutions both permits and makes necessary the expression of opinion, by a public man, on a great variety of topics. It is only natural, however, that many of the early speeches of men thus trained should have little enduring value. In the inception of such service, entered upon in comparative youth and before the character is fully formed, speeches are made upon nearly every measure that may be introduced. These may contribute something to an intelligent understanding of an issue at the time, or even to its settlement ; but amid our rapidly changing political conditions, interest in both the speech and the question is soon lost. In most cases such oratorical efforts remain little more than temporary contributions to an issue restricted to a neighborhood or a State.

Grover Cleveland had none of this training in politics and oratory. Until his inauguration as Mayor of Buffalo, in January, 1882, his experience and discipline were entirely professional. While an assistant to the District Attorney of Erie County, New York—his first independent position as a lawyer—he was constantly engaged in the work belonging to a prosecuting officer. His speeches then had the same characteristics that have distinguished his public utterances since he came into political prominence. They were short, concise, carefully prepared, and never labored or showy either in matter or in delivery. His manner of speaking was earnest, well adapted, then as now, to both subject and audience. His cases were submitted with clear and direct statements of the law and the facts, and his arguments were made with such care that neither judge, jury, nor culprit had reason to complain of being bored with the loose, rambling legal talks so often indulged in by prosecuting officials.

From 1866 to 1882—with the exception of the years between 1871 and 1874—he was engaged in the active and unremitting practice of his profession. He had for his associates the best lawyers of the large city in which he lived, and as he was brought into contact, before the Courts, with the recognized leaders of his profession, he met his growing responsibilities with confidence and success. He proved himself equal to each new duty. He was actively engaged in politics only so far as an interest in local affairs or in the struggles of his party were involved. He seldom made a political speech, but his increasing professional labors kept him in constant training as a speaker, and he easily met the demands of his new position in this respect as in all others. He took part in memorial meetings held for the purpose of paying the last tribute of respect to members of his profession, and the earliest speech in this volume is that on the character of Oscar Folsom, his former partner and dearest friend, in July, 1875. He made others of the same kind, and achieved such success that he was called upon to bear his part on these occasions at his old home even after his election to the Governorship of his State. His judgment of men was shown to be just and discriminating, and his habit of careful preparation stood him in good stead. Another part of his training and practice that contributed much to his skill in saying clearly what he had in mind, was his work in drawing indictments and other law papers. To a natural facility for expression, he thus added a most exacting training.

It was not, then, a man untrained to clear and accurate statement, or unused to effective and eloquent speech, that astonished his neighbors and the people—always ready to welcome the advent of a man with ideas and character—by those vigorous messages which soon commanded attention from the people of a great State. As the result of this fitness for important place, Mr. Cleveland had an advantage never before enjoyed by a public man. Almost from the beginning of his career—it was only a year after these earliest messages until he had become Governor of the great State of New York—he was able to make his appeal to the waiting people of a nation, on all the great problems in which they were interested.

In spite of the demonstrated possession of effective oratorical powers, Mr. Cleveland made but few speeches before his inauguration as President. Into these he condensed much thought and food for thought. They were prepared with care, as neither then nor since has he permitted even the most exacting public duties to make him careless either as to thought or form. He knew what he wanted to say, or studied until he found out, and then showed that he could say it to advantage. His speeches were quotable. They were filled with epigrams and pithy sentences, easy of recollection for reader or hearer, and as they were short, everyone interested in the question was sure to read and to recommend them to his associates. His manner of delivery was earnest, and he early learned the art of putting himself into sympathetic relations with his audience. He did not speak until he felt that he had something his countrymen needed to be told, and was early recognized as a man who did not make speeches merely for the sake of talking, or with the purpose of attracting attention to himself. He showed a willingness to discuss the various and varied problems of our social and political life, without pushing himself forward or shirking the expression of opinion.

One of Mr. Cleveland's claims to distinction lies in the fact that he was the first President to take the country entirely away from the prejudices and traditions of the Civil War, while still preserving the great moral lessons that made it so real as an influence on national life and character. It was his good fortune to restore perfect confidence between the elements of a people long widely sundered. This had been talked about by every President and public man for a full score of years ; but his predecessors could not escape from their environment, or fully recognize the fact that old things had passed away and that all things were become new. The war left many problems, some of them more serious than a civilized nation had ever before known. But struggle or dream as he might, during the long period under discussion, no President could get away from prejudice and partisanship. The one great overmastering issue had been settled by the stern arbitrament of war. When it no longer remained as a reality it was still left to do duty as a tradition. Giant abuses had followed its settlement and in order to correct them the courage of the soldier must give way to that civic courage so rare among men, and so valuable to a people. This could not be found at once, and yet no perfect readjustment was possible until it was found, and the man representing it was installed in a commanding place.

Mr. Cleveland was elected President, and as the result of his wisdom, prudence, and foresight the war became merely an episode in our country's history. It was a glorious memory ; not a living issue about which parties must divide or men quarrel. The "conscious nationality," for which Lowell had longed, had come at last. The last canvass had been conducted on the ideas of twenty years before ; we now found a man whose patriotic aspirations were not bounded by the next election. Our national horizon was enlarged, and with this wider view, new thoughts and sentiments were aroused. The past was now so secure that both duty and necessity compelled a great people to look to the future with earnestness and hope. Coming thus into the new conditions which he did so much to create, there is nowhere in Mr. Cleveland's utterances any regret that the past had left problems for him and his generation to solve. He turns always with confidence and hope to the new duties that lie before his country or confront its leaders and people.

When courage, tempered by conscience, were combined with the power inhering in a great office, the value of the resulting service was simply incalculable. Mr. Cleveland has always impressed his countrymen with his belief that, however bad the conditions or the men they had produced, the virtue and intelligence of his countrymen were potent to save from the gravest perils. Yet he is not one of those who, calling themselves optimists, affect to believe that things will come

right without an effort to make them so, and as he has always emphasized the doctrine that the individual must work
and struggle with temptation and danger in order that he may
find or create opportunity, so to him the nation, the State,
or the community, is only an aggregation of units, and cannot
escape, without effort, the consequences of weakness, selfishness, or wrongdoing.

He never looks upon a temporary abuse as a necessary
effect or fixture of government by the people. So, always
and everywhere, he emphasizes the necessity for patriotic
effort. His exhortation to care and watchfulness shows how
deeply seated is the sentiment of faith in the right. With him
appeal lies to the good sense, the ingrained probity, the moral
purposes of his fellow-men. He insists everywhere that if
these are good in private life, and if the individual finds them
desirable and necessary, it is still more important that the
same principles shall animate the mass when it takes the form
of organized society. His speeches and letters show not the
least sign of demagogy. He no more appeals to the base pas-
sions of men when they are associated, than he would if they
could be resolved into their original units.

His countrymen already know Mr. Cleveland as a man of
tender heart, kindly toward his neighbors and the world, considerate of the interests of all, and indifferent to nothing
human. They will find in his writings and speeches, here
massed together, new and emphatic evidence of this sentiment.
He is interested in political problems because, in his view,
their discussion and right settlement will promote the happiness of his fellow-men. He insisted upon the honest and
decent conduct of the affairs of a city, because he believed
that the health, prosperity, and happiness of its people would

be promoted, and he has shown that he believes the welfare of the people of a State or a great nation should be the first concern of the men chosen to direct its destinies.

He emphasizes, at all times, the duty of economy and thrift, both public and private, because of his conviction that a plain and prosperous people must be a contented and a happy one ; and insists, with even more emphasis, that fine houses, great fortunes, and material prosperity should be only means to an end, and that end the greatest good of all. He saves the taxpayers' money from misappropriation, when convinced that its expenditure is wrong or that it is about to be devoted to useless or questionable purposes. He refuses to permit the bestowal of a pension upon an unworthy claimant, because it would do violence to the sentiment of honesty that animates him. While his kindness of heart is everywhere apparent, in act as well as in speech, he does not permit himself to do an act of charity with money derived from taxation, when placed at his disposal by reason of his official position, even though it might commend itself as worthy if appeal were made to him as an individual.

So, while he is the most practical of men, he is made so because every action is dictated by honor and duty. This faculty has enabled him to appeal to his countrymen in his individual right. With exalted conceptions of the dignity of a great office, and the ability and courage to fix the very highest standard in act, as well as in theory, his countrymen have given him the perfect confidence that comes to few public men—a confidence that never comes to the servant of the people unless he is at the same time a high type of man, morally as well as intellectually.

A man of this kind deals only with the serious concerns of

life. He does not take a light view of them. Though his sense of humor is keen, and he can hold unworthy men or groveling ideas up to ridicule in the most effective way, he could not make a joke on any question that had a moral issue in it, or on the character of George Washington. It is an interesting fact that such serious discussion should be welcomed from a man of elevated character with a great official dignity behind it. The number of public men who can command the attention of their countrymen upon the most important business problems is not large, and much of Mr. Cleveland's unquestioned popularity arises from the fact that he is the one President, since the war period, who has gained the unreserved confidence of his countrymen on great fiscal questions. Whatever men may think of his party affiliations or his views of public policy, there is agreement in the judgment that he will conduct the financial affairs of the nation with unquestioned safety. The secret of all this lies in the fact that he applies to every question as it affects the public the well-grounded moral principles which, according to his view, ought to govern men in their individual relations.

It has been fortunate for Mr. Cleveland and his countrymen that he was a man of mature years and thought before he began to speak, and that, from the beginning of his public career, he has never spoken at random. He did not have to conduct any oratorical experiments at the expense of his hearers in order to make his art useful. He was forty-four years old when, in those remarkable messages to the Common Council of Buffalo, he began a public career which, in a little more than three years, led him to the White House. He had learned to write and speak well while he was engaged modestly in the practice of his profession. But he had something infinitely better and more effective than a gift for saying things plainly and well. He had something to say. He had gone in and out before his neighbors, studying their needs and forming an opinion about the best way to correct the evils that he saw about him. With this knowledge of the existence of abuses, and his habit of carefully studying every question as it came before him, he had no difficulty in mastering it in all its bearings and in suggesting a remedy.

His speeches and public papers are not mere pointers on the political weather-vane, or the exposition of something that has already become popular. He deems it his duty to direct attention to wrongs, and when he finds a great one he attacks it with the same intelligence and energy that he shows when dealing with the many smaller ones included in it. He does not seek to alarm or to punish only petty offenders who are weak, in order to impress the public, while big and strong ones are left to escape. He shirks nothing. He will veto, ruthlessly, an ordinance awarding a city contract to a political and personal friend, when he knows that the bid is too high, or that bad methods have been employed to secure it. He cannot be induced to sign a bill for the reason that a political friend may think it useful to his own party. If his power is enlarged, he considers that his responsibility is increased in even a greater ratio. While he may condemn the cowardice that unnecessarily puts responsibility upon him, he does not shirk it and make excuse because a legislative body has dealt unfairly with him and the public interests. He applies to each case the test of morality as well as that of good sense, and emphasizes his belief that principle, as well as policy, is involved in every measure brought to him for action, and in every cause upon which he may be called to express an opinion.

His utterances have a consistency seldom found in those of public men who have come to high places. This does not arise from an obstinate attachment to opinions simply because he has formed or expressed them. As he seeks to measure every question by its moral bearings, and has done so all his life, he is not forced to argue himself into the conclusion that the thing that was right when applied to the business management of his city, can be wrong because the affairs or the business of the United States are involved. He will not do a thing, or refuse to do it, in order to impress the public. So far as official action or the expression of opinion on any public question is concerned, his own candidacy for an office, or the seeking of support, is not in his thought. If votes come to him or his party because he has done an honest or a courageous thing, he welcomes them; but if he is expected to win them by either doing a wrong or winking at it, he will not so much as consider it, and that would be a bold man who would dare propose it; nor does he have to convince himself in order to carry out such a policy in a responsible place, or to avow his sympathy with a good cause. If the existence of an abuse is admitted, and measures are concerted to attack it, his countrymen are never left long in doubt about his attitude toward it, nor do they ask themselves whether he will have the courage to avow his convictions.

This is well shown by his position upon some of the important questions he has been called upon to deal with in executive place. As Mayor, Governor, and President, he has insisted that the abuse of the taxing power was the most serious known to government. In his speech, accepting the nomination of Mayor of Buffalo, he expressed the opinion that "much can be done to relieve our citizens from their present load of taxation," and he insisted that "a more rigorous scrutiny of all public expenditures will result in a great saving to the community." The message of 1887 is no more than this. There is a change of scene, the magnitude of the evils involved is greater, but the principle is the same. This insistence that none but necessary taxes shall be levied and that the resulting revenues must be expended with economy, runs like a thread through everything that he has said, and has been a guiding principle in all that he has done; and yet there is nowhere a suggestion of niggardliness, or of a desire or willingness to put up with bad work in order that a few dollars may be saved.

When, in 1882, he became a candidate for Governor, his attachment to the principle of a reformed civil service was as warm, his understanding of it as correct, and his arguments for it as strong as they are in his latest message, speech, or letter. He avowed his attachment to the doctrines of the Pendleton bill while it was pending and showed that he knew what it meant then as well as he did after he had applied its principles in a practical way, and had proved himself the best and most effective friend that genuine civil service reform ever had.

When an agitation looking to the reform of defective election laws was entered upon, he avowed his sympathy with it at the first opportunity, and that, too, when he was only a private citizen and had no responsibilities either to be shirked or assumed. He saw clearly that while abuses of the election laws were not causes, they were at least the most serious of the effects produced by a bad system.*

* The franchise is not debauched in the interest of good laws and honest government. It is by those who have special interests to subserve at the

For many years, the free coinage of silver has been one of
the most serious of our unsettled problems.   The question had
been juggled with so much, so many compromises and sub-
terfuges had been resorted to that the public mind and conscience were much confused.   To Mr. Cleveland it has always
been plain.   Its dangers were just as clear to his mind when
he was first called upon to express his opinion upon it as they
were in February, 1891, when he wrote a brief letter which revo-
lutionized public sentiment and made impossible the adoption of such a policy by his party or Congress.   In doing this
he saw clearly what the interests of the masses of his countrymen demanded, and he fearlessly took his place on their side.

He has the knack of making new arguments as they are
needed.   He does not use all his ammunition at once.   If there
is to be only a skirmish, he knows that a musket may be as
useful as a howitzer, so he saves something for another skirmish or the general engagement that is certain to follow.   The
greatest parliamentary orator of the last century had for a colleague a man whose only speech was " I say ditto to Mr.
Burke."   Mr. Cleveland does not resort to this even with himself.   He is not content to repeat, year after year, the same
recommendations on a given question.   He brings to its discussion new resources.   He became interested in the Indian
problem, and set forth his opinions in his first message as
President, with force and intelligence.   In each succeeding
message, special or annual, he treated it always from a different
point of view.   He had studied its new phases, in the mean-

people's expense, and not by those whose interests are in common with the
masses, that the ballot is corrupted.   There are no rich and powerful corporations interested in buying " floaters " or coercing employees to vote for
a reformation of our tariff laws.—*Interview in the Nashville American*,
February 11, 1890.

time, with the same care that he had taken while it was new and strange. When all his opinions on such a question are gathered together, they acquire almost as much a connected form as if, after a careful study, he had written an essay upon it.

An advantage of classification according to subjects chronologically is that it shows no posing while in one office for another of higher dignity. Close attention to the duty in hand, a careful study of existing conditions and surroundings, the waiting not for the morrow—all these are manifest, whether the office be Mayor, Governor, or President. In each, the same principles govern his action and his sayings ; but there is nothing in his record while Mayor, or in his utterances while holding that office, to show that its incumbent was looking for higher honors ; or in his policy or speeches, while Governor, to indicate that he thought the Presidency might be within his reach. In each, he attempts for himself to do his duty, and his exhortation to others is to watchfulness, economy, and strict attention to the work in hand of public service. One of the great men of history was wont to say that "No one rises so high as he who knows not whither he is going "; and its truth is certainly shown by the career of the man who became President of the United States, without looking for it or any of the places supposed to lead to it.

His speeches are all brief. He seizes upon the idea or point of first importance or of practical value, and presents it with skill and emphasis. He does not attempt to explain all the steps he has taken to reach a given conclusion. As he does not speak until he feels certain of his opinion upon a question, so, when he announces his conclusion, it has in it a positiveness akin to dogmatism. He does not permit official position, or the dignity of an office he has held, to tie his tongue. Dealing, as he does, with principles and policies, rather than with individuals, his wonted plainness of speech is not affected by such an artificial dignity.

He puts himself directly in touch with the people, with no reference to any place he may have held, and is so accustomed to study the interest of the masses of his fellow-countrymen, rather than the desires of a class, that he has no reason for concealment or evasion. He speaks to them in plain, simple language, with never an attempt to " divide a hair 'twixt south and southwest side." He goes straight to his point. If he believes that some newspapers "violate every instinct of American manliness, and in ghoulish glee desecrate every sacred relation of private life," he says so, and he says it to the assembled representatives of the oldest and most dignified educational institution in his country. If he wishes to rebuke insolent partisanship, he does it by vetoing a measure favored by his party in his own city, and insists upon it in language that nobody can misunderstand or misinterpret. At the time that he defeated this bad purpose, he declared : " I believe in an open and sturdy partisanship ; but parties were made for the people, and I am unwilling, knowingly, to give my assent to measures purely partisan, which will sacrifice or endanger their interests."* In this case, the just precept accompanied the saving action, and as showing his consistency he epitomized this opinion many years later, by declaring, in an interview, that " party honesty is party expediency."

Two chapters of this book are given up to his advice to members of his own party; but there is nowhere a line, the motive of which is partisan and nothing more. In every speech or letter to a Democratic meeting or club will be

* Message vetoing the amendments to the Buffalo charter, April 9, 1883.

found the expression of the loftiest patriotism. He believes in his party, but insists that it shall be true to its ideas and principles ; that it shall reach the people of the country through their conscience, and that it shall have the impulses and purposes of patriotism, not the hope that springs from selfishness in the individual or the mass, or the ambition that is aroused only by the love of power. In point of fact, he does not lower his standard when he addresses a meeting of his party friends, recognizing that if one-half of his fellow-countrymen make a public policy, it ought to be one that promotes the interests of all of them. Nothing ignoble is suggested or even left to inference ; there is nowhere a hint that questionable means might be employed by a candidate, in order to insure success, or by a party in order that it may secure or maintain supremacy.

Mr. Cleveland's writings and speeches have little of the personal or autobiographic element. He seldom draws directly upon his own career or public service for an illustration. He does not say : " I did so and so at such and such a time." And yet his opinions are, in large degree, the result of his own experience. Few of them have come from inheritance or from a merely scholastic study of a question. They reflect his early surroundings, or come from his close relations with, and intimate knowledge of, men. His life has been one of intelligent effort and great success ; so, if he seeks to enforce upon his countrymen the value of hard work, he but cons anew the lesson of his own life. He insists upon the most scrupulous regard for public honesty, because he believes this to be as plainly his duty as it is to pay his debts or to tell the truth. He appreciates Washington's tenderness for his mother because he himself showed the same filial love and devotion, and looked to his widowed mother for guidance and comfort during more than a quarter of a century after he had left his home. He sympathizes the more keenly with charities and the poor, because his early experiences made him acquainted with the hardships of plain people in all the relations of life.

It is not necessary, in considering Mr. Cleveland's style, to seek a model for it. He is simply an example of a man who uses speech to express his thoughts, having no sympathy with Voltaire's definition, which reverses this process. He fits manner to matter with ease, and expresses his ideas with no less of grace than of force ; but he never strives for effect or show. Some of his messages to Congress have a beauty and fineness of expression that make them rare and notable of their kind. Many of his speeches appeal to the educated, by the felicity of their expression, quite as distinctly as they do to the plain people of the land by their manly vigor and unquestioned good sense. At times, his utterance is Hebraic in its plainness of speech, as it is in the loftiness of thought and motive. Whether in commendation of the right, or in condemnation of the wrong, his meaning is as clear as sunshine, and no man, however plain, can have excuse for misunderstanding a single word ; and none, however refined, can, with the least reason, charge him with making appeal to groveling tastes, or with seeking to promote personal ambitions or interests.

In spite of the growing influence of the press, of which we hear so much these days, or, it may be, because of it, there has never been a time when the written or spoken words of the man fitted to lead had so much influence upon the formation of individual opinion, or upon that peculiar product called public sentiment. Whatever the man of vigorous mind and personality and rugged honesty may say, the people of this and every other free country are waiting to hear it as they never waited before.

In spite of the development of localism, there is an almost universal desire to hear something from the men who have risen so far superior to its trammels that they can be trusted to consider the good of all rather than the desires of the few. During recent years none has won this public confidence in so high a degree as the man whose thoughts, on a great variety of questions, are here brought together in collected form. Some of this may come because he has filled acceptably an exalted office ; but most of it arises from the fact that he has held the strong and sensible opinions that gave new dignity and importance to a place with great power and opportunities and that he has always expressed them with freedom and emphasis.

This is well shown by the position he has held as the apostle of a great idea since his retirement from the Presidency. Not only has he remained the first citizen of his country, but he has kept this place because he had gained and never abused the confidence of his countrymen. Behind all that he has said were the great, sturdy character, the trained intelligence, and the tender heart of a man who had risen superior to personal ambitions or comfort, one who had demonstrated, during all his public career, whether in or out of place, his devotion to the true interests of the people, and his indifference to praise or blame when advocacy of their interests demanded the telling of the whole truth. His countrymen have rewarded this unselfishness with the most devoted attention. In the remotest parts of the Union, that he has done so much to render more perfect, his words have been read with the same attention they commanded from those who listened to them in a banqueting hall or in a political meeting.

Such a position is not the result of accident or merely a tribute to an office from which its holder has retired, or to which he may even be called again. It is due to the fact that, though a people may wait long for a man of power, it knows him when he comes, and gives him the recognition he deserves. Such a man has a double claim to favor, that for things said as well as for things done. In the one case it makes Grover Cleveland the recognized friend of every good cause, whether he is able to promote it with official power or not; in the other, it makes him, in public station, the active promoter of the doctrines to which he may have given his adhesion as a citizen.

The works of such a man, still living among his countrymen and potent in every good cause, may well challenge attention and command study.

GEORGE F. PARKER.

NEW YORK, *June* 25, 1892.

CONTENTS.

THE WRITINGS AND SPEECHES OF

GROVER CLEVELAND.

CHAPTER I.

SPEECHES AND LETTERS ACCEPTING NOMINATIONS.

I.

Speech before City Convention, Buffalo, October 25, 1881.

GENTLEMEN OF THE CONVENTION:

I am informed that you have bestowed upon me the nomination for the office of Mayor. It certainly is a great honor to be thought fit to be the chief officer of a great and prosperous city like ours, having such important and varied interests. I hoped that your choice might fall upon some other and more worthy member of the city Democracy, for personal and private considerations have made the question of acceptance on my part a difficult one. But because I am a Democrat, and because I think no one has a right, at this time of all others, to consult his own inclinations as against the call of his party and fellow-citizens, and hoping that I may be of use to you in your efforts to inaugurate a better rule in municipal affairs, I accept the nomination tendered me.

I believe that much can be done to relieve our citizens from their present load of taxation, and that a more rigid scrutiny of all public expenditures will result in a great saving to the community.   I also believe that some extravagance in our city government may be corrected without injury to the public service.

There is, or there should be, no reason why the affairs of our city should not be managed with the same care and the same economy as private interests.   And when we consider that public officials are the trustees of the people, and hold their places and exercise their powers for the benefit of the people, there should be no higher inducement to a faithful and honest discharge of public duty.

These are very old truths; but I cannot forbear to speak in this strain to-day, because I believe the time has come when the people loudly demand that these principles shall be, sincerely and without mental reservation, adopted as a rule of conduct.   And I am assured that the result of the campaign upon which we enter to-day will demonstrate that the citizens of Buffalo will not tolerate the man or the party that has been unfaithful to public trusts.

I say these things to a convention of Democrats, because I know that the grand old party is honest, and they cannot be unwelcome to you.

Let us, then, in all sincerity, promise the people an improvement in our municipal affairs; and if the opportunity is offered us, as it surely will be, let us faithfully keep that promise.   By this means, and by this means alone, can our success rest upon a firm foundation and our party ascendency be permanently assured.   Our opponents will wage a bitter and determined warfare, but with united and hearty effort we shall achieve a victory for our entire ticket.

And at this day, and with my record before you, I trust it is unnecessary for me to pledge to you my most earnest endeavors to bring about this result; and, if elected to the position for which you have nominated me, I shall do my whole duty to the party, but none the less, I hope, to the citizens of Buffalo.

II.

Letter Accepting Nomination for Governor.

BUFFALO, N. Y., October 7, 1882.

DEAR SIR: I beg to acknowledge the receipt of your letter informing me of my nomination for Governor by the Democratic State Convention, lately held at the city of Syracuse.

I accept the nomination thus tendered to me, and trust that, while I am gratefully sensible of the honor conferred, I am also properly impressed with the responsibilities which it invites.

The platform of principles adopted by the convention meets with my hearty approval. The doctrines therein enunciated are so distinctly and explicitly stated that their amplification seems scarcely necessary. If elected to the office for which I have been nominated, I shall endeavor to impress them upon my administration and make them the policy of the State.

Our citizens for the most part attach themselves to one or the other of the great political parties; and, under ordinary circumstances, they support the nominees of the party to which they profess fealty.

It is quite apparent that under such circumstances the primary election or caucus should be surrounded by such safeguards as will secure absolutely free and uncontrolled action. Here the people themselves are supposed to speak; here they put their hands to the machinery of government, and in this place should be found the manifestations of the popular will.

When by fraud, intimidation, or any other questionable practice the voice of the people is here smothered, a direct blow is aimed at a most precious right, and one which the law should be swift to protect.

If the primary election is uncontaminated and fairly conducted, those there chosen to represent the people will go forth with the impress of the people's will upon them, and the benefits and purposes of a truly representative government will be attained.

Public officers are the servants and agents of the people to execute laws which the people have made, and within the limits of a constitution which they have established.

Hence the interference of officials of any degree, and whether State or Federal, for the purpose of thwarting or controlling the popular wish, should not be tolerated.

Subordinates in public place should be selected and retained for their efficiency, and not because they may be used to accomplish partisan ends. The people have a right to demand, here, as in cases of private employment, that their money be paid to those who will render the best service in return, and that the appointment to, and tenure of, such places should depend upon ability and merit. If the clerks and assistants in public departments were paid the same compensation and required to do the same amount of work as those employed in prudently conducted private establishments, the anxiety to hold these public places would be much diminished, and, it seems to me, the cause of civil service reform materially aided.

The system of levying assessments, for partisan purposes, on those holding office or place, cannot be too strongly condemned. Through the thin disguise of voluntary contributions, this is seen to be naked extortion, reducing the compensation which should be honestly earned and swelling a fund used to debauch the people and defeat the popular will.

I am unalterably opposed to the interference by the Legislature with the government of municipalities. I believe in the intelligence of the people when left to an honest freedom in their choice, and that when the citizens of any section of the State have determined upon the details of a local government, they should be left in the undisturbed enjoyment of the same. The doctrine of home rule, as I understand it, lies at the foundation of republican institutions, and cannot be too strongly insisted upon.

Corporations are created by the law for certain defined purposes, and are restricted in their operations by specific limitations. Acting within their legitimate sphere they should be protected; but when by combination, or by the exercise of unwarranted power, they oppress the people, the same authority which created should restrain them and protect the rights of the citizen. The law lately passed for the purpose of adjusting the relations between the people and corporations should be executed in good faith, with an honest design to effectuate its objects and with a due regard for the interests involved.

The laboring classes constitute the main part of our population. They should be protected in their efforts peaceably to assert their rights when endangered by aggregated capital, and all statutes on this subject should recognize the care of the State for honest toil, and be framed with a view of improving the condition of the workingman.

We have so lately had a demonstration of the value of our citizen soldiery in time of peril, that it seems to me no argument is necessary to prove that it should be maintained in a state of efficiency, so that its usefulness shall not be impaired.

Certain amendments to the constitution of our State, involving the management of our canals, are to be passed upon at the coming election. This subject affects divers interests, and, of course, gives rise to opposite opinions. It is in the hands of the sovereign people for final settlement; and as the question is thus removed from State legislation, any statement of my opinion in regard to it, at this time, would, I think, be out of place. I am confident that the people will intelligently examine the merits of the subject, and determine where the preponderance of interest lies.

The expenditure of money to influence the action of the people at the polls, or to secure legislation, is calculated to excite the gravest concern. When this pernicious agency is successfully employed, a representative form of government becomes a sham, and laws passed under its baleful influence cease to protect, but are made the means by which the rights of the people are sacrificed and the public treasury despoiled. It is useless and foolish to shut our eyes to the fact that this

evil exists among us, and the party which leads in an honest
effort to return to better and purer methods will receive the
confidence of our citizens and secure their support. It is
willful blindness not to see that the people care but little for
party obligations when they are invoked, to countenance and
sustain fraudulent and corrupt practices. And it is well, for
our country and for the purification of politics, that the people,
at times fully roused to danger, remind their leaders that party
methods should be something more than a means used to
answer the purposes of those who profit by political occupation.

The importance of wise statesmanship in the management of
public affairs cannot, I think, be overestimated. I am convinced, however, that the perplexities and the mystery often
surrounding the administration of State concerns grow, in a
great measure, out of an attempt to serve partisan ends rather
than the welfare of the citizen.

We may, I think, reduce to quite simple elements the duty
which public servants owe, by constantly bearing in mind that
they are put in place to protect the rights of the people, to
answer their needs as they arise, and to expend, for their
benefit, the money drawn from them by taxation.

I am profoundly conscious that the management of the
divers interests of a great State is not an easy matter, but I
believe, if undertaken in the proper spirit, all its real difficulties will yield to watchfulness and care.

Yours respectfully,
GROVER CLEVELAND.

III.

Serenade Speech in Albany, July 10, 1884.

FELLOW-CITIZENS:

I cannot but be gratified with this kindly greeting. I find
that I am fast reaching the point where I shall count the
people of Albany not merely as fellow-citizens, but as towns-
men and neighbors.

On this occasion, I am, of course, aware that you pay no compliment to a citizen, and present no personal tribute, but that you have come to demonstrate your loyalty and devotion to a cause in which you are heartily enlisted.

The American people are about to exercise, in its highest sense, their power of right and sovereignty. They are to call in review before them their public servants and the representatives of political parties, and demand of them an account of their stewardship.

Parties may be so long in power, and may become so arrogant and careless of the interests of the people, as to grow heedless of their responsibility to their masters. But the time comes, as certainly as death, when the people weigh them in the balance.

The issues to be adjudicated by the nation's great assize are made up and are about to be submitted.

We believe that the people are not receiving at the hands of the party which, for nearly twenty-four years, has directed the affairs of the nation, the full benefits to which they are entitled —of a pure, just, and economical rule—and we believe that the ascendency of genuine Democratic principles will insure a better government, and greater happiness and prosperity to all the people.

To reach the sober thought of the nation, and to dislodge an enemy intrenched behind spoils and patronage, involve a struggle, which, if we under-estimate, we invite defeat. I am profoundly impressed with the responsibility of the part assigned to me in this contest. My heart, I know, is in the cause, and I pledge you that no effort of mine shall be wanting to secure the victory which I believe to be within the achievement of the Democratic hosts.

Let us, then, enter upon the campaign, now fairly opened, each one appreciating well the part he has to perform, ready, with solid front, to do battle for better government, confidently, courageously, always honorably, and with a firm reliance upon the intelligence and patriotism of the American people.

IV.

Response to Official Notification at Albany, July 29, 1884.

MR. CHAIRMAN AND GENTLEMEN OF THE COMMITTEE:

Your formal announcement does not, of course, convey to me the first information of the result of the convention, lately held by the Democracy of the nation. And yet when, as I listen to your message, I see about me representatives from all parts of the land, of the great party which, claiming to be the party of the people, asks them to intrust to it the administration of their government, and when I consider, under the influence of the stern reality which present surroundings create, that I have been chosen to represent the plans, purposes, and the policy of the Democratic party, I am profoundly impressed by the solemnity of the occasion and by the responsibility of my position.

Though I gratefully appreciate it, I do not at this moment congratulate myself upon the distinguished honor which has been conferred upon me, because my mind is full of an anxious desire to perform well the part which has been assigned to me. Nor do I at this moment forget that the rights and interests of more than fifty millions of my fellow-citizens are involved in our efforts to gain Democratic supremacy. This reflection presents to my mind the consideration which, more than all others, gives to the action of my party, in convention assembled, its most sober and serious aspect.

The party and its representatives which ask to be intrusted, at the hands of the people, with the keeping of all that concerns their welfare and their safety, should only ask it with the full appreciation of the trust, and with a firm resolve to administer it faithfully and well. I am a Democrat—because I believe that this truth lies at the foundation of true Democracy. I have kept the faith—because I believe, if rightly and fairly administered and applied, Democratic doctrines and measures will insure the happiness, contentment, and prosperity of the people.

If, in the contest upon which we now enter, we steadfastly hold to the underlying principles of our party creed, and at all times keep in view the people's good, we shall be strong, because we are true to ourselves, and because the plain and independent voters of the land will seek, by their suffrages, to compass their release from party tyranny where there should be submission to the popular will, and their protection from party corruption where there should be devotion to the people's interests.

These thoughts lend a consecration to our cause; and we go forth, not merely to gain a partisan advantage, but pledged to give to those who trust us the utmost benefit of a pure and honest administration of national affairs. No higher purpose or motive can stimulate us to supreme effort, or urge us to continuous and earnest labor and effective party organization. Let us not fail in this, and we may confidently hope to reap the full reward of patriotic services well performed.

I have thus called to mind some simple truths; and, trite though they are, it seems to me we do well to dwell upon them at this time.

I shall soon, I hope, signify in the usual manner my acceptance of the nomination which has been tendered to me. In the meantime, I gladly greet you all as co-workers in a noble cause.

V.

Letter Accepting Nomination for President.

ALBANY, N. Y., August 18, 1884.

GENTLEMEN:

I have received your communication, dated July 28, 1884, informing me of my nomination to the office of President of the United States by the National Democratic Convention, lately assembled at Chicago. I accept the nomination with a grateful appreciation of the supreme honor conferred and a solemn sense of the responsibility which, in its acceptance, I assume. I have carefully considered the platform adopted by the convention and cordially approve the same. So plain a statement of Democratic faith, and the principles upon which that party appeals to the suffrages of the people, needs no supplement or explanation.

It should be remembered that the office of President is essentially executive in its nature. The laws enacted by the legislative branch of the government, the Chief Executive is bound faithfully to enforce. And when the wisdom of the political party, which selects one of its members as a nominee for that office, has outlined its policy and declared its principles, it seems to me that nothing in the character of the office or the necessities of the case requires more, from the candidate accepting such nomination, than the suggestion of certain well-known truths, so absolutely vital to the safety and welfare of the nation that they cannot be too often recalled or too seriously enforced.

We proudly call ours a government by the people. It is not such when a class is tolerated which arrogates to itself the management of public affairs, seeking to control the people, instead of representing them. Parties are the necessary outgrowths of our institutions; but a government is not by the people when one party fastens its control upon the country and perpetuates its power by cajoling and betraying the people instead of serving them. A government is not by the people when a result which should represent the intelligent will of free and thinking men is or can be determined by the shameless corruption of their suffrages.

When an election to office shall be the selection by the voters of one of their number to assume for a time a public trust, instead of his dedication to the profession of politics; when the holders of the ballot, quickened by a sense of duty, shall avenge truth betrayed and pledges broken, and when the suffrage shall be altogether free and uncorrupted, the full realization of a government by the people will be at hand. And of the means to this end not one would, in my judgment, be more effective than an amendment to the Constitution disqualifying the President from re-election. When we consider the patronage of this great office, the allurements of power, the temptations to retain public place once gained, and, more than all, the availability a party finds in an incumbent whom a horde of office-holders, with a zeal born of benefits received and fostered by the hope of favors yet to come, stand ready to aid with money and trained political service, we recognize in the eligibility of the President for re-election a most serious danger to that calm, deliberate, and intelligent political action which must characterize a government by the people.

A true American sentiment recognizes the dignity of labor and the fact that honor lies in honest toil. Contented labor is an element of national prosperity. Ability to work constitutes the capital and the wage of labor the income of a vast number of our population, and this interest should be jealously protected. Our workingmen are not asking unreasonable indulgence, but, as intelligent and manly citizens, they seek the same consideration which those demand who have other interests at stake. They should receive their full share of the care and attention of those who make and execute the laws, to the end that the wants and needs of the employers and employed shall alike be subserved and the prosperity of the country, the common heritage of both, be advanced. As related to this subject, while we should not discourage the immigration of those who come to acknowledge allegiance to our government and add to our citizen population, yet, as a means of protection to our workingmen, a different rule should prevail concerning those who, if they come or are brought to our land, do not intend to become Americans, but will injuriously compete with those justly entitled to our field of labor.

In a letter accepting the nomination to the office of Governor, nearly two years ago, I made the following statement, to which I have steadily adhered:

The laboring classes constitute the main part of our population. They should be protected in their efforts peaceably to assert their rights when endangered by aggregated capital, and all statutes on this subject should recognize the care of the State for honest toil, and be framed with a view of improving the condition of the workingman.

A proper regard for the welfare of the workingmen being inseparably connected with the integrity of our institutions, none of our citizens are more interested than they in guarding against any corrupting influences which seek to pervert the beneficent purposes of our government, and none should be more watchful of the artful machinations of those who allure them to self-inflicted injury.

In a free country the curtailment of the absolute rights of the individual should only be such as is essential to the peace and good order of the community. The limit between the proper subjects of governmental control and those which can be more fittingly left to the moral sense and self-imposed restraint of the citizen should be carefully kept in view. Thus laws unnecessarily interfering with the habits and customs of our people which are not offensive to the moral sentiments of the civilized world, and which are consistent with good citizenship and the public welfare, are unwise and vexatious.

The commerce of a nation, to a great extent, determines its supremacy. Cheap and easy transportation should therefore be liberally fostered. Within the limits of the Constitution, the general government should so improve and protect its natural water-ways as will enable the producers of the country to reach a profitable market.

The people pay the wages of the public employees, and they are entitled to the fair and honest work which the money thus paid should command. It is the duty of those intrusted with the management of their affairs to see that such public service is forthcoming. The selection and retention of subordinates in government employment should depend upon their ascertained fitness and the value of their work, and they should be neither expected nor allowed to do questionable party service. The interests of the people will be better protected; the estimate of public labor and duty will be immensely improved;

public employment will be open to all who can demonstrate their fitness to enter it; the unseemly scramble for place under government, with the consequent importunity which embitters official life, will cease, and the public departments will not be filled with those who conceive it to be their first duty to aid the party to which they owe their places, instead of rendering patient and honest return to the people.

I believe that the public temper is such that the voters of the land are prepared to support the party which gives the best promise of administering the government in the honest, simple, and plain manner which is consistent with its character and purposes. They have learned that mystery and concealment in the management of their affairs cover tricks and betrayal. The statesmanship they require consists in honesty and frugality, a prompt response to the needs of the people as they arise, and a vigilant protection of all their varied interests. If I should be called to the Chief Magistracy of the nation by the suffrages of my fellow-citizens, I will assume the duties of that high office with a solemn determination to dedicate every effort to the country's good, and with an humble reliance upon the favor and support of the Supreme Being, who, I believe, will always bless honest human endeavor in the conscientious discharge of public duty.

GROVER CLEVELAND.

VI.

Speech to the Committee on Notification, June 26, 1888.

MR. COLLINS AND GENTLEMEN OF THE COMMITTEE:

I cannot but be profoundly impressed when I see about me the messengers of the national Democracy, bearing its summons to duty. The political party to which I owe allegiance both honors and commands me. It places in my hand the proud standard and bids me bear it high at the front in a battle which it wages bravely, because conscious of right; confidently, because its trust is in the people, and soberly, because it comprehends the obligations which success imposes.

The message which you bring awakens within me the liveliest sense of personal gratitude and satisfaction, and the honor which you tender me is, in itself, so great that there might well be no room for any other sentiment. And yet I cannot rid myself of grave and serious thoughts when I remember that party supremacy is not alone involved in the conflict which presses upon us, but that we struggle to secure and save the cherished institutions, the welfare, and happiness of a nation of freemen.

Familiarity with the great office which I hold has but added to my apprehension of its sacred character and the consecration demanded of him who assumes its immense responsibilities. It is the repository of the people's will and power. Within its vision should be the protection and welfare of the humblest citizen, and with quick ear it should catch from the remotest corner of the land the plea of the people for justice and for right. For the sake of the people he who holds this office of theirs should resist every encroachment upon its legitimate functions, and, for the sake of the integrity and usefulness of the office, it should be kept near to the people and be administered in full sympathy with their wants and needs.

This occasion reminds me most vividly of the scene when, four years ago, I received a message from my party similar to that which you now deliver. With all that has passed since that day, I can truly say that the feeling of awe with which I heard the summons then is intensified many fold when it is repeated now. Four years ago I knew that our chief executive office, if not carefully guarded, might drift, little by little, away from the people, to whom it belonged, and become a perversion of all that it ought to be; but I did not know how much its moorings had already been loosened.

I knew four years ago how well devised were the principles of true Democracy for the successful operation of a government by the people and for the people; but I did not know how absolutely necessary their application then was for the restoration to the people of their safety and prosperity. I knew then that abuses and extravagances had crept into the management of public affairs; but I did not know their numerous forms, nor the tenacity of their grasp. I knew then something of the bitterness of partisan obstruction; but I did not know how bitter, how reckless, and how shameless it could be. I knew, too, that the American people were patriotic and just; but I did not know how grandly they loved their country, nor how noble and generous they were.

I shall not dwell upon the acts and the policy of the Administration now drawing to its close. Its record is open to every citizen of the land. And yet, I will not be denied the privilege of asserting, at this time, that in the exercise of the functions of the high trust confided to me I have yielded obedience only to the Constitution and the solemn obligation of my oath of office. I have done those things which, in the light of the understanding God has given me, seemed most conducive to the welfare of my countrymen and the promotion of good government. I would not, if I could, for myself nor for you, avoid a single consequence of a fair interpretation of my course.

It but remains for me to say to you, and through you to the Democracy of the Nation, that I accept the nomination with which they have honored me, and that I will, in due time, signify such acceptance in the usual formal manner.

VII.

Letter Accepting Renomination.

WASHINGTON, September 8, 1888.

HON. PATRICK A. COLLINS AND OTHERS, *Committee, etc.:*

GENTLEMEN: In addressing to you my formal acceptance of the nomination to the Presidency of the United States, my thoughts persistently dwell upon the impressive relation of such action to the American people, whose confidence is thus invited, and to the political party to which I belong, just entering upon a contest for continued supremacy.

The world does not afford a spectacle more sublime than is furnished when millions of free and intelligent American citizens select their Chief Magistrate, and bid one of their number to find the highest earthly honor and the full measure of public duty in ready submission to their will.

It follows that a candidate for this high office can never forget that, when the turmoil and the strife which attend the selection of its incumbent shall be heard no more, there must be, in the quiet calm which follows, a complete and solemn self-consecration by the people's chosen President of every faculty and endeavor to the service of a confiding and generous nation of freemen.

These thoughts are intensified by the light of my experience in the Presidential office, which has soberly impressed me with the severe responsibilities it imposes, while it has quickened my love for American institutions and taught me the priceless value of the trust of my countrymen.

It is of the highest importance that those who administer our government should jealously protect and maintain the rights of American citizens at home and abroad, and should strive to achieve for our country her proper place among the nations of the earth; but there is no people whose home interests are so great, and whose numerous objects of domestic concern deserve so much watchfulness and care.

Among these are the regulation of a sound financial system suited to our needs, thus securing an efficient agency of national wealth and general prosperity; the construction and equipment of means of defense, to insure our national safety and maintain the honor beneath which such national safety reposes; the protection of our national domain, still stretching beyond the needs of a century's expansion, and its preservation for the settler and the pioneer of our marvelous growth; a sensible and sincere recognition of the value of American labor, leading to the scrupulous care and just appreciation of the interests of our workingmen; the limitation and checking of such monopolistic tendencies and schemes as interfere with the advantages and benefits which the people may rightly claim; a generous regard and care for our surviving soldiers and sailors and for the widows and orphans of such as have died, to the end that, while the appreciation of their services and sacrifices is quickened, the application of their pension fund to improper cases may be prevented; protection against a servile immigration, which injuriously competes with our laboring men in the field of toil, and adds to our population an element ignorant of our institutions and laws, impossible of assimilation with our people, and dangerous to our peace and welfare; a strict and steadfast adherence to the principles of Civil Service Reform and a thorough execution of the laws passed for their enforcement, thus permitting to our people the advantages of business methods in the operation of their government; the guaranty to our colored citizens of all their rights of citizenship, and their just recognition and encouragement in all things pertaining to that relation; a firm, patient, and humane Indian policy, so that in peaceful relations with the government the civilization of the Indian may be promoted, with resulting quiet and safety to the settlers on our frontiers; and the curtailment of public expense by the introduction of economical methods in every department of the government.

The pledges contained in the platform adopted by the late convention of the National Democracy lead to the advancement of these objects and insure good government—the aspiration of every true American citizen, and the motive for every patriotic action and effort. In the consciousness that much has been done in the direction of good government by the present administration, and submitting its record to the fair inspection of my countrymen, I indorse the platform thus presented, with the determination that, if I am again called to the Chief Magistracy, there shall be a continuance of devoted endeavor to advance the interests of the entire country.

Our scale of Federal taxation and its consequences largely engross, at this time, the attention of our citizens, and the people are soberly considering the necessity of measures of relief.

Our government is the creation of the people, established to carry out their designs and accomplish their good. It was founded on justice, and was made for a free, intelligent, and virtuous people. It is only useful when within their control, and only serves them well when regulated and guided by their constant touch. It is a free government, because it guarantees to every American citizen the unrestricted personal use and enjoyment of all the reward of his toil and of all his income, except what may be his fair contribution to necessary public expense. Therefore, it is not only the right, but the duty, of a free people, in the enforcement of this guaranty, to insist that such expense should be strictly limited to the actual public needs. It seems perfectly clear that when the government, this instrumentality created and maintained by the people to do their bidding, turns upon them, and, through an utter perversion of its powers, extorts from their labor and capital tribute largely in excess of public necessities, the creature has rebelled against the creator and the masters are robbed by their servants.

The cost of the government must continue to be met by tariff duties collected at our custom houses upon imported goods, and by internal revenue taxes assessed upon spirituous and malt liquors, tobacco, and oleomargarine.

I suppose it is needless to explain that all these duties and assessments are added to the price of the articles upon which they are levied, and thus become a tax upon all those who buy these articles for use and consumption. I suppose, too, it is well understood that the effect of this tariff taxation is not limited to the consumers of imported articles, but that the duties imposed upon such articles permit a corresponding increase in price to be laid upon domestic productions of the same kind; which increase, paid by all our people as consumers of home productions and entering every American home, constitutes a form of taxation as certain and as inevitable as though the amount was annually paid into the hand of the tax gatherer.

These results are inseparable from the plan we have adopted for the collection of our revenue by tariff duties. They are not mentioned to discredit the system, but by way of preface to the statement that every million of dollars collected at our custom houses for duties upon imported articles and paid into the public treasury, represents many millions more which, though never reaching the national treasury, are paid by our citizens as the increased cost of domestic productions resulting from our tariff laws.

In these circumstances, and in view of this necessary effect of the operation of our plan for raising revenue, the absolute duty of limiting the rate of tariff charges to the necessities of a frugal and economical administration of the government seems to be perfectly plain. The continuance, upon the pretext of meeting public expenditures, of such a scale of tariff taxation as draws from the substance of the people a sum largely in excess of public needs, is surely something which, under a government based upon justice, and which finds its strength and usefulness in the faith and trust of the people, ought not to be tolerated.

While the heaviest burdens incident to the necessities of the government are uncomplainingly borne, light burdens become grievous and intolerable when not justified by such necessities.

Unnecessary taxation is unjust taxation.

And yet this is our condition. We are annually collecting at our custom houses, and by means of our internal revenue taxation, many millions in excess of all legitimate public needs. As a consequence, there now remains in the national treasury a surplus of more than one hundred and thirty millions of dollars.

No better evidence could be furnished that the people are exorbitantly taxed. The extent of the superfluous burden indicated by this surplus will be better appreciated when it is

suggested that such surplus alone represents taxation aggregating more than one hundred and eight thousand dollars in a
county containing fifty thousand inhabitants.

Taxation has always been the feature of organized government the hardest to reconcile with the people's ideas of freedom and happiness.   When presented in a direct form, nothing
will arouse popular discontent more quickly and profoundly
than unjust and unnecessary taxation.   Our farmers, me-
chanics, laborers, and all our citizens, closely scan the slightest
increase in the taxes assessed upon their lands and other property, and demand good reason for such increase.   And yet
they seem to be expected, in some quarters, to regard the
unnecessary volume of insidious and indirect taxation visited
upon them by our present rate of tariff duties with indifference,
if not with favor.

The surplus revenue now remaining in the treasury not only
furnishes conclusive proof of unjust taxation, but its existence
constitutes a separate and independent menace to the prosperity of the people.

This vast accumulation of idle funds represents that much
money drawn from the circulating medium of the country
which is needed in the channels of trade and business.

It is a great mistake to suppose that the consequences which
follow the continual withdrawal and hoarding by the government of the currency of the people are not of immediate
importance to the mass of our citizens, and only concern
those engaged in large financial transactions.

In the restless enterprise and activity which free and ready
money among the people produces is found that opportunity
for labor and employment, and that impetus to business and
production, which bring in their train prosperity to our citizens in every station and vocation.   New ventures, new
investments in business and manufacture, the construction of
new and important works, and the enlargement of enterprises
already established, depend largely upon obtaining money upon
easy terms with fair security; and all these things are stimu-

lated by an abundant volume of circulating medium. Even the harvested grain of the farmer remains without a market, unless money is forthcoming for its movement and transportation to the seaboard.

The first result of a scarcity of money among the people is the exaction of severe terms for its use. Increasing distrust and timidity are followed by a refusal to loan or advance on any terms. Investors refuse all risks and decline all securities, and in a general fright the money still in the hands of the people is persistently hoarded. It is quite apparent that when this perfectly natural, if not inevitable, stage is reached, depression in all business and enterprise will, as a necessary consequence, lessen the opportunity for work and employment, and reduce salaries and the wages of labor.

Instead, then, of being exempt from the influence and effect of an immense surplus lying idle in the national treasury, our wage-earners, and others who rely upon their labor for support, are most of all directly concerned in the situation. Others, seeing the approach of danger, may provide against it, but it will find those depending upon their daily toil for bread unprepared, helpless, and defenseless. Such a state of affairs does not present a case of idleness resulting from disputes between the laboring man and his employer, but it produces an absolute and enforced stoppage of employment and wages.

In reviewing the bad effects of this accumulated surplus and the scale of tariff rates by which it is produced, we must not overlook the tendency toward gross and scandalous public extravagance which a congested treasury induces, nor the fact that we are maintaining without excuse, in a time of profound peace, substantially the rates of tariff duties imposed in time of war, when the necessities of the government justified the imposition of the weightiest burdens upon the people.

Divers plans have been suggested for the return of this accumulated surplus to the people and the channels of trade. Some of these devices are at variance with all rules of good finance; some are delusive, some are absurd, and some betray, by their reckless extravagance, the demoralizing influence of a great surplus of public money upon the judgments of individuals.

While, such efforts should be made as are consistent with public duty, and sanctioned by sound judgment, to avoid danger by the useful disposition of the surplus now remaining in the treasury, it is evident that, if its distribution were accomplished, another accumulation would soon take its place if the constant flow of redundant income was not checked at its source by a reform in our present tariff laws.

We do not propose to deal with these conditions by merely attempting to satisfy the people of the truth of abstract theories, nor by alone urging their assent to political doctrine. We present to them the propositions that they are unjustly treated in the extent of present Federal taxation, that, as a result, a condition of extreme danger exists, and that it is for them to demand a remedy and that defense and safety promised in the guarantees of their free government.

We believe that the same means which are adapted to relieve the treasury of its present surplus and prevent its recurrence, should cheapen to our people the cost of supplying their daily wants. Both of these objects we seek in part to gain by reducing the present tariff rates upon the necessaries of life.

We fully appreciate the importance to the country of our domestic industrial enterprises. In the rectification of existing wrongs their maintenance and prosperity should be carefully and in a friendly spirit considered. Even such reliance upon present revenue arrangements as has been invited or encouraged should be fairly and justly regarded. Abrupt and radical changes which might endanger such enterprises, and injuriously affect the interests of labor dependent upon their success and continuance, are not contemplated or intended.

But we know the cost of our domestic manufactured products is increased, and their price to the consumer enhanced, by the duty imposed upon the raw material used in their manufacture. We know that this increased cost prevents the sale of our productions at foreign markets in competition with those countries which have the advantage of free raw material. We know that, confined to a home market, our manufacturing operations are curtailed, their demand for labor irregular, and the rate of wages paid uncertain.

We propose, therefore, to stimulate our domestic industrial enterprises by freeing from duty the imported raw materials which, by the employment of labor, are used in our home manufactures, thus extending the markets for their sale and permitting an increased and steady production with the allowance of abundant profits.

True to the undeviating course of the Democratic party, we will not neglect the interests of labor and our workingmen. In all efforts to remedy existing evils, we will furnish no excuse for the loss of employment or the reduction of the wage of honest toil. On the contrary, we propose, in any adjustment of our revenue laws, to concede such encouragement and advantage to the employers of domestic labor as will easily compensate for any difference that may exist between the standard of wages which should be paid to our laboring men and the rate allowed in other countries. We propose, too, by extending the markets for our manufacturers to promote the steady employment of labor, while by cheapening the cost of the necessaries of life we increase the purchasing power of the workingman's wages and add to the comforts of his home.

And before passing from this phase of the question I am constrained to express the opinion that, while the interests of labor should be always sedulously regarded in any modification of our tariff laws, an additional and more direct and efficient protection to these interests would be afforded by the restriction and prohibition of the immigration or importation of laborers from other countries, who swarm upon our shores, having no purpose or intent of becoming our fellow-citizens, or acquiring any permanent interest in our country, but who crowd every field of employment with unintelligent labor at wages which ought not to satisfy those who make claim to American citizenship.

The platform adopted by the late National Convention of our party contains the following declaration: "Judged by Democratic principles, the interests of the people are betrayed when by unnecessary taxation trusts and combinations are permitted and fostered which, while unduly enriching the few that combine, rob the body of our citizens by depriving them as purchasers of the benefits of natural competition."

Such combinations have always been condemned by the Democratic party. The declaration of its National Convention is sincerely made, and no member of our party will be found excusing the existence or belittling the pernicious results of these devices to wrong the people. Under various names they have been punished by the common law for hundreds of years; and they have lost none of their hateful features because they have assumed the name of trusts, instead of conspiracies.

We believe that these trusts are the natural offspring of a market artificially restricted; that an inordinately high tariff, besides furnishing the temptation for their existence, enlarges the limit within which they may operate against the people, and thus increases the extent of their power for wrong-doing.

With an unalterable hatred of all such schemes, we count the checking of their baleful operations among the good results promised by revenue reform.

While we cannot avoid partisan misrepresentation, our position upon the question of revenue reform should be so plainly stated as to admit of no misunderstanding.

We have entered upon no crusade of free trade. The reform we seek to inaugurate is predicated upon the utmost care for established industries and enterprises, a jealous regard for the interests of American labor, and a sincere desire to relieve the country from the injustice and danger which threaten evil to all the people of the land.

We are dealing with no imaginary danger. Its existence

has been repeatedly confessed by all political parties, and pledges of a remedy have been made on all sides.

Yet, when in the legislative body, where under the Constitution all remedial measures applicable to this subject must originate, the Democratic majority were attempting, with extreme moderation, to redeem the pledge common to both parties, they were met by determined opposition and obstruction; and the minority, refusing to co-operate in the House of Representatives, or propose another remedy, have remitted the redemption of their party pledge to the doubtful power of the Senate.

The people will hardly be deceived by their abandonment of the field of legislative action to meet in political convention and flippantly declare in their party platform that our conservative and careful effort to relieve the situation is destructive to the American system of protection. Nor will the people be misled by the appeal to prejudice contained in the absurd allegation that we serve the interests of Europe, while they will support the interests of America.

They propose in their platform thus to support the interests of our country by removing the internal revenue tax from tobacco and from spirits used in the arts and for mechanical purposes. They declare also that there should be such a revision of our tariff laws as shall tend to check the importation of such articles as are produced here. Thus, in proposing to increase the duties upon such articles to nearly or quite a prohibitory point, they confess themselves willing to travel backward in the road of civilization, and to deprive our people of the markets for their goods which can only be gained and kept by the semblance, at least, of an interchange of business, while they abandon our consumers to the unrestrained oppression of the domestic trusts and combinations which are in the same platform perfunctorily condemned.

They propose further to release entirely from import duties all articles of foreign production (except luxuries) the like of which cannot be produced in this country. The plain people of the land and the poor, who scarcely use articles of any description produced exclusively abroad and not already free, will find it difficult to discover where their interests are regarded in this proposition. They need in their homes cheaper domestic necessaries; and this seems to be entirely unprovided for in this proposed scheme to serve the country.

Small compensation for this neglected need is found in the further purpose here announced and covered by the declaration, that if, after the changes already mentioned, there still remains a larger revenue than is requisite for the wants of the government, the entire internal taxation should be repealed, "rather than surrender any part of our protective system."

Our people ask relief from the undue and unnecessary burden of tariff taxation now resting upon them. They are offered instead—free tobacco and free whisky.

They ask for bread and they are given a stone.

The implication contained in this party declaration, that desperate measures are justified or necessary to save from destruction or surrender what is termed our protective system, should confuse no one. The existence of such a system is entirely consistent with the regulation of the extent to which it should be applied and the correction of its abuses.

Of course, in a country as great as ours, with such a wonderful variety of interests, often leading in entirely different directions, it is difficult, if not impossible, to settle upon a perfect tariff plan. But in accomplishing the reform we have entered upon, the necessity of which is so obvious, I believe we should not be content with a reduction of revenue involving the prohibition of importations and the removal of the internal tax upon whisky. It can be better and more safely done within the lines of granting actual relief to the people in their means of living, and at the same time giving an impetus to our domestic enterprises and furthering our National welfare.

If misrepresentations of our purposes and motives are to gain credence and defeat our present effort in this direction, there seems to be no reason why every endeavor in the future to accomplish revenue reform should not be likewise attacked and with like result. And yet no thoughtful man can fail to see in the continuance of the present burdens of the people, and the abstraction by the government of the currency of the country, inevitable distress and disaster. All danger will be averted by timely action. The difficulty of applying the remedy will never be less, and the blame should not be laid at the door of the Democratic party if it is applied too late.

With firm faith in the intelligence and patriotism of our countrymen, and relying upon the conviction that misrepresentation will not influence them, prejudice will not cloud their understanding and that menace will not intimidate them, let us urge the people's interest, and public duty, for the vindication of our attempt to inaugurate a righteous and beneficent reform.

GROVER CLEVELAND.

CHAPTER II.

I.

As Mayor of Buffalo, January 2, 1882.

To the Honorable the Common Council:

In presenting to you my first official communication, I am by no means unmindful of the fact that I address a body, many of the members of which have had large experience in municipal affairs; and which is directly charged, more than any other instrumentality, with the management of the government of the city and the protection of the interests of all the people within its limits. This condition of things creates grave responsibilities, which, I have no doubt, you fully appreciate. It may not be amiss, however, to remind you that our fellow-citizens, just at this time, are particularly watchful of those in whose hands they have placed the administration of the city government, and demand of them the most watchful care and conscientious economy.

We hold the money of the people in our hands to be used for their purposes and to further their interests as members of the municipality; and it is quite apparent that when any part of the funds which the taxpayers have thus intrusted to us is diverted to other purposes, or when, by design or neglect, we allow a greater sum to be applied to any municipal purpose than is necessary, we have, to that extent, violated our duty. There surely is no difference in his duties and obligations, whether a person is intrusted with the money of one man or many. And yet it sometimes appears as though the office-holder assumes that a different rule of fidelity prevails between

him and the taxpayers than that which should regulate his conduct when, as an individual, he holds the money of his
neighbor.

It seems to me that a successful and faithful administration
of the government of our city may be accomplished, by bearing in mind that we are the trustees and agents of our fellow-
citizens, holding their funds in sacred trust, to be expended for
their benefit; that we should at all times be prepared to render
an honest account to them touching the manner of its expenditure, and that the affairs of the city should be conducted, as
far as possible, upon the same principles as a good business
man manages his private concerns.

I am fully persuaded that in the performance of your duties
these rules will be observed. And I, perhaps, should not do
less than to assure your honorable body that, so far as it is in
my power, I shall be glad to co-operate with you in securing
the faithful performance of official duty in every department
of the city government.

It seems to me that the duties which should be performed by
this officer [the City Auditor] have been entirely misapprehended. I understand that it has been supposed that he does
all that is required of him when he tests the correctness of the
extensions and footings of an account presented to him, copies
the same in a book and audits the same as charged, if the
extensions and footings are found correct. This work is certainly not difficult, and might well be done by a lad but slightly
acquainted with figures. The charter requires that this officer
"shall examine and report upon all unliquidated claims against
the city, before the same shall be audited by the common
council." Is it not very plain that the examination of a claim
means something more than the footing of the account by
which that claim is represented? And is it not equally plain
that the report provided for includes more than the approval
of all accounts which, *on their face*, appear correct? There is
no question but that he should inquire into the *merits* of the

claims presented to him; and he should be fitted to do so by a familiarity with the value of the articles and services embodied in the accounts. In this way he may protect the interests of the city; otherwise his services are worse than useless, so far as his action is relied upon.

.   .   .   .

I am utterly unable to discover any valid reason why the city offices should be closed and the employees released from their duties at the early hour in the day which seems now to be regarded as the limit of a day's work. I am sure no man would think an active private business was well attended to if he and all his employees ceased work at four o'clock in the afternoon. The salaries paid by the city to its officers and their employees entitle it to a fair day's work. Besides, these offices are for the transaction of public business; and the convenience of all our citizens should be consulted in respect to the time during which they should remain open.

I suggest the passage of an ordinance, prescribing such hours for the opening and closing of the city offices as shall subserve the public convenience.

It would be very desirable if some means could be devised to stop the practice, so prevalent among our city employees, of selling or assigning in advance their claims against the city for services to be rendered. The ruinous discounts charged and allowed greatly diminish the reward of their labors; in many cases habits of improvidence and carelessness are engendered, and in all cases this hawking and trafficking in claims against the city presents a humiliating spectacle.

In conclusion, I desire to disclaim any dictation as to the performance of your duties. I recognize fully the fact that with you rests the responsibility of all legislation which touches the prosperity of the city and the correction of abuses. I do not arrogate to myself any great familiarity with municipal affairs, nor any superior knowledge of the city's needs. I speak to you not only as the chief executive officer of the city, but as a citizen proud of its progress and commanding position. In this spirit the suggestions herein contained are made. If you deem them worthy of consideration, I shall still be anxious to aid the adoption and enforcement of any measures which you may inaugurate looking to the advancement of the interests of the city and the welfare of its inhabitants.

II.

Address as Governor, at Albany, January 1, 1883.

GOVERNOR CORNELL:

I am profoundly grateful for your pleasant words and kind wishes for my success. You speak in full view of labors that are past and duty well performed, and no doubt you generously suppose what you have safely encountered and overcome, another may not fear to meet.

But I cannot be unmindful of the difficulties that beset the path upon which I enter, and I shall be quite content if, when the end is reached, I may, like you, look back upon an official career honorable to myself and useful to the people of the State.

I cannot forbear at this time also to express my appreciation of the hearty kindness and consideration with which you have, at other times, sought to make easier my performance of official duty.

FELLOW-CITIZENS:

You have assembled to-day to witness the retirement of an officer, tried and trusted, from the highest place in the State, and the assumption of its duties by one yet to be tried. This ceremony, simple and unostentatious, as becomes the spirit of our institutions, is yet of vast importance to you and all the people of this great Commonwealth. The interests now transferred to new hands are yours; and the duties here newly assumed should be performed for your benefit and your good. This you have the right to demand and enforce by the means placed in your hands, which you well know how to use; and if the public servant should always know that he is jealously watched by the people, he surely would be none the less faithful to his trust.

This vigilance on the part of the citizen, and an active interest and participation in political concerns, are the safeguards of his rights; but sluggish indifference to political privileges invites the machinations of those who wait to betray the people's trust. Thus, when the conduct of public affairs receives your attention, you not only perform your duty as citizens, but protect your own best interests. While this is true, and while those whom you put in place should be held to strict account, their opportunity for usefulness should not be impaired, nor their efforts for good thwarted, by unfounded and querulous complaint and cavil.

Let us together, but in our different places, take part in the regulation and administration of the government of our State, and thus become, not only the keepers of our own interests, but contributors to the progress and prosperity which will await us.

I enter upon the discharge of the duties of the office to which my fellow-citizens have called me with a profound sense of responsibility; but my hope is in the guidance of a kind Providence, which I believe will aid an honest design; and the forbearance of a just people, which, I trust, will recognize a patriotic endeavor.

III.

Address as President, at Washington, March 4, 1885.

FELLOW-CITIZENS:

In the presence of this vast assemblage of my countrymen I am about to supplement and seal, by the oath which I shall take, the manifestation of the will of a great and free people. In the exercise of their power and right of self-government they have committed to one of their fellow-citizens a supreme and sacred trust; and he here consecrates himself to their service.

This impressive ceremony adds little to the solemn sense of responsibility with which I contemplate the duty I owe to all the people of the land. Nothing can relieve me from anxiety lest by any act of mine their interests may suffer, and nothing is needed to strengthen my resolution to engage every faculty and effort in the promotion of their welfare.

Amid the din of party strife the people's choice was made; but its attendant circumstances have demonstrated anew the strength and safety of a government by the people. In each succeeding year it more clearly appears that our democratic principle needs no apology, and that in its fearless and faithful application is to be found the surest guaranty of good government.

But the best results in the operation of a government wherein every citizen has a share, largely depend upon a proper limitation of purely partisan zeal and effort, and a correct appreciation of the time when the heat of the partisan should be merged in the patriotism of the citizen.

To-day the executive branch of the government is transferred to new keeping. But this is still the government of all the people, and it should be none the less an object of their affectionate solicitude. At this hour the animosities of political strife, the bitterness of partisan defeat, and the exultation of partisan triumph should be supplanted by an ungrudging acquiescence in the popular will, and a sober, conscientious concern for the general weal. Moreover, if, from this hour, we cheerfully and honestly abandon all sectional prejudice and distrust, and determine, with manly confidence in one another, to work out harmoniously the achievements of our national destiny, we shall deserve to realize all the benefits which our happy form of government can bestow.

On this auspicious occasion we may well renew the pledge of our devotion to the Constitution, which, launched by the founders of the republic and consecrated by their prayers and patriotic devotion, has for almost a century borne the hopes and the aspirations of a great people through prosperity and peace, and through the shock of foreign conflicts and the perils of domestic strife and vicissitudes.

By the Father of his Country our Constitution was commended for adoption as "the result of a spirit of amity and mutual concession." In that same spirit it should be administered, in order to promote the lasting welfare of the country, and to secure the full measure of its priceless benefits to us and to those who will succeed to the blessings of our national life. The large variety of diverse and competing interests subject to Federal control, persistently seeking the recognition of their claims, need give us no fear that "the greatest good to the greatest number" will fail to be accomplished, if, in the halls of national legislation, that spirit of amity and mutual concession shall prevail in which the Constitution had its birth. If this involves the surrender or postponement of private interests and the abandonment of local advantages, compensation will be found in the assurance that the common interest is subserved and the general welfare advanced.

In the discharge of my official duty I shall endeavor to be guided by a just and unrestrained construction of the Constitution, a careful observance of the distinction between the powers granted to the Federal government and those reserved to the State or to the people, and by a cautious appreciation of those functions which, by the Constitution and laws, have been especially assigned to the executive branch of the government.

But he who takes the oath to-day to preserve, protect, and defend the Constitution of the United States only assumes the solemn obligation which every patriotic citizen, on the farm, in the workshop, in the busy marts of trade, and everywhere should share with him. The Constitution which prescribes his oath, my countrymen, is yours; the government you have chosen him to administer for a time is yours; the suffrage which executes the will of freemen is yours; the laws and the entire scheme of our civil rule, from the town meeting to the

State capitals and the national capital, are yours. Your every voter as surely as your Chief Magistrate under the same high sanction, though in a different sphere, exercises a public trust. Nor is this all. Every citizen owes to the country a vigilant watch and close scrutiny of its public servants, and a fair and reasonable estimate of their fidelity and usefulness. Thus is the people's will impressed upon the whole framework of our civil polity—municipal, State, and Federal; and this is the price of our liberty and the inspiration of our faith in the republic.

It is the duty of those serving the people in public place closely to limit public expenditures to the actual needs of the government economically administered, because this bounds the right of the government to exact tribute from the earnings of labor or the property of the citizen, and because public extravagance begets extravagance among the people. We should never be ashamed of the simplicity and prudential economies which are best suited to the operation of a republican form of government and most compatible with the mission of the American people. Those who are selected for a limited time to manage public affairs are still of the people, and may do much by their example to encourage, consistently with the dignity of their official functions, that plain way of life which among their fellow-citizens aids integrity and promotes thrift and prosperity.

The genius of our institutions, the needs of our people in their home life, and the attention which is demanded for the settlement and development of the resources of our vast territory, dictate the scrupulous avoidance of any departure from that foreign policy commended by the history, the traditions, and the prosperity of our republic. It is the policy of independence, favored by our position and defended by our known love of justice and by our power. It is the policy of peace suitable to our interests. It is the policy of neutrality, rejecting any share in foreign broils and ambitions upon other continents, and repelling their intrusion here. It is the policy of

Monroe and of Washington and Jefferson: "Peace, commerce, and honest friendship with all nations; entangling alliance with none."

A due regard for the interests and prosperity of all the people demands that our finances shall be established upon such a sound and sensible basis as shall secure the safety and confidence of business interests and make the wage of labor sure and steady; and that our system of revenue shall be so adjusted as to relieve the people of unnecessary taxation, having a due regard to the interests of capital invested and workingmen employed in American industries, and preventing the accumulation of a surplus in the treasury to tempt extravagance and waste.

Care for the property of the nation, and for the needs of future settlers, requires that the public domain should be protected from purloining schemes and unlawful occupation.

The conscience of the people demands that the Indians within our boundaries shall be fairly and honestly treated as wards of the government, and their education and civilization promoted, with a view to their ultimate citizenship; and that polygamy in the Territories, destructive of the family relation and offensive to the moral sense of the civilized world, shall be repressed.

The laws should be rigidly enforced which prohibit the immigration of a servile class to compete with American labor, with no intention of acquiring citizenship, and bringing with them and retaining habits and customs repugnant to our civilization.

The people demand reform in the administration of the government and the application of business principles to public affairs. As a means to this end civil service reform should be in good faith enforced. Our citizens have the right to protection from the incompetency of public employees who hold their places solely as the reward of partisan service, and from the corrupting influence of those who promise and the vicious methods of those who expect such rewards. And those who worthily seek public employment have the right to insist that merit and competency shall be recognized instead of party subserviency or the surrender of honest political belief.

In the administration of a government pledged to do equal and exact justice to all men, there should be no pretext for anxiety touching the protection of the freedmen in their rights, or their security in the enjoyment of their privileges under the Constitution and its amendments. All discussion as to their fitness for the place accorded to them as American citizens is idle and unprofitable, except as it suggests the necessity for their improvement. The fact that they are citizens entitles them to all the rights due to that relation, and charges them with all its duties, obligations, and responsibilities.

These topics, and the constant and ever-varying wants of an active and enterprising population, may well receive the attention and the patriotic endeavor of all who make and execute the Federal law. Our duties are practical, and call for industrious application, an intelligent perception of the claims of public office, and, above all, a firm determination, by united action, to secure to all the people of the land the full benefits of the best form of government ever vouchsafed to man. And let us not trust to human effort alone; but, humbly acknowledging the power and goodness of Almighty God, who presides over the destiny of nations, and who has at all times been revealed in our country's history, let us invoke his aid and his blessing upon our labors.

CHAPTER III.

I.

To the New York Civil Service Reform Association.

MAYOR'S OFFICE,
BUFFALO, N. Y., October 28, 1882.

GENTLEMEN:

In answer to your letter of inquiry, dated October 20, 1882, in relation to civil service reform, I beg to refer you to my recent letter accepting the nomination for Governor, in which many of the matters referred to in your letter are touched upon, and I assure you that the sentiments therein expressed are sincerely and honestly entertained, and are stated without any mental reservation.

I have no hesitation in saying that I fully approve of the principles embodied in the Pendleton bill relating to this subject, and that I should be glad to aid in any practical legislation which would give them a place in the management of the affairs of the State and of municipalities, so far as they can be made applicable thereto. I believe that the interests of the people demand that a reform in the national and State administrative service should speedily become an accomplished fact, and that the public should receive honest and faithful service at the hands of well-fitted and competent servants. When contests between parties are waged for the purpose of securing places for professional politicians, of high or low degree, whose only recommendation for appointment is their supposed ability to do partisan service, the people are apt to be defrauded by the displacement of tried and faithful servants, well able to per-- form the duties for which they are paid with the people's money,

38

and the substitution of those who are unfit and incompetent. In this way, the interests of the party may be subserved, but the interests of the people are neglected and betrayed.

This pernicious system gives rise to an office-holding class, who in their partisan zeal, based upon the hope of personal advantage, arrogate to themselves an undue and mischievous interference with the will of the people in political action; this breeds the use of dishonest and reprehensible methods, which frequently result in the servants of the people dictating to their masters. If places in the public service are worth seeking, they should be the reward of merit and well-doing, and the opportunity to secure them on that basis should be open to all. Those holding these places should be assured that their tenure depends upon efficiency and fidelity to their trusts, and they should not be allowed to use them for partisan purposes. The money they earn they should receive and be allowed to retain, and no part of it should be exacted from them by way of political assessments.

It seems to me that very much or all of what we desire in the direction of civil service reform is included in the doctrine that the concerns of the State and nation should be conducted on business principles, and as nearly as possible in the same manner that a prudent citizen conducts his private affairs. If this principle is kept constantly in mind I believe the details of a plan by which its adoption may be secured will, without much difficulty, be suggested. You refer especially to mismanagement in schools, asylums, and institutions of charity and correction, and to the difficulty of securing the construction of an additional aqueduct in the city of New York. Without being fully acquainted in detail with the evils and obstacles surrounding these subjects, I believe they may be remedied and removed by a due regard to the dictates of humanity and decency and the application of the principles to which I have alluded.

Yours very respectfully,

GROVER CLEVELAND.

II.

From Message to the New York Legislature, January, 1883.

It is submitted that the appointment of subordinates in the several State departments, and their tenure of office or employment, should be based upon fitness and efficiency, and that this principle should be embodied in legislative enactment, to the end that the policy of the State may conform to the reasonable public demand on that subject.

III.

The Second Message to the New York Legislature, Jan., 1884.

New York, then, leads in the inauguration of a comprehensive State system of civil service. The principle of selecting the subordinate employees of the State on the ground of capacity and fitness, ascertained according to fixed and impartial rules, without regard to political predilections and with reasonable assurance of retention and promotion in case of meritorious service, is now the established policy of the State. The children of our citizens are educated and trained in schools maintained at common expense, and the people, as a whole, have a right to demand the selection for the public service of those whose natural aptitudes have been improved by the educational facilities furnished by the State. The application to the public service of the same rule which prevails in ordinary business, of employing those whose knowledge and training best fit them for the duties at hand, without regard to other considerations, must elevate and improve the civil service and eradicate from it many evils from which it has long suffered. Not the least gratifying of the results which this system promises to accomplish is relief to public men from the annoyance of importunity in the strife for appointments to subordinate places.

IV.

Letter t> New York Civil Service Reform Association.

ALBANY, October 24, 1884.

HON. GEORGE WILLIAM CURTIS:

DEAR SIR: While my letter of acceptance, in that part devoted to civil service reform, has verbal reference to subordinates in public affairs, I am of the opinion that there are other officials of a non-political character, to whose retention in place during the term for which they were appointed the same considerations should apply. I am, of course, a Democrat, attached to the principles of that party, and if elected I desire to remain true to that organization. But I do not think partisan zeal should lead to "arbitrary dismissal for party or political reasons" of officials of the class above referred to, who have attended strictly to their public duty, and have not engaged in party service, and who have not allowed themselves to be used as partisan instruments, or made themselves obnoxious to the people they should serve, by the use of their offices to secure party ends.

Yours very truly,

GROVER CLEVELAND.

V.

Letter to the National Civil Service Reform League.

ALBANY, December 25, 1884.

HON. GEORGE WILLIAM CURTIS, *President, etc.:*

DEAR SIR: Your communication dated December 20, addressed to me on behalf of the National Civil Service Reform League, has been received.

That a practical reform in the civil service is demanded is abundantly established by the fact that a statute, referred to in your communication, to secure such a result, has been passed in Congress with the assent of both political parties; and by the further fact that a sentiment is generally prevalent among patriotic people calling for the fair and honest enforcement of the law which has been thus enacted. I regard myself as pledged to this, because my conception of true Democratic faith and public duty requires that this, and all other statutes, should be in good faith and without evasion enforced, and because, in many utterances made prior to my election as President, approved by the party to which I belong and which I have no disposition to disclaim, I have in effect promised the people that this should be done.

I am not unmindful of the fact to which you refer, that many of our citizens fear that the recent party change in the National Executive may demonstrate that the abuses which have grown up in the civil service are ineradicable. I know that they are deeply rooted, and that the spoils system has been supposed to be intimately related to success in the main. tenance of party organization; and I am not sure that all those who profess to be the friends of this reform will stand firmly among its advocates, when they find it obstructing their way to patronage and place.

But, fully appreciating the trust committed to my charge, no such consideration shall cause a relaxation on my part of an earnest effort to enforce this law.

There is a class of government positions which are not within the letter of the civil service statute, but which are so disconnected with the policy of an administration that the removal therefrom of present incumbents, in my opinion, should not be made during the terms for which they were appointed, solely on partisan grounds and for the purpose of putting in their places those who are in political accord with the appointing power.

But many, now holding such positions, have forfeited all just claim to retention, because they have used their places for party purposes, in disregard of their duty to the people, and because, instead of being decent public servants, they have proved themselves offensive partisans, and unscrupulous manipulators of local party management.

The lessons of the past should be unlearned, and such officials, as well as their successors, should be taught that efficiency, fitness, and devotion to public duty are the conditions of their continuance in public place, and that the quiet and unobtrusive exercise of individual rights is the reasonable measure of their party service.

If I were addressing none but party friends, I should deem it entirely proper to remind them that, though the coming administration is to be Democratic, a due regard for the people's interest does not permit faithful party work to be always rewarded by appointment to office; and to say to them that while Democrats may expect all proper consideration, selections for office not embraced within the civil service rules will be based upon sufficient inquiry as to fitness, instituted by those charged with that duty, rather than upon persistent importunity or self-solicited recommendations on behalf of candidates for appointment.

Yours very truly,
GROVER CLEVELAND.

VI.

Accepting Letter of Resignation of Dorman B. Eaton.

EXECUTIVE MANSION,
WASHINGTON, September 11, 1885.

MY DEAR SIR:

I am in receipt of your letter tendering your resignation as a member of the Board of Civil Service Commissioners. I cannot refrain from expressing my sincere regret that you have determined to withdraw from a position in the public service where your intelligent performance of duty has been of inestimable value to the country. The friends of civil service reform, and all those who desire good government, fully appreciate your devotion to the cause in which you early enlisted, and they have seen with satisfaction that your zeal and faith have not led you to suppose that the reform in which you were engaged is unsuited to the rules which ordinarily govern progress in human affairs, or that it should at once reach perfection and universal acceptance. You have been willing patiently to accept good results as they, step by step, could be gained, holding every advance with unyielding steadfastness.

The success which, thus far, has attended the work of civil service reform is largely due to the fact that its practical friends have proceeded upon the theory that real and healthy progress can only be made as such of the people who cherish pernicious political ideas, long fostered and encouraged by vicious partisanship, are persuaded that the change contemplated by the reform offers substantial improvement and benefits. A reasonable toleration for old prejudices, a graceful recognition of every aid, a sensible utilization of every instrumentality that promises assistance, and a constant effort to demonstrate the advantages of the new order of things are the means by which this reform movement will, in the future, be further advanced, the opposition of incorrigible spoilsmen rendered ineffectual, and the cause placed upon a sure foundation. Of course, there should be no surrender of principle nor backward step, and all laws for the enforcement of the reform should be rigidly executed; but the benefits which its principles promise will not be fully realized unless the acquiescence of the people is added to the stern assertion of a doctrine and the vigorous execution of the laws.

It is a source of congratulation that there are so many friends of civil service reform marshaled on the practical side of the question, and that the number is not greater of those who profess friendliness for the cause, and yet mischievously, and with supercilious self-righteousness, discredit every effort not in exact accord with their attenuated ideas, decry with carping criticism the labor of those actually in the field of reform, and, ignoring the conditions which bound and qualify every struggle for a radical improvement in the affairs of government, demand complete and immediate perfection.

The reference in your letter to the attitude of the members of my cabinet toward the merit system established by the civil service law, besides being entirely correct, exhibits an appreciation of honest endeavor in the direction of reform, and a disposition to do justice to proved sincerity, which is most gratifying. If such treatment of those upon whom the duty rests of administering the government according to reform methods was the universal rule, and if the embarrassments and perplexities attending such an administration were fairly regarded by all those professing to be friendly to such methods, the avowed enemies of the cause would be afforded less encouragement.

I believe in civil service reform and its application in the most practicable form attainable, among other reasons, because it opens the door for the rich and the poor alike to a participation in public place holding. And I hope the time is at hand when all our people will see the advantage of a reliance for such an opportunity upon merit and fitness instead of upon the caprice or selfish interest of those who impudently stand between the people and the machinery of their government. In the one case, a reasonable intelligence, and the education which is freely furnished or forced upon the youth of our land, are the credentials to office; in the other, the way is found in favor, secured by a participation in partisan work often unfitting a person morally, if not mentally and physically, for the responsibilities and duties of public employment.

You will agree with me, I think, that the support which has been given to the present administration in its efforts to preserve and advance this reform, by a party restored to power after an exclusion for many years from participation in the places attached to the public service; confronted with a new system precluding the redistribution of such places in its interest; called upon to surrender advantages which a perverted partisanship had taught the American people belonged to success, and perturbed with the suspicions, always raised in such an emergency, that their rights in the conduct of this reform had not been scrupulously regarded, should receive due acknowledgment, and should confirm our belief that there is a sentiment among the people better than a desire to hold office, and a patriotic impulse upon which may safely rest the integrity of our institutions and the strength and perpetuity of our government.

I have determined to request you to retain your present position until the 1st day of November next, at which time your resignation may become operative. I desire to express my entire confidence in your attachment to the cause of civil service reform and your ability to render it efficient aid, and I indulge the hope and expectation that, notwithstanding the acceptance of your resignation, your interest in the object for which you have labored so assiduously will continue beyond the official term which you surrender.

Yours very truly,

GROVER CLEVELAND.

VII.

From the First Annual Message to Congress, December, 1885.

I am inclined to think that there is no sentiment more general in the minds of the people of our country than a conviction of the correctness of the principle upon which the law enforcing civil service reform is based. In its present condition the law regulates only a part of the subordinate public positions throughout the country. It applies the test of fitness to applicants for these places by means of a competitive examination, and gives large discretion to the commissioners as to the character of the examination and many other matters connected with its execution. Thus, the rules and regulations adopted by the commission have much to do with the practical usefulness of the statute and with the results of its application.

The people may well trust the commission to execute the law with perfect fairness and with as little irritation as is possible. But, of course, no relaxation of the principle which underlies it, and no weakening of the safeguards which surround it, can be expected. Experience in its administration will probably suggest amendment of the methods of its execution, but I venture to hope that we shall never again be remitted to the system which distributes public positions purely as rewards for partisan service. Doubts may well be entertained whether our government could survive the strain of a continuance of this system, which, upon every change of administration, inspires an immense army of claimants for office to lay siege to the patronage of government, engrossing the time of public officers with their importunities, spreading abroad the contagion of their disappointment, and filling the air with the tumult of their discontent.

The allurements of an immense number of offices and places, exhibited to the voters of the land, and the promise of their bestowal in recognition of partisan activity, debauch the suffrage and rob political action of its thoughtful and deliberative character. The evil would increase with the multiplication of offices consequent upon our extension, and the mania for office-holding, growing from its indulgence, would pervade our population so generally that patriotic purpose, the support of principle, the desire for the public good and solicitude for the nation's welfare would be nearly banished from the activity of our party contests and cause them to degenerate into ignoble, selfish, and disgraceful struggles for the possession of office and public place.

Civil service reform enforced by law came none too soon to check the progress of demoralization. One of its effects, not enough regarded, is the freedom it brings to the political action of those conservative and sober men who, in fear of the confusion and risk attending an arbitrary and sudden change in all the public offices with a change of party rule, cast their ballots against such a chance.

Parties seem to be necessary, and will long continue to exist; nor can it be now denied that there are legitimate advantages, not disconnected with office-holding, which follow party supremacy. While partisanship continues bitter and pronounced, and supplies so much of motive to sentiment and action, it is not fair to hold public officials, in charge of important trusts, responsible for the best results in the performance of their duties, and yet insist that they shall rely, in confidential and important places, upon the work of those not only opposed to them in political affiliation, but so steeped in partisan prejudice and rancor that they have no loyalty to their chiefs and no desire for their success. Civil service reform does not exact this, nor does it require that those in subordinate positions who fail in yielding their best service, or who are incompetent, should be retained simply because they are in place. The whining of a clerk discharged for indolence or incompetency, who, though he gained his place by the worst possible operation of the spoils system, suddenly discovers that he is entitled to protection under the sanction of civil service reform, represents an idea no less absurd than the clamor of the applicant who claims the vacant position as his compensation for the most questionable party work.

The civil service law does not prevent the discharge of the indolent or incompetent clerk, but it does prevent supplying his place with the unfit party worker. Thus, in both these phases, is seen benefit to the public service. And the people who desire good government, having secured this statute, will not relinquish its benefits without protest. Nor are they unmindful of the fact that its full advantages can only be gained through the complete good faith of those having its execution in charge. And this they will insist upon.

VIII.

Message on the Report of the Commission, March 26, 1886.

I transmit herewith the Report of the Civil Service Commission for the year ended on the 16th day of January last.

The exhibit thus made of the operations of the commission,

and the account thus presented of the results following the execution of the civil service law, cannot fail to demonstrate its usefulness and strengthen the conviction that this scheme for a reform in the methods of administering the government is no longer an experiment.

Wherever this reform has gained a foothold, it has steadily advanced in the esteem of those charged with public administrative duties, while the people who desire good government have constantly been confirmed in their high estimate of its value and efficiency.

With the benefits it has already secured to the public service plainly apparent, and with its promise of increased usefulness easily appreciated, this cause is commended to the liberal care and jealous protection of the Congress.

IX.

Order to Heads of Departments.

EXECUTIVE MANSION,
July 14, 1886.

I deem this a proper time especially to warn all subordinates in the several Departments, and all office-holders under the general government, against the use of their official positions in attempts to control political movements in their localities.

Office-holders are the agents of the people, not their masters. Not only are their time and labor due to the government, but they should scrupulously avoid, in their political action as well as in the discharge of their official duty, offending, by a display of obtrusive partisanship, their neighbors who have relations with them as public officials.

They should also constantly remember that their party friends, from whom they have received preferment, have not invested them with the power of arbitrarily managing their political affairs. They have no right as office-holders to dictate the political action of their party associates, or to throttle freedom of action within party lines, by methods and practices which pervert every useful and justifiable purpose of party organization.

The influence of Federal office-holders should not be felt in the manipulation of political primary meetings and nominating conventions. The use, by these officials, of their positions to compass their selection as delegates to political conventions is indecent and unfair; and proper regard for the proprieties and requirements of official place will also prevent their assuming the active conduct of political campaigns.

Individual interest and activity in political affairs are by no means condemned. Office-holders are neither disfranchised nor forbidden the exercise of political privileges; but their privileges are not enlarged nor is their duty to party increased to pernicious activity by office-holding.

A just discrimination in this regard, between the things a citizen may properly do and the purposes for which a public office should not be used, is easy in the light of a correct appreciation of the relation between the people and those intrusted with official place, and a consideration of the necessity under our form of government of political action free from official coercion.

GROVER CLEVELAND.

X.

Reasons for the Removal of William A. Stone.

EXECUTIVE MANSION,
November 23, 1886.

HON. A. H. GARLAND, *Attorney-General:*

DEAR SIR: I have read the letter of the 18th instant written to you by William A. Stone, lately suspended from office as district attorney for the western district of Pennsylvania, and the subject matter to which it refers has received my careful consideration.

I shall not impute to the writer any mischievous motive in

his plainly erroneous assumption that his case and that of
M. E. Benton, recently suspended and reinstated, rest upon
the same state of facts, but prefer to regard his letter as containing the best statement possible upon the question of his
reinstatement.

You remember, of course, that soon after the present administration was installed—and I think nearly a year and a half
ago—I considered with you certain charges which had been
preferred against Mr. Stone as a Federal official.   You remember, too, that the action we then contemplated was withheld by
reason of the excuses and explanations of his friends.   These
excuses and explanations induced me to believe that Mr.
Stone's retention would insure a faithful performance of official
duty, and that whatever offensive partisanship he had deemed
justifiable in other circumstances, he would, during his continuance in office, at his request, under an administration
opposed to him in political creed and policy, content himself
with a quiet and unobtrusive enjoyment of his political privileges.   I certainly supposed that his sense of propriety would
cause him to refrain from pursuing such a partisan course as
would wantonly offend and irritate the friends of the administration who insisted that he should not be retained in office,
either because of his personal merit or in adherence to the
methods which for a long time had prevailed in the distribution of Federal offices.

In the light of a better system, and without considering his
political affiliations, Mr. Stone, when permitted to remain in
office, became a part of the business organization of the present administration—bound by every obligation of honor to
assist within his sphere in its successful operation.   This obligation involved not only the proper performance of official duty,
but a certain good faith and fidelity, which, while not exacting
the least sacrifice of political principle, forbade active participation in purely partisan demonstrations of a pronounced type,
undertaken for the purpose of advancing partisan interests,
and conducted upon the avowed theory that the administration

of the government was not entitled to the confidence and respect of the people.

There is no dispute whatever concerning the fact that Mr. Stone did join others who were campaigning the State of Pennsylvania in opposition to the administration. It appears, too, that he was active and prominent, with noisy enthusiasm, in attendance upon at least two large public meetings; that the speeches at such meetings were largely devoted to abuse and misrepresentation of the administration; that he approved all this and actually addressed the meetings himself in somewhat the same strain; that he attended such meetings away from his home for the purpose of making such addresses; and that he was advertised as one of the speakers at each of said meetings.

I shall accept as true the statement of Mr. Stone that the time spent by him in thus demonstrating his willingness to hold a profitable office, at the hands of an administration which he endeavored to discredit with the people, and which had kindly overlooked his previous offenses, did not result in the neglect of ordinary official duty. But his conduct has brought to light such an unfriendliness toward the administration which he pretends to serve and of which he is nominally a part, and such a consequent lack of loyal interest in its success, that the safest and surest guarantee of his faithful service is, in my opinion, entirely wanting. His course, in itself such as should not have been entered upon while maintaining official relations to the administration, also renews and revives, with unmistakable interpretation of their character and intent, the charges of offensive partisanship heretofore made and up to this time held in abeyance.

Mr. Stone and others of like disposition are not to suppose that party lines are so far obliterated that the administration of the government is to be trusted, in places high or low, to those who aggressively and constantly endeavor, unfairly, to destroy the confidence of the people in the party responsible for such administration. While vicious partisan methods should not be allowed for partisan purposes to degrade or injure the public service, it is my belief that nothing tends so much to discredit our efforts, in the interest of such service, to treat fairly and generously the official incumbency of political opponents, as conduct such as is here disclosed.

The people of this country certainly do not require the best results of administrative endeavor to be reached with such agencies as these.

Upon a full consideration of all I have before me, I am constrained to decline the application of Mr. Stone for his reinstatement.

I inclose his letter with this, and desire you to acquaint him with my decision.

Yours truly,

GROVER CLEVELAND.

XI.

From Second Annual Message, December 6, 1886.

The continued operation of the law relating to our civil service has added the most convincing proofs of its necessity and usefulness. It is a fact worthy of note, that every public officer who has a just idea of his duty to the people testifies to the value of this reform. Its stanchest friends are found among those who understand it best, and its warmest supporters are those who are restrained and protected by its requirements.

The meaning of such restraint and protection is not appreciated by those who want places under the government, regardless of merit and efficiency, nor by those who insist that the selection for such places should rest upon a proper credential showing active partisan work. They mean to public officers, if not their lives, the only opportunity afforded them to attend to public business, and they mean to the good people of the country the better performance of the work of their government.

It is exceedingly strange that the scope and nature of this reform are so little understood, and that so many things not included within its plan are called by its name. When cavil yields more fully to examination, the system will have large additions to the number of its friends.

Our civil service reform may be imperfect in some of its details; it may be misunderstood and opposed; it may not always be faithfully applied; its designs may sometimes miscarry through mistake or willful intent; it may sometimes tremble under the assaults of its enemies, or languish under the misguided zeal of impracticable friends; but if the people of this country ever submit to the banishment of its underlying principle from the operation of their government, they will abandon the surest guarantee of the safety and success of American institutions.

I invoke for this reform the cheerful and ungrudging support of the Congress.

XII.

Order for Uniform Classification in the Departments.

To the United States Civil Service Commission:

Gentlemen: I desire to make a suggestion regarding Subdivision C, General Rule 3, of the amended Civil Service Rules promulgated February 2, 1888. It provides for the promotion of an employee, in a Department, who is below or outside of the classified service, to a place within said classified service in the same Department upon the request of the appointing officer, upon the recommendation of the commission and the approval of the President, after a non-competitive examination, in case such person has served continuously for two years in the place from which it is proposed to promote him, and "because of his faithfulness and efficiency in the position occupied by him," and "because of his qualifications for the place to which the appointing officer desires his promotion."

It has occurred to me that this provision must be executed with caution, to avoid the application of it to cases not intended and the undue relaxation of the general purposes and restrictions of the civil service law.

Non-competitive examinations are the exceptions to the plan of the Act, and the rules permitting the same should be strictly construed. The cases arising under the exception, above recited, should be very few, and when presented they should precisely meet all the requirements specified, and should be supported by facts which will develop the basis and reason of the application of the appointing officer, and which will commend them to the judgment of the commission and the President. The sole purpose of the provision is to benefit the public service, and it should never be permitted to operate as an evasion of the main feature of the law, which is competitive examinations.

As these cases will first be presented to the commission for recommendation, I have to request that you will formulate a plan by which their merits can be tested. This will naturally involve a statement of all the facts deemed necessary for the determination of such applications, including the kind of work which has been done by the person proposed for promotion, and the considerations upon which the allegations of the faithfulness, efficiency, and qualifications mentioned in the rule are predicated.

What has already been written naturally suggests another very important subject, to which I will invite your attention.

The desirability of the rule which I have commented upon would be nearly, if not entirely, removed, and other difficulties which now embarrass the execution of the civil service law would be obviated, if there was a better and uniform classification of the employees in the different Departments. The importance of this is entirely obvious. The present imperfect classifications, hastily made, apparently with but little care for uniformity, and promulgated after the last Presidential election and prior to the installation of the present administration, should not have been permitted to continue to this time.

It appears that in the War Department the employees were divided on the 19th day of November, 1884, into eight classes and sub-classes, embracing those earning annual salaries from $900 to $2000.

The Navy Department was classified November 22, 1884, and its employees were divided into seven classes and sub-classes, embracing those who received annual salaries from $720 to $1800.

In the Interior Department the classification was made on the 6th day of December, 1884. It consists of eight classes and sub-classes, and embraces employees receiving annual salaries from $720 to $2000.

On the 2d day of January, 1885, a classification of the employees in the Treasury Department was made, consisting of six classes and sub-classes; including those earning annual salaries from $900 to $1800.

In the Post Office Department the employees were classified on February 6, 1885, into nine classes and sub-classes, embracing persons earning annual salaries from $720 to $2000.

On the 12th of December, 1884, the Bureau of Agriculture was classified in a manner different from all the other Departments and presenting features peculiar to itself.

It seems that the only classification in the Department of State and the Department of Justice is that provided for by section 163 of the Revised Statutes, which directs that the employees in the several Departments shall be divided into four classes. It appears that no more definite classification has been made in these Departments.

I wish the commission would revise these classifications and submit to me a plan which will, as far as possible, make them uniform, and which will especially remedy the present condition which permits persons to enter a grade in the service in one Department without any examination, which in another

Department can only be entered after passing such examination. This, I think, should be done by extending the limits of the classified service rather than by contracting them.

GROVER CLEVELAND.

EXECUTIVE MANSION,
    March 21, 1888.

XIII.

Message Transmitting Report of the Civil Service Commission.

TO THE CONGRESS OF THE UNITED STATES:

Pursuant to the second section of Chapter XXVII of the laws of 1883, entitled "An Act to regulate and improve the civil service of the United States," I herewith transmit the fourth report of the United States Civil Service Commission, covering the period between the 16th day of January, 1886, and the 1st day of July, 1887.

While this report has especial reference to the operations of the commission during the period above mentioned, it contains, with its accompanying appendices, much valuable information concerning the inception of civil service reform and its growth and progress, which cannot fail to be interesting and instructive to all who desire improvement in administrative methods.

During the time covered by the report fifteen thousand eight hundred and fifty-two persons were examined for admission in the classified civil service of the government in all its branches; of whom ten thousand seven hundred and forty-six passed the examination, and five thousand one hundred and six failed. Of those who passed the examination, two thousand nine hundred and twenty-seven were applicants for admission to the departmental service at Washington, twenty-five hundred and forty-seven were examined for admission to the customs service, and five thousand two hundred and twenty-two for admission to the postal service. During the same period five hundred and forty-seven appointments were made from the eligible list to the departmental service, six hundred and forty-one to the customs service, and three thousand two hundred and fifty-four to the postal service.

Concerning separations from the classified service, the report only informs us of such as have occurred among employees in the public service who had been appointed from eligible lists under civil service rules. When these rules took effect they did not apply to the persons then in the service, comprising a full complement of employees who obtained their positions independently of the new law. The commission has no record of the separations in this numerous class; and the discrepancy apparent in the report between the number of appointments made in the respective branches of the service from the lists of the commission, and the small number of separations mentioned, is, to a great extent, accounted for by vacancies—of which no report was made to the commission—occurring among those who held their places without examination and certification, which vacancies were filled by appointment from the eligible lists.

In the departmental service there occurred between the 16th day of January, 1886, and the 30th day of June, 1887, among the employees appointed from the eligible lists under civil service rules, seventeen removals, thirty-six resignations, and five deaths. This does not include fourteen separations in the grade of special pension examiners, four by removal, five by resignation, and five by death.

In the classified customs and postal service the number of separations among those who received absolute appointments under civil service rules is given for the period between the 1st day of January, 1886, and the 30th day of June, 1887. It appears that such separations in the customs service for the time mentioned embraced twenty-one removals, five deaths, and eighteen resignations, and in the postal service two hundred and fifty-six removals, twenty-three deaths, and four hundred and sixty-nine resignations.

More than a year has passed since the expiration of the

period covered by the report of the commission. Within the time which has thus elapsed many important changes have taken place in furtherance of a reform in our civil service. The rules and regulations governing the execution of the law upon the subject have been completely remodeled, in such manner as to render the enforcement of the statute more effective and greatly increase its usefulness.

Among other things the scope of the examinations prescribed for those who seek to enter the classified service has been better defined and made more practical, the number of names to be certified from the eligible lists to the appointing officers from which a selection is made has been reduced from four to three, the maximum limitation of the age of persons seeking entrance to the classified service to forty-five years has been changed, and reasonable provision has been made for the transfer of employees from one Department to another in proper cases. A plan has also been devised providing for the examination of applicants for promotion in the service, which, when in full operation, will eliminate all chance of favoritism in the advancement of employees, by making promotion a reward of merit and faithful discharge of duty.

Until within a few weeks there was no uniform classification of employees in the different executive Departments of the government. As a result of this condition, in some of the Departments positions could be obtained without civil service examination, because they were not within the classification of such Department, while in other Departments an examination and certification were necessary to obtain positions of the same grade, because such positions were embraced in the classifications applicable to those Departments.

The exemption of laborers, watchmen, and messengers from examination and classification gave opportunity, in the absence of any rule guarding against it, for the employment, free from civil service restrictions, of persons under these designations who were immediately detailed to do clerical work.

All this has been obviated by the application to all the Departments of an extended and uniform classification, embracing grades of employees not theretofore included, and by the adoption of a rule prohibiting the detail of laborers, watchmen, or messengers to clerical duty.

The path of civil service reform has not at all times been pleasant or easy. The scope and purpose of the reform have been much misapprehended; and this has not only given rise to strong opposition, but has led to its invocation by its friends to compass objects not in the least related to it. Thus partisans of the patronage system have naturally condemned it. Those who do not understand its meaning either mistrust it, or, when disappointed because in its present stage it is not applied to every real or imaginary ill, accuse those charged with its enforcement with faithlessness to civil service reform. Its importance has frequently been underestimated; and the support of good men has thus been lost by their lack of interest in its success. Besides all these difficulties, those responsible for the administration of the government in its executive branches have been, and still are, often annoyed and irritated by the disloyalty to the service and the insolence of employees who remain in place as the beneficiaries and the relics and reminders of the vicious system of appointment which civil service reform was intended to displace.

And yet these are but the incidents of an advance movement, which is radical and far-reaching. The people are, notwithstanding, to be congratulated upon the progress which has been made, and upon the firm, practical, and sensible foundation upon which this reform now rests.

With a continuation of the intelligent fidelity which has hitherto characterized the work of the commission; with a continuation and increase of the favor and liberality which have lately been evinced by the Congress in the proper equipment of the commission for its work; with a firm but conservative and reasonable support of the reform by all its friends, and with the disappearance of opposition which must inevitably follow its better understanding, the execution of the civil service law cannot fail ultimately to answer the hopes in which it had its origin.

GROVER CLEVELAND.

EXECUTIVE MANSION,
WASHINGTON, July 23, 1888.

CHAPTER IV.

TAXATION AND REVENUE.

I.

First Message to the New York Legislature, January 2, 1883.

THE power of the State to exact from the citizen a part of his earnings and income for the support of the government, it is obvious, should be exercised with absolute fairness and justice. When it is not so exercised, the people are oppressed. This furnishes the highest and the best reason why laws should be enacted and executed which will subject all property—as all alike need the protection of the State—to an equal share in the burdens of taxation, by means of which the government is maintained. And yet it is notoriously true that personal property, not less remunerative than land and real estate, escapes to a very great extent the payment of its fair proportion of the expense incident to its protection and preservation under the law. The people should always be able to recognize, with the pride and satisfaction which are the strength of our institutions, in the conduct of the State, the source of undiscriminating justice, which can give no pretext for discontent.

Let us enter upon the discharge of our duties, fully appreciating our relations to the people, and determined to serve them faithfully and well. This involves a jealous watch of the public funds, and a refusal to sanction their appropriation except for public needs. To this end all unnecessary offices should be abolished, and all employment of doubtful benefit discontinued. If to this we add the enactment of such wise and well-considered laws as will meet the varied wants of our fellow-citizens and increase their prosperity, we shall merit and receive the approval of those whose representatives we are, and, with the consciousness of duty well performed, shall leave our impress for good on the legislation of the State.

II.

Interview in the New York Herald, December 10, 1883.

If Congress, at its present session, shall fail to reduce the revenues, now admitted to be larger than necessary, I have no doubt that the question will become an important issue in the Presidential election of next year, and that the election of Mr. Carlisle to the Speakership will tend to commit the Democratic party to advocate such a revision of the revenue laws as will secure a reduction of excessive revenue, by removing or lessening such duties as increase the cost of the necessaries of life rather than those which enhance the price of luxuries.

III.

Second Message to the New York Legislature, January 1, 1884.

The subject of taxation still remains a vexed question ; and the injustice and discrimination apparent in our laws on this subject, as well as the methods of their execution, call loudly for relief. There is no object so worthy of the care and attention of the Legislature as this. Strict economy in the management of State affairs by their agents should furnish the people a good government at the least possible cost. This is common honesty. But, to see to it that this cost is fairly and justly distributed, and the burden equally borne by those who have no peaceful redress if the State is unjust, is the best attribute of sovereignty and the highest duty to the citizen. The recognition of this duty characterizes a beneficent government ; but its repudiation marks the oppression of tyrannical power. The taxpayer need not wait till his burden is greater than he can bear, for just cause of complaint. However small his tax, he may reasonably protest if it represents more than his share of the public burden, and the State neglects all efforts to apply a remedy.

The tendency of our prosperity is in the direction of the accumulation of immense fortunes, largely invested in personal property ; and yet its aggregate valuation, as fixed for the purpose of taxation, is constantly decreased, while that of real estate is increased. For the year 1882, the valuation of personal property subject to taxation was determined at $351,021,-189, and real estate at $2,432,661,379. In 1883 the assessed valuation of personal property was fixed at $315,039,085, and real estate $2,557,218,240.

The present law permits, in the case of personal property, the indebtedness of its possessor to be deducted from its value, and allows no such deduction in favor of real estate, though it be represented by a mortgage which is a specific lien upon such real estate. Personal property, in need more than any other of the protection of the government, when discovered, escapes taxation to the extent of its owner's indebtedness, though such indebtedness is based upon the ordinary credit in the transaction of business, or is fictitious, and manufactured for the temporary purpose of evading taxation. But real property, the existence of which cannot be concealed, is, in contemplation of the law, taxed according to its full valuation, though the incumbrance upon it easily divests the owner of his title, though the interest and perhaps part of the principal must, as well as the tax, annually be met, and though, if sold, the amount due upon this lien must always be deducted from any sum agreed upon as the price of the land.

This statement does not necessarily lead to a deduction of the amount of any incumbrance upon real estate from its valuation for the purpose of taxation ; but it does suggest that both real and personal property should be placed upon the same footing, by abolishing, in all cases, any deduction for debts. This amendment, with some others regulating the manner in which local assessors should perform their duties, would do much toward ridding our present system of its imperfections.

If measures more radical in their nature, having for their object the exaction of taxes which are justly due, should be deemed wise, I hope their passage will not be prevented under the specious pretext that the means proposed are inquisitorial and contrary to the spirit of our institutions. The object is to preserve the honor of the State in its dealings with the citizen, to prevent the rich, by shirking taxation, from adding to the burdens of the poor, and to relieve the landholder from unjust discrimination. The spirit of our institutions dictates that this endeavor should be pursued, in a manner free from all demagogism, but with the determination to use every necessary means to accomplish the result.

The State of New York largely represents within her borders the development of every interest which makes a nation great. Proud of her place as leader in the community of States, she fully appreciates her immediate relations to the prosperity of the country ; and, justly realizing the responsibility of her position, she recognizes, in her policy and her laws, as of first importance, the freedom of commerce from all unnecessary restrictions. Her citizens have assumed the burden of maintaining, at their own cost and free to commerce, the waterway which they have built, and through which the products of the great West are transported to the seaboard. At the suggestion of danger she hastens to save her northern forests, and thus preserve to commerce her canals and vessel-laden rivers. The State has become responsible for a bureau of immigration, which cares for those who seek our shores from other lands, adding to the nation's population and hastening to the development of its vast domain ; while at the country's gateway a quarantine, established by the State, protects the nation's health.

Surely this great commonwealth, committed fully to the interests of commerce and all that adds to the country's prosperity, may well inquire how her efforts and sacrifices have been answered ; and she, of all the States, may urge that the interests thus by her protected, should, by the greater government administered for all, be fostered for the benefit of the American people.

Fifty years ago a most distinguished foreigner, who visited this country and studied its condition and prospects, wrote :

> When I contemplate the ardor with which the Americans prosecute commerce, the advantages which aid them, and the success of their undertakings, I cannot help believing that they will one day become the first maritime power of the globe. They are bound to rule the seas, as the Romans were to conquer the world. . . . The Americans themselves now transport to their own shores nine-tenths of the European produce which they consume, and they also bring three-fourths of the exports of the New World to the European consumer. The ships of the United States fill the docks of Havre and Liverpool, while the number of English and French vessels which are to be seen at New York is comparatively small.

We turn to the actual results reached since these words were written, with disappointment.

In 1840 American vessels carried eighty-two and nine-tenths per cent. of all our exports and imports ; in 1850, seventy-two and five-tenths ; in 1860, sixty-six and five-tenths ; in 1870, thirty-five and six-tenths ; in 1880, seventeen and four-tenths; in 1882, fifteen and five-tenths.

The citizen of New York, looking beyond his State and all her efforts in the interest of commerce and national growth, will naturally inquire concerning the causes of this decadence of American shipping.

While he sternly demands of his own government the exact limitation of taxation by the needs of the State, he will challenge the policy that accumulates millions of useless and unnecessary surplus in the national treasury, which has been not less a tax because it was indirectly and surely added to the cost of the people's life.

Let us anticipate a time when care for the people's needs, as they actually arise, and the application of remedies, as wrongs appear, shall lead in the conduct of national affairs ; and let us undertake the business of legislation with the full determination that these principles shall guide us in the performance of our duties as guardians of the interests of the state.

IV.

From the First Annual Message to Congress, December, 1885.

The fact that our revenues are in excess of the actual needs of an economical administration of the government justifies a reduction in the amount exacted from the people for its support. Our government is but the means, established by the will of a free people, by which certain principles are applied which they have adopted for their benefit and protection ; and it is never better administered, and its true spirit is never better observed, than when the people's taxation for its support is scrupulously limited to the actual necessity of expenditure, and distributed according to a just and equitable plan.

The proposition with which we have to deal is the reduction of the revenue received by the government, and indirectly paid by the people from customs duties. The question of free trade is not involved, nor is there now any occasion for the general discussion of the wisdom or expediency of a protective system.

Justice and fairness dictate that, in any modification of our present laws relating to revenue, the industries and interests which have been encouraged by such laws, and in which our citizens have large investments, should not be ruthlessly injured or destroyed. We should also deal with the subject in such manner as to protect the interests of American labor, which is the capital of our workingmen ; its stability and proper remuneration furnish the most justifiable pretext for a protective policy.

Within these limitations a certain reduction should be made in our customs revenue. The amount of such reduction having been determined, the inquiry follows—where can it best be remitted, and what articles can best be released from duty in the interest of our citizens ?

I think the reduction should be made in the revenue derived from a tax upon the imported necessaries of life. We thus directly lessen the cost of living in every family of the land, and release to the people in every humble home a larger measure of the rewards of frugal industry.

V.

From the Second Annual Message to Congress, December, 1886.

The income of the government, by its increased volume and through economies in its collection, is now more than ever in excess of public necessities. The application of the surplus to the payment of such portion of the public debt as is now at our option subject to extinguishment, if continued at the rate which has lately prevailed, would retire that class of indebtedness within less than one year from this date. Thus a continuation of our present revenue system would soon result in the receipt of an annual income much greater than necessary to meet government expenses, with no indebtedness upon which it could be applied. We should then be confronted with a vast quantity of money, the circulating medium of the people, hoarded in the treasury when it should be in their hands, or we should be drawn into wasteful public extravagance with all the corrupting national demoralization which follows in its train.

But it is not the simple existence of this surplus, and its threatened attendant evils, which furnish the strongest argument against our present scale of Federal taxation. Its worst phase is the exaction of such a surplus through a perversion of the relations between the people and their government, and a dangerous departure from the rules which limit the right of Federal taxation.

The indirect manner in which these exactions are made has a tendency to conceal their true character and their extent. But we have arrived at a stage of superfluous revenue which has aroused the people to a realization of the fact that the amount raised, professedly for the support of the government, is paid by them as absolutely, if added to the price of the things which supply their daily wants, as if it was paid at fixed periods into the hand of the tax-gatherer.

Those who toil for daily wages are beginning to understand that capital, though sometimes vaunting its importance and clamoring for the protection and favor of the government, is dull and sluggish, till, touched by the magical hand of labor, it springs into activity, furnishing an occasion for Federal taxation and gaining the value which enables it to bear its burden. And the laboring man is thoughtfully inquiring whether, in these circumstances and considering the tribute he constantly pays into the public treasury as he supplies his daily wants, he receives his fair share of advantage.

There is also a suspicion abroad that the surplus of our revenues indicates abnormal and exceptional business profits, which, under the system which produces such surplus, increase, without corresponding benefit to the people at large, the vast accumulations of a few among our citizens whose fortunes, rivaling the wealth of the most favored in anti-democratic nations, are not the natural growth of a steady, plain, and industrious republic..

Our farmers, too, and those engaged directly and indirectly in supplying the products of agriculture, see that, day by day, and as often as the daily wants of their households recur, they are forced to pay excessive and needless taxation, while their products struggle in foreign markets with the competition of nations which, by allowing a freer exchange of productions than we permit, enable their people to sell for prices which distress the American farmer. A sentiment prevails that the leading-strings, useful to a nation in its infancy, may well be, to a great extent, discarded in the present stage of American ingenuity, courage, and fearless self-reliance. And, for the privilege of indulging this sentiment with true American enthusiasm, our citizens are quite willing to forego an idle surplus in the public treasury.

And all the people know that the average rate of Federal taxation upon imports is, to-day, in time of peace, but little less, while, upon some articles of necessary consumption, it is actually more, than was imposed by the grievous burden willingly borne at a time when the government needed millions to maintain by war the safety and integrity of the Union.

It has been the policy of the government to collect the principal part of its revenues by a tax upon imports, and no change in this policy is desirable. But the present condition of affairs constrains our people to demand that, by a revision of our revenue laws, the receipts of the government shall be reduced to the necessary expense of its economical administration ; and this demand should be recognized and obeyed by the people's representatives in the legislative branch of the government.

In readjusting the burdens of Federal taxation, a sound public policy requires that such of our citizens as have built up large and important industries under present conditions should not be suddenly, and to their injury, deprived of advantages to which they have adapted their business ; but, if the public good requires it, they should be content with such consideration as shall deal fairly and cautiously with their interests, while the just demand of the people for relief from needless taxation is honestly answered.

A reasonable and timely submission to such a demand should certainly be possible without disastrous shock to any interest ; and a cheerful concession sometimes averts abrupt and heedless action, often the outgrowth of impatience and delayed justice.

Due regard should also be accorded, in any proposed readjustment, to the interests of American labor so far as they are involved. We congratulate ourselves that there is among us no laboring class, fixed within unyielding bounds and doomed, under all conditions, to the inexorable fate of daily toil. We recognize in labor a chief factor in the wealth of the republic ; and we treat those who have it in their keeping as citizens entitled to the most careful regard and thoughtful attention. This regard and attention should be awarded them, not only because labor is the capital of our workingmen, justly entitled to its share of government favor, but for the further and not less important reason that the laboring man, surrounded by his family in his humble home, as a consumer, is vitally interested in all that cheapens the cost of living and enables him to bring within his domestic circle additional comforts and advantages.

This relation of the workingman to the revenue laws of the country, and the manner in which it palpably influences the question of wages, should not be forgotten in the justifiable prominence given to the proper maintenance of the supply and protection of well-paid labor. And these considerations suggest such an arrangement of government revenues as shall reduce the expense of living, while it does not curtail the opportunity for work nor reduce the compensation of American labor, and injuriously affect its condition and the dignified place it holds in the estimation of our people.

But our farmers and agriculturists—those who from the soil produce the things consumed by all—are, perhaps, more directly and plainly concerned than any other of our citizens in a just and careful system of Federal taxation. Those actually engaged in, and more remotely connected with this kind of work, number nearly one-half of our population. None labor harder or more continuously than they. No enactments limit their hours of toil, and no interposition of the government enhances to any great extent the value of their products. And yet, for many of the necessaries and comforts of life, which the most scrupulous economy enables them to bring into their homes, and for their implements of husbandry, they are obliged to pay a price largely increased by an un-natural profit which, by the action of the government, is given to the more favored manufacturer.

I recommend that, keeping in view all these considerations, the increasing and unnecessary surplus of national income annually accumulating be released to the people, by an amendment to our revenue laws which shall cheapen the price of the necessaries of life, and give freer entrance to such im-ported materials as, by American labor, may be manufactured into marketable commodities.

Nothing can be accomplished, however, in the direction of this much needed reform, unless the subject is approached in a patriotic spirit of devotion to the interests of the entire country and with a willingness to yield something for the public good.

VI.

Third Annual Message to Congress.

To the Congress of the United States :

You are confronted at the threshold of your legislative duties with a condition of the national finances which imperatively demands immediate and careful consideration.

The amount of money annually exacted, through the oper-ation of present laws, from the industries and necessities of the people, largely exceeds the sum necessary to meet the ex-penses of the government.

When we consider that the theory of our institutions guar-antees to every citizen the full enjoyment of all the fruits of his industry and enterprise, with only such deduction as may be his share toward the careful and economical maintenance of the government which protects him, it is plain that the exaction of more than this is indefensible extortion, and a culpable betrayal of American fairness and justice. This wrong, inflicted upon those who bear the burden of national taxation, like other wrongs multiplies a brood of evil consequences. The public treasury, which should only exist as a conduit conveying the people's tribute to its legitimate objects of expenditure, becomes a hoarding-place for money needlessly withdrawn from trade and the people's use, thus crippling our national energies, suspending our country's development, preventing investment in productive enterprise, threatening financial disturbance, and inviting schemes of public plunder.

This condition of our treasury is not altogether new ; and it has more than once of late been submitted to the people's representatives in the Congress, who alone can apply a remedy. And yet the situation still continues, with aggravated incidents, more than ever presaging financial convulsion and wide-spread disaster.

It will not do to neglect this situation because its dangers are not now palpably imminent and apparent. They exist none the less certainly, and await the unforeseen and unexpected occasion when suddenly they will be precipitated upon us.

On the 30th day of June, 1885, the excess of revenues over public expenditures, after complying with the annual requirement of the Sinking-Fund Act, was $17,859,735.84; during the year ended June 30, 1886, such excess amounted to $49,405,545.20 ; and during the year ended June 30, 1887, it reached the sum of $55,567,849.54.

The annual contributions to the sinking fund during the three years above specified, amounting in the aggregate to $138,058,320.94, and deducted from the surplus as stated, were made by calling in for that purpose outstanding three per cent. bonds of the government. During the six months prior to June 30, 1887, the surplus revenue had grown so large by repeated accumulations, and it was feared the withdrawal of this great sum of money needed by the people would so affect the business of the country, that the sum of $79,864,100 of such surplus was applied to the payment of the principal and interest of the three per cent. bonds still outstanding, and which were then payable at the option of the government. The precarious condition of financial affairs among the people still needing relief, immediately after the 30th day of June, 1887, the remainder of the three per cent. bonds then outstanding, amounting with principal and interest to the sum of $18,877,500, were called in and applied to the sinking-fund contribution for the current fiscal year. Notwithstanding these operations of the Treasury Department representations of distress in business circles not only continued but increased, and absolute peril seemed at hand. In these circumstances the contribution to the sinking fund for the current fiscal year was at once completed by the expenditure of $27,684,283.55 in the purchase of government bonds not yet due, bearing four and four and one half per cent. interest, the premium paid thereon averaging about twenty-four per cent. for the former and eight per cent. for the latter. In addition to this the interest accruing during the current year upon the outstanding bonded indebtedness of the government was to some extent anticipated, and banks selected as depositories of public money were permitted somewhat to increase their deposits.

While the expedients thus employed to release to the people the money lying idle in the treasury served to avert immediate danger, our surplus revenues have continued to accumulate, the excess for the present year amounting on the first of December to $55,258,701.19, and estimated to reach the sum of $113,000,000 on the 30th of June next, at which date it is expected that this sum, added to prior accumulations, will swell the surplus in the treasury to $140,000,000.

There seems to be no assurance that, with such a withdrawal from use of the people's circulating medium, our business community may not in the near future be subjected to the same distress which was quite lately produced from the same cause. And while the functions of our national treasury should be few and simple, and while its best condition would be reached, I believe, by its entire disconnection with private business interests, yet when, by a perversion of its purposes, it idly holds money uselessly subtracted from the channels of trade, there seems to be reason for the claim that some legitimate means should be devised by the government to restore in an emergency, without waste or extravagance, such money to its place among the people.

If such an emergency arises there now exists no clear and undoubted executive power of relief. Heretofore the redemption of three per cent. bonds, which were payable at the option of the government, has afforded a means for the disbursement of the excess of our revenues ; but these bonds have all been retired, and there are no bonds outstanding the payment of which we have the right to insist upon. The contribution to the sinking fund, which furnishes the occasion for expenditure in the purchase of bonds, has been already made for the current year, so that there is no outlet in that direction.

In the present state of legislation the only pretense of any existing executive power to restore, at this time, any part of our surplus revenues to the people by its expenditure, consists in the supposition that the Secretary of the Treasury may enter the market and purchase the bonds of the government not yet due, at a rate of premium to be agreed upon. The only provision of law from which such a power could be derived is found in an appropriation bill passed a number of years ago ; and it is subject to the suspicion that it was intended as temporary and limiting in its application, instead of conferring a continuing discretion and authority. No condition ought to exist which would justify the grant of power to a single official, upon his judgment of its necessity, to withhold from or release to the business of the people, in an unusual manner, money held in the treasury, and thus affect, at his will, the financial condition of the country ; and if it is deemed wise to lodge in the Secretary of the Treasury the authority in the present juncture to purchase bonds, it should be plainly vested, and provided, as far as possible, with such checks and limitations as will define this official's right and discretion, and at the same time relieve him from undue responsibility.

In considering the question of purchasing bonds as a means of restoring to circulation the surplus money accumulating in the treasury, it should be borne in mind that premiums must, of course, be paid upon such purchase, that there may be a large part of these bonds held as investments which cannot be purchased at any price, and that combinations among holders who are willing to sell may unreasonably enhance the cost of such bonds to the government.

It has been suggested that the present bonded debt might be refunded at a less rate of interest, and the difference between the old and new security paid in cash, thus finding use for the surplus in the treasury. The success of this plan, it is apparent, must depend upon the volition of the holders of the present bonds ; and it is not entirely certain that the inducement which must be offered them would result in more financial benefit to the government than the purchase of bonds, while the latter proposition would reduce the principal of the debt by actual payment, instead of extending it.

The proposition to deposit the money held by the government in banks throughout the country, for use by the people, is, it seems to me, exceedingly objectionable in principle, as establishing too close a relationship between the operations of the government treasury and the business of the country, and too extensive a commingling of their money, thus fostering an unnatural reliance in private business upon public funds. If this scheme should be adopted it should only be done as a temporary expedient to meet an urgent necessity. Legislative and executive effort should generally be in the opposite direction, and should have a tendency to divorce, as much and as fast as can safely be done, the Treasury Department from private enterprise.

Of course, it is not expected that unnecessary and extravagant appropriations will be made for the purpose of avoiding the accumulation of an excess of revenue. Such expenditure, besides the demoralization of all just conceptions of public duty which it entails, stimulates a habit of reckless improvidence not in the least consistent with the mission of our people or the high and beneficent purposes of our government.

I have deemed it my duty thus to bring to the knowledge of my countrymen, as well as to the attention of their representatives charged with the responsibility of legislative relief, the gravity of our financial situation. The failure of the Congress heretofore to provide against the dangers which it was quite evident the very nature of the difficulty must necessarily produce, caused a condition of financial distress and apprehension since your last adjournment which taxed to the utmost all the authority and expedients within executive control ; and these appear now to be exhausted. If disaster results from the continued inaction of Congress, the responsibility must rest where it belongs.

Though the situation, thus far considered, is fraught with danger which should be fully realized, and though it presents features of wrong to the people as well as peril to the country, it is but a result growing out of a perfectly palpable and apparent cause, constantly reproducing the same alarming circumstances—a congested national treasury and a depleted monetary condition in the business of the country. It need hardly be stated that while the present situation demands a remedy, we can only be saved from a like predicament in the future by the removal of its cause.

Our scheme of taxation, by means of which this needless surplus is taken from the people and put into the public treasury, consists of a tariff or duty levied upon importations from abroad, and internal revenue taxes levied upon the consumption of tobacco and spirituous and malt liquors. It must be conceded that none of the things subjected to internal revenue taxation are, strictly speaking, necessaries ; there appears to be no just complaint of this taxation by the consumers of these articles, and there seems to be nothing so well able to bear the burden without hardship to any portion of the people.

But our present tariff laws, the vicious, inequitable, and illogical source of unnecessary taxation, ought to be at once revised and amended. These laws, as their primary and plain effect, raise the price to consumers of all articles imported and subject to duty, by precisely the sum paid for such duties. Thus the amount of the duty measures the tax paid by those who purchase for use these imported articles. Many of these things, however, are raised or manufactured in our own country, and the duties now levied upon foreign goods and products are called protection to these home manufactures, because they render it possible for those of our people who are manufacturers to make these taxed articles and sell them for a price equal to that demanded for the imported goods that have paid customs duty. So it happens that while comparatively a few use the imported articles, millions of our people, who never use and never saw any of the foreign products, purchase and use things of the same kind made in this country, and pay therefor nearly or quite the same enhanced price which the duty adds to the imported articles. Those who buy imports pay the duty charged thereon into the public treasury, but the great majority of our citizens, who buy domestic articles of the same class, pay a sum at least approximately equal to this duty to the home manufacturer. This reference to the operation of our tariff laws is not made by way of instruction, but in order that we may be constantly reminded of the manner in which they impose a burden upon those who consume domestic products as well as those who consume imported articles, and thus create a tax upon our people.

It is not proposed to relieve the country entirely of this taxation. It must be extensively continued as the source of the government's income ; and in a readjustment of our tariff the interests of American labor engaged in manufacture should be carefully considered, as well as the preservation of our manufacturers. It may be called protection, or by any other name, but relief from the hardships and dangers of our present tariff laws should be devised with especial precaution against imperiling the existence of our manufacturing interests. But this existence should not mean a condition which, without regard to the public welfare or a national exigency, must always insure the realization of immense profits instead of moderately profitable returns. As the volume and diversity of our national activities increase, new recruits are added to those who desire a continuation of the advantages which they conceive the present system of tariff taxation directly affords them. So stubbornly have all efforts to reform the present condition been resisted by those of our fellow-citizens thus engaged, that they can hardly complain of the suspicion, entertained to a certain extent, that there exists an organized combination, all along the line, to maintain their advantage.

We are in the midst of centennial celebrations, and with becoming pride we rejoice in American skill and ingenuity, in American energy and enterprise, and in the wonderful natural advantages and resources developed by a century's national growth. Yet, when an attempt is made to justify a scheme which permits a tax to be laid upon every consumer in the land for the benefit of our manufacturers, quite beyond a reasonable demand for governmental regard, it suits the purposes of advocacy to call our manufactures infant industries, still needing the highest and greatest degree of favor and fostering care that can be wrung from Federal legislation.

It is also said that the increase in the price of domestic manufactures resulting from the present tariff is necessary in order that higher wages may be paid to our workingmen, employed in manufactories, than are paid for what is called the pauper labor of Europe. All will acknowledge the force of an argument which involves the welfare and liberal compensation of our laboring people. Our labor is honorable in the eyes of every American citizen; and as it lies at the foundation of our development and progress, it is entitled, without affectation or hypocrisy, to the utmost regard. The standard of our laborers' life should not be measured by that of any other country less favored, and they are entitled to their full share of all our advantages.

By the last census it is made to appear that of the 17,392,099 of our population engaged in all kinds of industries, 7,670,493 are employed in agriculture, 4,074,238 in professional and personal service—2,934,876 of whom are domestic servants and laborers—while 1,810,256 are employed in trade and transportation, and 3,837,112 are classed as employed in manufacturing and mining.

For present purposes, however, the last number given should be considerably reduced. Without attempting to enumerate all, it will be conceded that there should be deducted from those whom it includes 375,143 carpenters and joiners, 285,401 milliners, dressmakers, and seamstresses, 172,726 blacksmiths, 133,756 tailors and tailoresses, 102,473 masons, 76,241 butchers, 41,309 bakers, 22,083 plasterers, and 4891 engaged in manufacturing agricultural implements, amounting in the aggregate to 1,214,023, leaving 2,623,089 persons employed in such manufacturing industries as are claimed to be benefited by a high tariff.

To these the appeal is made to save their employment and maintain their wages by resisting a change. There should be no disposition to answer such suggestions by the allegation that they are in a minority among those who labor, and therefore should forego an advantage, in the interest of low prices for the majority ; their compensation, as it may be affected by the operation of tariff laws, should at all times be scrupulously kept in view ; and yet, with slight reflection, they will not overlook the fact that they are consumers with the rest ; that they, too, have their own wants and those of their families to supply from their earnings, and that the price of the necessaries of life, as well as the amount of their wages, will regulate the measure of their welfare and comfort.

But the reduction of taxation demanded should be so

measured as not to necessitate or justify either the loss of employment by the workingman or the lessening of his wages; and the profits still remaining to the manufacturer, after a necessary readjustment, should furnish no excuse for the sacrifice of the interests of his employees, either in their opportunity to work, or in the diminution of their compensation. Nor can the worker in manufactures fail to understand that while a high tariff is claimed to be necessary to allow the payment of remunerative wages, it certainly results in a very large increase in the price of nearly all sorts of manufactures, which, in almost countless forms, he needs for the use of himself and his family. He receives at the desk of his employer his wages, and, perhaps before he reaches his home, is obliged, in a purchase for family use of an article which embraces his own labor, to return, in the payment of the increase in price which the tariff permits, the hard-earned compensation of many days of toil.

The farmer and agriculturist, who manufactures nothing, but who pays the increased price which the tariff imposes upon every agricultural implement, upon all he wears and upon all he uses and owns, except the increase of his flocks and herds and such things as his husbandry produces from the soil, is invited to aid in maintaining the present situation; and he is told that a high duty on imported wool is necessary for the benefit of those who have sheep to shear, in order that the price of their wool may be increased. They, of course, are not reminded that the farmer who has no sheep is by this scheme obliged, in his purchases of clothing and woolen goods, to pay a tribute to his fellow-farmer as well as to the manufacturer and merchant; nor is any mention made of the fact that the sheep-owners themselves and their households must wear clothing and use other articles manufactured from the wool they sell at tariff prices, and thus, as consumers, must return their share of this increased price to the tradesman.

I think it may be fairly assumed that a large proportion of the sheep owned by the farmers throughout the country are found in small flocks numbering from twenty-five to fifty. The duty on the grade of imported wool which these sheep yield is ten cents each pound, if of the value of thirty cents or less, and twelve cents if of the value of more than thirty cents. If the liberal estimate of six pounds be allowed for each fleece, the duty thereon would be sixty or seventy-two cents, and this may be taken as the utmost enhancement of its price to the farmer by reason of this duty. Eighteen dollars would thus represent the increased price of the wool from twenty-five sheep and thirty-six dollars that from the wool of fifty sheep; and, at present values, this addition would amount to about one-third of its price. If, upon its sale, the farmer receives this or a less tariff profit, the wool leaves his hands charged with precisely that sum, which, in all its changes, will adhere to it until it reaches the consumer. When manufactured into cloth and other goods and material for use, its cost is not only increased to the extent of the farmer's tariff profit, but a further sum has been added for the benefit of the manufacturer under the operation of other tariff laws. In the meantime the day arrives when the farmer finds it necessary to purchase woolen goods and material to clothe himself and family for the winter. When he faces the tradesman for that purpose he discovers that he is obliged not only to return, in the way of increased prices, his tariff profit on the wool he sold, and which then perhaps lies before him in manufactured form, but that he must add a considerable sum thereto to meet a further increase in cost caused by a tariff duty on the manufacture. Thus, in the end, he is aroused to the fact that he has paid upon a moderate purchase, as a result of the tariff scheme, which, when he sold his wool, seemed so profitable, an increase in price more than sufficient to sweep away all the tariff profit he received upon the wool he produced and sold.

When the number of farmers engaged in wool-raising is compared with all the farmers in the country, and the small proportion they bear to our population is considered; when it is made apparent, that, in the case of a large part of those who own sheep, the benefit of the present tariff on wool is illusory ; and above all, when it must be conceded that the increase of the cost of living caused by such tariff becomes a burden upon those with moderate means and the poor, the employed and unemployed, the sick and well, and the young and old, and that it constitutes a tax which, with relentless grasp, is fastened upon the clothing of every man, woman, and child in the land, reasons are suggested why the removal or reduction of this duty should be included in a revision of our tariff laws.

In speaking of the increased cost to the consumer of our home manufactures, resulting from a duty laid upon imported articles of the same description, the fact is not overlooked that competition among our domestic producers sometimes has the effect of keeping the price of their products below the highest limit allowed by such duty. But it is notorious that this competition is too often strangled by combinations quite prevalent at this time, and frequently called trusts, which have for their object the regulation of the supply and price of commodities made and sold by members of the combination. The people can hardly hope for any consideration in the operation of these selfish schemes.

If, however, in the absence of such combination, a healthy and free competition reduces the price of any particular dutiable article of home production below the limit which it might otherwise reach under our tariff laws, and if, with such reduced price, its manufacture continues to thrive, it is entirely evident that one thing has been discovered which should be carefully scrutinized in an effort to reduce taxation.

The necessity of combination to maintain the price of any commodity to the tariff point furnishes proof that someone is willing to accept lower prices for such commodity, and that such prices are remunerative ; and lower prices produced by competition prove the same thing. Thus, where either of these conditions exists, a case would seem to be presented for an easy reduction of taxation.

The considerations which have been presented touching

our tariff laws are intended only to enforce an earnest recommendation that the surplus revenues of the government be prevented by the reduction of our customs duties; and, at the same time, to emphasize a suggestion that, in accomplishing this purpose, we may discharge a double duty to our people by granting to them a measure of relief from tariff taxation in quarters where it is most needed and from sources where it can be most fairly and justly accorded.

Nor can the presentation made of such considerations be, with any degree of fairness, regarded as evidence of unfriendliness toward our manufacturing interests, or of any lack of appreciation of their value and importance.

These interests constitute a leading and most substantial element of our national greatness, and furnish the proud proof of our country's progress. But if, in the emergency that presses upon us, our manufacturers are asked to surrender something for the public good and to avert disaster, their patriotism, as well as a grateful recognition of advantages already afforded, should lead them to willing co-operation. No demand is made that they shall forego all the benefits of governmental regard; but they cannot fail to be admonished of their duty, as well as their enlightened self-interest and safety, when they are reminded of the fact that financial panic and collapse, to which the present condition tends, afford no greater shelter or protection to our manufactures than to our other important enterprises. Opportunity for safe, careful, and deliberate reform is now offered, and none of us should be unmindful of a time when an abused and irritated people, heedless of those who have resisted timely and reasonable relief, may insist upon a radical and sweeping rectification of their wrongs.

The difficulty attending a wise and fair revision of our tariff laws is not underestimated. It will require on the part of the Congress great labor and care, and especially a broad and national contemplation of the subject, and a patriotic disregard of such local and selfish claims as are unreasonable and reckless of the welfare of the entire country.

Under our present laws more than four thousand articles are subject to duty. Many of these do not in any way compete with our own manufactures and many are hardly worth attention as subjects of revenue. A considerable reduction can be made in the aggregate by adding them to the free list. The taxation of luxuries presents no features of hardship ; but the necessaries of life, used and consumed by all the people, the duty upon which adds to the cost of living in every home, should be greatly cheapened.

The radical reduction of the duties imposed upon raw material used in manufactures, or its free importation, is, of course, an important factor in any effort to reduce the prices of these necessaries ; it would not only relieve them from the increased cost caused by the tariff on such material, but the manufactured product being thus cheapened, that part of the tariff now laid upon such product, as a compensation to our manufacturers for the present price of raw material, could be accordingly modified. Such reduction, or free importation, would serve besides largely to reduce the revenue. It is not apparent how such a change can have any injurious effect upon our manufacturers. On the contrary, it would appear to give them a better chance in foreign markets with the manufacturers of other countries, who cheapen their wares by free material. Thus our people might have the opportunity of extending their sales beyond the limits of home consumption—saving them from the depression, interruption in business, and loss caused by a glutted domestic market, and affording their employees more certain and steady labor, with its resulting quiet and contentment.

The question thus imperatively presented for solution should be approached in a spirit higher than partisanship, and considered in the light of that regard for patriotic duty which should characterize the action of those intrusted with the weal of a confiding people. But the obligation to declared party policy and principle is not wanting to urge prompt and effective action. Both of the great political parties now represented in the government have, by repeated and authoritative declarations, condemned the condition of our laws which permits the collection from the people of unnecessary revenue, and have in the most solemn manner promised its correction ; and neither as citizens nor partisans are our countrymen in a mood to condone the deliberate violation of these pledges.

Our progress toward a wise conclusion will not be improved by dwelling upon the theories of protection and free trade. This savors too much of bandying epithets. It is a condition which confronts us—not a theory. Relief from this *condition* may involve a slight reduction of the advantages which we award our home productions, but the entire withdrawal of such advantages should not be contemplated. The question of free trade is absolutely irrelevant ; and the persistent claim made in certain quarters that all efforts to relieve the people from unjust and unnecessary taxation are schemes of so-called free-traders is mischievous, and far removed from any consideration for the public good.

The simple and plain duty which we owe the people is to reduce the taxation to the necessary expenses of an economical operation of the government, and to restore to the business of the country the money which we hold in the treasury through the perversion of governmental powers. These things can and should be done with safety to all our industries, without danger to the opportunity for remunerative labor which our workingmen need, and with benefit to them and all our people, by cheapening their means of subsistence and increasing the measure of their comforts.

The Constitution provides that the President " shall, from time to time, give to the Congress information of the state of the Union." It has been the custom of the Executive, in compliance with this provision, to exhibit annually to the Congress, at the opening of its session, the general condition of the country, and to detail, with some particularity, the operations of the different Executive Departments. It would be especially agreeable to follow this course at the present time, and to call attention to the valuable accomplishments of these Departments during the last fiscal year. But I am so much impressed with the paramount importance of the subject to which this communication has thus far been devoted that I shall forego the addition of any other topic, and shall only urge upon your immediate consideration the " state of the Union," as shown in the present condition of our treasury and our general fiscal situation, upon which every element of our safety and prosperity depends.

The reports of the heads of Departments, which will be submitted, contain full and explicit information touching the transaction of the business intrusted to them, and such recommendations relating to legislation in the public interest as they deem advisable. I ask for these reports and recommendations the deliberate examination and action of the legislative branch of the government.

There are other subjects not embraced in the departmental reports demanding legislative consideration and which I should be glad to submit. Some of them, however, have been earnestly presented in previous messages ; and as to them, I beg leave to repeat prior recommendations.

As the law makes no provision for any report from the Department of State, a brief history of the transactions of that important Department, together with other matters which it may hereafter be deemed essential to commend to the attention of the Congress, may furnish the occasion for a future communication.

GROVER CLEVELAND.

EXECUTIVE MANSION,
WASHINGTON, December 6, 1887.

VII.

Letter to Tammany Hall Celebration.

EXECUTIVE MANSION,
WASHINGTON, June 29, 1888.

To JAMES A. FLACK, *Grand Sachem:*

DEAR SIR : I regret that I am obliged to decline the courteous invitation which I have received to attend the celebration
by the Tammany Society of the birthday of our republic on
the 4th day of July next. The zeal and enthusiasm with
which your society celebrates this day afford proof of its steadfast patriotism as well as its care for all that pertains to the
advantage and prosperity of the people.

I cannot doubt that the renewal of a "love and devotion to
a pure Jeffersonian Democratic form of government," which
you contemplate, will suggest the inquiry whether the people
are receiving all the benefits which are due them under such a
form of government. These benefits are not fully enjoyed
when our citizens are unnecessarily burdened, and their earnings and incomes are uselessly diminished under the pretext
of governmental support.

Our government belongs to the people. They have decreed
its purpose; and it is their clear right to demand that its cost
shall be limited by frugality, and that its burden of expense
shall be carefully limited by its actual needs. And yet a useless and dangerous surplus in the national treasury tells no
other tale but extortion on the part of the government, and a
perversion of the people's intention. In the midst of our impetuous enterprise and blind confidence in our destiny, it is
time to pause and study our condition. It is no sooner appreciated than the conviction must follow that the tribute exacted
from the people should be diminished.

The theories which cloud the subject, misleading honest
men, and the appeals to selfish interests which deceive the understanding, make the reform, which should be easy, a difficult
task. Although those who propose a remedy for present evils

have always been the friends of American labor, and though they declare their purpose to further its interests in all their efforts, yet those who oppose reform attempt to disturb our workingmen by the cry that their wages and their employment are threatened.

They advocate a system which benefits certain classes of our citizens at the expense of every householder in the land—a system which breeds discontent, because it permits the duplication of wealth without corresponding additional recompense to labor, which prevents the opportunity to work by stifling production and limiting the area of our markets, and which enhances the cost of living beyond the laborer's hard-earned wages.

The attempt is made to divert the attention of the people from the evils of such a scheme of taxation, by branding those who seek to correct these evils as free-traders, and enemies of our workingmen and our industrial enterprises. This is so far from the truth that there should be no chance for such deception to succeed.

It behooves the American people, while they rejoice in the anniversary of the day when their free government was declared, also to reason together and determine that they will not be deprived of the blessings and the benefits which their government should afford.

Yours very truly,

GROVER CLEVELAND.

VIII.

From the Fourth Annual Message to Congress, December, 1888.

As you assemble for the discharge of the duties you have assumed as the representatives of a free and generous people, your meeting is marked by an interesting and impressive incident. With the expiration of the present session of the Congress the first century of our constitutional existence as a nation will be completed.

Our survival for one hundred years is not sufficient to assure us that we no longer have dangers to fear in the maintenance, with all its promised blessings, of a government founded upon the freedom of the people. The time rather admonishes us soberly to inquire whether in the past we have always closely kept in the course of safety, and whether we have before us a way, plain and clear, which leads to happiness and perpetuity.

When the experiment of our government was undertaken, the chart adopted for our guidance was the Constitution. Departure from the lines there laid down is failure. It is only by a strict adherence to the directions they indicate, and by restraint within the limitations they fix, that we can furnish proof to the world of the fitness of the American people for self-government.

The equal and exact justice of which we boast, as the underlying principle of our institutions, should not be confined to the relations of our citizens to each other. The government itself is under bond to the American people that, in the exercise of its functions and powers, it will deal with the body of our citizens in a manner scrupulously honest and fair, and absolutely just. It has agreed that American citizenship shall be the only credential necessary to justify the claim of equality before the law, and that no condition in life shall give rise to discrimination in the treatment of the people by their government.

The citizen of our republic in its early days rigidly insisted upon full compliance with the letter of this bond, and saw stretching out before him a clear field for individual endeavor. His tribute to the support of his government was measured by the cost of its economical maintenance, and he was secure in the enjoyment of the remaining recompense of his steady and contented toil. In those days the frugality of the people was stamped upon their government, and was enforced by the free, thoughtful, and intelligent suffrage of the citizen. Combinations, monopolies, and aggregations of capital were either avoided or sternly regulated and restrained. The pomp and glitter of governments less free offered no temptation and presented no delusion to the plain people, who, side by side, in friendly competition, wrought for the ennoblement and dignity of man, for the solution of the problem of free government, and for the achievement of the grand destiny awaiting the land which God had given them.

A century has passed. Our cities are the abiding-places of wealth and luxury; our manufactories yield fortunes never dreamed of by the fathers of the republic; our business men are madly striving in the race for riches, and immense aggregations of capital outrun the imagination in the magnitude of their undertakings.

We view with pride and satisfaction this bright picture of our country's growth and prosperity, while only a closer scrutiny develops a somber shading. Upon more careful inspection we find the wealth and luxury of our cities mingled with poverty and wretchedness and unremunerative toil. A crowded and constantly increasing urban population suggests the impoverishment of rural sections, and discontent with agricultural pursuits. The farmer's son, not satisfied with his father's simple and laborious life, joins the eager chase for easily acquired wealth.

We discover that the fortunes realized by our manufacturers are no longer solely the reward of sturdy industry and enlightened foresight, but that they result from the discriminating favor of the government, and are largely built upon undue exactions from the masses of our people. The gulf between employers and the employed is constantly widening, and classes are rapidly forming, one comprising the very rich and powerful, while in another are found the toiling poor.

As we view the achievements of aggregated capital, we discover the existence of trusts, combinations, and monopolies, while the citizen is struggling far in the rear, or is trampled to death beneath an iron heel.   Corporations, which should be carefully restrained creatures of the law and the servants of the people, are fast becoming the people's masters.

Still, congratulating ourselves upon the wealth and prosperity of our country, and complacently contemplating every incident of change inseparable from these conditions, it is our duty as patriotic citizens to inquire, at the present stage of our progress, how the bond of the government, made with the people, has been kept and performed.

Instead of limiting the tribute drawn from our citizens to the necessities of its economical administration, the government persists in exacting, from the substance of the people, millions, which, unapplied and useless, lie dormant in its treasury. This flagrant injustice, and this breach of faith and obligation, add to extortion the danger attending the diversion of the currency of the country from the legitimate channels of business.

Under the same laws by which these results are produced, the government permits many millions more to be added to the cost of the living of our people, and to be taken from our consumers, which unreasonably swell the profits of a small, but powerful minority.

The people must still be taxed for the support of the government under the operation of tariff laws.   But, to the extent that the mass of our citizens are inordinately burdened beyond any useful public purpose and for the benefit of a favored few, the government, under pretext of an exercise of its taxing power, enters gratuitously into partnership with these favorites, to their advantage and to the injury of a vast majority of our people.

This is not equality before the law.

The existing situation is injurious to the health of our entire body politic.   It stifles, in those for whose benefit it is permitted, all patriotic love of country, and substitutes in its place selfish greed and grasping avarice.   Devotion to American citizenship for its own sake and for what it should accomplish as a motive to our nation's advancement and the happiness of all our people, is displaced by the assumption that the government, instead of being the embodiment of equality, is but an instrumentality through which especial and individual advantages are to be gained.

The arrogance of this assumption is unconcealed. It appears in the sordid disregard of all but personal interests, in the refusal to abate for the benefit of others one iota of selfish advantage, and in combinations to perpetuate such advantages through efforts to control legislation and influence improperly the suffrages of the people.

The grievances of those not included within the circle of these beneficiaries, when fully realized, will surely arouse irritation and discontent. Our farmers, long-suffering and patient, struggling in the race of life with the hardest and most unremitting toil, will not fail to see, in spite of misrepresentations and misleading fallacies, that they are obliged to accept such prices for their products as are fixed in foreign markets, where they compete with the farmers of the world ; that their lands are declining in value while their debts increase ; and that, without compensating favor, they are forced by the action of the government to pay, for the benefit of others, such enhanced prices for the things they need that the scanty returns of their labor fail to furnish their support, or leave no margin for accumulation.

Our workingmen, enfranchised from all delusions and no longer frightened by the cry that their wages are endangered by a just revision of our tariff laws, will reasonably demand through such revision steadier employment, cheaper means of living in their homes, freedom for themselves and their children from the doom of perpetual servitude, and an open door to their advancement beyond the limits of a laboring class. Others of our citizens whose comforts and expenditures are measured by moderate salaries and fixed incomes, will insist upon the fairness and justice of cheapening the cost of necessaries for themselves and their families.

When to the selfishness of the beneficiaries of unjust discrimination under our laws there shall be added the discontent of those who suffer from such discrimination, we will realize the fact that the beneficent purposes of our government, dependent upon the patriotism and contentment of our people, are endangered.

Communism is a hateful thing, and a menace to peace and organized government. But the communism of combined wealth and capital, the outgrowth of overweening cupidity and selfishness, which insidiously undermines the justice and integrity of free institutions is not less dangerous than the communism of oppressed poverty and toil which, exasperated by injustice and discontent, attacks with wild disorder the citadel of rule.

He mocks the people who proposes that the government shall protect the rich and that they in turn will care for the laboring poor. Any intermediary between the people and their government, or the least delegation of the care and protection the government owes to the humblest citizen in the land, makes the boast of free institutions a glittering delusion and the pretended boon of American citizenship a shameless imposition.

A just and sensible revision of our tariff laws should be made for the relief of those of our countrymen who suffer under present conditions. Such a revision should receive the support of all who love that justice and equality due to American citizenship ; of all who realize that in this justice and equality our government finds its strength and its power to protect the citizen and his property ; of all who believe that the contented competence and comfort of many accord better with the spirit of our institutions than colossal fortunes unfairly gathered in the hands of a few ; of all who appreciate that the forbearance and fraternity among our people, which recognize the value of every American interest, are the surest guarantee of our national progress, and of all who desire to see the products of American skill and ingenuity in every market of the world with a resulting restoration of American commerce.

The necessity of the reduction of our revenue is so apparent as to be generally conceded. But the means by which this end shall be accomplished, and the sum of direct benefit which shall result to our citizens, present a controversy of the utmost importance. There should be no scheme accepted as satisfactory by which the burdens of the people are only apparently removed. Extravagant appropriations of public money, with all their demoralizing consequences, should not be tolerated, either as a means of relieving the treasury of its present surplus or as furnishing pretexts for resisting a proper reduction in tariff rates. Existing evils and injustice should be honestly recognized, boldly met, and effectively remedied. There should be no cessation of the struggle until a plan is perfected, fair and conservative toward existing industries, but which will reduce the cost to consumers of the necessaries of life, while it provides for our manufacturers the advantage of freer raw materials and permits no injury to the interests of American labor.

The cause for which the battle is waged is comprised within lines clearly and distinctly defined. It should never be compromised. It is the people's cause.

It cannot be denied that the selfish and private interests, which are so persistently heard when efforts are made to deal in a just and comprehensive manner with our tariff laws, are related to, if they are not responsible for, the sentiment largely prevailing among the people that the general government is the fountain of individual and private aid ; that it may be expected to relieve with paternal care the distress of citizens and communities, and that from the fullness of its treasury it should, upon the slightest possible pretext of promoting the general good, apply public funds to the benefit of localities and individuals. Nor can it be denied that there is a growing assumption that, as against the government and in favor of private claims and interests, the usual rules and limitations of business principles and just dealing should be waived.

These ideas have been, unhappily, much encouraged by

legislative acquiescence.   Relief from contracts made with the government is too easily accorded in favor of the citizen ; the failure to support claims against the government by proof is often supplied by no better consideration than the wealth of the government and the poverty of the claimant ; gratuities in the form of pensions are granted upon no other real ground than the needy condition of the applicant, or for reasons less valid ; and large sums are expended, for public buildings and other improvements, upon representations scarcely claimed to be related to public needs and necessities.

The extent to which the consideration of such matters subordinates and postpones action upon subjects of great public importance, but involving no special, private, or partisan interest, should arrest attention and lead to reformation.

A few of the numerous illustrations of this condition may be stated.

The crowded condition of the calendar of the Supreme Court, and the delay to suitors and denial of justice resulting therefrom, have been strongly urged upon the attention of the Congress, with a plan for the relief of the situation approved by those well able to judge of its merits.   While this subject remains without effective consideration, many laws have been passed providing for the holding of terms of inferior court at places to suit the convenience of localities, or to lay the foundation of an application for the erection of a new public building.

Repeated recommendations have been submitted for the amendment and change of the laws relating to our public lands, so that their spoliation and diversion to other uses than as homes for honest settlers might be prevented.   While a measure to meet this conceded necessity of reform remains awaiting the action of the Congress, many claims to the public lands and applications for their donation, in favor of States and individuals, have been allowed.

A plan in aid of Indian management, recommended by those well informed as containing valuable features in furtherance of the solution of the Indian problem, has thus far failed of legislative sanction, while grants of doubtful expediency to railroad corporations, permitting them to pass through Indian reservations, have greatly multiplied.

The propriety and necessity of the erection of one or more prisons for the confinement of United States convicts, and a post-office building in the national capital, are not disputed. But these needs yet remain unanswered, while scores of public buildings have been erected where their necessity for public purposes is not apparent.

A revision of our pension laws could easily be made, which would rest upon just principles and provide for every worthy applicant. But, while our general pension laws remain confused and imperfect, hundreds of private pension laws are annually passed which are the sources of unjust discrimination and popular demoralization.

Appropriation bills for the support of the government are defaced by items and provisions to meet private ends, and it is freely asserted by responsible and experienced parties that a bill appropriating money for public internal improvement would fail to meet with favor unless it contained items more for local and private advantage than for public benefit.

These statements can be much emphasized by an ascertainment of the proportion of Federal legislation which either bears upon its face its private character or which, upon examination, develops such a motive power.

And yet the people wait, and expect from their chosen representatives such patriotic action as will advance the welfare of the entire country ; and this expectation can only be answered by the performance of public duty with unselfish purpose. Our mission among the nations of the earth, and our success in accomplishing the work God has given the American people to do, require of those intrusted with the making and execution of our laws perfect devotion, above all other things, to the public good.

This devotion will lead us to resist strongly all impatience of constitutional limitations of Federal power, and to check persistently the increasing tendency to extend the scope of Federal legislation into the domain of State and local jurisdiction, upon the plea of subserving the public welfare. The preservation of the partitions between proper subjects of Federal and local care and regulation is of such importance under the Constitution, which is the law of our very existence, that no consideration of expediency or sentiment should tempt us to enter upon doubtful ground. We have undertaken to discover and proclaim the richest blessings of a free government, with the Constitution as our guide. Let us follow the way it points out. It will not mislead us. And surely no one who has taken upon himself the solemn obligation to support and preserve the Constitution can find justification or solace for disloyalty in the excuse that he wandered and disobeyed in search of a better way to reach the public welfare than the Constitution offers.

What has been said is deemed not inappropriate at a time when, from a century's height, we view the way already trod by the American people, and attempt to discover their future path.

The seventh President of the United States—the soldier and statesman, and at all times the firm and brave friend of the people—in vindication of his course as the protector of popular rights, and the champion of true American citizenship, declared:

The ambition which leads me on is an anxious desire and a fixed determination to restore to the people, unimpaired, the sacred trust they have confided to my charge ; to heal the wounds of the Constitution and to preserve it from further violation ; to persuade my countrymen, so far as I may, that it is not in a splendid government supported by powerful monopolies and aristocratical establishments that they will find happiness, or their liberties protection, but in a plain system, void of pomp—protecting all and granting favors to none—dispensing its blessings like the dews of heaven, unseen and unfelt save in the freshness and beauty they contribute to produce. It is such a government that the genius of our people requires—such an one only under which our States may remain, for ages to come, united, prosperous, and free.

IX.

To the Massachusetts Tariff Reform League.

EXECUTIVE MANSION,
WASHINGTON, December 24, 1888.

MESSRS. SHERMAN, HOAR, AND OTHERS, *Committee:*

GENTLEMEN : I am exceedingly sorry that I cannot be present at the dinner of the Massachusetts Tariff Reform League on the 28th instant. This is not merely a formal and common expression of regret ; it truly indicates how much I should enjoy meeting the members of your league, and how glad I should be to express in person my appreciation of their important services in a cause to which I am earnestly attached, and to acknowledge at the same time their frequent and encouraging manifestations of personal friendliness. I know, too, that it would be profitable and advantageous to be, even for a brief period, within the inspiring influence of the atmosphere surrounding patriotic and unselfish men, banded together in the interests of their fellow-countrymen, and devoted to the work of tariff reform.

This reform appears to me to be as far-reaching in its purposes as the destiny of our country, and as broad in its beneficence as the welfare of our entire people. It is because the efforts of its advocates are not discredited by any sordid motives that they are able boldly and confidently to attack the strongholds of selfishness and greed. Our institutions were constructed in purity of purpose and love for humanity. Their operation is adjusted to the touch of national virtue and patriotism, and their results, under such guidance, must be the prosperity and happiness of our people ; and so long as the advocates of tariff reform appreciate the sentiments in which our institutions had their origin, so long as they apprehend the sources which alone can guide their operations, so long as they, in a spirit of true patriotism, are consecrated to the service of their country, temporary defeat brings no discouragement. It but proves the stubbornness of the forces of com-

bined selfishness, and discloses how far the people have been
led astray and how great is the necessity of redoubled efforts
in their behalf.   To lose faith in the intelligence of the people
is a surrender and an abandonment of the struggle.   To arouse
their intelligence, and free it from darkness and delusion, gives
assurance of speedy and complete victory.

In the track of reform are often found the dead hopes of
pioneers and the despair of those who fall in the march.   But
there will be neither despair nor dead hopes in the path of
tariff reform ; nor shall its pioneers fail to reach the heights.
Holding fast their faith, and rejecting every alluring overture
and every deceptive compromise which would betray their
sacred trust, they themselves shall regain and restore the
patrimony of their countrymen, freed from the trespass of
grasping encroachment and safely secured by the genius of
American justice and equality.

Yours very truly,

GROVER CLEVELAND.

X.

To the Indiana Tariff Reform League.

NEW YORK, February 15, 1890.

EDGAR A. BROWN, ESQ., *President.*

MY DEAR SIR : Though my letters to Democratic and
tariff reform assemblages have lately been very frequent, I
cannot deny your request to say a word of encouragement to
the tariff reformers who will meet at the first annual convention of the Indiana Tariff Reform League on the 4th of
March.

I am very much pleased with the plan upon which your
league seems to be organized.   It conveys a suggestion of
practical work in the field of information and enlightenment.
This, if persistently carried out, cannot fail of success.   Of
course, we do not approach the American people, assuming

that they are ignorant or unpatriotic. But we know that they are busy people and apt to neglect the study of public questions. In the engrossment of their daily avocations, they are too ready to rely upon the judgment and avowed principles of the party with which they have affiliated as guides to their political actions. In this way they have become slow to examine for themselves the questions of tariff reform. If, in the lights of reasonable and simple arguments and of such object-lessons as are being constantly placed before them, our people can be induced to investigate the subjects, there need be no fear as to their conclusion.

The Democratic party—as the party of the people, opposed to selfish schemes, which ignore the public good, and pledged to the interests of all their countrymen instead of furtherance of the interests of the few who seek to pervert governmental powers for their enrichment—was never nearer to its fundamental principles than it was in its contests for tariff reform.

It certainly adds to the satisfaction with which we labor in this cause to be assured that in our efforts we not only serve our party, but all the people of the land.

Yours very truly,

GROVER CLEVELAND.

XI.

To the Tariff Reform Club, Hagerstown, Md.

NEW YORK, April 29, 1890.

HENRY KYD DOUGLASS, ESQ.

MY DEAR SIR : I thank you for your invitation to attend the meeting on the 2d day of May which inaugurates a tariff reform club at Hagerstown. I am sorry that I cannot be with you on this interesting occasion, which is to give birth to another of those agencies whose mission it is to rouse to practical thought and activity. Those who propose to juggle with the question of tariff reform will never again find their intended dupes asleep and uninformed. The people shall know the merits of this question, and shall know, too, that its fair and honest adjustment greatly concerns them.

With such a mission, and in the enforcement of such a principle, it is a glorious thing to be a true Democrat in these days. The zeal and enthusiasm which at this time prevail in our party demonstrate that Democracy is never in a more congenial element than when it battles for a principle which involves the real welfare and prosperity of the people. I hope that your meeting will be a great success, and that your Tariff Reform Club will never falter in usefulness and efficiency.

Yours very truly,

GROVER CLEVELAND.

XII.

To the Kensington Reform Club, Philadelphia.

NEW YORK, May 9, 1890.

F. A. HERWIG, *President.*

MY DEAR SIR : I desire through you to thank the Kensington Reform Club, formerly known as the Workingmen's Tariff Reform Association, for the courteous invitation I have received to attend a mass meeting on the evening of the 3d of June.

The terms in which the invitation is expressed convince me that the question of tariff reform is receiving the attention it deserves from those most vitally interested in its just and fair solution. I know that, with the feeling now abroad in our land and with the intense existence and activity of such clubs as yours, the claim, presumptuously made, that the people at the last election finally passed upon the subject of tariff adjustment will be emphatically denied ; that our workingmen and our farmers will continue to agitate this and all other questions involving their welfare with increased zeal, and in the light of increased knowledge and experience, until they are determined finally and in accordance with the American sentiment of fair play.

I use no idle form of words when I say that I regret my engagements and professional occupations will not permit me to meet the members of your club on the occasion of their mass meeting. Hoping that those who are fortunate enough to participate will find it to their profit, and that the meeting will in all respects be a great success,

I am, yours very truly,
GROVER CLEVELAND.

XIII.

To the President of the Custom Cutters' National Convention.

NEW YORK, January 20, 1891.

G. H. HUNTOON, ESQ.

DEAR SIR : I thank you for sending me your address made at the convention of the Custom Foremen Tailors' Association, and I have read the same with interest.

The question of tariff reform directly affects all the people of the land in a substantial way, and they ought to be interested in its discussion. I am afraid that a great many of our fellow-citizens are too apt to regard this as a political question, intricate and complex, affecting them in a remote way, and one which may well enough be left for politicians to wrangle over. This induces a neglect of the subject on the part of a great number of our people and a willingness to follow blindly the party to which they happen to belong in their action upon it.

It is a good sign to see practical men, such as belong to your association, discussing the question for themselves. If this is done intelligently, and with sincere intent to secure the truth, tariff reformers, I think, have no need to fear the result of such discussions.

Very truly yours,
GROVER CLEVELAND.

XIV.

To the Tariff Reform Club, Montclair, N. J.

NEW YORK, February 3, 1891.

ALEXANDER D. NOYES, ESQ.

DEAR SIR : I have received the invitation you sent me to attend a dinner given by the Tariff Reform Club of Montclair, N. J., on the 6th instant, and I regret that my engagements are such that I cannot accept the same.

It gives me great pleasure to note the growth of Democratic sentiments and strength in my native county, and to know that the cause of tariff reform has commended itself to the voters of the Sixth Congressional District. These circumstances furnish exceptional persuasion to an invitation to meet those who, by organized effort, are pushing on the good work in the county where I was born.

Nothing can excuse the Democratic party if, at this time, it permits the neglect or subordination of the question of tariff reform. In the first place, the principle involved is plainly and unalterably right. This, of itself, should be sufficient reason for constant activity in its behalf. Secondly, we have aroused a spirit of inquiry among our countrymen which it is our duty to satisfy ; and finally, there may be added to these considerations the promise of success held out to the party which honestly perseveres in the propagandism of sound and true political principles.

Yours very truly,

GROVER CLEVELAND.

XV.

To the Indiana Tariff Reform League, March, 1891.

You will not, I hope, think it amiss if I suggest the necessity of pushing, with more vigor than ever, the doctrine of your organization. I believe that the theories and practices which tariff reform antagonizes are responsible for many, if not all, of the evils which afflict our people. If there is a scarcity of the circulating medium, is not the experiment worth trying as a remedy, of leaving in the hands of the people, and for their use, the money which is needlessly taken from them under the pretext of necessary taxation ? If the farmer's lot is a hard one, in his discouraging struggle for better rewards of his toil, are the prices of his products to be improved by the policy which hampers trade in his best markets and invites the competition of dangerous rivals ?

Whether other means of relief may appear necessary to relieve present hardships, I believe the principle of tariff reform promises a most important aid in their rectification, and that the continued and earnest advocacy of this principle is essential to the lightening of the burdens of our countrymen.

Hoping that your organization may continue to be one of great usefulness and encouragement.

I am, yours very respectfully,
GROVER CLEVELAND.

XVI.

To the Young Men's Democratic Club, Canton, O.

NEW YORK, November 27, 1891.

CHAS. KRICHBAUM, ESQ., *President, etc.*

DEAR SIR : I regret that I am unable to attend the meeting to be held at Canton on the evening of the 3d of December, under the auspices of the Young Men's Democratic Club.

The value and significance of this occasion, it seems to me, are found in the evidence it furnishes of a determination to push the issue of tariff reform in a practical and effective manner. It is the duty of the Democratic party to do this ; and expediency, as well as duty, forbids any backward step or faltering.

No party can succeed which deliberately relinquishes a principle on the eve of its vindication ; and no party ought to succeed, which, having led honest men to the examination of a question vital to their interest and welfare, abandons their guidance and leaves them in unhappy doubt and perplexity.

The confidence born of mutual congratulation over partial success, and the assertion of the claims of any individual to pre-eminence or leadership, ought not to divert us from the duty we owe to the people. Our obligations, then, will not be discharged, until, in every hamlet and neighborhood throughout the land, our cause is so presented to our countrymen that they can no longer be deceived through blindness nor corrupted through indifference.

Yours very truly,

GROVER CLEVELAND.

CHAPTER V.

I.

At the Semi-Centennial of the City of Buffalo, July 3, 1882.

LADIES AND GENTLEMEN:

I OUGHT, perhaps, to be quite content on this occasion to assume the part of quiet gratification. But I cannot forbear expressing my satisfaction at being allowed to participate in the exercises of the evening, and I feel that I must give token of the pleasure I experience in gazing with you upon the fair face of our Queen City at the age of fifty. I am proud, with you, in contrasting what seem to us the small things of fifty years ago, with the beauty, and the greatness, and the importance of to-day. The achievements of the past are gained; the prosperity of the present we hold with a firm hand; and the promise of the future comes to us with no uncertain sound. It seems to me to-day that of all men the resident of Buffalo should be the proudest to name his home.

In the history of a city, fifty years but marks the period of youth, when all is fresh and joyous. The face is fair, the step is light, and the burden of life is carried with a song; the future, stretching far ahead, is full of bright anticipations, and the past, with whatever of struggle and disappointment there may have been, seems short, and is half forgotten. In this heyday of our city's life, we do well to exchange our congratulations, and to revel together in the assurances of the happy and prosperous future that awaits us.

And yet I do not deem it wrong to remind myself and you that our city, great in its youth, did not suddenly spring into existence clad in beauty and in strength. There were men fifty years ago, who laid its foundations broad and deep ; and who, with the care of jealous parents, tended it and watched its growth. Those early times were not without their trials and discouragements ; and we reap to-day the fruit of the labors and the perseverance of those pioneers. Those were the fathers of the city. Where are they? Fifty years added to manhood fill the cup of human life. Most have gone to swell the census of God's city, which lies beyond the stream of fate. A few there are who listlessly linger upon the bank, and wait to cross, in the shade of trees they have planted with their own hands. Let us tenderly remember the dead to-night, and let us renew our love and veneration for those who are spared to speak to us of the scenes attending our city's birth and infancy.

And in this, our day of pride and self-gratulation, there is, I think, one lesson at least which we may learn from the men who have come down to us from a former generation.

In the day of the infancy of the city which they founded, and for many years afterward, the people loved their city so well that they would only trust the management of its affairs in the strongest and best of hands ; and no man in those days was so engrossed in his own business but he could find some time to devote to public concerns. Read the names of the men who held places in this municipality fifty years ago, and food for reflection will be found. Is it true that the city of to-day, with its large population and with its vast and varied interests, needs less and different care than it did fifty years ago?

We boast of our citizenship to-night. But this citizenship brings with it duties not unlike those we owe our neighbor and our God. There is no better time than this for self-examination. He who deems himself too pure and holy to take part in the affairs of his city, will meet the fact that better men than he have thought it their duty to do so. He who cannot spare a moment, in his greed and selfishness, to devote to public concerns, will, perhaps, find a well-grounded fear that he may become the prey of public plunderers ; and he who indolently cares not who administers the government of his city, will find that he is living falsely, and in the neglect of his highest duty.

When our centennial shall be celebrated, what will be said of us ? I hope it may be said that we built and wrought well, and added much to the substantial prosperity of the city we had in charge. Brick and mortar may make a large city, but the encouragement of those things which elevate and purify, the exaction of the highest standard of integrity in official place, and a constant, active interest on the part of the good people in municipal government, are needed to make a great city.

Let it be said of us when only our names and memory are left, in the centennial time, that we faithfully administered the trust which we received from our fathers, and religiously performed our parts, in our day and generation, toward making our city not only prosperous, but truly great.

II.

Evacuation Day Celebration, New York, November 26, 1883.

MR. PRESIDENT AND GENTLEMEN OF THE CHAMBER OF
    COMMERCE :

My theme is too great for me, and I shall not attempt to cover it. The few words I shall speak will be upon a topic which makes but one element in the supremacy of the State of New York, and I fear that I shall treat of that in a very practical and perhaps uninteresting way.

I am free to confess that I am somewhat embarrassed to-night by my surroundings. Not only am I in the presence of a distinguished company, but I see about me what I suppose to be the guardians of the commerce of the State. This word " commerce " sounds very large to me ; because, whenever I have heard the greatness of a nation or a State spoken of, their commerce has been dwelt upon as a chief ingredient or factor in such greatness.   Here is the gateway of the commerce of our State ; and while the uttermost corner of our domain has felt and still feels its healthful influence, the tribute it has paid in passing this point has erected one of the largest cities in the world, and created many colossal fortunes.   I suppose, of course, I need not suggest that other cities and other States are quite willing to relieve the city and State of New York of a part or all of the commerce thus enjoyed ; and I doubt not the danger to be apprehended from any such competitors has received due care and attention.

I have lately seen a statement, by which it appears that for the year ending August 31, 1882, there were shipped from New Orleans to fifteen foreign ports 2,744,581 bushels of wheat and 639,342 bushels of corn.   This was transported in sixty-one steamers and two sailing vessels.   But for the year ending August 31, 1883, there were shipped from the same city to twenty-nine foreign ports 5,529,847 bushels of wheat and 7,161,168 bushels of corn, and this was transported in 278 steamers and twenty-four sailing vessels.   We thus find an increase, during the year specified, as follows : Increase in wheat, 2,785,266 ; increase in corn, 6,521,826 ; increase in number of ports, 14 ; increase in number of vessels, 239.

I expect there are other dangers to be apprehended from other quarters, which may threaten the perpetuity and volume of New York commerce.   Is there care enough taken to have champions of this all-important interest in the halls of legislation, and is it there distinctively enough represented ?   Bear in mind that you may labor and toil, in the whirl and excitement of business, to build new warehouses, and add to the city's wealth and to your own, but that, while you thus build, ignorant, negligent, or corrupt men among your lawmakers can easily and stealthily pull down.   Political duty and selfish interests lead in the same direction, and a neglect of this duty will, I believe, bring a sure punishment.

I venture the opinion that the commerce of your port should

be free from the annoying burdens and taxation to which it is now subjected, and yet a law passed by the last legislature, as a partial measure of relief, failed in its execution, for reasons, perhaps, in one sense commercial in their character, but far removed from any relations to the commerce of the port. I hasten to disclaim any insinuation that there are legislators sent from here who are not faithful to this great interest ; but I see no reason why they should not all be of that kind, nor why the commercial interests of this great city should not be more regarded in their selection.

The people of the State have lately taken it upon themselves to support the canals from funds raised by taxation, thus free-ing one branch of commerce from its burden. This means much to the farmer, who, by hours of toil, unknown to you, exacts from the soil barely sufficient to live and educate his children. He deems the advantage of a free canal to him in-direct and remote ; but this increased taxation he must meet. His land and farm buildings cannot be concealed ; and if, by chance, he is able to improve them, his betterments are within the gaze of the tax-gatherer, and bring a further increase of taxation. Are you sure that all the property of this great metropolis, where fortunes, which the farmer vainly works a lifetime to secure, are made and lost in a day, meets, with equal fairness, its share of taxation ? At any rate, cannot the city of New York afford to pay the expense necessary to the maintenance of its port—thus securing its commercial suprem-acy and controlling, free from State interference, this interest so directly important to you all.

We are apt, on such a day as this, to recall with pride what has been done within a hundred years to make us great, and we are quite sure to appropriate a full share of all that has been done in our day and generation. It is well, too, that we should deserve the praise of those who shall follow us and speak of us a hundred years hence ; but let us see to it that in our love for our State, and in our recognition of every duty which belongs to good citizenship, we are not behind those who lived a hun-dred years ago.

III.

At the Semi-Centennial of Rochester, N. Y., June 10, 1884.

Having been in the service of the State for nearly eighteen months, I feel, like any other loyal and grateful servant, that no flight of oratory or grace of diction could, if they were within my reach, do justice to the greatness and the goodness of my master. I shall not attempt to do more than to recall some of the elements which make ours a great State, and to suggest the pride which we should feel as citizens of this common-wealth.

The State of New York is not alone a vast area—though it includes within its borders more territory than seven of the original thirteen States combined, beautifully diversified with mountains and valleys, streams and lakes, forests and fields, and with farms where the wealth and variety of crops tell the story of fertility and adaptation to the most valuable products.

The State is not alone a busy workshop, with its continuous hum of machinery and its army of artisans and workmen— though its manufactures exceed in worth, variety, and volume any other State or Territory, and though their value is more than the aggregate produced in ten of the original States.

The State is not alone a pathway of commerce and a center of trade—though our waterways and railroads transport a nation's wealth, and though our metropolis rivals the money centers of the world, and is a distributing point for all lands.

The State is not alone an immense aggregation of people— though its population exceeds that of any sister State, amount-ing to more than one-tenth of all the States and Territories, and nearly exceeds that of eight of the original States.

Nor do all these things combined make up the State that we delight to call our own.

Our cities, busy, thrifty, and prosperous, are constantly in-creasing in population and wealth, and in the means to furnish to their people all that pertains to refinement and civilization.

Our villages, quiet, contented, and orderly, are everywhere; and by their growth and enterprise give proof of proper and economical management.

Our colleges and seminaries on every hill, and our common schools on every hand, are evidences of the faith of the people in popular and thorough education. Our numerous charitable institutions enlist the care of the State for the unfortunate poor. Our churches, and the tolerant and almost universal observance of religious duties by every sect and creed, teach obedience to the law and prepare our people for good citizenship. Our soldiery, well disciplined and equipped, stand ready to defend our homes, while they beget a martial spirit and patriotic sentiment. A wise and firm administration of the law by our courts gives no occasion for disorders and outbreaks that arise from the miscarriage of justice.

Surely we have enough to cause us to congratulate ourselves upon the claim we have to State citizenship. And yet I cannot forget how much the continuance of all that makes us proud to-day depends upon the watchfulness and independence of the people and their effective participation and interest in State affairs. With a bad government, notwithstanding all our advantages, our State will not be great. Remember that the government of the State was made for the people, and see to it that it be by the people. A sturdy independence and a determination to hold the public servant to a strict accountability will teach him to keep well in view the line between the people's interests and narrow and selfish partisanship; and I am sure that a man, after faithful service in official place, reaps no mean reward, if, at the end, he shall retire with the confidence and affection of a thoughtful and intelligent community, still retaining the proud title of a citizen of the Empire State.

IV.

*At the Two Hundred and Fiftieth Anniversary of Harvard
College, November 9, 1886.*

MR. PRESIDENT AND GENTLEMEN:

I find myself to-day in a company to which I am much
unused, and when I see the alumni of the oldest college in the
land surrounding in their right of sonship the maternal board
at which I am but an invited guest, the reflection that for me
there exists no alma mater gives rise to a feeling of regret,
which is tempered only by the cordiality of your welcome and
your reassuring kindness.

If the fact is recalled that only twelve of my twenty-one predecessors in office had the advantage of a collegiate or university education, a proof is presented of the democratic sense
of our people, rather than an argument against the supreme
value of the best and most liberal education in high public
positions.   There certainly can be no sufficient reason for any
space or distance between the walks of a most classical education and the way that leads to a political place.   Any disin-
clination on the part of the most learned and cultured of our
citizens to mingle in public affairs, and the consequent abandonment of political activity to those who have but little
regard for student and scholar in politics, are not favorable
conditions under a government such as ours, and if they have
existed to a damaging extent, very recent events appear to
indicate that the education and conservatism of the land are
to be hereafter more plainly heard in the expression of the
popular will.

Surely the splendid destiny which awaits a patriotic effort
in behalf of our country will be sooner reached if the best of
our thinkers and educated men shall deem it a solemn duty
of citizenship to engage actively and practically in political
affairs, and if the force and power of their thought and learning shall be willingly or unwillingly acknowledged in party
management.

If I am to speak of the President of the United States I desire to mention, as the most pleasant and characteristic feature of our system of government, the nearness of the people to their President and other high officials. A close view afforded our citizens of the acts and conduct of those to whom they have intrusted their interests, serves as a regulator and check upon temptation and pressure in office, and is a constant reminder that diligence and faithfulness are the measure of public duty ; and such a relation between President and people ought to leave but little room, in popular judgment and conscience, for unjust and false accusations and for malicious slanders invented for the purpose of undermining the people's trust and confidence in the administration of their government.

No public officer should desire to check the utmost freedom of criticism as to all official acts, but every right-thinking man must concede that the President of the United States should not be put beyond the protection which American love of fair play and decency accords to every American citizen. This trait of our national character would not encourage, if their extent and tendency were fully appreciated, the silly, mean, and cowardly lies that every day are found in the columns of certain newspapers, which violate every instinct of American manliness, and in ghoulish glee desecrate every sacred relation of private life.

There is nothing in the highest office that the American people can confer which necessarily makes the President altogether selfish, scheming, and untrustworthy. On the contrary, the solemn duties which confront him tend to a sober sense of responsibility ; the trust of the American people and an appreciation of their mission among the nations of the earth should make him a patriotic man, and the tales of distress which reach him from the humble and lowly, and needy and afflicted in every corner of the land, cannot fail to quicken within him every kind impulse and tender sensibility.

After all, it comes to this : The people of the United States have one and all a sacred mission to perform, and your President, not more surely than any other citizen who loves his country must assume part of the responsibility of the demonstration to the world of the success of popular government. No man can hide his talent in a napkin, and escape the condemnation which his slothfulness deserves, or evade the stern sentence which his faithlessness invites.

Be assured, my friends, that the privilege of this day, so full of improvement, and the enjoyments of this hour, so full of pleasure and cheerful encouragements, will never be forgotten ; and in parting with you now let me express my earnest hope that Harvard's alumni may always honor the venerable institution which has honored them, and that no man who forgets and neglects his duty to American citizenship will find his alma mater here.

V.

At the Centennial of Clinton, N. Y., July 13, 1887.

I am inclined to content myself on this occasion with an acknowledgment, on behalf of the people of the United States, of the compliment which you have paid to the office which represents their sovereignty. But such an acknowledgment suggests an idea which I cannot refrain from dwelling upon for a moment.

That the office of President of the United States does represent the sovereignty of sixty millions of free people, is, to my mind, a statement full of solemnity ; for this sovereignty I conceive to be the working out or enforcement of the divine right of man to govern himself and a manifestation of God's plan concerning the human race.

Though the struggles of political parties to secure the incumbency of this office, and the questionable methods sometimes resorted to for its possession, may not be in keeping with this idea, and though the deceit practiced to mislead the people in their choice, and its too frequent influence on their suffrage may surprise us, these things should never lead us astray in our estimate of this exalted position and its value and dignity.

And though your fellow-citizen who may be chosen to perform for a time the duties of this highest place should be badly selected, and though the best attainable results may not be reached by his administration, yet the exacting watchfulness of the people, freed from the disturbing turmoil of partisan excitement, ought to prevent mischance to the office which represents their sovereignty, and should reduce to a minimum the danger of harm to the State.

I by no means underestimate the importance of the utmost care and circumspection in the selection of the incumbent. On the contrary, I believe there is no obligation of citizenship that demands more thought and conscientious deliberation than this. But I am speaking of the citizen's duty to the office and its selected incumbent.

This duty is only performed when, in the interest of the entire people, the full exercise of the powers of the Chief Magistracy is insisted on, and when, for the people's safety, a due regard for the limitations placed upon the office is exacted. These things should be enforced by the manifestation of a calm and enlightened public opinion. But this should not be simulated by the mad clamor of disappointed interest, which, without regard for the general good, or allowance for the exercise of official judgment, would degrade the office by forcing compliance with selfish demands.

If your President should not be of the people and one of your fellow-citizens, he would be utterly unfit for the position, incapable of understanding the people's wants and careless of their desires. That he is one of the people implies that he is subject to human frailty and error. But he should be permitted to claim but little toleration for mistakes ; the generosity of his fellow-citizens should alone decree how far good intentions should excuse his shortcomings.

Watch well, then, this high office, the most precious possession of American citizenship. Demand for it the most complete devotion on the part of him to whose custody it may be intrusted, and protect it not less vigilantly against unworthy assaults from without.

Thus will you perform a sacred duty to yourselves and to those who may follow you in the enjoyment of the freest institutions which Heaven has ever vouchsafed to man.

———

VI.

At the Constitution Centennial, Philadelphia, September 17, 1887.

I deem it a very great honor and pleasure to participate in these impressive exercises.

Every American citizen should on this centennial day rejoice in his citizenship.

He will not find the cause of his rejoicing in the antiquity of his country, for among the nations of the earth his stands with the youngest. He will not find it in the glitter and the pomp that bedeck a monarch and dazzle abject and servile subjects, for in his country the people themselves are rulers. He will not find it in the story of bloody foreign conquests, for his government has been content to care for its own domain and people.

He should rejoice because the work of framing our Constitution was completed one hundred years ago to-day, and also because, when completed, it established a free government. He should rejoice because this Constitution and government have survived so long, and also because they have survived so many blessings and have demonstrated so fully the strength and value of popular rule. He should rejoice in the wondrous growth and achievements of the past one hundred years, and also in the glorious promise of the Constitution through centuries to come.

We shall fail to be duly thankful for all that was done for

us one hundred years ago, unless we realize the difficulties of the work then in hand, and the dangers avoided in the task of forming "a more perfect union" between disjointed and inharmonious States, with interests and opinions radically diverse and stubbornly maintained.

The perplexities of the convention which undertook the labor of preparing our Constitution are apparent in these earnest words of one of the most illustrious of its members :

The small progress we have made after four or five weeks of close attendance and continued reasonings with each other, our different sentiments on almost every question—several of the last producing as many noes as yeas—is, methinks, a melancholy proof of the imperfection of the human understanding. We, indeed, seem to feel our own want of political wisdom, since we have been running about in search of it. We have gone back to ancient history for models of government, and examined the different forms of those republics which, having been formed with the seeds of their own dissolution, now no longer exist. In this situation of this assembly, groping as it were in the dark to find political truth, and scarce able to distinguish it when presented to us, how has it happened, sir, that we have not heretofore once thought of humbly applying to the Father of Light to illuminate our understandings ?

And this wise man, proposing to his fellows that the aid and blessing of God should be invoked in their extremity, declared :

I have lived, sir, a long time, and the longer I live the more convincing proofs I see of the truth that God governs in the affairs of men. And if a sparrow cannot fall to the ground without his notice, is it probable that an empire can rise without his aid ? We have been assured, sir, in the sacred writings that "except the Lord build the house, they labor in vain that build it." I firmly believe this ; and I also believe that without his concurring aid we shall succeed in this political building no better than the builders of Babel. We shall be divided by our little partial, local interests, our projects will be confounded, and we ourselves shall become a reproach and a byword down to future ages ; and, what is worse, mankind may hereafter, from this unfortunate instance, despair of establishing governments by human wisdom, and leave it to chance, war, and conquest.

In the face of all discouragements, the fathers of the republic labored on for four long, weary months, in alternate hope and fear, but always with rugged resolve, never faltering in a sturdy endeavor sanctified by a prophetic sense of the value to posterity of their success, and always with unflinching faith in the principles which make the foundation of a government by the people.

At last their task was done. It is related that upon the back of the chair occupied by Washington as the president of the Convention a sun was painted, and that as the delegates were signing the completed Constitution one of them said : " I have often and often, in the course of the session, and in the solicitude of my hopes and fears as to its issue, looked at that sun behind the president without being able to tell whether it was rising or setting. But now at length I know that it is a rising and not a setting sun."

We stand to-day on the spot where this rising sun emerged from political night and darkness ; and in its own bright meridian light we mark its glorious way. Clouds have sometimes obscured its rays, and dreadful storms have made us fear ; but God has held it in its course, and through its life-giving warmth has performed his latest miracle in the creation of this wondrous land and people.

As we look down the past century to the origin of our Constitution, as we contemplate its trials and its triumphs, as we realize how completely the principles upon which it is based have met every national peril and every national need, how devoutly should we confess, with Franklin, " God governs in the affairs of men ; " and how solemn should be the reflection that to our hands is committed this ark of the people's covenant, and that ours is the duty to shield it from impious hands. We receive it sealed with the tests of a century. It has been found sufficient in the past ; and in all the future years it will be found sufficient, if the American people are true to their sacred trust.

Another centennial day will come, and millions yet unborn will inquire concerning our stewardship and the safety of their Constitution. God grant that they may find it unimpaired ;

and as we rejoice in the patriotism and devotion of those who lived a hundred years ago, so may others who follow us rejoice in our fidelity and in our jealous love for constitutional liberty.

————

VII.

At the Dinner of the Historical and Scientific Societies of Philadelphia, September 17, 1887.

On such a day as this, and in the atmosphere that now surrounds him, I feel that the President of the United States should be thoughtfully modest and humble. The great office he occupies stands to-day in the presence of its maker; and it is especially fitting for this servant of the people and creature of the Constitution, amid the impressive scenes of this centennial occasion, by a rigid self-examination to be assured concerning his loyalty and obedience to the law of his existence. He will find that the rules prescribed for his guidance require for the performance of his duty, not the intellect or attainments which would raise him far above the feeling and sentiment of the plain people of the land, but rather such a knowledge of their condition, and sympathy with their wants and needs as will bring him near to them. And though he may be almost appalled by the weight of his responsibility and the solemnity of his situation, he cannot fail to find comfort and encouragement in the success of the fathers of the Constitution, wrought from their simple, patriotic devotion to the rights and interests of the people. Surely he may hope that, if reverently invoked, the spirit which gave the Constitution life, will be sufficient for its successful operation and the accomplishment of its beneficent purposes.

Because they are brought nearest the events and scenes which marked the birth of American institutions, the people of Philadelphia should, of all our citizens, be more imbued with the broadest patriotism. The first Continental Congress and

the Constitutional Convention met here, and Philadelphia still
has in her keeping Carpenter's Hall, Independence Hall and
its bell, and the grave of Franklin.

As I look about me and see here represented the societies
that express so largely the culture of Philadelphia, its love of
art, its devotion to science, its regard for the broadest knowledge, and its studious care for historical research—societies
some of which antedate the Constitution—I feel that I am in
notable company.   To you is given the duty of preserving for
your city, for all your fellow-countrymen, and for mankind,
the traditions and the incidents related to the freest and best
government ever vouchsafed to man.   It is a sacred trust,
and as time leads our government further and further from
the date of its birth, may you solemnly remember that a nation
exacts of you that these traditions and incidents shall never
be tarnished nor neglected, but that, brightly burnished, they
may always be held aloft, fastening the gaze of a patriotic
people and keeping alive their love and reverence for the
Constitution.

VIII.

*At the Washington Inauguration Centennial, New York,
April* 30, 1889.

Wherever human government has been administered in
tyranny, in despotism, or in oppression, there has been found,
among the governed, yearning for a freer condition and the
assertion of man's nobility.   These are but the faltering steps
of human nature in the direction of the freedom which is its
birthright ; and they presage the struggle of men to become a
free people, and thus reach the plane of their highest and best
aspirations.   In this relation, and in their cry for freedom, it
may be truly said, the voice of the people is the voice of
God.

In sublime faith and rugged strength our fathers cried out

to the world, " We, the people of the United States, in order to form a more perfect union, establish justice, insure domestic tranquillity, provide for the common defense, promote the general welfare, and secure the blessings of liberty to ourselves and our posterity, do ordain and establish this Constitution for the United States of America."

Thus " our people," in a day, assumed a place among the nations of the earth. Their mission was to teach the fitness of man for self-government, and their destiny was to outstrip every other people in national achievement and material greatness.

One hundred years have passed. We have announced and approved to the world our mission, and made our destiny secure.

Our churches, our schools and universities, and our benevolent institutions, which beautify every town and hamlet, and look out from every hillside, testify to the value our people place upon religious teaching, upon advanced education, and upon deeds of charity. That our people are still jealous of their individual rights and freedom is proved by the fact that no one in place or power has dared openly to assail them. The enthusiasm which marks the celebration of the centennial of the inauguration of their first Chief Magistrate shows the popular appreciation of the value of the office, which, in our plan of government, stands above all others, for the sovereignty of the people, and is the repository of their trust.

Surely such a people can be safely trusted with their free government ; and there need be no fear that they have lost the qualities which fit them to be its custodians. If they should wander, they will return to duty in good time. If they should be misled, they will discover the true landmarks none too late for safety; and if they should even be corrupted they will speedily be found seeking with peace-offerings their country's holy altar.

Let us, then, have an abiding faith in " our people." Let petulance and discontent with popular action disappear before the truth that in any and all circumstances, the will of the people, however it may be exercised, is the law of our national existence—the arbiter, absolute and unchangeable, by which we must abide. Other than existing situations and policies can only justify themselves when they may be reached by the spread of political intelligence and the revival of unselfish and patriotic interest in public affairs. Ill-natured complaints of popular incompetency, and self-righteous assertions of superiority over the body of the people, are impotent and useless.

But there is danger, I fear, that the scope of the words "our people" and all they import are not always fully apprehended. It is only natural that those in the various walks of life should see "our people" within the range of their own vision, and find just about them the interests most important and the most worthy the care of the government. The rich merchant or capitalist, in the center of wealth and enterprise, hardly has a glimpse of the country blacksmith at his forge or the farmer in his field; and these, in their turn, know but little of the laborers, who crowd our manufactories and inhabit their own world of toil, or of the thousands who labor in our mines. If representatives of every element of our population and industries should be gathered together, they would find but little of purely selfish and personal interest in common ; and upon a superficial glance but little would be seen to denote that only one people was represented. Yet, in the spirit of our institutions, all these, so separated in station and personal interest, are a common brotherhood and are "our people"; all of equal value before the law ; all having, by their suffrage, the same voice in governmental affairs ; all demanding with equal force protection and defense ; and all, in their persons and property, equally entitled to their government's scrupulous care.

IX.

On Taking the Chair at the Celebration of the Organization of the Supreme Court, February 4, 1890.

LADIES AND GENTLEMEN :

We are accustomed to express, on every fit occasion, our reverence for the virtue and patriotism in which the foundations of our republic were laid, and to rejoice in the blessings vouchsafed to us under free institutions. Thus we have lately celebrated, with becoming enthusiasm, the centennial of the completion of our Constitution and the inauguration of our first President.

To-day we have assembled to commemorate an event connected with our beginning as a people, which, more than any other, gave safety and the promise of perpetuity to the American plan of government, and which, more than any other, happily illustrated the wisdom and enlightened foresight of those who designed our national structure.

In the work of creating our nation, the elements of a free government were supplied by concessions of sovereign States, by surrender of accustomed rights, and by the inspiration of pure and disinterested patriotism. If, from these elements, there had not been evolved that feature in our Federal system which is our theme to-day, the structure might have been fair to look upon and might have presented a semblance of solidity and strength ; but it would have been only a semblance ; and the completed edifice would have had within its foundations the infirmity of decay and ruin.

It must be admitted that it is hardly within the power of human language so to compass diverse interests and claims, within the lines of a written constitution, as to free it entirely from disputes of construction ; and certainly diverse constructions were apt to lurk in the diction of a constitution declared by the president of the convention which formulated it, to be " the result of a spirit of amity and of that mutual deference and concession which the peculiarity of our political situation rendered indispensable."

It is fairly plain and palpable, both from reason and a review of events in our history, that without an arbiter to determine, finally and conclusively, the rights and duties embraced in the language of the Constitution, the union of States and the life of the American nation must have been precarious and disappointing. Indeed, there could hardly have been a well-grounded hope that they would long survive the interpretation of the national compact by every party upon whom it rested, and the insistence of each, to the last extremity, upon such an interpretation as would secure coveted rights and benefits, and absolve from irksome duties and obligations.

In the creation of the world, the earth was without form and void, and darkness was upon the face of the deep, until God said : " Let there be light, and there was light."

In the creation of our new nation, our free institutions were without the form and symmetry of strength, and the darkness of hopelessness brooded over the aspirations of our people, until a light in the temple of Justice and Law, gathered from the Divine fountain of light, illumined the work of the fathers of our republic.

On this centennial day we will devoutly thank Heaven for the revelation, to those who formed our government, of this source of strength and light, and for the inspiration of disinterested patriotism and consecrated devotion which established the tribunal which we to-day commemorate.

Our fathers had sacrificed much to be free. Above all things they desired freedom to be absolutely secured to themselves and their posterity. And yet, with all their enthusiasm for this sentiment, they were willing to refer to the tribunal which they devised all questions arising under their newly formed Constitution, affecting the freedom and the protection and safety of the citizen. Though bitter experience had taught them that the instrumentalities of government might trespass upon freedom, and though they had learned in a hard school the cost of the struggle to wrest liberty from the grasp of power, they refused, in the solemn work they had in hand, to take counsel of undue fear or distracting perturbation ; and they calmly and deliberately established, as a function of their government, a check upon unauthorized freedom and a restraint upon dangerous liberty. Their attachment and allegiance to the sovereignty of their States were warm and unfaltering ; but these did not prevent them from contributing a fraction of that sovereignty to the creation of a Court which should guard and protect their new nation, and save and perpetuate a government which should, in all time to come, bless an independent people.

I deem myself highly honored by the part assigned to me in these commemorative exercises. As in eloquent and fitting terms we shall be led, by those chosen to address us, to the contemplation of the history of that august tribunal organized one hundred years ago ; as the lives and services of those who in the past have presided over its councils are rehearsed to us ; as our love and veneration for our fellow-countrymen who now fill its high and sacred places are quickened ; and as we are reminded of the manner in which our national Court has at all times illustrated the strength and beneficence of free institutions, let us be glad in the possession of this rich heritage of American citizenship, and gratefully appreciate the wisdom and patriotism of those who gave to us the Supreme Court of the United States.

X.

At the Celebration of the Semi-Centennial of the German Young Men's Association, Buffalo, May 11, 1891.

MR. PRESIDENT AND LADIES AND GENTLEMEN :

I am glad to meet here to-night so many old friends and acquaintances, and to join them in the felicitations which have called us together. At this moment I recall with perfect vividness another evening nearly eight years ago, when, in a beautiful building standing on this spot and then just completed, we inaugurated with songs and rejoicing a grand national Sänger-fest.   That was a proud day for Buffalo, and a prouder one still for our German fellow-townsmen, who then welcomed as their guests a large and notable assemblage from many States, representing their national love of music ; and, at the same time, were permitted to exhibit to their visitors, as a monument of the enterprise and activity of the German Young Men's Association, the grand and imposing Music Hall in which their festival of song was held.

The disaster which soon after overtook the association, involving the destruction of their splendid building, brought no discouragement to the members of the organization.   To-night we meet in another and more magnificent Music Hall, built upon the ashes of the first, to celebrate the close of fifty years in the life of an association that exhibits to every observer the courage and determination which inevitably lead to usefulness and success.

I shall not assume such a familiarity with the career of the association as would enable me to present in detail the results of its past efforts.   In any event it would ill become me to enter upon this field, in view of the fact that the able and honorable gentleman now at the head of the association was also its first president, and for fifty years has watched its progress and been devoted to its interests.   Surely there has seldom been an organization which numbered among its members, at the end of half a century, so competent a chronicler of its history and achievements.

I understand that among the prominent purposes of the German Young Men's Association are the propagation and promotion of a knowledge of German literature and the cultivation and encouragement of the best elements of German character.

So far as the first of these objects is concerned, I hope I may be permitted to say that, while the efforts of the association in the direction mentioned are most praiseworthy and patriotic, such an undertaking can by no means be monopolized by any association. The value and importance of German literature are too keenly appreciated to be neglected in any part of the world, where there are those who seek to know the past triumphs of science, poetry, music, and art, or where there are those who strive to keep pace with their present development and progress. It is not too much to say that all nations which make claim to high civilization encourage the study of German literature, and that the extent to which this study is pursued by a people furnishes a standard of their enlightenment.

On behalf of the American people, I am inclined, also, to claim to-night that the German character which the association undertakes to cultivate is so interwoven with all the growth and progress of our country that we have a right to include it among the factors which make up a sturdy and thrifty Americanism. With our early settlers came the Germans. They suited themselves to every condition of our new world. Many of them fought for American independence, and many, who in the trade of war came to fight against us, afterward settled on our soil, and contributed greatly to the hardihood and stubborn endurance which our young nation so much needed.

As years were added to the new republic, the tide of German immigration increased in volume. Those who thus came to us brought with them a love of liberty which readily assimilated them to our institutions, and their natural love of order made them good citizens. By their love of music and social enjoyments they shed a bright light upon the solemn and constant routine of American work, while, at the same time, they abundantly proved that reasonable recreation was entirely consistent with wholesome and conservative accumulation. They were found in every part of our land. Among the pioneers of the far West, they struggled against discouragements and hardships—counteracting privation by frugality, and never for a moment losing sight of the better day promised by the future to undaunted courage and persistent industry. In our

cities and towns they were found in the front ranks of successful business and trade; and by the choice of their fellow-
citizens they held public positions of trust and influence.
Everywhere they illustrated the value and the sure reward of
economy and steady work.

Thus, before the American nation had lived one hundred
years, our German population had grown to millions, and
constituted an important ingredient in the mass of American
activity. Then there came a time when the government of the
country of their adoption was assaulted by rebellious hands;
and then our German fellow-citizens had presented to them an
opportunity to prove the depth and breadth of their attachment
to the land in which they lived and wrought, and to exhibit how
completely they had become patriotic American citizens. They
allowed not a moment for uncertainty, but flocked by thousands
to the standard of the Union and bravely devoted themselves
to its defense. In every battle the German soldiers fought with
courage and persistence, and died with fortitude. This common
baptism of blood, and this partnership in peril, brought closer
together every element of our people, and made them all—
more than ever and in every sense—Americans. This leads
me to say that any opposing claims to ownership in the valuable
traits of German character admit of a fair compromise. No
one will begrudge the satisfaction to be derived from analyzing
these elements and establishing their German origin; and all
will concede that the more they are cultivated the more our
country will gain. But when all this is done, let us call these
traits, so far as they are here exhibited, American. They have
been with us since our beginning; they have influenced every
day of our country's life; they are among the traits which our
government was formed to foster, and they are essential to our
country's safety and prosperity.

I hardly think there is any city in the land that should appreciate the value of German population better than Buffalo.
On every side, within your limits, are seen the evidences of the
thrift of your German fellow-townsmen and monuments of

their industry and enterprise. No one can dispute their contribution to your immense municipal growth, and you do well
to recognize it in the selection of those charged with the administration of your city government. Even now there stands
at its head, performing his duties acceptably to the entire
community, one who has won his way to the confidence of his
fellow-citizens solely by the German-American traits of honesty, industry, and economy. I know that he will forgive me
for saying that when I knew him first, not many years ago, he
was occupying an honorable, but very humble position, and gave
no symptom of his present prominence. I will not dispute the
right of anyone to call him a German ; but I claim the satisfaction of also calling this old friend of mine a first-rate
American.

In the light of the suggestions I have made, it is a pleasant
thing to learn the significant fact that the membership of the
German Young Men's Association is quite largely made up of
those who have no title to German parentage or origin.

I cannot resist the temptation to introduce here the thought
that no such association can exist and escape a responsibility
to our people and our government. Wherever our countrymen
are gathered together with the professed purpose of mutual
improvement, or in furtherance of any useful object, they ought
to do something for their country. Its welfare and progress
depend so clearly upon what the people are taught and what
they think that patriotism should pervade their every endeavor
in the direction of mental or social improvement. Our government was made by the people ; and by the people it must
be constantly watched and maintained. Like every other
mechanism it requires guidance and care. Without this, like
many another mechanism, it will not only fail to do its work, but
it may injure and wound those who stand idly near. We cannot
afford, in the heedless race for wealth, nor in the absorbing
struggle for the promotion of selfish ends, to neglect, for a day,
our duty to our government.

So, as the members of the German Young Men's Association

contemplate the steadfast love of country which belongs to the German character, let them enforce the lesson that this sentiment is absolutely essential to the strength and vigor of American institutions.   If they find that German industry and frugality lead to national happiness and comfort, let them insist that these characteristics be rooted in our soil ; and if they find that the justice and equality which our free institutions promise, and which the Germans love, are withheld from them and the American people, let them demand from the government which they support a scrupulous redemption of its pledges.

As this association crosses the threshold which lies midway in the first century of its existence, its members may well recall with pride and congratulation what it has thus far done for the promotion of a knowledge of German literature and the cultivation of German character ; and, as they enter upon the second half century of organized effort, they should be more than ever determined to pursue these purposes, not only because they may thus keep alive a fond remembrance of the Fatherland, but because they may thus, in a higher, better spirit, aid in the cultivation of those sentiments which purify and strengthen a genuine and patriotic Americanism.

CHAPTER VI.

I.

At the Oswegatchie Fair, Ogdensburg, N. Y., October 5, 1883.

LADIES AND GENTLEMEN :

WHEN I received the invitation of the president of this fair to be with you to-day, I could hardly see my way to accept, because I find that the duties of the office to which I have been called are of such a nature that I can scarcely do all that crowds upon me, with quite constant attention. But the more I considered the question of visiting you, the stronger the desire became to accept the invitation. I remembered that I had never been here but once, many years ago, and then for only a night. I wanted to know more of the largest county in the State. I wanted to see your thriving and pleasant city. I thought of the opportunity I should have of seeing something of the kind and quality of your products ; and, more than all, I wanted to see, and become better acquainted with, the people here, who, from lack of familiarity, seemed so far away. And then, too, I reflected that I was the servant of the people of the State ; and inasmuch as they could not all come to see how their servants are doing their duty, it is no more than right that these servants should occasionally go to their masters and report—or at least answer to their names. Thus I am here ; but I came upon the express condition that I shall not make a speech. And the little talk I may have here with my friends of St. Lawrence County I do not regard as either a speech or an address.

I have not come to you with any pretense of special knowl-

edge of the things which are here the subject of interest.   I
am obliged to confess that I am not a farmer, and know but
little about it.   My experience of a few weeks on a farm, when
a boy, resulted in but little addition to my knowledge of agriculture, and I am sure was of but little benefit to the proprie-
tor of the cornfield in which I worked.   I suppose, too, you
have, from time to time, heard enough of transparent flattery,
having for its text the nobility of those who till the soil and
the simplicity which characterizes the greatness of a farming
community.   I am glad to meet you as fellow-citizens, all
engaged in one way or another in developing the resources of
a great State, and maintaining and adding to its high supremacy, as well as increasing your own wealth and comfort.
The farm, furnished with fine and well-kept buildings, is not
only a proof of its owner's thrift and competency, but that
much has been added to the wealth of the State.

Broad fields, well tilled, not only secure comfort and an
income to the farmer, but build up the commerce of the State
and easily supply the wants of the population.   None of these
things result except by labor.   This is the magic wand whose
touch creates wealth and a great State.   So all of us who work
are, in our several ways, engaged in building to a higher reach
and nobler proportions the fabric of a proud commonwealth.
Those who make and execute the laws, join with those who
toil from day to day with their hands in their several occupations, all alike engaged in building up and protecting the
State.

The institution of fairs such as this must, it seems to me, have
a wholesome and beneficial effect.   In addition to the competition engendered, which spurs to more effect and better methods,
the opportunity is afforded to profit by the experience of
others.   The State has shown an appreciation of the value of
experiment in agriculture, by establishing and maintaining, at
considerable expense, a farm for the express purpose of devis-
ing and proving the value of new plans and operations in
farming.   The results are freely offered to all ; and thus the

farmer may gain a knowledge of methods which will render his labor more profitable without the risk of loss in time which he himself might spend in experiment. I have no doubt that the soil of the State of New York is tilled well and intelligently. And still I suppose much of our farming might be improved by a closer regard to successful experiment, and by learning the lessons of approved science as applied to agriculture. I do not fear, however, that the farmers of New York will stop short of the highest excellence. The people of this State are not given to that.

While I, in this manner, urge you to claim from the soil all it has to yield, by the aid of intelligent efforts in its cultivation, I cannot refrain from reminding you that, as citizens, you have something else to do. You have the responsibility of citizenship upon you, and you should see to it that you do your duty to the State, not only by increasing its wealth by the cultivation and improvement of the soil, but by an intelligent selection of those who shall act for you in the enactment and execution of your laws. Weeds and thistles, if allowed in your fields, defeat your toil and efforts. So abuses in the administration of your government lead to the dishonor of your State, choke and thwart the wishes of the people, and waste their substance.

I have heard it said that a farm or business never does better than when it is managed by its owner. So it is with your government. It accomplishes its purposes and operates well only when it is managed by the people and for the people. It was designed and constructed to be used in just this way. None of you would attempt to turn the soil of a field without putting a strong hand on the plow. A plow was constructed to be thus operated, and it can do its work in no other way. The machinery of the government will not do its work unless the strong, steady hands of the people are put upon it. This is not done when the people say that politics is a disgraceful game, and should be left untouched by those having private concerns and business which engages their attention. This neglect serves to give over the most important interests to those who care but little for their protection, and who are willing to betray their trust for their own advantage.

Manifestly, in this matter, the people can only act through agents of their selection.   But that selection should be freely and intelligently made by the careful exercise of their suffrages. I have said this duty should not be neglected.   A careless or mistaken performance may be as fatal as neglect.   All cannot personally know the applicants for office ; but, by careful inquiry, their characters for fair dealing and honesty, and the manner in which they have fulfilled the ordinary duties of life, may be discovered as well as the ability they have shown in the management of their own affairs.   Do their neighbors and those who know them well trust them, and are they willing to put in their hands important interests ?   Are their personal habits and their personal and private relations good, and pure, and clean ?

I believe that, in the selection of those who shall act for the people in the government, no better rule can be adopted than the one suggested by these inquiries.   If they are answered satisfactorily, the people will probably conclude that they have found the men they wish to put in public places, even though they lack a knowledge of the arts and wiles which tricksters use to deceive and mislead.

Be diligent, then, in your business, and willing and anxious to improve and expand it.   This you owe to yourselves, to your families, and to the public.   Be also diligent and careful in the performance of your political duty.   This you owe none the less to yourselves and to the State.   With every obligation thus discharged, your welfare and prosperity will be secured, and you may congratulate yourselves upon the honorable part you bear in the support and maintenance of a free and beneficent government.

II.

At the State Fair at Elmira, September 8, 1884.

It affords me great pleasure to meet you here to-day, and to have an opportunity of inspecting the annual exhibition which illustrates the condition of the agriculture of our State. I regard these annual fairs as something connected with the State government, because, to some extent, at least, they are fostered and aided by public funds, and I am sure that no good citizen is inclined to complain of the appropriation of a small part of the people's money to the encouragement of this important interest.

The fact that this is done furnishes a distinct recognition by the State of the valuable relation which the farmers and its farms bear to the prosperity and welfare of the commonwealth. We boast of our manufactures, exceeding, as they largely do, those of any other State ; but our supremacy is clearly shown when we recall the fact that, in addition to our lead in manufactures, the value of our farms and their products is second only among the States.

There is a fixedness and reliability in agricultural pursuits which is not always found in other branches of human effort. The soil remains in its place, ready to be tilled ; and the farmer, with ruddy health and brawny arm, depends alone upon the work of his hands and a kind Providence for a reward of his labor. Thus our farmers are the most independent of our citizens. They produce, or have within their reach, all they need for their necessities and for their comfort. Their crops may be more abundant at one harvest than at another, and their products may command a higher price at one market time than another. These conditions may expand or contract their ability to indulge in luxuries or in expenditures not absolutely needful, but they should never be in want of the necessities or comforts of life.

This is the sure result of patient and well-regulated farming. When the farmer fails and becomes bankrupt in his business, we may, I think, confidently look for shiftlessness ; or a too ambitious desire to own more land or stock than he can pay for ; or an intermeddling with matters that bear no relation to his farm ; or such mismanagement and ignorance as demonstrate that he has mistaken his vocation. Fortunes may be quickly amassed in speculation and lost in a day, leaving a bad example and, perhaps, demoralization and crime. The tradesman or the manufacturer, by the vicissitudes of trade, or through the allurements of the short road to wealth, may in a day be overcome and bring disaster and ruin upon hundreds of his neighbors. But in the industrious, intelligent, and contented farmer the State finds a safe and profitable citizen, always contributing to its wealth and prosperity. The real value of the farmer to the State and nation is not, however, fully appreciated until we consider that he feeds the millions of our people who are engaged in other pursuits, and that the product of his labor fills the avenues of our commerce and supplies an important factor in our financial relations with other nations.

I have not come here to attempt to please you with cheap and fulsome praise, nor to magnify your worth and your importance ; but I have come as the Chief Executive of the State to acknowledge on its own behalf that our farmers yield a full return for the benefits they receive from the State government. I have come to remind you of the importance of the interests which you have in charge, and to suggest that, notwithstanding the farmer's independence, he cannot and must not be unmindful of the value and importance to the interests he holds of a just and economical government. It is his right and his duty to demand that all unjust and inequitable burdens upon agriculture and its products, however caused, should be removed, and that, while the furtherance of the other interests of the State have due regard, this important one should not be neglected. Thus, by his labor as farmer and in the full performance of his duty as citizen, he will create and secure to himself his share of the result of his toil and save and guard for all the people a most important element in the prosperity of the State.

III.

At the Virginia State Fair, Richmond, October 12, 1886.

FELLOW-CITIZENS OF VIRGINIA :

While I thank you most sincerely for your kind reception and recognize in its heartiness the hospitality for which the people of Virginia have always been distinguished, I am fully aware that your demonstration of welcome is tendered not to an individual, but to an incumbent of an office which crowns the government of the United States. The State of Virginia, the Mother of Presidents, seven of whose sons have filled that high office, to-day greets a President who for the first time meets Virginians upon Virginia soil.

I congratulate myself that my first introduction to the people of Virginia occurs at a time when they are surrounded by the exhibits of the productiveness and prosperity of their State. Whatever there may be in honor in her history, and however much of pride there may be in her traditions, her true greatness is here exemplified. In our sisterhood of States the leading and most commanding place must be gained and kept by that commonwealth which, by the labor and intelligence of her citizens, can produce the most of those things which meet the necessities and desires of mankind.

But the full advantage of that which may be yielded to a State by the toil and ingenuity of her people is not measured alone by the money value of the products. The efforts and the struggles of her farmers and her artisans not only create new values in the field of agriculture and in the arts and manufactures, but they, at the same time, produce rugged, self-reliant, and independent men, and cultivate that product which, more than all others, ennobles a State—a patriotic, earnest American citizenship.

This will flourish in every part of the American domain.

Neither drought nor rain can injure it, for it takes root in true hearts, enriched by love of country.   There are no new varieties in this production.   It must be the same wherever seen, and its quality is neither sound nor genuine unless it grows to deck and beautify an entire and united nation, nor unless it supports and sustains the institutions and the government founded to protect American liberty and happiness.

The present administration of the government is pledged to return for such husbandry not only promises, but actual tenders of fairness and justice, with equal protection and a full participation in national achievements.   If, in the past, we have been estranged and the cultivation of American citizenship has been interrupted, your enthusiastic welcome of to-day demonstrates that there is an end to such estrangement, and that the time of suspicion and fear is succeeded by an era of faith and confidence.

In such a kindly atmosphere and beneath such cheering skies I greet the people of Virginia as co-laborers in the field where grows the love of our united country.

God grant that in the years to come Virginia—the Old Dominion, the Mother of Presidents, she who looked on the nation at its birth—may not only increase her trophies of growth in agriculture and manufactures, but that she may be among the first of all the States in the cultivation of true American citizenship.

IV.

To the annual Grange Picnic of Pennsylvania.

EXECUTIVE MANSION,
WASHINGTON, August 27, 1888.

DEAR SIR :

I hope I need not assure you that I should very much enjoy meeting the large representation of farmers who will gather at Williams Grove to-morrow.   I shall not plead confinement here by official business as my excuse for declining the courteous invitation I have received to be present at the picnic, but shall frankly say to you that the opportunity, long contemplated, to enjoy two or three days of rest and recreation unexpectedly presents itself in such a manner that, if I avail myself of it, I must, therefore, forego the pleasure of visiting Williams Grove. I am sure that I am not calculating too much upon the kindness and consideration of those managing the picnic when I believe they will be content with my non-attendance, if I am enabled thereby to improve the opportunity I am offered to enjoy a much-needed rest and freedom from official care.

I have heard of the character of your exhibition; and the large congregation of farmers and others interested in subjects relating to farming which are there brought together, the exhibits, the discussion, and the comparison of views which necessarily are the accompaniment of such a meeting, cannot fail to be of the utmost use to those directly interested; and what is useful to them is useful to all our people.

The reflection is an interesting and consoling one that in the midst of political turmoil, in the feverish anxiety of the marts of trade, and in the rush and hurry of financial operations, our agriculturists pursue the even tenor of their way at all times, furnishing the most stable support of our country's prosperity, and quietly supplying the most reliable source of our greatness and strength. When our farmers are prosperous and contented, the welfare and advancement of the nation are secured.

Hoping that the picnic of 1888 will exceed all prior ones in the enjoyments and benefits accorded to those in attendance,
I am,
Yours very truly,
GROVER CLEVELAND.

V.

To a Steubenville (O.) Lodge of the Farmers' Alliance.

NEW YORK, March 24, 1890.

J. A. HILL, ESQ., *Corresponding Secretary, etc.*

DEAR SIR : I have received your letter, accompanied by a copy of the declaration of principles of the Farmers' Alliance.

I see nothing in this declaration that cannot be fully indorsed by any man who loves his country, who believes that the object of our government should be the freedom, prosperity, and happiness of all our people, and who believes that justice and fairness to all are necessary conditions to its useful administration.

It has always seemed to me that the farmers of the country were especially interested in an equitable adjustment of our tariff system. The indifference they have shown to that question, and the ease with which they have been led away from a sober consideration of their needs and their rights as related to this subject, have excited my surprise.

Struggle as they may, our farmers must continue to be purchasers and consumers of numberless things enhanced in cost by tariff regulations. Surely they have the right to insist that this cost shall not be increased for the purpose of collecting unnecessary revenue or to give undue advantage to domestic manufactures. The plea that our infant industries need the protection which thus impoverishes the farmer and consumer is, in view of our natural advantages and the skill and ingenuity of our people, a hollow pretext.

Struggle as they may, our farmers cannot escape the conditions which fix the price of what they produce and sell, according to the rates which prevail in foreign markets flooded with the competition of countries enjoying freer exchange of trade than we. The plausible presentation of the blessings of a home market should not deceive our depressed and impoverished agriculturists. There is no home market for them which does not take its instructions from the seaboard, and the seaboard transmits the word of the foreign markets.

Because my conviction that there should be a modification of our tariff laws arose principally from an appreciation of the wants of the vast army of consumers, comprising our farmers, our artisans, and our workingmen, and because their condition has led me to protest against present impositions, I am especially glad to see these sections of my fellow-countrymen arousing themselves to the importance of tariff reform.

Yours very truly,

GROVER CLEVELAND.

CHAPTER VII.

TO COMMERCIAL AND BUSINESS ASSOCIATIONS.

I.

At the Commercial Exchange, Philadelphia, September 16, 1887.

I AM glad I have an opportunity to meet so large a representation of the business men of Philadelphia. It is well that we should not entirely forget, in the midst of our centennial jubilee, that the aim and purpose of good government tend, after all, to the advancement of the material interests of the people and the increase of their trade and commerce. The thought has sometimes occurred to me that, in the hurry and rush of business, there might well be infused a little more patriotism than we are wont to see, and a little more recognition of the fact that a wholesome political sentiment is closely related not only to the general good, but to the general success of business. Of course, our citizens engaged in business are quick to see the bearings of any policy which the government may adopt, as it affects their personal success and their accumulation. But I would like to see that broad and patriotic sentiment among them which can see beyond their peculiar personal interests, and which can recognize that the advancement of the entire country is an object for which they may well strive, even sometimes to the diminution of their constantly increasing profits.

Must we always look for the political opinions of our business men precisely where they suppose their immediate pecuniary advantage is found ? I know how vain it is to hope for the eradication of a selfish motive in all the affairs of life ; but I am reminded that we celebrate, to-day, the triumph of patriotism over selfishness. Will anyone say that the concessions of the Constitution were not well made, or that we are not to-day in the full enjoyment of the blessings resulting from a due regard for all the conflicting interests represented by the different States which were united a hundred years ago?

I believe the complete benefits promised to the people by our form of government can only be secured by an exercise of the same spirit of toleration for each other's rights and interests in which it had its birth. This spirit will prevail when the business men of the country cultivate political thought ; when they cease to eschew participation in political action ; and when such thought and action are guided by better motives than purely selfish and exclusive benefit.

I am of the opinion that there is no place in the country where such a condition can be so properly and successfully maintained as here, among the enlightened and enterprising business men of Philadelphia.

II.

Before the Milwaukee Merchants' Association, October 7, 1887.

I feel like thanking you for remembering on this occasion the President of the United States ; for I am sure you but intend a respectful recognition of the dignity and importance of the high office I, for the time being, hold in trust for you and for the American people.

It is a high office, because it represents the sovereignty of a free and mighty people. It is full of solemn responsibility and duty, because it embodies, in a greater degree than any other office on earth, the suffrage and the trust of such a people. As an American citizen, chosen from the mass of his fellow-countrymen to assume for a time this responsibility and this duty, I acknowledge with patriotic satisfaction your tribute to the office which belongs to us all.

And because it belongs to all the people the obligation is manifest on their part to maintain a constant and continuous watchfulness and interest concerning its care and operation. Their duty is not entirely done when they have exercised their suffrage and indicated their choice of the incumbent. Nor is their duty performed by settling down to bitter, malignant, and senseless abuse of all that is done or attempted to be done by the incumbent selected. The acts of an administration should not be approved as a matter of course, and for no better reason than that it represents a political party ; but more unpatriotic than all others are those who, having neither party discontent nor fair ground of criticism to excuse or justify their conduct, rail because of personal disappointment ; who misrepresent for sensational purposes, and who profess to see swift destruction in the rejection of their plans for governmental management.

After all, we need have no fear that the American people will permit this high office of President to suffer. There is a patriotic sentiment abroad which, in the midst of all party feeling and of party disappointment, will assert itself and will insist that the office which stands for the people's will shall, in all its vigor, minister to their prosperity and welfare.

III.

To the New York Chamber of Commerce.

EXECUTIVE MANSION,
WASHINGTON, November 4, 1887.

MESSRS. HENRY HENTZ, CHARLES WATROUS, AND OTHERS,
Committee:

GENTLEMEN : I have received your invitation to attend the annual banquet of the Chamber of Commerce of the State of New York on the evening of the 15th instant. It would certainly give me great pleasure to be present on that occasion and meet those who, to a great extent, have in charge the important business interests represented in your association. I am sure, too, that I should derive profit as well as pleasure from such a meeting.

Those charged by the people with the management of their government cannot fail to enhance their usefulness by a familiarity with business conditions and intimacy with business men, since good government has no more important mission than the stimulation and protection of the activities of the country.

This relation between governments and business suggests the thought that the members of such associations as yours owe to themselves and to all the people of the land a thoughtful discharge of their political obligations, guided by their practical knowledge of affairs, to the end that there may be impressed upon the administration of our government a business character and tendency free from the diversion of passion, and unmoved by sudden gusts of excitement.

But the most wholesome purpose of their political action will not be accomplished by an insistence upon their exclusive claims and selfish benefits, regardless of the welfare of the people at large. Interdependence is so thoroughly an element in our national existence that a patriotic and generous heed to the general good sense will best subserve every particular interest.

I regret that my official duties and engagements prevent the acceptance of your courteous invitation, and, expressing the hope that the banquet may be a most enjoyable and interesting occasion to those present,

I am,

Very truly yours,

GROVER CLEVELAND.

IV.

POLITICAL SELFISHNESS AND ITS ANTIDOTES.*

MR. CHAIRMAN AND GENTLEMEN:

When I see about me this gathering of business men and merchants, I find it impossible to rid myself of the impressive thought that here is represented that factor in civilized life which measures the progress of a people, which constitutes the chief care of every enlightened government, and which gives to a country the privilege of recognized membership in the community of nations.

Our business men cannot, if they would, escape the responsibility which this condition casts upon them—a responsibility most exacting and invested with the seriousness which always results from a just apprehension of man's relation to his fellowman and the obligation due from a citizen to his government. They can find no pretext for indifference in the self-complacent claim that under American institutions, as in other times and in foreign lands, business men and merchants have only gained a recognition of their importance and value as it has been forced from a government in which they had no representation and from rulers who looked upon their vocation with contempt. They cannot absolve themselves from loyal duty to a government which has, at all times, invited them to a high place in public counsels and which has always ungrudgingly conceded their indispensable value in the growth and progress of our republic.

These considerations plainly point out your responsibility and duty as members of the guild of business and as belonging to the fellowship of trade.

But we cannot avoid other reflections leading in the same direction and related to you alone—the business men of Boston. The scene of your activity is the commercial center of a great

* An address delivered at the banquet of the Merchants' Association of Boston, December 12, 1889.

and ancient commonwealth, rich in patriotic traditions. It was upon the waters of your harbor that the first active and physical defiance and opposition were made to odious and unfair imperial legislation affecting colonial trade ; and the first battle by Americans for liberty of the person, and for freedom from unjust and oppressive restraint upon business, was fought within sight of your warehouses.

You have, besides, inherited a trust which shades with sober sentiment your obligation to your country and your fellow-citizens. With the birth of American trade there arose on the spot merchants of strong sense and enlightened enterprise, chiefs among their fellows, independent and self-reliant, willing to chance their success upon their own effort and foresight, inflexibly honest and intensely jealous of their commercial honor. Upon your wharves and in your counting rooms they wrought out their well-earned fortunes. Their ships were found in every ocean-path, and they made their country known in the trade transactions of the world. Abroad they gained willing confidence and credit by their commercial integrity and probity, and at home they were the pride of their countrymen.

These were the old Boston merchants. You, their business heirs and successors, will pardon me if I remind you to-night that the commanding influence of these men did not rest upon immense fortunes, made in a day ; but resulted from their well-known honor and scrupulous good faith, which led them to concede to all even the uttermost fraction of right. Nor did they forget their duties of citizenship. They jealously watched the operations of their government, and exacted from it only economy and honesty and a just measure of care and security for themselves and the interests they had in charge.

The Boston merchant of to-day has not less integrity and virtue than his predecessor ; but surely we are not called upon, by the fear of controversy, to close our eyes to the fact that his environment is vastly different. There is among our people less of meaning embodied in the sentiment that the government upon which we have staked all our hopes and aspirations, requires, for its successful maintenance, a patriotic regard for the aggregate of the happiness and prosperity of all our people and a willing consent to a fair distribution of the benefits of our free institutions.

Equal rights and impartial justice are stipulations of the compact we have entered into with each other as American citizens ; and so nicely adjusted is this plan of our political association, that favoritism for the sole advantage of any section of our membership inevitably results in an encroachment upon the benefits justly due to others. But these things sit so lightly upon the consciences of many that a spirit of selfishness is abroad in the land, which has bred the habit of clamorous importunity for government aid in behalf of special interests—imperfectly disguised under the cloak of solicitude for the public good.

Can we see no contrast between the sturdy self-reliance of the Boston merchant in the days that are past, and the attitude you are invited to assume as dependents upon the favor of the government and beneficiaries under its taxing power ? Is there not a difference between the ideas that formerly prevailed concerning the just and wholesome relations which should exist between the government and the business of the country, and the present tendency toward a government partnership in trade ? And was there a hint in former days that especial advantages thus once secured, constituted a vested right which in no event should in the least be disturbed ?

Political selfishness cheapens in the minds of the people their apprehension of the character and functions of the government ; it distorts every conception of the duty of good citizenship, and creates an atmosphere in which iniquitous purposes and designs lose their odious features. It begins when a perverted judgment is won to the theory that political action may be used solely for private gain and advantage, and when a tender conscience is quieted by the ingenious argument that such gain and advantage are identical with the public welfare. This stage having been reached, and self-interest being now fully aroused, agencies are used and practices permitted in the accomplishment of its purposes, which, seen in the pure light of disinterested patriotism, are viewed with fear and hatred. The independent thought, and free political preference of those whom Fate has made dependent upon daily toil for hard-earned bread, are strangled and destroyed by intimidation and the fear of loss of employment. Vile, unsavory forms rise to the surface of our agitated political waters, and gleefully anticipate, in the anxiety of selfish interest, their opportunity to fatten upon corruption and debauched suffrage.

This train of thought leads us to consider the imminent danger which threatens us from the intimidation and corruption of our voters.

It is too late to temporize with these evils, or to speak of them otherwise than in the plainest terms. We are spared the labor of proving their existence, for all admit it. That they are terribly on the increase all must concede.

Manifestly, if the motives of all our citizens were unselfish and patriotic, and if they sought in political action only their share of the advantage accruing from the advance of our country at all points toward her grand destiny, there would be no place or occasion for the perversion of our suffrage. Thus the inauguration of the intimidation and corruption of our voters may be justly charged to selfish schemes seeking success through political action. But these evils have been neglected by honest men, disgusted with all political endeavor; they have been tolerated by respectable men who, in weakness of patriotic sentiment, have regarded them as only phases of shrewd political management, and they have been actually encouraged by the honors which have been bestowed upon those who boast of their use of such agencies in aid of party supremacy.

Many of us, therefore, may take to ourselves a share of blame, when we find confronting us these perils which threaten the existence of our free institutions, the preservation of our national honor, and the perpetuity of our country. The condition annexed to the founding of our government upon the suffrage of the people was that the suffrage should be free and pure. We consented to abide by the honest preponderance of political opinion, but we did not consent that a free vote, expressing the intelligent and thoughtful sentiment of the voter, should be balanced by a vote of intimidation and fear, or by an unclean, corrupt vote disgracefully bought and treacherously sold.

Let us look with a degree of pity and charity upon those who yield to fear and intimidation in the exercise of their right of suffrage. Though they ought not thus to yield, we cannot forget that, as against their free ballot, they see in the scale their continued employment, the comforts of their homes, and the maintenance of their families. We need not stifle our scorn and contempt for the wretch who basely sells his vote, and who for a bribe betrays his trust of citizenship. And yet the thought will intrude itself that he but follows, in a low and vulgar fashion, the example of those who proceed upon the theory that political action may be turned to private gain.

But whether we pity or whether we hate, our betrayal is none the less complete ; nor will either pity or hate restore our birthright. But we know that when political selfishness is destroyed our dangers will disappear ; and though the way to its stronghold may be long and weary, we will follow it—fighting as we go. There will be no surrender, nor will there be desertions from our ranks. Selfishness and corruption have not yet achieved a lasting triumph, and their bold defiance will but hasten the day of their destruction.

As we struggle on, and confidently invite a direct conflict with these intrenched foes of our political safety, we have not failed to see another hope, which has manifested itself to all the honest people of the land. It teaches them that though they may not immediately destroy at their source the evils which afflict them, they may check their malign influence and guard themselves against their baneful results. It assures them, that, if political virtue and rectitude cannot at once be thoroughly restored to the republic, the activity of baser elements may be discouraged. It inspires them with vigilant watchfulness and a determination to prevent as far as possible their treacherous betrayal by those who are false to their obligations of citizenship.

This hope, risen like the Star in the East, has fixed the gaze of our patriotic fellow-countrymen ; and everywhere—in our busy marts of trade and on our farms, in our cities and in our villages, in the dwellings of the rich and in the homes of the poor, in our universities and in our workshops, in our banking houses and in the ranks of inexorable toil—they greet with enthusiastic acclaim the advent of ballot reform.

There are no leaders in this cause. Those who seem to lead the movement are but swept to the front by the surging force of patriotic sentiment. It rises far above partisanship ; and only the heedless, the sordid, and the depraved refuse to join in the crusade.

This reform is predicated upon the cool deliberation of political selfishness in its endeavor to prostitute our suffrage to the purposes of private gain. It is rightly supposed that corruption of the voter is entered upon with such business calculation that the corrupter will only pay a bribe when he has ocular proof that the suffrage he has bargained for is cast in his interest. So, too, it is reasonably expected that if the employee or laborer is at the time of casting his ballot removed from the immediate control of his employer, the futility of fear and intimidation will lead to their abandonment.

The change demanded by this reform in the formalities surrounding the exercise of the privilege of suffrage has given rise to real or pretended solicitude for the rights of our voters ; and the fear has been expressed that inability on the part of electors to conform to the requirements of the proposed change might produce great inconvenience, and in some cases result in disfranchisement. It has even been suggested that the inauguration of the new plan might encroach upon constitutional guarantees.

It will not do to accuse of hostility to the reform all those who present these objections; but it is not amiss to inspect their ranks for enemies in disguise. Though the emergency which is upon us is full of danger, and though we sadly need relief, all rights should be scrupulously preserved. But there should be no shuffling, and no frivolous objections should be tolerated. When a dwelling is in flames we use no set phrase of speech to warn its inmates, and no polite and courtly touch to effect their rescue. Experience has often demonstrated how quickly obstacles, which seemed plausible if not convincing when urged against a measure of reform, are dissipated by the test of trial, and how readily a new order of things adjusts itself to successful use.

I remember the inauguration of another reform; and I have seen it grow and extend, until it has become firmly established in our laws and practice. It is to-day our greatest safeguard against the complete and disgraceful degradation of our public service. It had its enemies, and all of them are not yet silenced. Those openly and secretly unfriendly said in the beginning that the scheme was impracticable and unnecessary; that it created an office-holding class; that it established burdensome and delusive tests for entry in the public service which should be open to all; that it put in the place of real merit and efficiency, scholastic acquirements; that it limited the discretion of those charged with the selection of public employees, and that it was unconstitutional. But its victory came,—wrought by the force of enlightened public sentiment,—and upon its trial every objection which had been urged against it was completely discredited.

As it has been with civil service reform, so will it be with ballot reform, except that the coming victory will be more speedily achieved and will be more complete.

And as the grand old State of Massachusetts was foremost to adopt and demonstrate the practicability and usefulness of civil service reform, so has she been first to adopt a thorough scheme of ballot reform and to prove in practice its value and the invalidity of the objections made against it. We thank Massachusetts to-night for all that she has done for these reforms ; and we of New York hope that our Empire State will soon be keeping step with her sister States in the enforcement of an effective and honest measure of ballot reform.

In conclusion let me say that good men have no cause for discouragement. Though there are dangers which threaten our welfare and safety, the virtue and patriotism of the American people are not lost, and we shall find them sufficient for us. If in too great confidence they slumber, they will not always sleep. Let them but be aroused from lethargy and indifference by the consciousness of peril, and they will burst the bonds of political selfishness, revive their political freedom, and restore the purity of their suffrage.

Thus will they discharge the sacred trust committed to their keeping ; thus will they still proudly present to the world proof of the value of free institutions ; thus will they demonstrate the strength and perpetuity of a government by the people ; thus will they establish American patriotism throughout the length and breadth of our land ; and thus will they preserve for themselves and for posterity their God-given inheritance of freedom and justice and peace and happiness.

V.

At the New York Chamber of Commerce Banquet, November 19, 1889.

As I speak of the honorary members of the Chamber of Commerce, I shall, first of all, avail myself of the opportunity here afforded to express my thanks for the action of that body which placed my name upon its roll of honor. It is a source of great gratification to me to be thus related, though only nominally, to the vast business interests which this organization has in its charge and keeping, and I think and trust that I do not in the least underestimate the improvement and benefit which may result to me from such relationship.

The business of a country is its life blood ; and all who are directly or indirectly connected with it, who are acquainted with its operations and are able to discern the manner in which it may be benefited or injured, and the causes which affect it, should be, for these reasons, better able to perform well their duties as citizens.

Good government is the object of every patriotic aspiration of our people. But good government is so unlike a thing to be gained by dreaming of it, and is something so practical and palpable, that it is best judged by business tests ; and thus the condition of the business of a country is properly considered a reliable indicator of the nature of its government and the manner in which such government is administered.

Of course, the conception of business here intended must not be confused with the selfish scurry and sordid clutching after wealth which we see about us every day—heedless of the rights of others and utterly regardless of any obligation to aid in the nation's growth and greatness. This is not the business of a country ; nor should the narrow and circumscribed success of such endeavor be recognized as evidence of a benefi-cent government or of wholesome laws. The active, strong impulse which, starting from important centers, steadily per-meates the entire land, giving to our tradesmen, everywhere, healthy prosperity, to our toilers remunerative labor, and to our homes comfort and contentment, constitute phases of the business of our country which we love to recognize as proofs of the value of our free institutions and demonstrations of the benign operation of just legislation. But when these factors of general thrift and happiness are wanting, we may well fear that we are not in the enjoyment of all the blessings of good government.

Since business, properly defined, is thus closely related to government, it plainly follows that, if those intrusted with pub-lic affairs were more identified with men like those forming the active membership of this Chamber of Commerce, and were better informed concerning the interests which such men represent, the country would be the gainer. I do not hesitate to say that we should have more business men in our national legislature. If this should be conceded, and the question of reaching that result is presented, but two modes can be suggested—either to make business men of those elected or choose business men in the first instance. The latter plan is manifestly the best, and, indeed, the only practical one.

I must confess that, fresh from public employment, as I look about me here, I feel like a good judge of valuable material, when he sees it in abundance unused and going to waste before his eyes. It is well for you to be conversant with markets, and you are obliged to study them. But it is undeniable that the laws of your country and their execution are so related to markets that they, too, are worthy of your attention. I know that participation in the public service would involve an interruption of your ordinary vocations, but is it not your duty to suffer this for the sake of the good you can accomplish ? Nor is the subject devoid of an inducement based upon self-interest, for you must agree with me that business men upon Congressional committees, or upon the floor of Congress, could accomplish much more in the direction of their own protection than by periodically seeking admission to committee rooms, or awaiting the convenience of legislators who need their instructions.

I cannot be mistaken when I say that some dangers which beset our political life might be avoided or safely met if our business men would more actively share in public affairs, and that nothing would better befit the character and object of your organization than a practical movement in this direction.

I hasten now to say that I have not forgotten the topic with which I started. I am embarrassed in treating of it because, in theory, the honorary members are those who have rendered useful public service. As the last and least of these members I feel that I can do little more than acknowledge my gratitude for the privilege of being counted with the grand men whose names stand above me on the roll—the living and the dead.

There has been much discussion lately concerning the disposition which should be made of our ex-Presidents, and many plans have been suggested for putting us out of the way. I am sure we are very sorry to make so much trouble, but I do hope that, whatever conclusion may be reached, the recommendation of a Kentucky newspaper editor, to take us out and shoot us, will not be adopted. Prior to the 4th day of last March I did not appreciate as well as I do now the objections to this proceeding, but I have had time to reflect upon the subject since and I find excellent reasons for opposing this plan.

If I should be allowed to express myself upon this question I would suggest that the best way to deal with your troublesome ex-Presidents is to let them alone and give them the same chance to earn an honest living that other people have. And if for any reason you desire to honor them, it cannot be done better than by putting their names upon the roll of honorary membership of the New York Chamber of Commerce.

VI.

At the Piano and Organ Manufacturers' Banquet, New York, April 24, 1890.

MR. CHAIRMAN AND GENTLEMEN :

The words of the toast to which I am to respond may just at this time appear to have a somewhat threatening sound. In the midst of unusual thought and discussion among our fellow-citizens upon economic subjects, the phrase " our American industries " is very commonly used ; and the furtherance of these industries is claimed to be the patriotic purpose of those in both political parties who lead in such thought and discussion.

Thus it happens that the announcement of "Our American Industries," as a topic of discourse, has almost come to be a signal for combat between those not at all loath to fly at each other in wordy warfare over the subject of tariff reform. But if there are any persons here who now feel an inclination to gird up their loins for the fray, I hasten to assure them that, though I have been suspected of having some opinions on that question, I am sure that at this particular time the toast I have in charge is not loaded, and that there will be no explosion.

And yet, while I think I can keep the peace and mention my subject without any warlike sensation, I cannot avoid feeling the weight and impediment of another difficulty, which is calculated to appall and discourage me. This is the vastness of my subject. It embraces the toil of the pioneer in the far West, the most delicate operations of manufacture, the most pronounced triumphs of art, and the most startling results of inventive genius.

How can I compass these things within the limits allotted to me on this occasion, and where shall I begin, as I stand before this assemblage of American citizens and am confronted with the ideas which "Our American Industries" suggests?

I can do little more than to speak of the present condition of these industries as indicating the greatest and swiftest national growth and advancement the world has ever seen. We have only one hundred years of history ; but in all that time American ingenuity and investigation have been active and restless. We have begrudged to Nature everything she seeks to hide, and have laid in wait to learn the secret of her processes. We have not believed that the greatest advance yet reached in mechanical skill and art has exhausted American invention, and when other nations have started first in any field of progress, we have resolutely given chase and struggled for the lead.

We now invite the old nations of Europe to see our steam

plows turning furrows in wheatfields as large as some of their principalities. We astonish them with the number and the length of our railroads, and the volume and speed of our transportation. With odds against us, for which American skill and industry are in no wise to blame, we force our products and manufactures into their markets. Our Edison lighted the Eiffel Tower, and by his display of the wonders of electricity lent success to the American exhibits at the Paris Exposition.

It appears that some of our industries suit the people of foreign lands so well that they desire to own them ; and daily we hear of English syndicates purchasing our manufacturing establishments. Our people seem to endure this raid upon them with wonderful complacency, though we cannot forget that, less than two years ago, they were very solemnly warned against the dangers and seductions of British gold.

I hope I am not too late in expressing my thanks for the privilege of meeting on this occasion an assemblage representing one of our industries which, so far as I know, is not infected by the wholesale influence of British gold, and which embraces only such manufactures as are honestly and fairly American.

This means a great deal ; and I do not envy the American citizen who has no pride in what you have accomplished. Of course, we do not forget that many who have contributed to our glory in this direction bear names which betray their foreign lineage. But we claim them all as Americans ; and I believe that you will, in the enthusiasm and vigor of true American sentiment and independence, stubbornly hold the place which has been won by you and others of your guild, under the banner of " A fair field and no favor."

I have within the last few days received as a gift—perhaps suggested by my contemplated presence here—a book entitled " A History of the American Pianoforte," which I shall read with much interest.

In glancing through it my eye fell upon a passage which

arrested my attention, as furnishing a slight set-off against the indebtedness we owe to those of foreign birth among our piano and organ manufacturers. I know you will permit me to quote it, as evidence of the share our free institutions may claim in the success of your industry. The writer, claiming priority for the United States for some particular things done in the progress of piano manufacturing by two certain makers, who, though manufacturing in this country, were, as he says, "originally Britons, one English and the other evidently Scotch," clinches the argument in our favor, as follows :

Notwithstanding this circumstance, America is entitled to the honor of the achievements pointed out, because it is a well demonstrated fact, although, perhaps, a subtlety, that the social and governmental institutions of this country, in so far as they promote mental freedom, have a stimulating and immediate influence upon the inventive faculties of persons brought up in Europe and settling here.

I cannot forbear, in conclusion, a reference to the manner in which your busy manufactories and the salesrooms of your wares are related to the love and joy and hopes and sadness and grief and the worship of God which sanctify the American family circle.

In many a humble home throughout our land, the piano has gathered about it the most sacred and tender associations. For it, the daughters of the household longed by day and prayed in dreams at night. For it fond parents saved and economized at every point and planned in loving secrecy. For it, a certain Christmas Day, on which the arrival of the piano gave a glad surprise, was marked as a red-letter day in the annals of the household.

With its music and with simple song each daughter in her turn touched with love the heart of her future husband. With it, the sacred hymn and the family prayer are joined in chastened memory. With it, closed and silent, are tenderly remembered the days of sickness, the time of death, and the funeral's solemn hush.

When the family circle is broken and its members are scattered, happy is the son or daughter who can place among his or her household goods the old piano.

VII.

At the Chamber of Commerce Banquet, New York, November 18, 1890.

MR. PRESIDENT AND GENTLEMEN :

This volunteer business I did not calculate upon, and I think it would best befit me now only to thank you for the kindness which you have extended to me. I do not believe it would be fair for me to disturb the contentment which ought to remain to you after the delicious dinner which you have eaten; and I know that, after the oratory and the dinner speeches you have heard, it would ill become me to obtrude any random thoughts. I do not believe that when people are under the influence of sweet music, a boy around the edges ought to be shooting off a blunderbuss.

I shall go home to-night with some confused ideas in my mind ; you are not to blame for them, but I suppose my condition and circumstances are to blame. We have heard about literature and business, about education and business, and about foreign commerce, and a good deal about reciprocity ; and that is where my trouble comes in. We have been told that it would be a grand thing to have reciprocity with Spanish-speaking people. Now, if it is good for Spanish-speaking people, how would it do with the people who speak our own language ?

We have heard that our breadstuffs go across the water, and that the people need them there. That means a market for them, doesn't it ? I had an idea that a bird in the hand is worth two in the bush, and that, perhaps, if you had a market, it might be well to cultivate it, instead of trying to manufacture another.

We have heard that England and France have within a few days rushed to our rescue in a financial way, prompted thereto by the noble sentiment of reciprocity. If they are so willing and glad to extend to us the hand of reciprocity in financial matters, how would it do to give them a chance in commercial and other matters ?

Now, as I said, these difficulties of mine are entirely attributable to my own neglected education, and incidentally and indirectly, I think they are attributable to the fact that I am only an honorary member of this institution, instead of being an active one. This being the case, I have not that intimate familiarity with the subject which would probably clear up my doubts.

I have spoken of being an honorary member of this institution ; and I have prized that distinction very highly, indeed, but never more so than to-night, because I see there may be at some time a possibility of my attending a banquet of the Chamber of Commerce, without being called upon for a speech; that I may come here and enjoy the good things which you set before me, without that gloomy foreboding which an undigested and indigestible speech brings over a man. I have almost accomplished it to-night, and as progress is the order of the day, I have no doubt but that it will be finally arranged to my liking.

To-night I find myself facing this audience under circumstances which gave me no intimation that I was to make a speech. That was a mercy in itself, for I enjoyed my dinner before the collapse came. Therefore, as I speak of my association with this Chamber of Commerce, though my relations are not so intimate as to understand all questions which are, perhaps, easy to you, and though I have not reached that stage when I can confidently come here without being called upon to make a speech, I am glad to believe that the promise is favorable.

I am very strongly tempted to say something in answer to some remarks which my friend Depew made, but everybody seems to have pitched on to him, and even Mr. Schurz, who promised to stand by him, did not do so at all ; and although he is well able to stand up against any number of us, I do not know that I ought to make any reference to some things which he has said ; and yet, when he spoke of the nomination my friend Springer made, I could not help but think that perhaps Springer had learned from him how to do it. Now, it was a very innocent thing that my friend Springer said. It amounted to nothing. But I can tell you a circumstance which involves in it modesty, accountability to the people of the country, and ambition, and, when I have done, I think you will agree with me, that perhaps Mr. Depew was more to blame before the eyes of the people than Mr. Springer was.

The first time I ever saw Mr. Depew in a public place was in Albany. I was then Governor of the State, and we had a banquet in commemoration of a certain military company, or something of that kind, and I was invited and went. I was to make a speech. I prepared myself most elaborately, and did the very best I could. Now, mind you, at that time I was a quiet, unambitious man, quite content with the situation I occupied, and happy with the delusion that I was doing something for the good of the State. Mr. Depew arose—I shall repeat only what he said—and congratulated those present that at last they had elected a Governor who could do that most difficult of all things, make an after-dinner speech. That made me very happy indeed. He spoke of some other traits, and of some other things which were very complimentary, and he then said, " Gentlemen, I know of nothing more proper, I know of nothing more in keeping with the services of this gentleman than that the party with which he is affiliated should nominate him in the coming convention for the highest office in the gift of the people."

Now, the effect of that on a young man can be easily imagined, if not described. And then he went on and said : " When that is done, the party with which I am proud to be affiliated, I hope, will nominate as his competitor that noble citizen, that grand man and statesman whose name I have no doubt rises to the lips of every man here present—though it does not to mine." Well, I did not know what to make of that then, nor why he did not mention the name of the citizen and statesman, but subsequent events have made me rather suspicious that at that moment our friend was struck with a fit of extreme modesty. Doesn't that excuse Mr. Springer? I think so. There was an administration of the Federal Government with which I was connected, and with which I had something to do—at all events, I have been held to an accountability for all its shortcomings—and I long ago made up my mind, that when the opportunity came that I could do it without injuring myself, I might, perhaps, have something to say about Mr. Depew's candidacy for the Presidency. Now, see the selfishness of this thing. See the mean political selfishness of that idea. Not so with Mr. Depew. Why, within four weeks, I think, in his magnanimity, and in his generous heart, though at a festive board, where we are all apt to say kind and generous things, he said such complimentary things of me as visited upon him, I am informed, the condemnation of members of his party. Indeed, I hear that one enthusiastic adherent of his from the West, on account of those complimentary and courteous things, which he said regardless of Presidential consequences, while I was waiting for an opportunity when I could say a kind thing of him, without hurting myself, wrote to him : " While you have been for years my ideal of a man that has Presidential timber in him, and while I have been strongly your advocate for that office, after seeing what you said of that miserable fellow Cleveland, I wouldn't vote for you for poundmaster."

Now this carries with it an acknowledgment of the kindness and goodness of Mr. Depew, and also a confession of my own disposition, for I confess to you that the time has not yet come when I have thought I could safely, and without harm to myself, launch out on that subject in regard to him ; but I hope the time will come. I am watching for it.

Now, gentlemen, there seems nothing left to me but to thank you again for your hearty recognition of me, and to say of the Chamber of Commerce that I sincerely hope that it may long exist in the prosperity which has marked it for so many years, and that these banquets may constantly increase in pleasure to those who are fortunate enough to be their invited guests.

———

VIII.

At the Jewelers' Association Annual Dinner, New York, November 21, 1890.

MR. PRESIDENT AND GENTLEMEN:

The sentiment assigned to me suggests a theme so vast and so animating that I am embarrassed in my attempt to deal with it. You surely will not expect me on this occasion to voice all the thoughts and feelings which the mention of " Our Country " inspires. If I should do this, I should merely tax your time and patience by the expression of reflections which spontaneously fill your minds. Besides, if I should launch upon this subject in true American style, I know I could not avoid the guilt of making a Fourth of July speech late in the month of November.

I hasten to declare that I do not fight shy of my subject because I do not love it. On the contrary, I love it so well that I am anxious to observe all the proprieties related to it ; and I cannot rid myself of the idea that our American eagle soars higher and better in the warm days of July than in the cool atmosphere of the present season.

And yet, I am far from believing that at any time and in any assemblage of Americans the sentiment " Our Country " is not a proper one to propose ; though I have sometimes thought that it speaks so eloquently for itself that it needs no interpreter. There seems absolutely to be no necessity for arousing enthusiasm on this topic, and there is not the slightest danger that any of us will forget what we have accomplished as a nation or what we propose to accomplish, or that we will fix

too narrow a limit upon the progress, development, and greatness of our country. Sometimes those who, unfortunately,
cannot claim this as their country accuse us of dwelling with
some exaggeration upon these things, but every American is
entirely certain that such imputations arise from ignorance of
our achievements or from envy and disappointed rivalry. At
any rate, it is a habit to glorify our country, and we propose
to continue it. We all do it without prompting, and we like
it. We can stand any amount of it without disturbance, and
whether others like it or not, we know, and we propose to declare on every occasion, that America is the finest and the
best and the greatest country on the face of the globe. That
proposition is not original with me, but has been a settled fact
in the American mind for many years.

Though this might be said to dispose of the subject by a
short cut, and though I have declined to deal with it in all its
aspects, the American disposition to glorify our country is
strong with me ; and I am disinclined to abandon my allotted
sentiment in a manner quite so summary. If I am to retain
it for a few moments, I know of no better way to deal with it
than to divide it and consider one branch or part of my text,
as is sometimes done with a long text in the pulpit. I, therefore, propose to say something about the word " our " as related to the sentiment, " Our Country."

This is " our " country, because the people have established
it, because they rule it, because they have developed it, because they have fought for it, and because they love it. And
still each generation of Americans holds it only in trust for
those who shall come after them, and they are charged with
the obligation to transmit it as strong as it came to their hands.
It is not ours to destroy, it is not ours to sell, and it is not
ours to neglect and injure. It is ours as our families are ours,
and as our churches and schools are ours—to protect and defend, to foster and improve. As its strength and its fitness to
reach its promised destiny depend upon its unity, one of our
highest duties toward it is to cultivate and encourage kindli-

ness among our people, to the end that all may heartily co-operate in performing the terms of our trust. As it exists for us all, so all should be accorded an equal share in its benefits. It is so constructed that its work is badly done and its operation perverted, when special and exclusive advantages are awarded to any particular class of our people. If we permit grasping selfishness to influence us in the care of our trust, we are untrue to our obligations and our covenants as Americans.

Our country is "ours" for the purpose of securing through its means justice, happiness, and prosperity to all—not for the purpose of permitting the selfish and designing to be enriched at the expense of their confiding fellow-countrymen. It is our duty, then, to defend and protect our country, while it remains in our hands, from that selfishness which, if permitted, will surely undermine it, as clearly as it is our duty to defend it against armed enemies.

Nor are we discharged from our obligations as trustees of our country if we merely preserve it in the same condition as when we received it. The march of progress and civilization throughout the world imposes on us the duty of improving the subject of our trust so that it may be transmitted to others in such an advanced condition of prosperity and growth as shall bear witness to our faithfulness and our devotion to its interests. He who hid his talent in a napkin and added nothing to it was condemned as unfaithful, when called upon to give an account of his stewardship.

Let us, then, rejoice in the greatness of "Our Country"; but let us remember that it will be our blame if it is not made greater ; let us boast of the country which is ours, but let our boasting be tempered with the reflection that its possession is charged with a sacred trust ; let us constantly bear in mind that while it is ours to use patriotically and transmit to coming generations, our relation to it is made more serious by the fact that, in its broadest and most solemn meaning, our country is something which, as an example and interpreter of freedom, belongs to the world, and which, in its blessed mission, belongs to humanity.

IX.

At the Banquet of the National Association of Builders,
New York, February 12, 1891.

Mr. President and Gentlemen :

When American citizens are gathered together on occasions like this, and the hour of feasting is supplemented by toast and sentiment, it is surely fitting that "Our Country" should be prominent among the topics proposed for thought and speech. Evidence is thus furnished of the ever present love and affection of our people for their country, prompting them, at all times and in all places, to yield to her ready recognition and homage.

The conspicuous place which this sentiment occupies in American thought is the result of our relations to the land which we possess and to the government under which we live. Our vast domain belongs to our people. They have fought for it, and have labored hard for its development and growth. Our government, too, was fashioned and established by and for our people, and is sustained and administered at their behest. Subjects of other lands, less free than ours, and those who owe obedience to governments further removed from popular control, may boast of their country, in a spirit of natural pride and patriotism and as sharers in its splendor and glory. They thus exhibit their submission and allegiance and a habitual regard for constituted authority. But the enthusiasm which warms our hearts at the mention of "Our Country" grows out of our sense of proprietary and individual right in American institutions. It is mingled with no servile gratitude to any ruler for scant freedom generously conceded to us, nor with admiration of monarchical pomp and splendor. The words, "Our Country," suggest to us not only a broad domain which is ours, but also a government which is ours, based upon our will, protected and guarded by our love and affection, vouchsafing to us freedom limited only by our self-imposed restraints, and securing to us, as our right, absolute and impartial justice.

When we consider the extensive growth of our country—its cities and villages, and all the physical features which contribute so much to give to it a foremost place in the civilization of the age—we are bound to acknowledge that the builders of our land have had much to do with securing for us the commanding position we hold among the nations of the earth. It may, indeed, be said that all the nations which have ever existed, have, like us, been largely indebted, for the grandeur and magnificence of which they could boast, to those belonging to the vocation represented in this assembly. It will be impossible to find a complete description of any country, ancient or modern, which does not mention the size and character of its buildings, and its public and private edifices.

I do not intend to do injustice, in the enthusiasm of this hour, to any of the trades and occupations which have contributed to make our country and other countries great. But truth and candor exact the confession that the chief among these occupations in all times past has been that of the builder. He began his work in the early days of created things, and has been abroad among the sons of men ever since. The builder's advent was signalized by a service to mankind of which not another craft can boast. No one has the hardihood to deny that the construction of the ark was the turning-point in the scheme for the perpetuation of the human race. The builder's work in that emergency saved mankind from a watery grave ; and if we suffer at the hands of his successors in these modern times, we should allow his first job to plead loudly in his behalf. If in these days we are vexed by the failure of the builder to observe plans and specifications, let us bear in mind that in his first construction he, fortunately for us, followed them implicitly. The gopher wood was furnished, the ark was pitched within and without, it was built three hundred cubits long, fifty cubits broad, and thirty cubits high; the window was put in, the door was placed in the side, and it had a lower, second, and third story. If we are now and then prompted almost to profanity, because the builder has not completed our house within the time agreed, let us recall with gratitude the fact that the ark was fully completed and finished in a good and workmanlike manner and actually occupied, seven days before the waters of the flood were upon the earth. If a feeling like paralysis steals over us when a long account for extra work is placed before our affrighted eyes, let us be reconciled to our fate by the thought that there was no charge for extra work in the construction of the ark, and that the human race was saved without that exasperating incident.

We sometimes hear things which are calculated to convey the impression that there is an irrepressible conflict raging between our builders and the rest of our people. If any such thing exists, I desire to suggest, in behalf of the builders, that it may to a great extent arise from the uncertainty prevailing among employers concerning their wants and what they can afford to have. These are days when the free-born and ambitious American citizen does not like to be outdone by his neighbor or anyone else. If, as a result of this, a man with fifty thousand dollars to spend for a home, is determined to have one as good and as extravagant as that of another man, who has twice the amount to invest for the same purpose, the builder certainly ought not to be blamed if he fails to perform that miracle. On the other hand, it has sometimes seemed to me that when an honest, confiding man applies to a builder for an estimate of the cost of a construction which he contemplates, he ought to receive more definite and trustworthy figures than those frequently submitted to him. I am inclined to think, however, that on the whole the relations of the builder with his fellow-men have been fairly amicable. If this were not so, and if disputes and misunderstandings were ordinary incidents of building contracts, it is quite apparent that the buildings which have been put up in our country would have caused enough of quarrels not only to endanger our social fabric, but to transfer much of the wealth now in the hands of the builders and their patrons to the pockets of the members of that peaceful and honest profession to which I have the honor to belong. This latter result would not be altogether mournful; the legal profession are so patriotic, and so easily satisfied, that I am quite certain they are contented with existing conditions.

The National Association of Builders gives promise in its declared objects and purposes of much usefulness. It recognizes the fact that the relation its members bear to vast numbers of our wage-earners furnishes the opportunity for them to do an important and beneficent work in the way of reconciling differences between employers and employees and averting unprofitable and exasperating conflicts. All must commend the desire of the organization for the adoption of effective precautions against accident and injury to employees, and for some provision for such as are injured or incapacitated for work. And all our people ought especially to appreciate the efforts of your association to aid in the establishment of trade schools for the education and improvement of apprentices. Of course, no one will deny that a workman in your vocation, who labors intelligently and with some knowledge of the underlying reason for his plan of work, does more and better service than one who pursues his round of daily toil, unthinkingly, and as a mere matter of routine or imitation. Herein is certainly a palpable advantage to the workman, to the builder, and to his patron. But the value of a trade school education is not thus limited. The apprentice not only becomes a better workman by means of the education and discipline of such a school, but that very process must also tend to make him a better citizen. While he learns the things which give him an understanding of his work and fit his mind and brain to guide his hand, he also stimulates his perception of that high service which his country claims of him as a citizen.

For this service he and all of us have placed in our hands the suffrage of freemen. It is only faithfully used when its exercise represents a full consciousness of the responsibilities and duties which its possession imposes, and when it is guided and controlled by a pure conscience and by thoughtful, intelligent, and independent judgment.

" Neither walls, theaters, porches, nor senseless equipage, make states ; but men who are able to rely upon themselves."

As a concluding thought, let me suggest, that though the builders of the United States may erect grand and beautiful edifices which shall be monuments of their skill and evidences of our nation's prosperity, their work is not well done nor their duty wholly performed unless, in pursuance of their contract of citizenship, they join with all their fellow-countrymen in building and finishing in beautiful proportions, the grandest and most commanding of all earthly structures—" Our Country."

X.

Before the Commercial Club, Providence, R. I., June 27, 1891.

MR. PRESIDENT AND GENTLEMEN :

I suppose from the name of the organization which extends to us the hospitalities of this occasion, that its membership is mainly, at least, made up of those engaged in business enterprises, and that its object is the discussion of topics related to the progress and development of such enterprises.

I never attend a gathering of business men, and recall the restless activity which they represent, and the strain of brain which they willingly bear for the sake of profit and success, without wondering that they are content to be so thoroughly engrossed in the immediate details of their occupations, as often to lead to an habitual neglect of those affairs, which though outside of their counting houses, exchanges and manufactories, have an intimate relation to their prosperity. No one can be oblivious to the fact that matters of legislation, and the course of governmental policy, are so important to the business in which we engage that our individual efforts in its prosecution may be easily promoted or thwarted by the conduct of those who make and execute our laws. Yet, in business circles we find but few men who are willing to forego their ordinary work to engage in the business of legislation. Indeed this unfortunate condition has reached such a pass that our business men think and often speak of politics as something quite outside of their interest and duty, which, if not actually disreputable, may well be left to those who have a taste for it.

I am by no means unmindful of the spasmodic interference of business interests in politics, spurred on by a selfish desire to be aided, especially and exclusively through legislative action. Such interference, based upon such motives, is more blameworthy than inactivity, because it amounts to an attempt to pervert governmental functions—which is worse than a neglect of political responsibility. But I speak of a heedlessness of the duty resting upon every one of us as American citizens, to participate thoughtfully and intelligently in the general conduct of the government which is ours, and which has been left to our management.

I seek to remind you of the interest which you and all of us have as members of our American body politic, in wholesome general laws and honest administration. This interest is represented by the share to which each of us is entitled, in the aggregate of advantage which such laws and such administration secure. This interest and this duty are surely worth all the attention we can bestow upon them; and the penalty of their neglect we shall surely not escape. In order that the patriotism and intelligence of the country shall prevail in our legislation, the patriotic and intelligent men of the country must see to it that they are properly represented in our national councils. If they fail in this they will be governed by those who simply make a trade of politics. If it is well that our legislation be influenced by the enlightened and practical business sense of the people, our business men must see to it that those they trust are chosen as their lawmakers. If they are indifferent on the subject, the vast interests which so greatly concern them and all their fellow-citizens will be left at the mercy of those who neither understand them nor care for them ; and I do not believe these dangers will be effectively averted until they are better understood by the people and more thoroughly resisted.

It seems to me that private and special legislation, as it at present prevails, is an evil chargeable to a great extent to the listlessness and carelessness of the people.

There is a kind of legislation which, upon its face and concededly, is private and special, and which engrosses far too much of the time and attention of our lawmakers. The people have a right to claim from their representatives their best care and attention to the great subjects of legislation in which the entire country is interested. This is denied them if their representatives take their seats burdened with private bills, in which their immediate neighbors are exclusively interested, and which they feel they must be diligent in advancing, if they would secure their continuance in public life. They are thus led by the exigencies of their situation as they view it, not only to the support of private bills of questionable propriety, but to the neglect of a study and understanding of the important questions involved in general legislation. Nor does the pernicious effect of such special and private legislation stop here. The importance of a successful championship of these private bills, measured by a standard which ought not for a moment to be recognized, seems so vital to those having them in charge that they are easily led to barter their votes for measures as bad as theirs or worse, in order to secure the support of similarly situated colleagues. Thus is inaugurated a system called log-rolling, which comes frightfully near actual legislative corruption ; and thus the people at large lose not only the attention to their affairs which is due to them, but are often no better than robbed of the money in the public treasury.

I have hardly done more than to present a very general outline of some of the palpably bad accompaniments of legislation, confessedly special and private. The details might easily be filled in, which would furnish proof of the elements of its mischievous character which I have pointed out.

I have not, however, mentioned the aspect of special and private legislation which seems to me most pernicious. I refer to the habit which it engenders among our people of looking to the government for aid in the accomplishment of special and individual schemes, and the expectation which it creates and fosters, that legislation may be invoked for the securing of individual advantages and unearned benefits.

The relations of our countrymen toward their government should be founded upon their love for it as the fountainhead of their national life ; their faith in it as the power which preserves them a free people ; their reverence for it as the perfect work of the highest patriotism ; their confidence in its justice and equality, and their pride in its ownership and management. These should furnish at all times sufficient motive for a lively interest in public affairs, and should supply abundant incentive to popular watchfulness of legislative and executive methods. In the light of these considerations, no thoughtful American can shut his eyes to the truth, that when our people regard their government as the source of individual benefit and favoritism, and when their interest in it is measured by the extent to which they hope to realize such benefit and favoritism, our popular government is in dangerous hands and its entire perversion is alarmingly imminent.

These perils are not alone chargeable to legislation which is confessedly special and private. Measures of a general character, and apparently proposed for the public good, frequently originate in selfish calculations, or so completely subserve in their details selfish plans, that they also tend toward the fatal point of sordidness among the people and unjust paternalism in the government. No matter what plausible pretexts may be advanced for such legislation, if it has in it these elements, it ought to be condemned. Neither the cry of protection to American interests, nor pretended solicitude for the public good, ought to succeed in concealing schemes to favor the few at the expense of the many ; nor should the importance to the country of legislative action upon any subject divert us from inquiry concerning the selfish motives and purposes which may be hidden behind the proposal of such legislation.

It is quite time that our business men, and all American citizens who love their country, bestir themselves for battle against the evil tendencies of private and special legislation, whatever guise it may assume. At this time no more important truth can be presented to the people than that they should support their government in love and patriotism, and remain unselfishly content with the blessings and advantages which our free institutions were established to bestow, with justice and equality, upon every citizen throughout the length and breadth of our land.

CHAPTER VIII.

TO RELIGIOUS AND CHARITABLE ORGANIZATIONS.

I.

At the Laying of the Corner Stone of the " Fitch Institute," Buffalo, May 10, 1882.

MR. FITCH:

IT falls to my lot on this occasion to extend to you, on behalf of the city of Buffalo, a hearty greeting and a cordial welcome. I am to attempt to express to you the sentiments of gratitude and appreciation which our citizens cherish toward you, their former fellow-citizen.

I am sure I shall do no act during my official career, as Chief Executive of our beautiful and prosperous city, which more accords with my own feelings, or which will afford me so much pleasure. You, sir, have known and watched the growth and progress of our city since its day of small things; and in the full strength of your earlier years you were identified with its important and successful enterprises. The way of the world, too, often is to forget and neglect the scene of a successful struggle with life; and those who amass wealth are too apt to enjoy the fruit, unmindful of the soil whereon it grew.

We joyfully and gratefully acknowledge to-day that human nature has a different phase. You left the activities of our city's business life, years ago, laden with the prizes earned and gathered by untiring industry, prudent management, and honorable dealing. But the occasion which we celebrate assures us that your heart has still been with us, and that, in the day of independent affluence, you have not been unmindful of the city where you conquered success. You return to us to-day bearing gifts to our people which will make them happier and better.

The extent and value of your princely munificence certainly call for the warmest gratitude on the part of all of us, inasmuch as it adds so greatly to the beauty, advancement, and substantial prosperity of the city. But the object and purpose of your noble charity touch our hearts more deeply, and awaken our love and affection.

You have given a fortune away, and have directed that it " be applied to the physical, moral, and intellectual benefit of the worthy poor of Buffalo without distinction of creed or sex." This comprises all the elements of the most Christian and disinterested benevolence.

The poor are to be relieved. And not only their physical, but their moral and intellectual wants are to be provided for. And all this is to be done for the worthy poor, because they are poor and worthy, and not because they profess any creed, or religious belief. A common humanity is the only necessary credential. This opens your charity to the family of man, and stamps upon it the seal of genuine and pure philanthropy.

You have not built for yourself a monument of brass, but have secured for yourself in the grateful hearts of thousands living, and those yet unborn, a more enduring monument than brass or marble. We feel that your greatest compensation to-day consists in your self-approval of a noble work well done, and that our words of thanks are cold and cheerless. And yet, on behalf of our citizens, and on behalf of the worthy poor of Buffalo, we thank you for all you have done for us.

You witness on this occasion the beginning of the building which is to perpetuate your goodness. We pray Heaven that you may live long to witness its completion and continued usefulness. And may your declining years be sustained and soothed by the sweet solace of an approving conscience, and the benisons of thousands of the poor people who shall rise up and call you blessed.

I have been directed by the Common Council to present to you resolutions expressing their sentiments toward you, and extending to you the freedom of the city.

II.

Message to the Buffalo Common Council, June 5, 1882.

My attention has been called, by a committee from the Society for the Prevention of Cruelty to Children, to the number of small boys and girls found upon our streets at late hours in the night.

I have reason to believe that many of these children are allowed, and some are obliged, by their parents, thus to remain in the streets for the ostensible purpose of earning money by selling newspapers or blacking boots. In truth, however, after a certain hour in the evening, the most, if not all the money they receive, they obtain by begging or by false pretenses. In the meantime they are subjected to the worst influences, leading directly to profligacy, vagrancy, and crime.

The importance of caring for children who are uncared for by their natural guardians, or who are unmindful of parental restraint, must be apparent to all. In the future, for good or evil, their influence will be felt in the community; and certainly the attempt to prevent their swelling the criminal class is worth an effort.

It seems to me that no pretext should be permitted to excuse allowing young girls to be on the streets at improper hours, since the result must necessarily be their destruction.

The disposition of the boy—child though he be—to aid in his own support or that of others, in an honest, decent way, ought not to be discouraged. But this does not call for his being in the street at late hours, to his infinite damage morally, mentally, and physically, and to the danger of society.

I respectfully suggest that this subject be referred to the committee on ordinances and the attorney, and that a committee from the Society for the Prevention of Cruelty to Children be invited to co-operate with them in an effort to frame an ordinance which will remedy the evil herein considered.

GROVER CLEVELAND, *Mayor*.

III.

At the Laying of the Corner Stone of the Y. M. C. A. Building in Buffalo, September 7, 1882.

LADIES AND GENTLEMEN:

I desire to express the sincere pleasure and gratification I experience in joining with you in the exercises of this afternoon. An event is here marked which I deem a most important one, and one well worthy of the attention of all good citizens. We, this day, bring into a prominent place an institution which, it seems to me, cannot fail to impress itself upon our future with the best results.

Perhaps a majority of our citizens have heard of the Young Men's Christian Association; and perchance the name has suggested, in an indefinite way, certain efforts to do good and to aid generally in the spread of religious teaching. I venture to say, however, that a comparatively small part of our community has really known the full extent of the work of this Association; and many have thought of it as an institution well enough in its way—a proper enough outlet for a superabundance of religious enthusiasm—doing, of course, no harm, and perhaps very little good. Some have aided it by their contributions from a sense of Christian duty, but more have passed by on the other side.

We have been too much in the habit of regarding institutions of this kind as entirely disconnected from any considerations of municipal growth or prosperity, and have too often considered splendid structures, active trade, increasing commerce, and growing manufactures as the only things worthy of our care as public-spirited citizens. A moment's reflection reminds us that this is wrong.   The citizen is a better business man if he is a Christian gentleman, and surely business is not the less prosperous and successful if conducted on Christian principles.   This is an extremely practical, and perhaps not a very elevated, view to take of the purposes and benefits of the Young Men's Christian Association.   But I assert that if it did no more than to impress some religious principles upon the business of our city, it would be worthy of generous sup-port.   And when we consider the difference, as a member of the community, between the young man who, under the influ-ence of such an association, has learned his duty to his fellows and to the State, and that one who, subject to no moral restraint, yields to temptation and thus becomes vicious and criminal, the importance of an institution among us which leads our youth and young men in the way of morality and good citizenship must be freely admitted.

I have thus only referred to this association as in some man-ner connected with our substantial prosperity.   There is a higher theme connected with this subject which touches the welfare, temporal and spiritual, of the objects of its care. Upon this I will not dwell.   I cannot, however, pass on with-out invoking the fullest measure of honor and consideration due to the self-sacrificing and disinterested efforts of the men—and women, too—who have labored amid trials and discouragements to plant this Association firmly upon sure foundation.   We all hope and expect that our city has en-tered upon a course of unprecedented prosperity and growth. But to my mind not all the signs about us point more surely to real greatness than the event which we here celebrate.

Good and pure government lies at the foundation of the wealth and progress of every community.

As the Chief Executive of this proud city, I congratulate all my fellow-citizens that to-day we lay the foundation stone of an edifice which shall be a beautiful adornment, and, what is more important, shall inclose within its walls such earnest Christian endeavors as must make easier all our efforts to administer, safely and honestly, a good municipal government. I commend the Young Men's Christian Association to the cheerful and generous support of every citizen, and trust that long after the men who have wrought so well in establishing these foundations shall have surrendered lives well spent, this building shall stand a monument of well directed, pious labor, to shed its benign influence on generations yet to come.

IV.

To the Cardinal Gibbons Reception Committee.

Executive Mansion,
Washington, January 26, 1887.

My Dear Sir:

I have received from you, as one of the Committee of the Catholic Club of Philadelphia, an invitation to attend a banquet to be given by the club, on Tuesday evening, February 8, in honor of His Eminence Cardinal Gibbons. The thoughtfulness which prompted this invitation is gratefully appreciated; and I regret that my public duties here will prevent its acceptance. I should be glad to join in the contemplated expression of respect to be tendered to the distinguished head of the Catholic Church in the United States, whose personal acquaintance I very much enjoy, and who is so worthily entitled to the esteem of all his fellow-citizens.

I thank you for the admirable letter which accompanies my invitation, in which you announce as one of the doctrines of your club "that a good and exemplary Catholic must *ex necessitate rei* be a good and exemplary citizen," and that "the teachings of both human and Divine law thus merging in the one word, duty, form the only union of Church and State that a civil and religious government can recognize."

I know you will permit me, as a Protestant, to supplement this noble sentiment by the expression of my conviction that the same influence and result follow a sincere and consistent devotion to the teachings of every religious creed which is based upon Divine sanction.

A wholesome religious faith thus inures to the perpetuity, the safety and the prosperity of our Republic, by exacting the due observance of civil law, the preservation of public order, and a proper regard for the rights of all; and thus are its adherents better fitted for good citizenship and confirmed in a sure and steadfast patriotism. It seems to me, too, that the conception of duty to the State which is derived from religious precept involves a sense of personal responsibility, which is of the greatest value in the operation of the government by the people. It will be a fortunate day for our country when every citizen feels that he has an ever-present duty to perform to the State which he cannot escape from or neglect without being false to his religious as well as his civil allegiance.

Wishing for your club the utmost success in its efforts to bring about this result,

I am,

Yours sincerely,

GROVER CLEVELAND.

————

V.

At the Laying of the Y. M. C. A. Building Corner Stone, Kansas City, Mo., October 13, 1887.

In the busy activities of our daily life we are apt to neglect instrumentalities which are quietly, but effectually, doing most important service in molding our national character. Among these, and challenging but little notice compared with their valuable results, are the Young Men's Christian Associations scattered throughout our country. All will admit the supreme importance of that honesty and fixed principle which rest upon Christian motives and purposes, and all will acknowledge the sad and increasing temptations which beset our young men and lure them to their destruction.

To save these young men, oftentimes deprived of the restraints of home, from degradation and ruin, and to fit them for usefulness and honor, these associations have entered the field of Christian effort and are pushing their noble work. When it is considered that the subjects of their efforts are to be the active men for good or evil in the next generation, mere worldly prudence dictates that these associations should be aided and encouraged.

Their increase and flourishing condition reflect the highest honor upon the good men who have devoted themselves to this work, and demonstrate that the American people are not entirely lacking in appreciation of its value. Twenty years ago but one of these associations owned a building, and that was valued at only $11,000. To-day more than one hundred such buildings, valued at more than $5,000,000, beautify the different cities of our land and beckon our young men to lives of usefulness.

I am especially pleased to be able to participate to-day in laying the corner stone of another of these edifices in this active and growing city; and I trust that the encouragement given the Young Men's Christian Association located here may be commensurate with its assured usefulness, and in keeping with the generosity and intelligence which characterize the people of Kansas City.

VI.

To the Evangelical Alliance, Washington, December 9, 1887.

Mr. President:

I am glad to meet so large a delegation from the Evangelical Alliance of the United States. I understand the purpose of this Alliance to be the application of Christian rules of conduct to the problems and exigencies of social and political life.

Such a movement cannot fail to produce the most valuable

results. All must admit that the reception of the teachings of Christianity results in the purest patriotism, in the most scrupulous fidelity to public trust, and in the best type of citizenship. Those who manage the affairs of government are by this means reminded that the law of God demands that they should be courageously true to the interests of the people, and that the Ruler of the Universe will require of them a strict account of their stewardship. The people, too, are thus taught that their happiness and welfare will be best promoted by a conscientious regard for the interest of a common brotherhood, and that the success of a government by the people depends upon the morality, the justice, and the honesty of the people.

I am especially pleased to know that your efforts are not cramped and limited by denominational lines, and that your credentials are found in a broad Christian fellowship. Manifestly, if you seek to teach your countrymen toleration you yourselves must be tolerant; if you would teach them liberality for the opinions of each other, you yourselves must be liberal; and if you would teach them unselfish patriotism, you yourselves must be unselfish and patriotic. There is enough of work in the field you have entered to enlist the hearty co-operation of all who believe in the value and efficacy of Christian teaching and practice.

Your noble mission, if undertaken in a broad and generous spirit, will surely arrest the attention and respectful consideration of your fellow-citizens; and your endeavors, consecrated by benevolence and patriotic love, must exert a powerful influence in the enlightenment and improvement of our people, in illustrating the strength and stability of our institutions, and in advancing the prosperity and greatness of our beloved land.

VII.

Before the Northern and Southern Presbyterian Assemblies at Philadelphia, May 23, 1888.

I am very much gratified by the opportunity here afforded me to meet the representatives of the Presbyterian Church.

Surely a man never should lose his interest in the welfare of the Church in which he was reared; and yet I will not find fault with any of you who deem it a sad confession made when I acknowledge that I must recall the days now long past, to find my closest relation to the grand and noble denomination which you represent. I say this because those of us who inherit fealty to our Church, as I did, begin early to learn those things which make us Presbyterians all the days of our lives; and thus it is that the rigors of our early teaching, by which we are grounded in our lasting allegiance, are especially vivid, and perhaps the best remembered. The attendance upon church service three times each Sunday, and upon Sabbath school during the noon intermission, may be irksome enough to a boy of ten or twelve years of age to be well fixed in his memory; but I have never known a man who regretted these things in the years of his maturity. The Shorter Catechism, though thoroughly studied and learned, was not, perhaps, at the time perfectly understood, and yet, in the stern labors and duties of after life, those are not apt to be the worst citizens who were early taught: "What is the chief end of man?"

Speaking of these things and in the presence of those here assembled, the most tender thoughts crowd upon my mind—all connected with Presbyterianism and its teachings. There are present with me now memories of a kind and affectionate father, consecrated to the cause, and called to his rest and his reward in the midday of his usefulness; a sacred recollection of the prayers and pious love of a sainted mother, and a family circle hallowed and sanctified by the spirit of Presbyterianism.

I certainly cannot but express the wish and hope that the Presbyterian Church will always be at the front in every movement which promises the temporal as well as the spiritual advancement of mankind. In the turmoil and the bustle of everyday life few men are foolish enough to ignore the practical value to our people and our country of the Church organizations established among us, and the advantage of Christian example and teachings.

The field is vast, and the work sufficient to engage the efforts of every sect and denomination; but I am inclined to believe that the Church which is most tolerant and conservative, without loss of spiritual strength, will soonest find the way to the hearts and affections of the people. While we may be pardoned for insisting that our denomination is the best, we may, I think, safely concede much that is good to all other Churches that seek to make men better.

I am here to greet the delegates of two General Assemblies of the Presbyterian Church. One is called ''North'' and the other ''South.'' The subject is too deep and intricate for me; but I cannot help wondering why this should be. These words, so far as they denote separation and estrangement, should be obsolete. In the councils of the nation, and in the business of the country, they no longer mean reproach and antagonism. Even the soldiers who fought for the North and for the South are restored to fraternity and unity. This fraternity and unity are taught and enjoined by our Church. When shall she herself be united, with all the added strength and usefulness that harmony and union insure?

VIII.

To a Meeting for Promoting the Free Library Movement, New York, March 6, 1890.

MR. CHAIRMAN AND LADIES AND GENTLEMEN:

The few words I shall speak on this occasion, I intend rather as a pledge of my adherence to the cause in which you are enlisted, than an attempt to say anything new or instructive.

I gladly join, with the enthusiasm of a new convert, in the felicitations of those who have done noble and effective work in the establishment and maintenance in our city of a free circulating library; and it seems to me they have abundant cause for congratulation in a review of the good which has already been accomplished through their efforts, and in the contemplation of the further usefulness which awaits their continued endeavor.

In every enlightened country the value of popular education is fully recognized, not only as a direct benefit to its recipients, but as an element of strength and safety in organized society. Considered in these aspects, it should nowhere be better appreciated than in this land of free institutions, consecrated to the welfare and happiness of its citizens, and deriving its sanction and its power from the people. Here the character of the people is inevitably impressed upon the government, and here our public life can no more be higher and purer than the life of the people, than a stream can rise above its fountain or be purer than the spring in which it has its source.

That we have not failed to realize these conditions is demonstrated by the establishment of free public schools on every side, where children are not only invited but often obliged to submit themselves to such instruction as will better their situation in life and fit them to take part intelligently in the conduct of the government.

Thus in our schools the young are taught to read, and in this manner the seed is sown from which we expect a profitable return to the state, when its beneficiaries shall repay the edutional advances made to them by an intelligent and patriotic performance of their social and political duties.

And yet, if we are to create good citizenship, which is the object of popular education, and if we are to insure to the country the full benefit of public instruction, we can by no means consider the work as completely done in the schoolroom. While the young gathered there are fitting themselves to assume in the future their political obligations, there are others upon whom these obligations already rest, and who now have the welfare and safety of the country in their keeping. Our work is badly done if these are neglected. They have passed the school age, and have perhaps availed themselves of free instruction; but they, as well as those still in school, should, nevertheless, have within their reach the means of further mental improvement and the opportunity of gaining that additional knowledge and information which can only be secured by access to useful and instructive books.

The husbandman who expects to gain a profitable return from his orchards not only carefully tends and cultivates the young trees in his nurseries as they grow to maturity, but he generously enriches and cares for those already in bearing and upon which he must rely for ripened fruit.

Teaching the children of our land to read is but the first step in the scheme of creating good citizens by means of free instruction. We teach the young to read so that, both as children and as men and women, they may read. Our teaching must lead to the habit and the desire of reading, to be useful; and only as this result is reached, can the work in our free schools be logically supplemented and made valuable.

Therefore, the same wise policy and intent which open the doors of our free schools to our young also suggest the completion of the plan thus entered upon, by placing books in the hands of those who, in our schools, have been taught to read.

A man or woman who never reads and is abandoned to unthinking torpor, or who allows the entire mental life to be bounded by the narrow lines of a daily recurring routine of effort for mere existence, cannot escape a condition of barrenness of mind which not only causes the decay of individual contentment and happiness, but which fails to yield to the state its justly expected return of usefulness in valuable service and wholesome political action.

Another branch of this question should not be overlooked.

It is not only of great importance that our youth and our men and women should have the ability, the desire, and the opportunity to read, but the kind of books they read is no less important. Without guidance and without the invitation and encouragement to read publications which will improve as well as interest, there is danger that our people will have in their hands books whose influence and tendency are of a negative sort, if not positively bad and mischievous. Like other good things, the ability and opportunity to read may be so used as to defeat their beneficent purposes.

The boy who greedily devours the vicious tales of imaginary daring and blood-curdling adventure, which in these days are far too accessible to the young, will have his brain filled with notions of life and standards of manliness which, if they do not make him a menace to peace and good order, will certainly not tend to make him a useful member of society.

The man who devotes himself to the flash literature now much too common will, instead of increasing his value as a citizen, almost surely degenerate in his ideas of public duty and grow dull in his appreciation of the obligations he owes his country.

In both these cases there will be a loss to the state. There is danger also that a positive and aggressive injury to the community will result; and such readers will certainly suffer deprivation of the happiness and contentment which are the fruits of improving study and well-regulated thought.

So, too, the young woman who seeks recreation and entertainment in reading silly and frivolous books, often of doubtful moral tendency, is herself in the way of becoming frivolous and silly, if not of weak morality. If she escapes this latter condition, she is almost certain to become utterly unfitted to bear patiently the burden of self-support, or to assume the sacred duties of wife and mother.

Contemplating these truths, no one can doubt the importance of securing for those who read, as far as it is in our power, facilities for the study and reading of such books as will instruct and innocently entertain, and which will, at the same time, improve and correct the tastes and desires.

There is another thought somewhat in advance of those already suggested, which should not pass unnoticed.

As an outgrowth of the inventive and progressive spirit of our people, we have among us legions of men, and women too, who restlessly desire to increase their knowledge of the new forces and agencies, which, at this time, are being constantly dragged from their lurking-places and subjected to the use of man. These earnest inquirers should all be given a chance and have put within their reach such books as will guide and inspire their efforts. If, by this means, the country shall gain to itself a new inventor, or be the patron of endeavor which shall add new elements to the sum of human happiness and comfort, its intervention will be well repaid.

These considerations, and the fact that many among us having the ability and inclination to read are unable to furnish themselves with profitable and wholesome books, amply justify the beneficent mission of our Free Circulating Library. Its plan and operation, so exactly adjusted to meet a situation which cannot safely be ignored and to wants which ought not to be neglected, establish its claim upon the encouragement and reasonable aid of the public authorities and commend it most fully to the support and generosity of private benefaction.

The development which this good work has already reached in our city has exhibited the broad field yet remaining untouched, and the inadequacy of present operations. It has brought to view also instances of noble individual philanthropy and disinterested private effort and contribution.

But it certainly seems that the time and money directed to this object are confined to a circle of persons far too narrow, and that the public encouragement and aid have been greatly disproportioned to private endeavor.

The city of New York has never shown herself willing to be behind other cities in such work as is done by our Free Circulating Library, and, while her people are much engrossed in business activity and enterprise, they have never yet turned away from a cause once demonstrated to them to be so worthy and useful as this.

The demonstration is at hand. Let it be pressed upon our fellow-citizens, and let them be shown the practical operation of the project you have in hand and the good it has accomplished, and the further good of which it is capable through their increased liberality, and it will be strange if they fail to respond generously to your appeal to put the city of New York in the front rank of the cities which have recognized the usefulness of free circulating libraries.

IX.

At the Ninth Annual Meeting of the Actors' Fund of America, January 3, 1890.

MR. PRESIDENT, AND LADIES AND GENTLEMEN:

If my appearance here to-day serves no other purpose, I hope I may say, without offense to anyone, that it illustrates the progress of our time in toleration and liberality of sentiment.

I was reared and taught in the strictest school of Presbyterianism. I remember well the precious precepts and examples of my early days, and I acknowledge that to them I owe every faculty of usefulness I possess, and every just apprehension of the duties and obligations of life. But though still clinging to these with unabated faith and steadfastness, I meet and congratulate you on this occasion, not only without the least vestige of moral compunction, but with great pleasure and satisfaction.

It is not necessary to remind this audience that, whether right or wrong, such a condition could not always be anticipated, for the time is within the remembrance of us all when, in many quarters of our country, very little good was acknowledged to exist in the dramatic profession. We are certain there has been a change in the relation your profession bears to the people at large; and, while much of this change is undoubtedly due to the growth of more liberal ideas, it will not do to overlook the fact that you yourselves have, by a constant regard to the ethics of your calling, contributed perhaps in a greater degree to the breaking down of old prejudices and misconceptions. At all events, we, as laymen, know that we are freer from bigoted intolerance; and you, as members of the dramatic profession, must feel that you are greatly relieved from unjust suspicions.

We all see less and less reason why our ministers should quote Shakspere from their pulpits and we be prohibited from seeing and hearing his works better interpreted on the stage. We see still less consistency in permitting the perusal of books of fiction, which only sometimes teach wholesome moral lessons, and at the same time prohibiting attendance upon the well-regulated and conventional play, where virtue is always triumphant and villainy is always circumvented.

But while I can say that I am not at all perplexed at this moment by my Presbyterianism, I cannot claim that my position before such an audience as this is entirely free from embarrassment. I have been told by one of my best friends, and, at the same time, one of the best actors I ever saw, that at a play an audience of actors are critical, but kind and patient. This reflection is, of course, reassuring as far as it goes. But, since I agreed to meet you here to-day, it has often occurred to me that I had no guarantee of your kindness and patience except at a play; and that perhaps when you see your places on the stage occupied by those not of your brotherhood, you may still be critical, but neither kind nor patient. In these circumstances, I may as well confess now and here, that, in strict accordance with the promptings of weak and unamiable human nature, I have stifled all misgivings as to what I may inflict upon you—if I have not rid myself of anxiety—by the reflection that, however much I may fall short of your approbation, I cannot possibly take of you excessive

reprisals for the dreary speaking and acting that have at times
been inflicted upon me when some of your profession have
been upon the stage and I in the audience.

It is very doubtful whether there is much appropriateness in
the ideas I have thus far presented, in the light of the fact that
we have met to review the work of a noble charity; for, though
this particular enterprise has its rise within the limits of the
dramatic profession, surely, in the things which pertain to the
relief of the sick and suffering, and to the aid and comfort of
the unfortunate and afflicted, all who are charitably inclined
belong to one fraternity. The sentiment of charity arouses all
that is worth having in human nature, and in its work it weaves
the bands which hold mankind in gentle kinship.

I cannot refrain from speaking of one characteristic of the
charity you have in charge, which to me is especially gratifying. Necessarily, in the administration of many benevolent
enterprises, the conditions of participation in their benefits are
so exacting and the investigations practiced are so searching
and unsparing, that humiliation and sadness often accompany
relief. It is a most happy arrangement of the work of your
organization that it is done directly, promptly, and without
humiliating incidents; that your relief is extended to all in any
way related to your profession, from the highest to the lowest
grade; and that they require no other certificate than their
needy condition. Thus there is given to your charitable
efforts a sort of cordiality and heartiness which makes your
assistance doubly welcome.

I remember well how impressed I was by this feature of
your charity, when, six or seven years ago, I first knew of the
existence of your organization, and was urged, as Governor of
the State, to attend an entertainment to be given for its benefit; and how it determined me to set aside my objections and
accept the invitation which was so cordially and persuasively
presented. I have always felt grateful to those who tendered
that invitation, not only for the enjoyment which the entertainment afforded, but also because I was thus introduced to a

charity in which I have ever since taken a lively interest. You at that time placed my name upon your roll of honorary membership, and I am very proud of it—all the more so because if not the first, it was among the first, there recorded.

I feel, then, that I am nearly enough related to you and your active membership to join in your felicitations upon the good you have already accomplished and upon the promise of extended usefulness in the future. The record of charitable accomplishments which has been presented by your president must be full of satisfaction, and must, of necessity, bring home to you the feeling that you have been amply paid for all you have done for this beneficent organization, by the consciousness that you have in this way aided in alleviating the sorrow and the distress of your "forlorn and shipwrecked" brethren.

The highest and best development of your charity, and the most important purpose of your Fund, will be reached when you are able to provide a home for those in your profession who, through age, sickness, or infirmity, are unfitted longer to work and struggle. It must be perfectly apparent that, in such a retreat, managed and superintended by those who, from professional experience and sympathy, are conversant with the history and peculiar needs of those whom it shelters, poverty would lose much of its humiliation, and disability need not rob the unfortunate of self-respect. I hope the day is not far distant when this important instrumentality will be added to your means of usefulness.

You will not, I trust, deem it amiss if, in conclusion, I present a thought which is apt to be prominent in my mind on occasions like this.

Considering, as I do, the dramatic profession as furnishing favorable conditions for the development of thoughtful men, I am not fully satisfied that its members appreciate, as soberly as they ought, their duty to our country. You must yourselves confess that the tendency of your occupation is somewhat in the direction of isolation, and a separation from familiar contact with the ordinary affairs of life. These lead not only to your being misunderstood by many of your fellow-citizens, but to the loss of the advantage which your intelligence might contribute to the common welfare. You are patriotic in sentiment, but you are too apt to think that you perform your full duty when you do well your professional work and when you keep the peace and obey the laws. Pardon me if I say to you that all these things, and all your readily acknowledged charitable undertakings, will not atone for a neglect to discharge your duty as it is related to the affairs of your country. This government of ours is constructed upon the theory that every thoughtful, intelligent, and honest citizen will directly interest himself in its operation; and unless this is forthcoming, its best objects and purposes will not be accomplished.

As the welfare of your country is dear to you, as you desire an honest and wise administration of your government, and as your interests and prosperity, in common with those of your fellow-citizens, are bound up in the maintenance of our free institutions, do not forget that these things can only be secured by conscientious political thought and careful political action.

X.

Before the State Charities Aid Association, New York, May 1, 1891.

MR. PRESIDENT, AND LADIES AND GENTLEMEN:

When I consented to say a few words on this occasion, I knew that others would attend, and ably and thoroughly present the work and achievements of the State Charities Aid Association. This knowledge gave rise in my mind to considerable doubt and hesitation, because it seemed to me that in this condition of the matter, the little I could say must appear useless—if nothing worse. It occurred to me, however, in settling the question, that my participation in this meeting would probably benefit one person at least—and that was myself. If this suggests a motive for my appearance, which seems to have a slight color of selfishness, I hasten to declare that I would be glad to share the good effects of the influence of this occasion with all my fellow-townsmen who might be inclined to place any value upon disinterested and well-directed charitable effort.

There are benefits originating in charitable activity, which reach others besides those directly relieved. It is clear that those actually engaged in the ministrations of charity derive a benefit therefrom. Physical exercise and outdoor athletic recreation strengthen the muscles and invigorate the bodily powers. So charitable exercise and humane work strengthen the best tendencies of human nature and invigorate the moral health. These are the natural and expected rewards of actual participation in physical exercise and in the activity of charity. But the thought I have in my mind relates to certain benefits resulting from charitable efforts which may accrue to those who, simply as observers, are brought within its influence. Those who go out to witness the physical exercise of others, or to watch athletic sports, receive a benefit by breathing the fresh air, if in no other way. So, those who witness charitable exercise and humane work, and even those who only put themselves in the way of hearing of the results of such exercise and work, cannot fail to derive benefit and advantage from the atmosphere surrounding them. They will be cured of much moral dyspepsia, they will be relieved of the atrophy of selfishness; they are apt to be better fitted for all the duties of life, while the flexibility and mobility of their inclinations toward charitable giving will, almost surely, be increased.

It is well, therefore, to keep before those not actively enlisted in charity, the work that is being done by others—to the end, that, by a process of absorption or leavening, the charitable and kindly feeling which should characterize American civilization may be quickened among our people.

I hope I have not placed too much stress upon the value of the benevolent sentiment which may be cultivated by the contemplation of charitable work, by those who are simply bystanders—even though they remain bystanders. I cannot help thinking, that, in a country like ours, where so much depends upon the virtue of individuals, the improvement of every impulse or inclination which makes men better and more unselfish, is most important to our citizenship.

Besides, we do not expect that those who thus feel the influence which is spread abroad by the charitable activity of others, will long remain mere bystanders. What they see and feel ought to lead to hearty co-operation—if not in time and effort, certainly in pecuniary assistance.

We commemorate, to-night, the successes in humane work of a volunteer association of men and women so organized that their labor and influence is found in every neighborhood of our State. Theirs is a labor of love and disinterested humanity. They ask no public appropriation of money, nor do they seek compensation for their services. What they have done for the dependent poor and unfortunate cannot be over-valued. The part they have taken in rescuing the State from the disgrace of its neglect of the pauper insane, and their instrumentality in placing these afflicted ones within the reach of proper care and treatment, are sufficient to entitle these earnest workers to the gratitude of every good citizen. If there is difficulty in obtaining the small amount of money—beyond their own contributions—which is necessary to continue the work of their organization, it must be that its mission is not understood or that the bystanders, of whom I have spoken, either do not comprehend the necessities of the situation, or are resisting the beneficent influences of the association's existence and labors.

I have left to others the agreeable task of recounting, in detail, the direct benefits to the poor, the wretched, and the unfortunate, which have been wrought by the association. I have spoken of the improvement which the influence and example of its members should make in the character of our people. I desire now to suggest a way by which the work of the association may be made useful to our State charitable institutions themselves, altogether aside from the correction of any wrongs and abuses in their management.

We all know that there is among our people a readiness to suspect the existence of neglect and cruelty in the conduct of these institutions. This is evidenced by the unquestioning credence which is accorded to the most sensational reports concerning the ill-treatment of the paupers in our poorhouses, of the insane in our asylums, and of the sick in our hospitals. We all know, too, that, though these reports are sometimes unfounded and often grossly exaggerated, no amount of official denial, and frequently no exoneration through official investigation, can reassure the public, or shake the belief easily rooted in the minds of compassionate citizens, that terrible outrages are committed behind the doors which only open to official bidding. It is hardly necessary to suggest that these apprehensions and convictions have their rise in sentiments of humanity and pity, coupled with what is construed to be a desire for the concealment of the actual situation.

It is perfectly plain that such a want of confidence on the part of the people, in the proper management of our public charitable institutions, must remove the chief supports of their usefulness and prevent their fulfillment of the purposes of their maintenance. The avoidance of such conditions can in no way be better secured, nor can a surer safeguard against such groundless and sensational accusations be provided, than by the frequent visitation and inspection of these institutions by prudent, intelligent, and sensible men and women in their localities, respected and trusted by the entire community, and volunteering in the service. The further removed they are from official limitations and regulation, the more implicit faith and confidence will their neighbors and fellow-citizens place in their reports and representations. It would be exceedingly difficult for unfounded accusations and tales of horror to gain a foothold against the testimony of such disinterested and unpaid visitors, and the quiet existence of conditions, which, if known, might justify accusation and suspicion, would be impossible under their watchful visitations.

I do not overlook the fact that such visitation and inspection might be regarded, with some reason, as an interference with necessary official management and administration and might thus cause irritation and trouble. But the danger of such consequences I am sure could be avoided by care in the selection of the visitors and by the employment of only those of good judgment and conservative disposition. Indeed, visitors of that kind must, of necessity, be selected, if any good purpose is to be accomplished through their efforts. At any rate, I believe the wholesome checks to the improper treatment of the unfortunate wards of the State and the protection of our charitable institutions against unjust attack, which volunteer visitation and inspection would secure, much more than counterbalance the risk of any objectionable results.

Besides, in considering this plan of charitable work, we have something more reliable and satisfactory to guide us than mere theory and presumption. For ten years the members and agents of the State Charities Aid Association have been permitted by law to visit and inspect the county, city, and town poorhouses and almshouses within the State. The far-reaching good which has resulted from these limited ministrations of the Association can hardly be estimated; and I have never heard of any instance where harm has resulted.

With such a demonstration before us, and thus having reason and experience to support us, we are abundantly justified in asking that the Association's right of visitation and inspection be extended, so that it shall apply to all the asylums and other charitable institutions which are under State management.

In conclusion, I desire to congratulate the members of the Charities Aid Association on the grand results of their labors, and to acknowledge the beneficence and usefulness of their undertaking. I believe the encouragement of such endeavors as theirs is a duty devolving upon every citizen of the State.

Their mission should be better understood and our people should be constantly reminded that charity not only aids and relieves the poor and distressed, but that, by its influence and inspiration, it improves and broadens the best elements of American citizenship.

CHAPTER IX.

I.

Memorial Tribute to Oscar Folsom, before the Erie County Bar Association Meeting, July 26, 1875.

IT has been said, "Light sorrows speak, great grief is dumb," and the application of this would enforce my silence on this occasion. But I cannot go so far, nor let the hour pass without adding a tribute of respect and love for my departed friend. He was my friend in the most sacred and complete sense of the term. I have walked with him, talked with him, ate with him, and slept with him—was he not my friend?

I must not, dare not, recall the memories of our long and loving friendship. And let not my brethren think it amiss if I force back the thoughts which come crowding to my mind. I shall speak coldly of my friend; but the most sacred tribute of a sad heart, believe me, is unspoken.

In the course of a life not entirely devoid of startling incidents, I can truly say I never was so shocked and overwhelmed as when I heard, on Friday night, of the death of Oscar Folsom. I had an engagement with him that evening, and was momentarily expecting him when I received the intelligence of his injury; and before I reached the scene of the accident I was abruptly told of his death; I shall not attempt to describe my emotions. Death seemed so foreign to this man, and the exuberance of his life was so marked and prominent, that the idea of his dying, or his death, seemed to me incongruous and out of place. And before I saw him dead I found myself reflecting, "How strange he would look, dying or dead."

I had seen him in every other part of the drama of life but this, and for this he seemed unfitted.

His remarkable social qualities won for him the admiration of all with whom he came in contact, while his great, kind heart caused all to love him who knew him well. He was remarkably true in his friendships, and having really made a friend he "grappled him with hooks of steel." Open and frank himself, he opposed deceit and indirection. His remarkable humor never had intentional sting; and though impulsive and quick, he was always just. In the practice of his profession and in the solution of legal questions he saw which was right and just, and then expected to find the law leading him directly there.

It is not strange to find joined to a jovial disposition a kind and generous heart; but he had, besides these, a broad and correct judgment and a wonderful knowledge of men and affairs; and the instances are numerous in my experience when his strong common sense has aided me easily through difficulties. Such was my friend.

The sadness of his taking off has no alleviation. I shall not dwell upon the harrowing circumstances. On Friday afternoon Oscar Folsom, in the midday of life, was cherishing bright anticipations for the future. Among them, he had planned a home in an adjoining town, where he calculated upon much retirement and quiet. He had already partially perfected his arrangements, which were soon to be fully consummated. Within forty-eight hours he reached the town of his anticipated residence. But God had intervened. The hands of loving friends bore him to a home, but not the home he had himself provided. He found peace in the home that God provides for the sons of men, and quiet—ah! such quiet—in the grave. I know how fleeting and how soon forgotten are the lessons taught by such calamities. "The gay will laugh, the solemn brow of care plod on, and each one as before pursue his favorite phantom." But it seems to me that long, long years will intervene before pleasant memories of his life will be unmingled with the sad admonitions furnished by the death of Oscar Folsom.

Let us cherish him in loving remembrance, and heed well the lessons of his death ; and let our tenderest sympathy extend to a childless father, a widowed wife, and fatherless child.

II.

When presiding over the New York State Bar Association,
Albany, January 8, 1884.

GENTLEMEN OF THE ASSOCIATION :

At a late hour I was solicited to preside at your meeting. I should certainly have felt that I must decline, but for two considerations. I was assured that no address would be expected of me, and that even a little speech, on assuming the chair, might be dispensed with. This disposed of one objection to my consent.

The other consideration sprang up in my mind when I reflected that there would be here an assemblage of my professional brethren, and the impulse was irresistible to be among them for a time, though necessarily brief, and to feel about me the atmosphere from which, for a twelve-month, I have been excluded. I beg to assure you, gentlemen, that in the crowd of official duties which for the past year have surrounded me, I have never lost sight of the guild to which I am proud to belong, nor have I lost any of the love and care for the noble profession I have chosen. On the contrary, as I have seen the controlling part which the lawyers of the State assume in the enacting of her laws, and in all other works that pertain to her progress and her welfare, I have appreciated more than ever the value and usefulness of the legal profession. And, when I have seen how generally my professional brethren have been faithful to their public trusts, my pride has constantly increased.

And yet from the outside world I come within the grateful circle of professional life to say to you that much is to be done before the bar of this State will, in all its parts, be what we all could wish. We hold honorable places, but we hold places of power—if well used, to protect and save our fellows; if prostituted and badly used, to betray and destroy. It seems to me that a profession so high and noble in all the purposes of its existence should be only high and noble in all its results. But we know it is not so. There is not a member of the bar in this assemblage who has not shuddered when he thought of the wicked things he had the power to do safely ; and he has shuddered again when he recalled those, whom he was obliged to call professional brothers, who needed but the motive to do these very things.

An association like this, to be really useful, must be something more than a society devoted to the laudation of the profession. It should have duties to perform, earnest in their nature, and not the less boldly met because they are disagreeable. Those who steal our livery to aid them in the commission of crime should be detected and exposed ; and this association, or branches of it, should have watchmen on the walls to protect the honor and fair fame of the bar of the State.

Your words are fair, when, in your constitution, you declare the objects of this association to be " to elevate the standard of integrity, honor, and courtesy in the legal profession " ; and I have no doubt you have done much in that direction ; but I hope I may be pardoned for reminding you here that frequently, to insure health and vigor, the bad, diseased limbs of the tree must be lopped off.

My thought has carried me further than I intended. Be assured I have spoken in no censorious spirit. I congratulate the State Bar Association on all it has done, and for one am determined to aid its work as well during my temporary professional exile as when I shall again gladly mingle in the contests of the bar.

III.

At the Laying of the Corner Stone of the New Academy of Medicine, New York, October 2, 1889.

The congratulation and the satisfaction which attend this hour especially belong to the members of the Academy of Medicine. This is as it should be, for the exercises of to-day signalize an achievement wrought by their activity and energy, and give proof of their devotion and attachment to their chosen profession. To the members of this organization the corner stone which we now lay is an honor, for it is a monument which marks an important advance in the attainment of the purpose of the Academy, as declared in its constitution : "the promotion of the science and art of medicine."

In these extensive foundations is also found proof of the progressive ideas of these earnest men and their constantly enlarging estimate of what is necessary to meet the purposes to which their energy is directed. I have lately seen a pamphlet containing the constitution and by-laws of the Academy, with a prefatory note published only three years ago. In this note it is declared that, from the inception of the Academy, one of its chief objects has been the procurement of a building or hall where its meetings might be held, where a library and museum could be garnered, and where the profession could meet on common ground. The statement is added with much apparent satisfaction that the efforts put forth in this direction have culminated in the purchase of a commodious building centrally situated, thus "providing a library, hall, and audience room, which will, for some time, answer the Academy's wants and those of the profession." It is already found that the commodious building which, three years ago, was deemed sufficient headquarters for the usefulness of the Academy, is too small and cramped to answer the beneficent purposes of the organization, and the erection of a structure three or four times as large has been entered upon. It is thus evident that the members of the Academy of Medicine, not forgetting the mission they have undertaken to promote the science and art of medicine, and, seeing broader avenues leading to this object, have promptly, and with an energy which never fails, begun their preparations for wider activity and more important results.

I have spoken of the mission of the Academy. The nobility and sacred character of this mission have been often dwelt upon. It is an old story, but it will never lose its interest while humanity is touched with human woe ; while self-sacrifice receives the homage of Christian hearts ; while the sufferings and sorrows of our fellow-men start the tear of pity ; nor while their alleviation brings comfort and satisfaction to the soul of sympathy.

These reflections easily and naturally lead to the thought that the members of the Academy of Medicine are not entitled to the absolute monopoly of congratulation to-day. All your fellow-citizens may well claim a share, not only because they are interested in the promotion of the science and art of medicine, by reason of their liability to accident and disease, but because such advance in any profession, as is here demonstrated, adds to the glory and renown of our common country. I am here to claim for the laymen among your fellow-citizens a part of the pride which grows out of the progress and achievement of our medical profession. I base this claim upon the fact that, in this favored land of ours, all interests are so interwoven and all activities lead, or should lead, so directly to the accomplishment of our common national destiny that none of us can be indifferent to an important advance among us in any science or industry.

I am sure that you are not inclined to ignore the aid you have received, in the project you have undertaken, from the laymen among your fellows. Nor can you forget that underlying all that you have done and all that you have received are our free American institutions, which encourage and give scope to every worthy effort, and which offer fitting rewards for intelligent and well-directed labor in every condition of life.

You will not, therefore, I trust, deem it impertinent if I remind you that none of us is absolved from the duty of aiding in the maintenance in complete integrity of these free institutions, and that this requires the thoughtful care and attention of every citizen. You do much for your country when you raise the standard and enlarge the usefulness of your profession ; but you do not accomplish all you can, nor do you discharge your full duty of citizenship, unless you also attempt to better the condition of public affairs and give to political topics and movements the benefit of your trained thought and well-informed judgment. In this way you assist in making safe and sure the foundations upon which must rest the success and value of all your professional efforts and accomplishments.

I hope, when we shall celebrate here the discovery of our country, that we may point out on this spot, in your completed building, a splendid monument of the progress of our medical education, a monument which shall not only prove to the stranger that our physicians are proud of their profession, but one which shall also be a reminder that those who govern within its walls do not forget, in their devotion to the science and art of medicine, their other duties of citizenship.

IV.

Before the Medical Alumni Association of New York City, February 15, 1890.

MR. PRESIDENT AND GENTLEMEN :

I feel that I ought, first of all, to acknowledge the courtesy which affords me the opportunity of pleasantly meeting this evening so many of the medical fraternity. I hasten to follow this by the expression of my thanks for the permission to say the few words which I suppose are expected of me thus early in the speech-making stage of this entertainment. I recognize in this favor the utmost kindness, based, I have no doubt, upon your knowledge of physical and mental conditions. You evidently know as well as I do that of all congested, distended and flatulent conditions, the worst and most painful arise from the combination of a stomach full of good things to eat and drink, held in uncomfortable solution by an undigested speech.

I interpret my invitation to be here to-night as a recognition of the relationship which exists between the professions of medicine and law. At any rate I am quite proud in the assumption that I am entitled, in a fashion, to represent the law side of this professional reunion.

There are many things which we have in common, and many points where we diverge in our professional ways. We, with the clergy, enjoy the distinction of belonging to the learned professions. This has a pleasant sound and conveys to us an idea calculated to inspire the greatest self-satisfaction and to fill us with a feeling of arrogant superiority. These sentiments are, however, at once much tempered, or are destroyed, by the reflection that we are all obliged to recognize as professional brethren those who demonstrate by their conduct that mere membership in our brotherhoods will not, of itself, raise us above the ordinary scale of morality, or exalt us above the plane of everyday human nature. Neither you nor I can deny that both of our professions have at this moment representatives not engaged in active practice, but resting in retirement and seclusion within the walls of certain penal institutions scattered throughout the land. And I will concede, if you will, that there are others now at large, in both professions, who are entitled to the same retirement and seclusion.

Perhaps, in passing, I might also say with bated breath that it is sometimes broadly hinted that even the clergy occasionally do things which better befit the unregenerate.

I do not indulge in these reflections for the sake of saying unpleasant things, but rather to suggest humility and modesty, and to introduce the declaration that I am prepared now and here to disavow with you the claim of any special goodness or greatness for our profession, except such as grows out of active sympathy with everything which helps and benefits our fellow-men, and except such as result from a conscientious and honest discharge of professional duty.

We occupy common ground in the similarity of the treatment we receive at the hands of the outside world, and in the opportunity we have to make things even with those who despitefully use us.

I have no doubt that it is very funny for people to caricature doctors as playing into the hands of undertakers, and to represent lawyers as being on such good terms with the evil one as to preclude the least chance of their salvation. Those who indulge in this sort of merriment are well people and people who have no law suits on hand. They grow very serious when their time comes and they grow sick or are caught in the meshes of the law. Then they are very respectful and very appreciative of our skill and learning. If sick they would fain have the doctor by their side day and night ; and if they are troubled with a law suit they sit like Mordecai at the lawyer's gate and are unwilling that he should attend to any business but theirs. They are ready to lay their fortunes at our feet and to give and promise all things if they can but recover their health or win their suit. These are the days in which the lawyer, if he is wise, will suggest to his clients the payment of a round retainer or a fee in advance. I mention this as indicating a difference at this time in our situations in favor of the lawyer which gives him a slight advantage over his medical brother.

When the patient recovers, or the client has succeeded in his suit, the old hardihood and impenitence return. The patient insists that his strong constitution carried him through, and the client declares that he always knew there was nothing in the case of his adversary. They haggle over our bills and wonder how we can charge so much for so little work.

But sometimes the life or the law suit cannot be saved. In such a case we must not overlook a difference in our situations, with features in favor of the doctor. The defeated client is left in a vigorous and active condition, not only in the complete enjoyment of his ancient privilege of swearing at the Court, but also with full capacity to swear at his lawyer. The defeated patient, on the contrary, is very quiet indeed and can only swear at his doctor if he has left his profanity in a phonograph to be ground out by his executor.

A point of resemblance between us is found in the fact that in neither profession do we manage well in treating our own cases. Doctors solemnly advise their patients that it is dangerous to eat this or drink that, or do many other things which make existence pleasant ; and after marking out a course for their poor patients which, if followed, robs life of all which makes it worth living, they hasten away to tempt instant death, according to their own teachings, by filling themselves with all the good things and indulgence within the reach of their desires. So the lawyer, safe and wise when he counsels others, deals so poorly with his own legal affairs as to have originated the saying that a lawyer who tries his own case has a fool for a client ; and it seems almost impossible for a lawyer to draw his own will in such manner as not to yield a passage through it for a coach and four.

Another point of resemblance between the two professions consists in the disposition of the members of both to quarrel with each other. I am bound to say, however, that a difference is to be noted in this matter in favor of the amiability of the Bar. Our quarrels are mostly of the Pickwickian sort and strictly in the line of business. They keep us in fighting trim and serve a very good purpose in impressing our clients with our zeal and devotion to their interest. Our asseveration of the rectitude and justice of their side of the cause in hand, and our demonstration of contempt and indignation for the baseless pretenses of their antagonist and for that prostitution of professional effort which advocates such pretenses, is a part of our trade. At the same time I suppose our clients would suspect us of bad faith and disloyalty if they knew how temporary and free from bitterness our quarrels are. Of course, I personally know but little of the quarrels of doctors, except that they are constant and well sustained. I am not to be blamed, however, if I share in the common belief of those outside of the profession, that you are very belligerent and quarrel a great deal for the sake of quarreling. You seem to quarrel in squads, in sections, in schools and in colleges. You certainly have not, as we have, the excuse that your warfare pleases and exhilarates your patients ; for neither they nor anyone else know what you are quarreling about.

It is extremely pleasant to turn from these things to the acknowledgment of certain obligations we, as lawyers, often owe to the medical fraternity. When, burdened with a troublesome case, we feel that the facts are against us ; when we languish in the chill darkness of adverse legal principles ; and when discouragement broods over our efforts, if we can bring from afar and inject into our cause some question of medical science, our drooping law suit immediately becomes animated and interesting, for we know that whatever our theory may be concerning this medical question, we shall find generous and considerate doctors who will support it. Of course fully as many will dispute and denounce it ; but with a jury in the box who have not the slightest idea of what the doctors are talking about, neither litigant need feel discouraged.

You are not, I trust, unprepared for the distinct expression in conclusion, that nothing is more noble or useful than worthy membership in our professions. In both are found that culture and enlightened education which make them learned professions; and in both are found that dignity, integrity, and devotion which entitle them to be called honorable professions. Our membership should lead us to acknowledge the responsibilities to our fellow-men, which our situations impose, and our obligation to our country, which we cannot innocently evade. May I not suggest that our entire duty is not done if we never look beyond our professional routine, and if we limit our endeavor to strictly professional labor ? If our positions give us influence, that influence should be exerted in every direction for the good of our fellow-countrymen. There are also maladies and evils afflicting the body politic which require remedies and corrections ; and there are suits to be tried before the tribunal of public opinion in which the anxious suitors are a free, generous, and confiding people.

CHAPTER X.

ON EDUCATIONAL AND PATRIOTIC QUESTIONS.

I.

At St. Stephen's Hall, Buffalo, December 5, 1881.

LADIES AND GENTLEMEN :

I DESIRE to acknowledge the honor you have conferred upon me by this call to the chair. My greatest regret is that I know so little of the conditions that have given birth to the Land League. I know, in a general way, that it is designed to secure to Ireland those just and natural rights to which Irishmen are entitled. I understand, also, that these are to be obtained by peaceful measures and without doing violence to any just law of the land. This should meet with the support and countenance of every man who enjoys the privilege of American citizenship and lives under American laws. Our sympathy is drawn out by a bond of common manhood. We are here to-night to welcome an apostle of this cause, one who can, from personal experience, recount the scenes of that troubled isle ; who can tell us the risks that are taken and the pains that are suffered by those who lead the van in this great movement. I congratulate you upon having Father Sheehy with you, and I will not delay the pleasure of his presentation to you.

II.

At St. James' Hall, Buffalo, at a Mass Meeting to Protest Against the Treatment of American Citizens Imprisoned Abroad, April 9, 1882.

FELLOW-CITIZENS :

This is the formal mode of address on occasions of this kind, but I think we seldom realize fully its meaning, or how valuable a thing it is to be a citizen.

From the earliest civilization, to be a citizen has been to be a free man, endowed with certain privileges and advantages, and entitled to the full protection of the state. The defense and protection of the personal rights of its citizens have always been the paramount and most important duties of a free, enlightened government.

And perhaps no government has this sacred trust more in its keeping than this—the best and freest of them all; for here the people who are to be protected are the source of those powers which they delegate upon the express compact that the citizen shall be protected. For this purpose we choose those who, for the time being, shall manage the machinery which we have set up for our defense and safety.

And this protection adheres to us in all lands and places as an incident of citizenship. Let but the weight of a sacrilegious hand be put upon this sacred thing, and a great, strong government springs to its feet to avenge the wrong. Thus it is that a native-born American citizen enjoys his birthright. But when, in the westward march of empire, this nation was founded and took root, we beckoned to the Old World, and invited hither its immigration, and provided a mode by which those who sought a home among us might become our fellow-citizens. They came by thousands and hundreds of thousands; they came and

> Hewed the dark old woods away,
> And gave the virgin fields to day ;

they came with strong sinews and brawny arms to aid in the growth and progress of a new country ; they came and upon our altars laid their fealty and submission ; they came to our temples of justice, and under the solemnity of an oath renounced all allegiance to every other state, potentate, and sovereignty, and surrendered to us all the duty pertaining to such allegiance. We have accepted their fealty and invited them to surrender the protection of their native land.

And what should be given them in return ? Manifestly,

good faith and every dictate of honor demand that we give them the same liberty and protection here and elsewhere which we vouchsafe to our native-born citizens. And that this has been accorded to them is the crowning glory of American institutions.

It needed not the statute, which is now the law of the land, declaring that, " all naturalized citizens while in foreign lands are entitled to and shall receive from this government the same protection of persons and property which is accorded to native-born citizens," to voice the policy of our nation.

In all lands where the semblance of liberty is preserved, the right of a person arrested to a speedy accusation and trial is, or ought to be, a fundamental law, as it is a rule of civilization.

At any rate, we hold it to be so, and this is one of the rights which we undertake to guarantee to any native-born or naturalized citizen of ours, whether he be imprisoned by order of the Czar of Russia or under the pretext of a law administered for the benefit of the landed aristocracy of England.

We do not claim to make laws for other countries, but we do insist that, whatever those laws may be, they shall, in the interests of human freedom and the rights of mankind, so far as they involve the liberty of our citizens, be speedily administered. We have a right to say, and do say, that mere suspicion, without examination or trial, is not sufficient to justify the long imprisonment of a citizen of America. Other nations may permit their citizens to be thus imprisoned. Ours will not. And this, in effect, has been solemnly declared by statute.

We have met here to-night to consider this subject, and to inquire into the cause and the reasons and the justice of the imprisonment of certain of our fellow-citizens now held in British prisons without the semblance of a trial or legal examination. Our law declares that the government shall act in such cases. But the people are the creators of the government.

The undaunted apostle of the Christian religion, imprisoned and persecuted, appealing, centuries ago, to the Roman law and the rights of Roman citizenship, boldly demanded : " Is it lawful for you to scourge a man that is a Roman, and un-condemned ? "

III.

At the Albany High School, June 12, 1883.

I accepted the invitation of your principal to visit your school this morning with pleasure, because I expected to see much that would gratify and interest me. In this I have not been disappointed ; but I must confess that if I had known that my visit here involved my attempting to address you, I should have hesitated, and quite likely have declined the invitation.

I hasten to assure you now that there is not the slightest danger of my inflicting a speech upon you, and that I shall do but little more than express my pleasure in the proof I have of the excellence of the methods and management of the school, and of the opportunities which those who attend have within their reach of obtaining a superior education.

I never visit a school in these days without contrasting the advantages of the scholar of to-day with those of a time not many years in the past. Within my remembrance, even, the education which is freely offered to you was only secured by those whose parents were able to send them to academies and colleges. And thus, when you entered this school, very many of you began where your parents left off.

The theory of the State, in furnishing more and better schools for the children, is that it tends to fit them to perform better their duties as citizens, and that an educated man or woman is apt to be more useful as a member of the community.

This leads to the thought that those who avail themselves of the means thus tendered them are in duty bound to make such use of their advantages as that the State shall receive, in return, the educated and intelligent citizens and members of the community, which it has the right to expect from its schools. You who will soon be the men of the day, should consider that you have assumed an obligation to fit yourselves by the education, which you may, if you will, receive in this school, for the proper performance of any duty of citizenship, and to fill any public station to which you may be called. And it seems to me to be none the less important that those who are to be the wives and mothers should be educated, refined, and intelligent. To tell the truth, I should be afraid to trust the men, educated though they should be, if they were not surrounded by pure and true womanhood. Thus it is that you all, now and here, from the oldest to the youngest, owe a duty to the State which can only be answered by diligent study and the greatest possible improvement. It is too often the case that in all walks and places the disposition is to render the least possible return to the State for the favors which she bestows.

If the consideration which I have mentioned fails to impress you, let me remind you of what you have often heard, that you owe it to yourselves, and the important part of yourselves, to seize, while you may, the opportunities to improve your minds and store in them, for your own future use and advantage, the learning and knowledge now fairly within your reach.

None of you desires or expects to be less intelligent or educated than your fellows. But, unless the notions of scholars have changed, there may be those among you who think that in some way or manner, after the school day is over, there will be an opportunity to regain any ground now lost, and to complete an education without a present devotion to school requirements. I am sure this is a mistake. A moment's reflection ought to convince all of you that when you have once entered upon the stern, uncompromising, and unrelenting duties of mature life, there will be no time for study. You will have a contest then forced upon you which will strain every nerve and engross every faculty. A good education, if you have it, will aid you, but if you are without it you cannot stop to acquire it. When you leave the school you are well equipped for the van in the army of life, or you are doomed to be a laggard, aimlessly and listlessly following in the rear.

Perhaps a reference to truths so trite is useless here. I hope it is. But I have not been able to forego the chance to assure those who are hard at work that they will surely see their compensation, and those, if any such there are, who find school duties irksome, and neglect or slightingly perform them, that they are trifling with serious things and treading on dangerous ground.

IV.

At the Annual Saengerfest in Buffalo, July 16, 1883.

I have come to join my fellow-townsmen and their visitors in the exercises which inaugurate a festival of music and of song, and a season of social enjoyments.

It may be safely said, I think, that no one who has called this his home, who has enjoyed a residence in this beautiful city, and has learned the kindness of its people, ever forgets these things, or fails to experience a satisfaction in whatever adds to the prestige of the city and the pride and enjoyment of its inhabitants.

And thus it is that I am here to-night, at my home, claiming, as an old citizen of Buffalo, my full share of the pleasure which Buffalonians appropriate to themselves on this occasion.

I am glad that our State has within its borders a city containing sufficient German enterprise, and enough of the German love of music, to secure to itself the honor and distinction of being selected as the place where this national festival is held.

I desire to feel free, to-night, from official responsibilities and restraint, and, as a private citizen, to join in welcoming our guests to my home ; but I will not forbear, as the Executive of the great State of New York, and on behalf of all its people, to extend to those here assembled from other States a hearty greeting.

At this moment the reflection is uppermost in my mind that we owe much to the German element among our people. Their thrift and industry have added immensely to our growth and prosperity. The sad and solemn victims of American overwork may learn of them that labor may be well done and at the same time that recreation and social enjoyment have their place in a busy life. They have also brought to us their music and their song, which have done much to elevate, refine, and improve, and to demonstrate that nature's language is as sweet as when the morning stars sang together.

I am inclined to think that a music-loving people are not apt to be a bad people ; and it may well be hoped that occasions like this will tend to make the love and cultivation of music more universal in our land.

We hear, sometimes, of the assimilation of the people of different nationalities, who have made their home upon American soil. As this process goes on, let the German's love of music be carefully included, to the end that the best elements of human nature may be improved and cultivated, and American life be made more joyous and happy.

I must not detain you longer ; better things await you.

To the stranger guest, I pledge a cordial hospitality at the hands of the Germans of Buffalo. I know the warmth of heart and the kindliness of disposition of those having you in charge, and no other guarantee is needed.

To my fellow-townsmen, who have labored thus far so faithfully in preparation for this occasion, I cannot forbear saying that your most difficult and delicate work will not be done until your guests depart declaring the twenty-third the most successful and enjoyable Saengerfest upon the list, and confessing that the most cordial and hospitable entertainers are the Germans of Buffalo.

V.

Accepting the Bartholdi Statue, October 28, 1886.

The people of the United States accept with gratitude from their brethren of the French Republic the grand and completed work of art we here inaugurate.

This token of the affection and consideration of the people of France demonstrates the kinship of republics, and conveys to us the assurance that in our efforts to commend to mankind the excellence of a government resting upon popular will, we still have beyond the American continent a steadfast ally.

We are not here to-day to bow before the representation of a fierce and warlike god, filled with wrath and vengeance, but we joyously contemplate instead our own deity keeping watch and ward before the open gates of America, and greater than all that have been celebrated in ancient song. Instead of grasping in her hand thunderbolts of terror and of death, she holds aloft the light which illumines the way to man's enfranchisement.

We will not forget that Liberty has here made her home; nor shall her chosen altar be neglected. Willing votaries will constantly keep alive its fires, and these shall gleam upon the shores of our sister republic in the east. Reflected thence and joined with answering rays, a stream of light shall pierce the darkness of ignorance and man's oppression, until Liberty enlightens the world.

VI.

At the Unveiling of the Garfield Statue, Washington, May 12, 1887.

FELLOW-CITIZENS :

In performance of the duty assigned to me on this occasion, I hereby accept, on behalf of the people of the United States, this completed and beautiful statue.

Amid the interchange of fraternal greetings between the survivors of the Army of the Cumberland and their former foes upon the battlefield, and while the Union General and the people's President awaited burial, the common grief of these magnanimous soldiers and mourning citizens found expression in the determination to erect this tribute to American greatness ; and thus, to-day, in its symmetry and beauty, it presents a sign of animosities forgotten, an emblem of a brotherhood redeemed, and a token of a nation restored.

Monuments and statues multiply throughout the land, fittingly illustrative of the love and affection of our grateful people and commemorating brave and patriotic sacrifices in war, fame in peaceful pursuits, or honor in public station.

But from this day forth there shall stand at our seat of government this statue of a distinguished citizen who, in his life and services, combined all these things and more, which challenge admiration in American character—loving tenderness in every domestic relation, bravery on the field of battle, fame and distinction in our halls of legislation, and the highest honor and dignity in the Chief Magistracy of the nation.

This stately effigy shall not fail to teach every beholder that the source of American greatness is confined to no condition, nor dependent alone for its growth and development upon favorable surroundings. The genius of our national life beckons to usefulness and honor those in every sphere, and offers the highest preferment to manly ambition and sturdy honest effort, chastened and consecrated by patriotic hopes and aspirations. As long as this statue stands, let it be proudly remembered that to every American citizen the way is open to fame and station, until he

> Moving up from high to higher,
> Becomes on Fortune's crowning slope
> The pillar of a people's hope,
> The center of a World's desire.

Nor can we forget that it also teaches our people a sad and distressing lesson ; and the thoughtful citizen who views its fair proportions cannot fail to recall the tragedy of a death which brought grief and mourning to every household in the land. But, while American citizenship stands aghast and affrighted that murder and assassination should lurk in the midst of a free people and strike down the head of their government, a fearless search and the discovery of the origin and hiding place of these hateful and unnatural things should be followed by a solemn resolve to purge forever from our political methods and from the operation of our government, the perversions and misconceptions which gave birth to passionate and bloody thoughts.

If, from this hour, our admiration for the bravery and nobility of American manhood, and our faith in the possibilities and opportunities of American citizenship be renewed; if our appreciation of the blessing of a restored Union and love for our government be strengthened, and if our watchfulness against the dangers of a mad chase after partisan spoils be quickened, the dedication of this statue to the people of the United States will not be in vain.

VII.

At the Banquet of the Hibernian Society, Philadelphia, September 17, 1887.

I should hardly think my participation in the centennial celebration was satisfactory if I had not the opportunity of meeting the representative of the society which, through its antiquity and associations, bears close relations on the events of the time we commemorate. That you celebrate this occasion is a reminder of the fact that in the troublous and perilous days of our country those whose names stood upon your roll of membership fought for the cause of free government and for the homes which they had found upon our soil.

No society or corporation, I am sure, has in its charter, or in its traditions and history, a better or more valuable certificate of its patriotic worth and character than you have, and which is found in the words of Washington, who, in 1782, declared of the Friendly Sons of St. Patrick, of which this association is the successor, that it "has always been noted for the firm adherence of its members to the glorious cause in which we are engaged." These are priceless words, and they render most fitting the part which the members of the Hibernian Society are to-day assuming.

I noticed upon a letter which I have received from your secretary that one object of your society is stated to be "for the relief of emigrants from Ireland," and this leads me to reflect how nearly allied love of country is to a kindly humanity, and how naturally such a benevolent purpose of this society, as the assistance and relief of your stranger and needy emigrants, follows the patriotism in which it had its origin.

Long may the Hibernian Society live and prosper, and long may its benevolent and humane work be prosecuted. And when another centennial of the Constitution is celebrated, may those who shall then form its membership be as fully inspired with the patriotism of its history and traditions, and as ready to join in the general felicitation, as the men I see about me here.

VIII.

At the Fellowcraft Club, New York, May 14, 1889.

MR. PRESIDENT AND GENTLEMEN :

I think I should be glad to depart to-night from what I suppose to be the custom here, and say a few words to you without the least reference to the occupations in which I understand the members of this club are principally engaged, and without speaking of the newspapers and those who make and manage them. But I do not see how I am to accomplish these things, because, in the first place, the atmosphere is against me, and in the second place, the newspaper press and what it does are so interwoven with our life that they can hardly be eliminated from the discussion of any subject.

I want to speak of American citizenship; and I am prompted at the outset to say that I cannot see why, among those who have to do with the newspaper press, all things that pertain to good citizenship should not have the highest place; and that I never could discover why those connected with newspapers should not be judged by the same rules as are applied to the rest of us, nor why they are not charged with certainly as serious duties and responsibilities as other citizens. I protest against the theory, which appears to have gained some headway in certain quarters, that they are a little outside of the mass of ordinary citizens; and in their defense and vindication, I deny the proposition that they deliberately acknowledge fealty and devotion to their newspapers first and to their country afterward. Of course, if crowded, I should be obliged to confess that, in my opinion, there are exceptions, and that, occasionally, there are found among the editors and managers of newspapers, as everywhere else, those whose personal resentments, or extreme and misguided partisanship, lead them to pitiable conclusions; but against these I put the great number who, day by day, labor to make our country better and our people more thoughtful and intelligent.

The warmth of my desire to see good American citizenship more prevalent, and the value of it better appreciated by our people, arises in a great degree, I suppose, from my recent experience in discharging the duties of an office which afforded an opportunity of observing the motive power and strength of selfish interests in governmental affairs; and in comparison, how weak, if judged by their accomplishments, are disinterested love of country and dutiful solicitude for the public good.

Ours is not a government which operates well by its own momentum. It is so constructed that it will only yield its best results when it feels the constant pressure of the hands of the people. This condition suggests the importance of patriotism and devotion to the general and public welfare in all branches of the government. But this is impossible if the representatives of the people in the State or nation look no higher than the promotion of personal benefit, or the local interests of their immediate constituents, or the accomplishment of some purpose in aid of their own retention in place. The man who enters upon a legislative career, having charged himself especially or exclusively with the passage of measures in which he or his personal supporters are alone interested, or with the success of some private enterprise, is apt to be false to himself and untrue to his trust. His mind is preoccupied to such an extent, and his selfish purposes assume such large proportions in his sight, that a scheme for a new public building for his town or district, or for a bridge across a river, or for the right of way for a railroad, or for the allowance of a claim against the government, crowds out all consideration on his part of great and broad general subjects. Thus he furnishes no intelligent aid in legislation for the public good, and it is fortunate for the people if he does not deliver questionable votes in exchange for like favors in behalf of his pet scheme or schemes.

I do not indulge in the statement of an imaginary case. And what I have thus presented is but an illustration of the perversions that are creeping into every branch of our public service. Thoughtful men will not deny that danger lurks in the growing tendency of to-day to regard public office as something which may be sought and administered for private ends, instead of being received and held as a public trust.

Now I plead for the cultivation of a sentiment among the people which will condemn this conduct and these ideas, and which will impress upon those who act for and represent us in every official capacity the truth that their duty is only performed by activity for the public good and by the utmost care that the spirit of our institutions suffers no impairment.

As a stream will not rise above its source, so it is manifest that, to reach this better condition, selfishness and listlessness among the people themselves must give way to a sincere and earnest desire for the preservation and increase of that sentiment of true American citizenship which recognizes in the advancement of the entire country something more to be desired than the direct and immediate attainment of purely private ends.

Here is a field in which all can labor and find plenty to do. Those active in the work will have their love of country enlivened, and they will not fail to receive encouraging response to their efforts.

It will be a mistake for us to relax effort because we cannot reach the highest point of useful activity, or because we may not be able to deal directly with evils in the highest places. A good beginning is made when communities and individuals are led to appreciate properly the value of public spirit and unselfishness in matters connected with their home affairs and with the interest of their neighborhoods. The men who have learned the lesson of good citizenship, as related to the concerns of the school district, the village, or the city, will soon strive effectively to impress that lesson upon those who have to do with the concerns of the State and of the nation.

I am sure that we can none of us confidently say that even here, in this grand and busy city, there is no room for an increase of public spirit, or that too much attention is paid to the cultivation of American citizenship. I do not mean to say that we are behind in these things, but intend merely to intimate that we should as far excel in this direction as we do in every other.

Nor is there the least danger that we shall have among us too many reminders that our city is something more than a swift-running mill which grinds the grists of fortune, and that we have in our history and traditions things well worthy of commemoration in palpable and lasting form. Thus the project now on foot to build in an appropriate location a permanent and beautiful arch, to replace a temporary one which added so much to our splendid Centennial display, should not be allowed to miscarry. Such a structure will lead the minds of our citizens away from sordid things, and will suggest to them not only the impressive thoughts connected with our first President's inauguration, but will constantly remind them how grandly the event was celebrated in this city one hundred years afterward. By such means is public spirit fostered, and the way opened for a wider prevalence of good citizenship in its highest and broadest sense.

Let us, on the threshold of a new century, charged as we are with the maintenance, in our day and generation, of the integrity of our government, pledge ourselves to labor, each in his own sphere, for the revival of pure and simple patriotism and for the increase of that unselfish love of our entire country in which our safety lies.

And now I cannot refrain from suggesting as a closing thought that the responsibility of men like those who constitute the membership of this club, in every part and every phase a movement in the direction of public spirit and good citizenship, is made apparent when it is conceded that no agency can accomplish more in the cause than a free, courageous, and patriotic press.

IX.

At the Cornell Alumni Society Meeting, December 21, 1889.

Mr. President and Gentlemen :

I am confident that however well a man may think he has computed the factors which fix his status among his fellows, and however closely he may have inventoried his social assets and the claims he may hold to dignity and consideration, an item is quite likely now and then to escape his scrutiny. As a result he is liable to awaken some morning and find himself, if not famous, at least entitled to some distinction or consideration which had not before entered into his calculation.

If I am not the inventor of this weighty proposition I may

safely claim to be a striking and convincing illustration of its truth.

When a committee having the arrangements for this occasion in charge came to me with an invitation to be present, I listened to their proposition with that placid fortitude which one acquires in encounters with those anxious to demonstrate their unselfish patriotism by accepting office in the Federal service. I confess that the impressive representation made by the committee of the importance of the occasion, which in these days I hear so often, had little or no effect upon me, and that the thought I was giving to the subject was solely directed to determining the manner in which I might most courteously announce my declination. At this juncture one of my visitors mentioned the fact that I had been the only Governor of the State of New York, who, during his incumbency, had attended a meeting of the Trustees of Cornell University as *ex officio* a member of that body.

This was an entirely unexpected announcement. I need hardly say that conditions changed in an instant, when I understood that I had done an important thing, entirely proper and creditable, which my gubernatorial predecessors had not done. Somewhat puffed up by this newly found superiority, and by the additional importance which I imagined it gave me, I was ready to acknowledge the character of the obligation which was imposed by my relations thus established to an important institution of learning, and the duty I owed to those who ate and drank in its honor.

So I came here to insist upon a proper recognition of my kinship to you all, and, I fear, with some idea of exploiting, in rather a patronizing way, my importance in that relationship.

But I am entirely cured of all this ; for when I see here the alumni of Cornell and others connected with her, and when I recall the pride which the people of New York have in her success and achievements, and when I remember the interest and inspiration aroused by my visit to her home more than six years ago, I am quite willing to rest the satisfaction I experience from the privilege of being with you to-night, upon the interest which every citizen of our country and our State ought to feel in an institution which has done so much, and which promises so much for the instruction and improvement of the people of the nation and the State.

As I speak of the nation in its relation to your university, I at once encounter a thing which seems not only to underlie the establishment of the institution, but which presents a feature full of gratification and congratulation. In the grant of aid made by the general government, which did so much toward the founding of the university, I find it provided that the institutions which sought the benefit of its benefaction must "teach such branches of learning as are related to agriculture and the mechanic arts, in order to promote the liberal and practical education of the industrial classes in the several pursuits and professions in life."

When we consider the relations of the State to the university, we find the charter giving her a corporate existence upon the same condition contained in the Federal grant. We find, too, that the State guided in her direction the benefits of that grant, and at the same time permitted her to extend, to additional branches of science and learning, her plan of instruction. Nor should we overlook the fact that in her charter the State required her several departments of study to be open to applicants for admission at the lowest rate of expense consistent with her welfare and efficiency, and without distinction as to rank, class, previous occupation, or locality.

To my mind these things mean a great deal. They mean that both the nation and the State deemed the instruction of the people in agriculture and the mechanical arts as a fit subject for governmental care. This seems natural enough when we consider the broad area of our country, with its variety of soil and climate, waiting the magic transformation of agriculture, and when we remember that the American people surpass all others in ingenuity and mechanical faculty. They mean, too, the recognition of the fact that the good of the nation and the State is subserved by the education of all the people without distinction of rank or class, thus keeping in view the principle, upon which our institutions rest, that the people are the rulers of the land, and that their intelligence and education are the surest safeguards of our perpetuity, our prosperity, and our progress. They mean, also, that our nation and our State have made an offer of educational facilities and have exacted from their beneficiaries a compensating return of good citizenship.

These thoughts immediately suggest that those who close with this offer and accept its benefits incur an obligation to the nation and State which cannot be avoided or compromised. It is an obligation to realize thoughtfully and carefully the trust they hold as citizens, to interest themselves in public questions and to discharge their political duties with a patriotic intent and purpose of securing and protecting the welfare of their entire country. No man has a right to be heedless and listless under the responsibility he bears as an American citizen. An educated man has certainly no excuse for indifference ; and most of all, the man is derelict to his obligation who calls your university his Alma Mater and yet fails to discharge his full duty of citizenship. His graduation is proof that he has worthily earned the honors which your university can bestow ; but, wherever he may go and whatever may be his way of life, his diploma is evidence that he owes service to the nation.

Of this service he should at all times be proud. He is everywhere, if he is true to his duty, in the ranks of those who are engaged in the noble work of aiding to reach its grand and ultimate destiny, the best and freest nation the world has ever seen. If he retains his allegiance to the Empire State of New York, his pride should be enhanced; because, if he is faithful to his pledge, he is striving to advance the interest of the greatest commonwealth which the government of the United States numbers among its jewels.

Thus in the nation and in the State he wears the badge of

his obligation to good citizenship placed upon him within the walls of Cornell University. Happy and dutiful are her graduates, if, for the welfare of their country, for the honor of their university, and for the vindication of their own rectitude and good faith they respond patriotically to this obligation.

Concerning the debt of affection due from you to the university herself, I hardly need say, in this company, that all the alumni of Cornell, wherever in this broad land they may be, should love and revere their Alma Mater, beneath whose sheltering roof they have been fitted for usefulness and well equipped for the conflict of life. Their loyalty to her should never fail, and when the student life of their sons makes their fathers' names again familiar in the old university and upon her rolls, the sons should come to her halls laden with a father's devotion to her welfare, and they should be spurred to their best endeavor by a father's appreciation of her benefits and advantages.

Let me, in closing, leave the alumni of Cornell University the thought that they cannot honor their Alma Mater more, nor illustrate her value and usefulness better, than by keeping alive and active at all times a sober apprehension of the duty they owe to " the Nation, the State, and the University."

X.

At a Meeting to Demand New Legislation Concerning the Adirondack Park, New York, January 24, 1891.

MR. PRESIDENT, AND LADIES AND GENTLEMEN :

I rise to say a word in support of the resolutions that have been read. I have come here to be instructed as to the progress that has been made in a cause to which a few years ago, as Governor of your State, I gave considerable attention, and to testify to my continued interest in forest preservation. When, as Governor, this subject was brought to my mind, I gave it careful study, and I was thoroughly satisfied that the destruction of the Adirondack forests was jeopardizing our rivers as means of transportation, and that their preservation was essential to the health and comfort of future generations.

It is a most important matter, worthy the attention of all. Therefore it was that I recommended to the legislators of the State the passage of measures calculated to prohibit the further sale of forest lands in the possession of the State, and that such lands as we had, together with such as should come into our hands for the non-payment of taxes, should be preserved for a park. Something of that sort was done or attempted through an act providing for a forest commission, but the necessary amount of public feeling could not then be aroused to accomplish much.

I have listened with a great deal of interest to the suggestions which have been made here. To my conservative mind many of them seem radical. I have had the same advantages of observation as some of the previous speakers. I am an Adirondacker. I go to the Adirondacks every year. I have seen the great waste places and the desolation of which you have heard ; but, ladies and gentlemen, I have been on the edge of another great waste, on the margin of another great wilderness. I refer to the Capitol at Albany. Now, make no mistake : if you wish to preserve your forests from waste, there must be considerable cultivation done up there.

But, after all, there is no reason for discouragement. A little reminiscence of a previous struggle like this will teach you that. There was a suggestion made when I was in Albany that an effort should be made to have a reservation at Niagara Falls for the purpose of preserving the great natural beauty of the place. I must confess that that project seemed to me a rather discouraging one to attempt. I was full of sympathy, but not full of hope. Its warmest supporters hardly dared to predict that their hopes would be realized, yet they were realized, and I will tell you how.

If we had then gone to the Legislature with a bill asking

for so much money to buy so much land around the Falls, we certainly would have failed. We might have gone there and pleaded that we only wanted $1,500,000 until we were black in the face, and we would have been answered every time that the $1,500,000 we asked for was only an entering wedge. Our opponents would have pointed to the Capitol Building at Albany and shaken their heads.

What did we do? We got the Legislature to pass a law authorizing an appraisal of the lands we wanted to preserve. As good luck would have it, the appraisal amounted to just about the amount we said the lands would cost. We had continued to win supporters for our project. We then asked the State to buy the lands, and, to her credit be it said, she did so.

Our success then was largely due to an argument we may use here. We wanted to awaken the people's pride. I used to say to people that Niagara Falls was a great natural wonder by which we were known throughout the world. When you go to Europe, you are asked about Niagara Falls. I have never been to Europe, but I take that for granted for the sake of argument. When we told people that they began to take a sort of personal pride in Niagara. So we must make them feel that they have a personal interest in the splendid Adirondack region, which will make them demand its preservation. I would propose that we have a committee of 128 able-bodied citizens, each of whom shall go to Albany, take a legislator by the ear, and show him the great import of the work for which we ask his support.

The trouble is that the waste of our means of transportation is too remote to affect them. They will shrug their shoulders and say that the Hudson River will continue to flow as long as they live, and future generations—well, perhaps future generations can get along without rivers. Tell them that the work is essential to the preservation of health, and they will answer you that they are healthy enough. These arguments are weak to us, but to a member of the Legislature, when linked with the question of expense, they become strong.

We must take up the great task before us by easy stages. Let us begin on what we already have. Let us demand that the State shall preserve the great amount of Adirondack lands it now owns. That will not antagonize anybody. Let us demand that railroads shall not go in there on public lands except upon the consent of the State and the Forest Commission. That is but right and cannot antagonize anybody. We must not ask that somebody be given a license to go into the Adirondack region and blow up all the destructive dams, but we can with reason ask the State to see that no dam shall exist which is an injury to public lands and public forests.

Let us begin at once to protect what we have. That will demonstrate to the people the value of our work. Having done that, I believe that securing new lands and finally getting such a great State Park as we need will be an easy matter. Rome was not built in a day. A great Adirondack Park cannot be acquired by a single act.

I believe that we must have the co-operation of those who now own Adirondack lands. This is especially true of the clubs which have purchased preserves there for sporting purposes. Their desire to preserve the natural beauty of the region is as strong as ours is. If we could get these clubs to hold lands adjoining State lands, doing more or less exchanging for State lands, the region under preservation would be so much larger. I believe that it would be perfectly feasible to frame a law, agreeable to these clubs, that would give the State a right to protect, not a title to, private preserves adjoining a park.

Don't, then, let us shock our lawmakers, economical at least on matters of this kind, by asking for too much at once. Don't let us oppose any association, society, or individual that is working on the same line as we are. We need all the help we can get. Let us get to work to do something now, for, although it may be but an inch of the mile we ultimately want, we must remember that a little done now is worth a great deal in the future. I move the adoption of the resolution as offered.

XI.

At the Annual Banquet of the New England Society of Brooklyn, December 21, 1891.

MR. PRESIDENT AND GENTLEMEN :

As this is the first time I have attended a dinner given by a New England Society, I beg to express the gratification it affords me to enter upon my new experience in the City of Brooklyn and among those whom I have always regarded as especially my friends.

You are by no means to suppose that my failure heretofore to be present on occasions like this is accounted for by any doubt I have had as to my qualifications for admission. From the time the first immigrant of my name landed in Massachusetts, down to the day of my advent, all the Clevelands from whom I claim descent were born in New England. The fact that I first saw the light in the State of New Jersey I have never regarded as working a forfeiture of any right I may have derived from my New England lineage, nor as making me an intruder or merely tolerated guest in an assemblage of this kind. I resent, of course, with becoming spirit, the imputation that my birth in New Jersey constitutes me a foreigner and an alien ; and I have never been able to see any humor in the suggestion that my native State is not within the Union. To my mind the regularity with which she votes the Democratic ticket entitles her to a high rank among the States that are really useful. At any rate, I shall always insist that New Jersey is a good State to be born in, and I point to the fact that, after an absence of more than fifty years, I have returned to find a temporary home within her limits as fully demonstrating that my very early love for her is not extinguished.

Assuming that you agree with me that my birth in New Jersey has not stamped me with indelible ineligibility, and anticipating your demand for affirmative support of my qualification to mingle with those who celebrate Forefathers' Day and sing the praises of the men who first settled in New England, I can do no better than to rest my case upon the statement that Bean Hill, in the town of Norwich and State of Connecticut, was the birthplace of my father. I hope that in making this statement I shall not remind you of the man who loudly boasted of his patriotic sacrifice in defense of his country on the ground that he had permitted his wife's relatives to join the army. At any rate, it seems to me that the claim I make is entirely valid, with no embarrassment connected with it, except the admission by inference that for some purposes and on some occasions a father's birthplace may be of more value to a man than his own. I have nothing further to urge on the subject of my eligibility except to mention, as something which should be credited to me upon my own account, the fact that I have lately demonstrated my preference for New England and my love for that section of our country where my ancestors lived and died, by establishing a summer home in the State of Massachusetts.

I think all of us are old enough to remember the prophetic words put opposite certain dates in the old almanacs, " About these days look out for snow." If almanacs were now made up as they used to be, it would not be amiss to set opposite the latter days of December, " About these days look out for glorification of the Pilgrims." This would be notice to those consulting the almanac that a time was foretold when the people of the country would be reminded that there were Pilgrims who came to New England, and there set in motion the forces which created our wondrous nation.

No one will deny that the Pilgrims to New England were well worthy of all that is done or can be done to keep them in remembrance. But we cannot recall their history, and what they did and established, and what they taught, without also recalling that there have been Pilgrims from New England who, finding their way to every part of the land, have taken with them those habits, opinions, and sentiments which, having an early origin in American soil, should be best suited to American life everywhere, and should be the best guarantees in every situation, of the preservation, in their integrity and purity, of American institutions.

We have heard much of abandoned lands in New England. If farms have been abandoned there, we know that larger and more productive farms have been developed in newer States by the Pilgrims from New England. If the population of New England has suffered a drain, we shall find that the vigorous activity lost to her has built up new cities and towns on distant and unbroken soil and impressed upon these new creations the truest and best features of American civilization.

While all will admit the debt our great country owes to New England influences, and while none of us should be unmindful of the benefits to be reasonably expected from the maintenance and spread of these influences, a thought is suggested which has further relation to the mission and duty of the Pilgrims from New England and their descendants, wherever they may be scattered throughout the land. If they are at all true to their teachings and their traditions, they will naturally illustrate, in a practical way, the value of education and moral sentiment in the foundations of social life and the value of industry and economy as conditions of thrift and contentment. But these Pilgrims and their descendants and all those who, with sincere enthusiasm, celebrate Forefathers' Day, will fail in the discharge of their highest duty if, yielding to the temptation of any un-American tendency, they neglect to teach persistently that in the early days there was, and that there still ought to be, such a thing as true and distinctive Americanism, or if they neglect to give it just interpretation.

This certainly does not mean that a spirit of narrowness or proscription should be encouraged, nor that there should be created or kept alive a fear concerning such additions to our population from other lands as promise assimilation with our conditions and co-operation in our aims and purposes. It does, however, mean the insistence that every transfer of allegiance from another government to our own, should signify the taking on at the same time of an aggressive and affirmative devotion to the spirit of American institutions. It means that with us, a love of our government for its own sake and for what it is, is an essential factor of citizenship, and that it is only made full and complete by the adoption of the ideas and habits of thought which underlie our plan of popular rule. It means that one fills a place in our citizenship unworthily who regards it solely as a vantage ground where he may fill his purse and better his condition. It means that our government is not suited to a selfish, sordid people, and that in their hands it is not safe.

This is a time when there is pressing need for the earnest enforcement of these truths ; and occasions like this cannot be better improved than by leading us to such self-examination and self-correction as shall fit us to illustrate and teach the lessons of true Americanism. When we here recall the landing of the Pilgrims, let us remember that they not only sought "Freedom to worship God," but they also sought to establish the freedom and liberty of manhood. When we dwell upon their stern and sturdy traits, let us remember that these nurtured the spirit which achieved American independence, and that in such soil alone can its fruits ripen to bless our people. When we contemplate how completely conscience guided their lives and conduct, let us resolve that conscience shall find a place in every phase of our citizenship ; and when we learn of their solicitude and care for their new-found home, let us acknowledge that unselfish love of country can alone show us the path of political duty.

With such preparation as this—leaving no place for the ignoble thought that our government can, without perversion, hold out unequal rewards and encourage selfish beings—we shall teach that this heritage of ours has been confided from generation to generation to the patriotic keeping and loving care of true Americanism, and that this alone can preserve it ; to shelter a free and happy people—protecting all, defending all, and blessing all.

CHAPTER XI.

TO POLITICAL CLUBS AND ORGANIZATIONS.

I.

At the Manhattan Club, December 5, 1882.

IT is not without considerable embarrassment that I attempt
to say a few words in response to those so well spoken, and to
express my thanks for the kindness and good will of which
this occasion is an evidence. This scene and these surroundings are new and strange to me, and, notwithstanding all that
is calculated to reassure and comfort me in the kindness of
your welcome, when I am reminded of the circumstances
which give rise to this reunion, a sense of grave responsibility weighs upon me and tempers every other sentiment.

We stand to-night in the full glare of a grand and brilliant
manifestation of popular will, and in the light of it how vain
and small appear the tricks of politicians and the movements
of party machinery. He must be blind who cannot see that
the people well understand their power and are determined to
use it when their rights and interests are threatened. There
should be no skepticism to-night as to the strength and perpetuity of our popular government. Partisan leaders have
learned, too, that the people will not unwittingly and blindly
follow, and that something more than unmeaning devotion to
party is necessary to secure their allegiance.

I am quite certain, too, that the late demonstration did not
spring from any pre-existing love for the party which was
called to power, nor did the people place the affairs of state in
our hands to be by them forgotten. They voted for themselves and in their own interests. If we retain their confidence

we must deserve it, and we may be sure they will call on us to give an account of our stewardship. We shall utterly fail to read aright the signs of the times if we are not fully convinced that parties are but the instruments through which the people work their will, and that when they become less or more the people desert or destroy them. The vanquished have lately learned these things, and the victors will act wisely if they profit by the lesson.

I have read and heard much of late touching the great responsibility which has been cast upon me, and it is certainly predicated upon the fact that my majority was so large as to indicate that many, not members of the party to which I am proud to belong, supported me. God knows how fully I appreciate the responsibility of the high office to which I have been called, and how much I sometimes fear that I shall not bear the burden well. It has seemed to me, however, that the citizen who has been chosen by his fellows to discharge public duties owes no less nor more to them, whether he was elected by a small or a large majority. In either event, he owes to the people who have honored him his best endeavor to protect their rights and further their interests.

But if it is merely intended to remind me that, as a member of a party, attached to its principles, and anxious for its continued supremacy, my conduct should be such as to give hope and confidence to those who are surely with us, I have to say that this responsibility should be shared by all the members of the party. An administration is only successful, in a partisan sense, when it appears to be the outgrowth and result of party principles and methods. You who lead and others who follow, should all strive to commend to the people in this, the time of our opportunity, not an administration alone, but a party which shall appear adequate to their wants and useful to their purposes.

The time-honored doctrines of the Democratic party are dear to me. If honestly applied in their purity I know the affairs of the government would be fittingly and honestly administered, and I believe that all the wants of the people would be met. They have survived all changes, and good and patriotic men have clung to them, through all disasters, as the hope of political salvation. Let us hold them as a sacred trust, and let us not forget that an intelligent, reading, and thinking people will look to the party which they put in power to supply all their various needs and wants. And the party which keeps pace with the development and progress of the time, which keeps in sight its landmarks and yet observes those things which are in advance, and which will continue true to the people as well as to its traditions, will be the dominant party of the future.

In conclusion, may I bespeak for myself your kind support and consideration ? My only aspiration is to perform, faithfully, the duties of the office to which the people of my State have called me, and I hope and trust that proud endeavor will light the way to a successful administration.

II.

At a Reception Given by the Democratic Club, New York, April 27, 1889.

MR. PRESIDENT :

Many incidents of my short residence in this good city have served to fill my cup of gratitude, and to arouse my appreciation of the kindness and consideration of those with whom I have made my home. The hospitality of the citizens of New York, for which they have long been distinguished, has outdone itself in my welcome. The members of my profession have, upon my return to its activities, received me with fraternal greetings, and personal friends have not permitted me to feel like a stranger in a strange city.

And yet I can truly say to-night that none of these things

will be more vividly and gratefully remembered than the opportunity afforded me by this occasion to greet the political friends I see about me. While I believe that no man is more susceptible than I to every personal kindness, and while I am sure that no one values more his personal friendships, it should not be regarded as strange when I say that these are not more cherished than my loyalty and attachment to Democratic faith and my obligation to the cardinal principles of its party organization.

I have been honored by my party far beyond my deserts ; indeed, no man can deserve its highest honors. After six years of public service, I return to you, my party friends. Six years have I stood as your representative in the State and nation, and now I return again to the ranks, more convinced than ever that the cause of true Democracy is the cause of the people—their safeguard and their hope.

I come to you with no excuses or apologies, and with no confession of disloyalty. It is not given to man to meet the various and conflicting views of party duty and policy which prevail within an organization where individual opinion is so freely tolerated as in the Democratic party. Because these views are various and conflicting some of them must be wrong, but when they are honestly held and advocated they should provoke no bitterness or condemnation. But when they are proclaimed merely as a cover and pretext for personal resentment and disappointment, they should be met by the exposure and contempt which they deserve.

If one charged with party representation, with sincere design and purpose keeps the party faith, that should be a fulfillment of his party obligation.

No man can lay down the trust which he has held in behalf of a generous and confiding people, and feel that at all times he has met, in the best possible way, the requirements of his trust ; but he is not derelict in duty if he has conscientiously devoted his effort and his judgment to the people's service.

I have deliberately placed in close connection loyalty to

Democratic principles and devotion to the people's interest, for, in my view, they belong together and should mean the same thing.

But, in this day of party feeling and attachment, it is well for us to pause and recall the fact that the only justification for the existence of any party is the claim that, in profession and intent, its objects and its purposes are the promotion of the public good and the advancement and the welfare and prosperity of the entire country. There never was a party platform or declaration of principles that did not profess these things and make them the foundation of party creed, and any body of men that should associate themselves together proclaiming openly that their purpose was supremacy in the government with the sole intent of distributing offices and the spoils of victory among their associates, would be treated with ridicule and scorn. Thus we are brought face to face with the proposition that parties no more than individuals should be untruthful or dishonest.

Of course in the supremacy of party there are advantages to its members—and this is not amiss. But when high party aims and professions are lost sight of and abandoned, and the interests of office holding and personal pelf are all that remain to inspire party activity, not only is the support expected from patriotic people forfeited, but the elements of cohesion and of effective and lasting political strength are gone. The honest differences of opinion which must always exist upon questions of principle and of public policy, should be sufficient occasion for the existence of parties, and should point to the field of their usefulness. The study of these questions cannot fail to result in more valuable citizenship and more intelligent and better equipped partisans.

When we seek for the cause of the perpetuity of the Democratic party and its survival through every crisis and emergency, and in the face of all opposition, we find it in the fact that its corner stone is laid in devotion to the rights of the people and in its sympathy with all things that tend to the advancement of their welfare and happiness. Though heresy may sometimes have crept into its organization, and though party conduct may at times have been influenced by the shiftiness which is the habitual device of its opponents, there has always remained deeply imbedded in its nature and character that spirit of true Americanism and that love of popular rights which has made it indestructible in disaster and defeat, and has constituted it a boon to the country in its hour of triumph and supremacy.

The great founder of our party, as he consecrated himself by a solemn oath to the faithful performance of the duties of the Presidential office, and as he pledged himself to the preservation, protection, and defense of the Constitution, after presenting to his assembled countrymen the causes of congratulation, found in the condition of our country and the character of our people, impressively added : " With all these blessings, what more is necessary to make us a happy and prosperous people ? Still one thing more, fellow-citizens : a wise and frugal government which shall restrain men from injuring one another, shall leave them otherwise free to regulate their own pursuits of industry and improvement, and shall not take from the mouth of labor the bread it has earned. This is the sum of good government, and this is necessary to close the circle of our felicities."

In the lexicon of true Democracy these words are not obsolete, but they still furnish the inspiration for our efforts and an interpretation of our political faith.

Happily the party creed which we profess is not within such narrow lines as that obedience does not permit us to move abreast with the advanced thought of the country and to meet and test every question and apply a principle to every situation.

True Democracy, stanch in its adhesion to fundamental doctrine, is at the same time, in a proper sense, progressive. It recognizes our growth and our expansion, and the birth of new thought and sentiment. It will judge them all by safe standards, and in every phase of national development it will be prepared to meet as they arise every need of the people and every popular want. True Democracy honestly advocates national brotherhood, to the end that all our countrymen may aid in the achievement of the grand destiny which awaits us as a nation ; and it condemns the pretext of liberality and har-́ mony which, when partisan advantage is to be gained, gives way for inflammatory appeals to sectional hate and passion. It insists upon that equality before the law which concedes the care and protection of the government to simple manhood and citizenship. It does not favor the multiplication of offices and salaries merely to make partisans, nor use the promise and bestowal of place for the purpose of stifling the press and bribing the people. It seeks to lighten the burdens of life in every home and to take from the citizen for the cost of government the lowest possible tribute.

We know that we have espoused the cause of right and justice. We know that we have not permitted duty to country to wait upon expediency. We know that we have not trafficked our principles for success. We know that we have not deceived the people with false promises and pretenses. And we know that we have not corrupted or betrayed the poor with the money of the rich.

Who shall say that these things promise no reward and that triumph shall not follow the enlightened judgment and the sober second thought of our countrymen ? There are to-day no weak, weary, and despondent members of the true Democracy, and there should be none. Thoughtful attention to political topics is thoroughly aroused. Events day by day are leading men to review the reasons for their party affiliations and the supporters of the principles we profess are constantly recruited by intelligent, young, and sturdy adherents.

Let us deserve their confidence, and, shunning all ignoble practices, let us remain steadfast to Democratic faith and to the cause of our country. If we are true and loyal to these, the day of our triumph will surely and quickly come, and our victory shall be fairly, nobly won, through the invincible spirit of true Democracy.

_____

III.

At the Thurman Birthday Banquet, Columbus, O., November 13, 1890.

MR. PRESIDENT AND GENTLEMEN:

I follow the promptings of a heart full of devotion and veneration, as I tender from the Democracy of the great State of New York her tribute of affection for the man whom we honor to-night. I am commissioned to claim for my State her full share of the glory which has been shed upon the American name and character by one whose career and example cannot be pre-empted, and whose renown cannot be limited in ownership to the neighbors and friends of any locality. We contest every exclusive pretension to his fame and greatness, because he is a neighbor to all the people of the land ; because he is the friend of all who love their country ; because his career splendidly illustrates the best and strongest elements of our national character ; and because his example belongs to all his countrymen.

It is fitting that those who have faith in our destiny as a nation, who believe that there are noble things which belong distinctively to our character as a people, and who prize at its true worth pure American citizenship, should gather here to-night. It is given us to contemplate the highest statesmanship, the most unyielding and disinterested devotion to the interests of the people, and the most valuable achievements in the cause of our country's welfare, all of which have been stimulated and accomplished through the influence and impulse of true, unperverted, sturdy Americanism. We rejoice in the example afforded on this occasion of genuine American citizenship, revealed to us as a safe and infallible interpreter of duty in all the emergencies of a long and honorable public career, and as an unfailing guide to usefulness and fame.

In this presence and in the atmosphere of these reflections, we should not miss the lesson they commend to us, nor fail to renew our appreciation of the value of this citizenship, and revive our apprehension of the sentiments and conditions in which it has its rise and growth.

And first of all we should be profoundly grateful that the elements which make up the strength and vigor of American citizenship are so naturally related to our situation and are so simple. The intrigues of monarchy which taint the individual character of the subject ; the splendor which dazzles the popular eye and distracts the attention from abuses and stifles discontent ; the schemes of conquest and selfish aggrandizement which make a selfish people, have no legitimate place in our national life. Here the plain people of the land are the rulers. Their investiture of power is only accompanied with the conditions that they should love their country, that they should jealously guard and protect its interests and fair fame, and that all the intelligence with which they are endowed should be devoted to an understanding of its needs and the promotion of its welfare.

These are the elements of American citizenship, and these are the conditions upon which our free institutions were intrusted to our people, in full reliance, at the beginning and for all time to come, upon American manhood, consecrated by the highest and purest patriotism.

A country, broad and new, to be subdued to the purposes of man's existence, and promising vast and independent resources, and a people intelligently understanding the value of a free nation and holding fast to an intense affection for its history and its heroes, have had much to do with molding our American character and giving it hardihood and vigor. But it should never be forgotten that the influence which, more than all other things, has made our people safe depositories of governmental power, and which has furnished the surest guarantee of the strength and perpetuity of the republic, has its source in the American home. Here our patriotism is born and entwines itself with the growth of filial love, and here our children are taught the story of our freedom and independence. But above all, here in the bracing and wholesome atmosphere of uncomplaining frugality and economy, the mental and moral attributes of our people have been firmly knit and invigorated. Never could it be said of any country so truly as of ours, that the permanency of its institutions depends upon its homes.

I have spoken of frugality and economy as important factors in American life. I find no fault with the accumulation of wealth, and am glad to see energy and enterprise receive their fair reward. But I believe that our government, in its natural integrity, is exactly suited to a frugal and economical people ; and I believe it is safest in the hands of those who have been made strong and self-reliant in their citizenship, by self-denial and by the surroundings of an enforced economy. Thrift and careful watchfulness of expenditure among the people tend to secure a thrifty government ; and cheap and careful living on the part of individuals ought to enforce economy in the public expenditures.

When, therefore, men in high places of trust, charged with the responsibility of making and executing our laws, not only condemn but flippantly deride cheapness and economy within the homes of our people, and when the expenditures of the government are reckless and wasteful, we may be sure that something is wrong with us, and that a condition exists which calls for a vigorous and resentful defense of Americanism, by every man worthy to be called an American citizen.

Upon the question of cheapness and economy, whether it relates to individuals or to the operations of the government, the Democratic party, true to its creed and its traditions, will unalterably remain attached to our plain and frugal people. They are especially entitled to the watchful care and protection of their government; and when they are borne down with burdens greater than they can bear, and are made the objects of scorn by hard taskmasters, we will not leave their side. As the great German Reformer, insisting upon his religious convictions, in the presence of his accusers, exclaimed, " I can do nought else. Here I stand. God help me," so, however much others may mock and deride cheapness and the poor and frugal men and women of our land, we will stand forth in defense of their simple Americanism, defiantly proclaiming, " We can do nought else. Here we stand."

Thus, when the question is raised whether our people shall have the necessaries of life at a cheaper rate, we are not ashamed to confess ourselves " in full sympathy with the demand for cheaper coats " ; and we are not disturbed by the hint that this seems " necessarily to involve a cheaper man or woman under the coats."

When the promoter of a party measure which invades every home in the land with higher prices, declares that " cheap and nasty go together, and this whole system of cheap things is a badge of poverty ; for cheap merchandize means cheap men, and cheap men mean a cheap country," we indignantly repudiate such an interpretation of American sentiment.

And when another one, high in party councils, who has become notorious as the advocate of a contrivance to perpetuate partisan supremacy by outrageous interference with the suffrage, announces that the " cry for cheapness is un-American," we scornfully reply that his speech does not indicate the slightest conception of true Americanism.

I will not refer to other utterances of like import from similar sources. I content myself with recalling the most prominent and significant. The wonder is that these things were addressed by Americans to Americans.

What was the occasion of these condemnations of cheapness, and what had honest American men and women done, or what were they likely to do, that they should be threatened with the epithets " cheap," " nasty," and " un-American ?"

It is hard to speak patiently as we answer these questions. Step by step a vast number of our people had been led on, following blindly in the path of party. They had been filled with hate and sectional prejudice ; they had been cajoled with misrepresentations and false promises ; they had been corrupted with money and by appeals to their selfishness. All these things led up to their final betrayal to satisfy the demands of those who had supplied the fund for their corruption.

This betrayal was palpable ; and it was impossible to deny or conceal the fact that the pretended relief tendered to the people in fulfilment of a promise to lighten the burden of their life, made by the party intrusted with the government, was but a scheme to pay the debt incurred by the purchase of party success, while it further increased the impoverishment of the masses.

The people were at last aroused and demanded an explanation. They had been taught for one hundred years that in the distribution of benefits their government should be administered with equality and justice. They had learned that wealth was not indispensable to respectability and that it did not entitle its possessors to especial governmental favors. Humble men with scanty incomes had been encouraged, by the influence and the spirit of our institutions, to practice economy and frugality to the end that they might enjoy to the utmost the reward of their toil. The influence of the American home was still about them. In their simplicity they knew nothing of a new dispensation which made cheapness disreputable, and they still loved the cheap coats of Lincoln and Garfield, and hundreds of their countrymen whom they held in veneration. And thus these unsophisticated Americans, unconscious of their wrong-doing, demanded the redemption of party pledges and clamored for cheapness, in order that they might provide the necessaries and comforts of life for themselves and their families at the lowest possible cost.

The leaders of the party, which was caught in the act of

robbery and which was arraigned by the people for a violation of its trust, were forced by their sad predicament to a desperate expedient. To attempt to reverse the current of true Americanism and discredit the most honorable sentiments belonging to American manhood, were the disgraceful tasks of those who insulted our people by the announcement of the doctrine that to desire cheapness was to love nastiness, and to practice economy and frugality was un-American.

Thus we do plainly see that when the path pointed out by patriotism and American citizenship is forsaken by a party in power for schemes of selfishness and for unscrupulous conspiracies for partisan success, its course inevitably leads to unjust favoritism, neglect of the interest of the masses, entire perversion of the mission of republican institutions, and, in some form, to the most impudent and outrageous insult to true American sentiment.

It cannot be denied that political events in the past have gone far toward encouraging arrogant party assumption. Every thoughtful and patriotic man has at times been disappointed and depressed by the apparent indifference and demoralization of the people.

But such reflections have no place in the felicitations of tonight. This is a time when faith in our countrymen should be fully re-established. The noise of a recent political revolution is still heard throughout the land ; the people have just demonstrated that there is a point beyond which they cannot be led by blind partisanship, and that they are quite competent to examine and correctly decide political questions concerning their rights and their welfare. They have unmercifully resented every attack upon true American manhood, and have taught party leaders that, though slow to anger, they take terrible revenges when betrayed. They permit us to forgive our honored guest for all the cheap coats he has ever worn, for they have declared them to be in fashion. They have also decreed that the Decalogue has a place in our politics, for they enforced the command, "Thou shalt not steal," and rendered an emphatic verdict against those who have borne false witness.

Nothing could so well accompany the honors we pay our distinguished guest as the celebration on his birthday of the victory which has just been achieved in vindication of American citizenship—for in him we honor the man who has best illustrated true American manhood. Our rejoicing and his are increased, as we also celebrate to-night the triumph of a Democratic principle for which he fought and fell but two short years ago ; and to complete our joy and his, we are permitted to indulge in true Democratic enthusiasm over the steadfastness and devotion to its creed exhibited by our party, which, knowing no discouragement, has fought to victory in the people's cause.

Who can now doubt our countrymen's appreciation of that trait, so well illustrated in the character of Allen G. Thurman, which prompted him throughout his long career, at all times and in all circumstances, and without regard to personal consequences, to do the things which his conscience and judgment approved, and which seemed to him to be in the interests of his country and in accordance with the Democratic faith ? Who can now doubt that conscience and courage point out the way to public duty?

If we entertain more solemn thoughts on this occasion, let them be concerning the responsibility which awaits us as our fellow-countrymen place in our keeping their hopes and their trust. We shall fail in our obligation to them if we stifle conscience and duty by ignoble partisanship ; but we shall meet every patriotic expectation if, in all we do, we follow the guidance of true and honest Democracy, illumined by the light of genuine American citizenship.

IV.

THE CAMPAIGN OF EDUCATION.*

MR. PRESIDENT AND GENTLEMEN :

I suppose I have a correct understanding of what is meant by "The Campaign of Education." Assuming this to be so, I desire, before going further, to acknowledge the valiant services in this campaign of the organization whose invitation brings us together to-night. I may be permitted, I hope, to make this acknowledgment as a citizen interested in all that promises the increased prosperity of the country ; and I shall also venture to do so as a Democrat who recognizes, in the principle for which the campaign has thus far proceeded, a cardinal and vital doctrine of Democratic creed. If I thus acknowledge the useful services, in a Democratic cause, of any who have not claimed long affiliation with my party, I feel that my Democratic allegiance is strong enough to survive such an indulgence in fairness and decency. I am, too, at all times willing that the Democratic party should be enlarged ; and, as tending in that direction, I am willing to accept and acknowledge in good faith honest help from any quarter when a struggle is pending for the supremacy of Democratic principles. Indeed, I have an idea that, in the campaign of education, it was deemed important to appeal to the reason and judgment of the American people, to the end that the Democratic party should be reinforced as well as that the activity and zeal of those already in our ranks should be stimulated. If this be treason in the sight of those who, clothed in Democratic uniform, would be glad to stand at the entrance of our camp and drive back recruits, I cannot help it. I have come here to-night, among other things, to rejoice in the numerous accessions we have received in aid of Democratic endeavor and to give credit wherever it is due for the work of conversion.

* In response to the Toast, " The Campaign of Education : its result is a signal tribute to the judgment of the American people," delivered at the Reform Club Dinner, New York, December 23, 1890.

The grand and ultimate object of the campaign of education was the promotion of the welfare of the country and the
relief of the people from unjust burdens. In aid of this purpose and, of course, subordinate and accessory to its accomplishment, it became necessary, first of all, to arouse the Democratic organization to an apprehension of the fact that the
campaign involved a Democratic principle, in the advocacy of
which the party should be active and aggressive.

Let it be here confessed that we, as a party, had, in these
latter days, been tempted by the successes our opponents had
gained solely by temporary shifts and by appeals to prejudice
and selfish interests, into paths which avoided too much the
honest insistence upon definite and clearly defined principle
and fundamental Democratic doctrine. To be sure, some
earnest men in the party could but ill conceal their dissatisfac-
tion with the manner in which cardinal principles were rele-
gated to the rear and expediency substituted as the hope of
success ; but the timid, the heedless, and those who, though
nominally belonging to the organization, were not of the faith,
constantly rendered ineffective all attempts to restore the party
to the firm and solid ground of Democratic creed.

If these things are confessed, let it also be conceded that
when the time came and the cries of a suffering people were
heard, and when, for their relief, a genuine Democratic remedy
was proposed, the party easily recognized its duty and gave
proof of its unconquerable Democratic instincts. As soon as
the campaign of education was inaugurated, the party was
quickly marshaled as of the olden time, aggressive, courageous, devoted to its cause and heedless of discouragement or
defeat. Day by day, and hour by hour, expediency and time-
serving were thrown to the winds. Traitors were silenced,
camp-followers fell away or joined the scurvy band of floaters,
while the sturdy Democratic host confidently pressed on, bearing aloft the banner of tariff reform. If any have wondered
in the past at the tenacity and indestructibility of our party,
their wonder should cease when, in the light of the last three

years, it is seen how gloriously it springs to the front at the call of duty to the people, and in obedience to the summons of party loyalty and obligation.

Thus the education of the campaign meant, as related to the Democracy, its awakening in response to the signal for its return to the propagandism of Democratic doctrine.

The thoroughly aroused enthusiasm and determination of the party, and its allied thousands of good and earnest men, drawn from the non-partisan intelligence and honesty of the land, saw no obstacle too formidable for attack and no end which was not within their reach. In a sublime confidence, almost amounting to audacity, they were willing to attempt the education of those high in the counsels of the Republican party, and those who formulated that party's policy, so far as such a thing existed.

I am afraid, however, that if this task may be considered a step in the campaign of education, the word education, as applied to those who were to be affected, must be construed as meaning the instillation of such fear and terror in the minds of unregenerate men as leads them to flee from the wrath to come.

But even in this unpromising field we are able to report progress. No one who remembers the hilarity with which the leaders of the Republican party greeted the message of tariff reform, and the confidence with which they prepared to meet and crush the issue presented, can fail to see how useful a lesson has been taught them in our campaign of education.

Within twenty-four hours after the submission to Congress of the question of tariff reform, sundry Senators and Representatives belonging to the Republican party were reported to have ventilated their partisan exultation jauntily in the public press.

If it be true that a Senator from Nebraska said, " It is a big card for the Republicans," this big card cannot appear remarkably useful to him now, for his State to-day contains a big curiosity in the shape of a Democratic Governor-elect.

If the junior Senator from New York declared that his party

would carry this State by the largest majority ever known if they could be given the platform proposed; the reply will come when, in a few days, a Democratic colleague is placed by his side.

If a Senator from Maine declared, "It is a good enough platform for the Republicans—we want nothing better," how is it that he is now so diligently endeavoring to find out the meaning of the word Reciprocity?

If a New Hampshire Senator believed that "the Republicans want nothing better with which to sweep the country," the trouble his State is giving him to-day must lead him to suspect there is a mistake somewhere.

If a Senator from Wisconsin gleefully said he was glad to see us "show our hand" he cannot fail to be convinced, when he soon gives place to a real good, sound Democrat, that there was, after all, more in the hand than he cared to see.

If the present Speaker of the House sarcastically said, "It only shows what fools all the other Presidents have been," he may well be excused, since he has lately so thoroughly learned, that, in the sight of the people, infallibility is not an attribute always to be found in the Speaker's chair.

If the Representative from Ohio whose name is associated with a bill which has given his party considerable trouble of late, said, "If the Democratic party had hired Burchard to write a stump speech it could not have suited us better," it must be that circumstances leading to his approaching retirement from public life have suggested a modification of his judgment, and caused him to suspect that Mr. Burchard has at least one formidable competitor.

As our campaign has proceeded, other unusual symptoms have been apparent among those prominent in directing the opposition. Some of them have become insubordinate and discontented, and at times actually disobedient to party orders. Some have left the ship. One shrewd and weather-wise navigator has clambered off, and, in a frail bark, with the word "Reciprocity" painted on its stern, was last seen hovering near, prepared to climb aboard again, or sail away, as wind and wave would appear to make most safe. At the present stage of the campaign the unwieldy party hulk of Bourbon Republicanism is still afloat, but damaged and badly leaking. On board, some are still working at the pumps against the awful odds of opening seams ; many, mutinous and discontented, short of provisions and of grog, are loudly and angrily disputing as to whether bad seamanship or overloading is the cause of their wretched plight, while accusations of guilty responsibility are heard on every side. If, from this turbulence, there shall emerge any who, actually pricked in conscience, desire a better life, they will be gladly welcomed. I cannot, however, keep out of my mind the story of the pious deacon who, having, in his efforts to convert a bad sinner, become so excited by his incorrigibility that he gave him a thorough drubbing, afterward explained and justified his course by declaring that he believed he had "walloped saving grace into an impenitent soul."

Of course, we do not overlook the fact that before their present predicament was reached, and in their first battle with us, the enemy gained a victory over tariff reform. This is confessed ; and we may here only refer to the methods by which that victory was gained for the purpose of saying that we thoroughly understand them, and that if the beneficiaries of those methods are satisfied with the condition they have wrought, we also are not without compensation. That we have cause for satisfaction, even in the remembrance of temporary defeat, is evidenced by the fact that among those who ought to rejoice in success there is quite a general sentiment that "the least said of it the better."

I have spoken of the campaign of education as it has affected the two great party organizations. It remains to mention another and a more important and gratifying feature of its progress. I refer to the manner in which access has been gained to the plain people of the land, and the submission to their reason and judgment of the objects and purposes for which the campaign was undertaken.

The Democratic party is willing to trust the ordinary intelligence of our people for an understanding of its principles. It does not seat itself above the common feelings and sympathies of humanity, and in an arrogant assumption of superior learning formulate political doctrines suited only to those favored with advanced educational opportunities. It recognized the fact at the outset of the campaign of education that it was not the ignorance of the people which had led them to submit to the evils of bad government, but that it was partly owing to the busy activity of their occupations, and the consequent neglect of political subjects, and partly to the rigidity of their party ties and their unquestioning confidence in party leadership. Having once settled upon their political affiliations, they have been wont to turn from a watchfulness of public affairs to the daily routine of their labor with much virtuous satisfaction in the reflection that they were not politicians.

Therefore the labor of their education in the campaign has consisted in persuading them to hear us ; to examine the theories in party organizations and the ends to which they lead ; to recall the promises of political leadership and the manner in which such promises have been redeemed ; and to counsel with us as to the means by which their condition could be improved.

Never was more intelligent, honest, and effective effort made in a noble cause than that made by the Democratic party and its allies in this work. Our fellow-countrymen were approached, not by fabricated extracts from English journals and a lying demagogic cry of British gold ; not by fraudulent pictures of the ruin of American industries if the justice of governmental favoritism was questioned ; not by a false presentation of the impoverishment and distress of our laboring men which would follow their independent political thought and action ; not by a disgraceful proposition for the purchase of their suffrages ; and not by the cruel intimidation, by selfish employers, of those dependent on them for the wages of their toil

We have been content to rely upon the intelligence and thoughtfulness of the people for the success of our cause. We have solicited the most thorough examination of its merits. For the purpose of such examination we have put before the people plain and honest exposition of the justice and beneficence of our principle. This has been done by the systematic and industrious distribution of tariff reform literature, by the effective and conscientious arguments of a well-informed and unsubsidized press, and by an extensive discussion on the platform of the question involved.

These are the weapons we have used in our campaign of education. It is a cause of congratulation to-night that our work has been done in a manner so decent, and in its best sense so purely American.

Need I speak of the results of our labors? This happy assemblage, called together " To celebrate the victories achieved in the cause of tariff reform," tells the story of our success.

We will rejoice to-night, not only in our success and the manner of its achievement, but as American citizens we will especially rejoice in the proof which our victory affords of the intelligence, the integrity, and the patriotism of our fellow-countrymen. We have again learned that, when roused to thought and action, they can be trusted to determine rightly any questions involving their interests and the welfare of their country.

Let us not fail to realize the fact that our work is not done. Our enemies are still alive, and have grown desperate. Human selfishness is not easily overcome, and the hope of private gain at the expense of the masses of our people is not yet abandoned. It would be shameful, and a pitiable disgrace, if by over-confidence we should lose the ground we have gained, or if we should fail to push further our advantage. The result of our labor thus far is, indeed, " a signal tribute to the judgment of the American people." In full faith in this judgment our work should continue upon the lines thus far followed until the enemies of tariff reform are driven from their last intrenchment. As the people have trusted us, let us, above all things, be true to them. Let the light of our campaign be carried into every part of the land where it has not been seen ; and where it has been kindled let it be kept brightly burning, still showing the way to better days for the people, and disclosing the plans of insidious foes.

In the years to come, when we look back with patriotic satisfaction upon our participation in the glorious struggle for tariff reform and recall its happy termination, it will delight us to remember every incident of discouragement as well as of triumph in the people's cause. Then, when we are asked to speak of our proudest political endeavor, and to give the best illustrations of American intelligence, and to pay the highest tribute to the judgment of the American people, we will rehearse the history and the grand result of "the campaign of education."

V.

THE PRINCIPLES OF TRUE DEMOCRACY.*

MR. PRESIDENT AND GENTLEMEN :

As I rise to respond to the sentiment which has been assigned to me, I cannot avoid the impression made upon my mind by the announcement of the words "True Democracy." I believe them to mean a sober conviction or conclusion touching political topics, which, formulated into a political belief or creed, inspires a patriotic performance of the duties of citizenship. I am satisfied that the principles of this belief or creed are such as underlie our free institutions, and that they may be urged upon our fellow-countrymen, because, in their purity and integ-

*A speech in response to the toast : "The Principles of True Democracy : They are Enduring because They are Right, and Invincible because They are Just," at the banquet of the Young Men's Democratic Association, Philadelphia, January 8, 1891.

rity, they accord with the attachment of our people for their government and their country. A creed based upon such principles is by no means discredited because illusions and perversions temporarily prevent their popular acceptance, any more than it can be irretrievably shipwrecked by mistakes made in its name or by its prostitution to ignoble purposes. When illusions are dispelled, when misconceptions are rectified, and when those who guide are consecrated to truth and duty, the ark of the people's safety will still be discerned in the keeping of those who hold fast to the principles of true democracy.

These principles are not uncertain nor doubtful. The illustrious founder of our party has plainly announced them. They have been reasserted and followed by a long line of great political leaders, and they are quite familiar. They comprise: Equal and exact justice to all men; peace, commerce, and honest friendship with all nations—entangling alliance with none; the support of the State governments in all their rights; the preservation of the general government in its whole constitutional vigor; a jealous care of the right of election by the people; absolute acquiescence in the decisions of the majority; the supremacy of the civil over the military authority; economy in the public expenses; the honest payment of our debts and sacred preservation of the public faith; the encouragement of agriculture, and commerce as its handmaid, and freedom of religion, freedom of the press, and freedom of the person.

The great President and intrepid Democratic leader whom we especially honor to-night, who never relaxed his strict adherence to the Democratic faith nor faltered in his defense of the rights of the people against all comers, found his inspiration and guidance in these principles. On entering upon the Presidency he declared his loyalty to them; in his long and useful incumbency of that great office he gloriously illustrated their value and sufficiency; and his obedience to the doctrines of true Democracy, at all times during his public career, permitted him on his retirement to find satisfaction in the declaration: "At the moment when I surrender my last public trust, I leave this great people prosperous and happy and in the full enjoyment of liberty and peace, and honored and respected by every nation of the world.''

Parties have come and parties have gone. Even now the leaders of the party which faces in opposition the Democratic host, listen for the footsteps of that death which destroys parties false to their trust.

> Touched by thine
> The extortioner's hard hand foregoes the gold
> Wrung from the o'erworn poor.
>
> .   .   .   .   .
>
> Thou, too, dost purge from earth its horrible
> And old idolatries ; from the proud fanes,
> Each to his grave, their priests go out, till none
> Is left to teach their worship.

But there has never been a time, from Jefferson's day to the present hour, when our party did not exist, active and aggressive and prepared for heroic conflict. Not all who have followed the banner have been able by a long train of close reasoning to demonstrate, as an abstraction, why Democratic principles are best suited to their wants and the country's good; but they have known and felt that as their government was established for the people, the principles and the men nearest to the people and standing for them could be the safest trusted. Jackson has been in their eyes the incarnation of the things which Jefferson declared. If they did not understand all that Jefferson wrote, they saw and knew what Jackson did. Those who insisted upon voting for Jackson after his death felt sure that, whether their candidate was alive or dead, they were voting the ticket of true Democracy. The devoted political adherent of Jackson who, after his death, became involved in a dispute as to whether his hero had gone to Heaven or not, was prompted by Democratic instinct when he disposed of the question by declaring, ''I tell you, sir, that if Andrew Jackson has made up his mind to go to Heaven you may depend upon it he's there.'' The single Democratic voter in more than one town who, year after year, deposited his single Democratic ballot undismayed by the number of his misguided opponents, thus discharged his political duty with the utmost pride and satisfaction in his Jacksonian Democracy.

Democratic steadfastness and enthusiasm, and the satisfaction arising from our party history and traditions, certainly ought not to be discouraged.   But it is hardly safe for us because we profess the true faith, and can boast of distinguished political ancestry, to rely upon these things as guarantees of our present usefulness as a party organization, or to regard their glorification as surely making the way easy to the accomplishment of our political mission.

The Democratic party, by an intelligent study of existing conditions, should be prepared to meet all the wants of the people as they arise, and to furnish a remedy for every threatening evil.   We may well be proud of our party membership; but we cannot escape the duty which such membership imposes upon us, to urge constantly upon our fellow-citizens of this day and generation the sufficiency of the principles of true Democracy for the protection of their rights and the promotion of their welfare and happiness, in all their present diverse conditions and surroundings.

There should, of course, be no suggestion that a departure from the time-honored principles of our party is necessary to the attainment of these objects.   On the contrary, we should constantly congratulate ourselves that our party creed is broad enough to meet any emergency that can arise in the life of a free nation.

Thus, when we see the functions of government used to enrich a favored few at the expense of the many, and see also its inevitable result in the pinching privation of the poor and the profuse extravagance of the rich; and when we see in operation an unjust tariff which banishes from many humble homes the comforts of life, in order that, in the palaces of wealth, luxury may more abound, we turn to our creed and find that it enjoins "equal and exact justice to all men."

Then, if we are well grounded in our political faith, we will not be deceived, nor will we permit others to be deceived, by any plausible pretext or smooth sophistry excusing the situation. For our answer to them all, we will point to the words which condemn such inequality and injustice, as we prepare for the encounter with wrong, armed with the weapons of true Democracy.

When we see our farmers in distress, and know that they are not paying the penalty of slothfulness and mismanagement; when we see their long hours of toil so poorly requited that the money-lender eats out their substance, while for everything they need they pay a tribute to the favorites of governmental care, we know that all this is far removed from the "encouragement of agriculture" which our creed commands. We will not violate our political duty by forgetting how well entitled our farmers are to our best efforts for their restoration to the independence of a former time and to the rewards of better days.

When we see the extravagance of public expenditure fast reaching the point of reckless waste, and the undeserved distribution of public money debauching its recipients, and by pernicious example threatening the destruction of the love of frugality among our people, we will remember that "economy in the public expense" is an important article in the true Democratic faith.

When we see our political adversaries bent upon the passage of a Federal law, with the scarcely denied purpose of perpetuating partisan supremacy, which invades the States with election machinery designed to promote Federal interference with the rights of the people in the localities concerned, discrediting their honesty and fairness, and justly arousing their jealousy of centralized power, we will stubbornly resist such a dangerous and revolutionary scheme, in obedience to our pledge for "the support of the State governments in all their rights."

Under anti-Democratic encouragement we have seen a constantly increasing selfishness attach to our political affairs. **A** departure from the sound and safe theory that the people should support the government for the sake of the benefits resulting to all, has bred a sentiment manifesting itself with astounding boldness, that the government may be enlisted in the furtherance and advantage of private interests, through their willing agents in public place.   Such an abandonment of the idea of patriotic political action on the part of these interests, has naturally led to an estimate of the people's franchise so degrading that it has been openly and palpably debauched for the promotion of selfish schemes.   Money is invested in the purchase of votes with the deliberate calculation that it will yield a profitable return in results advantageous to the investor.   Another crime akin to this in motive and design is the intimidation by employers of the voters dependent upon them for work and bread.

Nothing could be more hateful to true and genuine Democracy than such offenses against our free institutions.   In several of the States the honest sentiment of the party has asserted itself, in the support of every plan proposed for the rectification of this terrible wrong.   To fail in such support would be to violate that principle in the creed of true Democracy which commands " a jealous care of the right of election by the people," for certainly no one can claim that suffrages purchased or cast under the stress of threat or intimidation represent the right of election by the people.

Since a free and unpolluted ballot must be conceded as absolutely essential to the maintenance of our free institutions, I may perhaps be permitted to express the hope that the State of Pennsylvania will not long remain behind her sister States in adopting an effective plan to protect her people's suffrage. In any event the Democracy of the State can find no justification in party principle, nor in party traditions, nor in a just apprehension of Democratic duty, for a failure earnestly to support and advocate ballot reform.

I have thus far attempted to state some of the principles of true Democracy, and their application to present conditions.

Their enduring character and their constant influence upon those who profess our faith have also been suggested. If I were now asked why they have so endured and why they have been invincible, I should reply in the words of the sentiment to which I respond: "They are enduring because they are right, and invincible because they are just."

I believe that among our people the ideas which endure, and which inspire warm attachment and devotion, are those having some elements which appeal to the moral sense. When men are satisfied that a principle is morally right, they become its adherents for all time. There is sometimes a discouraging distance between what our fellow-countrymen believe and what they do, in such a case; but their action in accordance with their belief may always be confidently expected in good time. A government for the people and by the people is everlastingly right. As surely as this is true so surely is it true that party principles which advocate the absolute equality of American manhood, and an equal participation by all the people in the management of their government, and in the benefit and protection which it affords, are also right. Here is common ground where the best educated thought and reason may meet the most impulsive and instinctive Americanism. It is right that every man should enjoy the result of his labor to the fullest extent consistent with his membership in civilized community. It is right that our government should be but the instrument of the people's will, and that its cost should be limited within the lines of strict economy. It is right that the influence of the government should be known in every humble home as the guardian of frugal comfort and content, and a defense against unjust exactions, and the unearned tribute persistently coveted by the selfish and designing. It is right that efficiency and honesty in public service should not be sacrificed to partisan greed; and it is right that the suffrage of our people should be pure and free.

The belief in these propositions, as moral truths, is nearly universal among our countrymen. We are mistaken if we suppose the time is distant when the clouds of selfishness and perversion will be dispelled and their conscientious belief will become the chief motive force in the political action of the people.

I understand all these truths to be included in the principles of true Democracy. If we have not at all times trusted as implicitly as we ought to the love our people have for the right, in political action, or if we have not always relied sufficiently upon the sturdy advocacy of the best things which belong to our party faith, these have been temporary aberrations which have furnished their inevitable warning.

We are permitted to contemplate to-night the latest demonstration of the people's appreciation of the right, and of the acceptance they accord to Democratic doctrine when honestly presented. In the campaign which has just closed with such glorious results, while party managers were anticipating the issue in the light of the continued illusion of the people, the people themselves and for themselves were considering the question of right and justice. They have spoken, and the Democracy of the land rejoice.

In the signs of the times and in the result of their late State campaign, the Democracy of Pennsylvania must find hope and inspiration. Nowhere has the sensitiveness of the people, on questions involving right and wrong, been better illustrated than here. At the head of your State government there will soon stand a disciple of true Democracy, elected by voters who would have the right and not the wrong when their consciences were touched. Though there have existed here conditions and influences not altogether favorable to an unselfish apprehension of the moral attributes of political doctrine, I believe that if these features of the principles of true Democracy are persistently advocated, the time will speedily come when, as in a day, the patriotic hearts of the people of your great Commonwealth will be stirred to the support of our cause.

It remains to say that, in the midst of our rejoicing and in the time of party hope and expectation, we should remember that the way of right and justice should be followed as a matter of duty and regardless of immediate success. Above all things let us not for a moment forget that grave responsibilities await the party which the people trust; and let us look for guidance to the principles of true Democracy, which "are enduring because they are right, and invincible because they are just."

VI.

At the Democratic Club, New York, April 13, 1891.

MR. PRESIDENT AND GENTLEMEN:

I desire, first of all, to express my thanks to the promoters of this occasion, for the pleasure which a place in this goodly company affords me, and to congratulate the Democratic Club upon the indication of prosperity and enterprise supplied by its ownership of this beautiful and commodious house. The maintenance of such a center for the cultivation and dissemination of true Democratic principles, together with the activity and earnestness of members of the club, furnish the most gratifying evidence that those who abide here fully realize the value and importance of unremitting political endeavor and thorough organization in behalf of true Democracy.

It seems to me that the atmosphere which pervades this place is ill-suited to selfish and ignoble designs; and I feel at this moment that I am surrounded by influences which invite patriotic partisanship and disinterested devotion to party principles. This sensation is most agreeable—for I am glad to be called a partisan if my partisanship is patriotic. If a partisan is correctly defined as "one who is violently and passionately devoted to a party or interest," I must plead guilty to the charge of being a Democratic partisan, so long as the Democracy is true to its creed and traditions, and so long as conditions exist which, to my understanding, make adherence to its doctrines synonymous with patriotism.

It is a glorious thing to belong to a party which has a history beginning with the first years of our government, and full of achievements interwoven with all that has made our country great and kept our people free. It is an inspiring thing to know that by virtue of our party membership we are associated with those who resist the attempt of arrogant political power to interfere with the independence and integrity of popular suffrage, who are determined to relieve our countrymen from unjust and unnecessary burdens, who are intent upon checking extravagance in public expenditures, and who test party purposes by their usefulness in promoting the interests and welfare of all the people of the land.

These considerations furnish to those who love their country the highest and best incentives to constant and faithful effort in the cause of true Democracy.

We are reminded on this occasion that we not only have a proud history and glorious traditions, but that our party had an illustrious founder, whose services and teachings have done as much to justify and make successful our government by the people and for the people, as any American who ever lived. A claim to such political ancestry is, of itself, sufficient to lend honor and pride to membership in a party which preserves in their vigor and purity the principles of that Democracy which was established by Thomas Jefferson.

These principles were not invented for the purpose of gaining popular assent for a day, nor only because they were useful in the early time of the Republic. They were not announced for the purpose of serving personal ambitions, nor merely for the purpose of catching the suffrages of the people. They were laid as deep and broad as the truths upon which the fabric of our government rested. In the spirit of prophecy, they were formulated and declared, not only as suited to the experiments of a new government, but as sufficient in every struggle and every emergency which should beset popular rule, in all times to come and in all stages of our country's growth and development.

The political revolution which accompanied the birth of our party was not accomplished while the principles of Democracy were kept laid away in a napkin, nor was the unanimity of their first acceptance secured by the senseless and noisy shouting of partisan bigotry and the refusal to receive converts to the faith. No man believed more implicitly in the political instruction of the people than the great founder of our party; and the first triumph of Democratic principles, under his leadership, was distinctly the result of a campaign of education. So, too, in the light of our last great victory, no man who desires Democratic success will deny the supreme importance of a most thorough and systematic presentation to our fellow-citizens of the reasons which support the avowed and accepted purposes of our party. Those who now sneer at efforts in that direction are our enemies—whether they confront us as confessed opponents, or whether they are traitors skulking within our camp.

It seems to me that this is peculiarly a time when the Democratic party should be mindful of its relations to the country, of its responsibilities as the guardian of sacred principles, and of its duty to a confiding people. In the rejoicing which success permits, let us remember that the mission of our party is continued warfare. We cannot accomplish what we promise to the people if we allow ourselves to be diverted from the perils which are still in our way. Blindness to danger, and neglect of party organization and discipline, are invitations to defeat. We cannot win permanent and substantial success by putting aside principle and grasping after temporary expedients. We shall court disaster if we relax industry in commending to the intelligence of our countrymen the creed which we profess; and we tempt humiliating failure and disgrace when we encourage or tolerate those who, claiming fellowship with us, needlessly and often from the worst of motives, seek to stir up strife and sow discord in the councils of our party.

As we celebrate to-night the birthday of the father of

Democracy, let us reinforce our Democratic zeal and enthusiasm and renew our faith and trust in the aroused intelligence of our countrymen. Let the reflections prompted by the surroundings of this occasion, confirm us in the assurance that we shall patriotically discharge our political duty and well maintain our party loyalty, if in all we do as Democrats we bravely and consistently hold fast to the truths which illumine the path laid out by our great guide and leader.

VII.

Before the "Cleveland Democracy" at Buffalo, N. Y., May 12, 1891.

MR. PRESIDENT AND GENTLEMEN:

As I stand for the first time face to face with the Cleveland Democracy, I experience mingled emotions of responsibility and pride. My sense of responsibility arises from my relation to your organization as its godfather, and my pride from the noble manner in which you have borne my name. I acknowledge your right to require of me at this time an account of the manner in which I have kept the political faith to which you are devoted. This right grows out of the fact that the word "Democracy," as it stands in the name of your organization, means so much and is so worthy of your care, that its significance should not be in the least clouded by any prefix which is not in keeping with Democratic aims and purposes.

In giving an account of my political behavior, I can only offer a record of political conduct familiar to all my countrymen, and supplement this record by the declaration that I have done the best I could to deserve the confidence in me which you have so gracefully manifested. For the character of the record thus presented, you yourselves are answerable with me —for it has been made under the influence and encouragement of the sentiments and doctrines which the Cleveland Democracy have cultivated and enforced. When we started together in political life and responsibility, your accepted creed taught that politics was something more than adroit jugglery; that there was still such a thing as official duty, and that it meant obligation to the people ; that the principles of our government were worthy of conscientious study ; and that the doctrines of true Democracy, honestly and bravely enforced, promised the greatest good to all our countrymen, and exacted, through the length and breadth of our land, impartial governmental care and indiscriminating justice.

You were not content to allow these truths to remain with you as mere idle beliefs. They supplied constant and aggressive motives for your political activity and were your inspiration as you went forth to do battle in the Democratic cause, resting your hope of triumph upon an unwavering faith in the thoughtful and well-informed intelligence of the American people.

Thus you were found doing valiant service in the campaign of education. As the smoke of the last stubbornly fought battle cleared away, no soldiers on the field were found surrounded by more trophies of victory than the forces of the Cleveland Democracy.

Surely your rewards are most abundant. You have not only aided in the advancement of the Democratic standard, but you have also contributed your full share in demonstrating that the people can be trusted when aroused to thoughtfulness and duty.

When I suggest to you that much sturdy fighting still awaits all those enlisted in the Democratic ranks, I feel that I am speaking to veterans who have no fear of hard campaigning. We may be sure that unless we continue active, watchful warfare, we shall lose what we have gained in the people's cause. Insidious schemes are started on every side to allure them to their undoing. Awakened to a sense of wrong and injustice, promises of redress and benefit are held up to their sight, ''like

Dead Sea fruits, that tempt the eye but turn to ashes on the lips." The selfish and designing will not forego the struggle, but will constantly seek to regain their vantage ground through tempting fallacies and plausible pretexts of friendliness.

I believe the most threatening figure which to-day stands in the way of the safety of our government and the happiness of our people, is reckless and wicked extravagance in our public expenditures. It is the most fatal of all the deadly brood born of governmental perversion. It hides beneath its wings the betrayal of the people's trust, and holds powerless in its fascinating glance the people's will and conscience. It brazenly exhibits to-day a Billion Dollar Congress. But lately, a large surplus remained in the people's public treasury after meeting all expenditures, then by no means economical. This condition was presented to the American people as positive proof that their burden of taxation was unjust because unnecessary; and yet, while the popular protest is still heard, the harpy of Public Extravagance devours the surplus and impudently calls upon its staggering victims to bring still larger supplies within the reach of its insatiate appetite. A few short years ago a pension roll amounting to fifty-three millions of dollars was willingly maintained by our patriotic citizens. To-day, Public Extravagance decrees that three times that sum shall be drawn from the people, upon the pretext that its expenditure represents the popular love of the soldier. Not many years ago a river and harbor bill, appropriating eleven millions of dollars, gave rise to a loud popular protest. Now, Public Extravagance commands an appropriation of twenty-two millions for the same purposes, and the people are silent. To-day, millions are paid for barefaced subsidy; and this is approved or condoned at the behest of Public Extravagance, and thus a new marauder is turned loose, which, in company with its vicious tariff partner, bears pilfered benefit to the households of favored selfish interests.

We need not prolong the details. Turn where we will, we see the advance of this devouring and destructive creature,

Our Democratic faith teaches us that the useless exaction of money from the people, upon the false pretext of public necessity, is the worst of all governmental perversions, and involves the greatest of all dangers to our guarantees of justice and equity. We need not unlearn this lesson to apprehend the fact that behind the fact that such exaction, and as its source of existence, is found Public Extravagance. The ax will not be laid at the root of the unwholesome tariff tree, with its vicious inequality and injustice, until we reach and destroy its parent and support.

But the growth of Public Extravagance in these latter days, and its unconcealed and dreadful manifestations, force us to the contemplation of other crimes, of which it is undoubtedly guilty, besides unjust exactions from the people.

Our government is so ordained that its lifeblood flows from the virtue and patriotism of our people, and its health and strength depend upon the integrity and faithfulness of their public servants. If these are destroyed, our government, if it endures, will endure only in name, failing to bless those for whom it was created, and failing in its mission as an example to mankind.

Public Extravagance, in its relation to inequitable tariff laws, not only lays an unjust tribute upon the people, but is responsible for unfair advantages bestowed upon special and favored interests as the price of partisan support. Thus the exercise of the popular will, for the benefit of the country at large, is replaced by sordid and selfish motives directed to personal advantage, while the encouragement of such motives, in public place for party ends, deadens the official conscience.

Public Extravagance directly distributes gifts and gratuities among the people, whose toleration of waste is thus secured, or whose past party services are thus compensated, or who are thus bribed to future party support. This makes the continuance of partisan power a stronger motive among public servants than the faithful discharge of the people's trust, and sows the seeds of contagious corruption in the body politic.

But to my mind, the saddest and most frightful result of Public Extravagance is seen in the readiness of the masses of our people, who are not dishonest, but only heedless, to accustom themselves to that dereliction in public place which it involves. Evidence is thus furnished that our countrymen are in danger of losing the scrupulous insistence upon the faithful discharge of duty on the part of their public servants, the regard for economy and frugality which belongs to sturdy Americanism, the independence which relies upon personal endeavor, and the love of an honest and well-regulated government, all of which lie at the foundation of our free institutions.

Have I overstated the evils and dangers with which the tremendous growth of Public Extravagance threatens us? Every man who loves his country well enough to pause and think of these things must know that I have not.

Let us, then, as we push on in our campaign of education, especially impress upon our countrymen the lesson which teaches that Public Extravagance is a deadly, dangerous thing, that frugality and economy are honorable, that the virtue and watchfulness of the people are the surest safeguards against abuses in their government, and that those who profess to serve their fellow-citizens in public place must be faithful to their trust.

VIII.

Before the Business Men's Democratic Association, New York, January 8, 1892.

Mr. President and Gentlemen:

No one can question the propriety of the celebration of this day by the organization whose invitation has called us together. Its right to celebrate on this occasion results from the fact that it is an organization attached to the doctrines of true Democracy, having a membership composed of business men, who, in a disinterested way, devote themselves to honest party work, and who labor for the growth and spread of the political principles which they profess.

This anniversary has not gained its place as a festival day in the calendar of Democracy by chance or through unmeaning caprice; nor is it observed by the Democratic party merely because a battle was fought on the 8th day of January, many years ago, at New Orleans. That battle in itself had no immediate political significance, and, considered solely as a military achievement in comparison with many other battles fought by Americans both before and since, it need not be regarded as an event demanding especial commemoration.

The Democratic zest and enthusiasm of our celebration of the day grow out of the fact that the battle of New Orleans was won under the generalship of Andrew Jackson. So, while the successful general in that battle is not forgotten to-night, Democrats, wherever they are assembled throughout our land to celebrate the day, are honoring the hero who won the battles of Democracy, and are commemorating the political courage and steadfastness which were his prominent characteristics.

It is well that there are occasions like this where we may manifest that love and affection for Andrew Jackson which have a place in every Democratic heart. It is needless to attempt an explanation of this love and affection. They are Democratic instincts. So strong is our conviction that Jackson's Democracy derived its strength and vigor from the steadfast courage, the honesty of purpose and the sturdy persistency which characterized the man, that we willingly profess the belief that these same conditions are essential to the usefulness and success of the Democratic party in these latter days. Thus, wherever party principle or policy may lead us, we have constantly before us an unquestioned example of the spirit in which our work should be undertaken.

It may not be unprofitable for us, at this time, to recall some incidents in the career of Andrew Jackson, and note their bearing upon the position of our party in its present relations to the people. We may thus discover an incentive for the cultivation and preservation of that Jacksonian spirit which ought to belong to Democratic effort.

When General Jackson was sent with troops to protect our border against disturbers of the peace whose retreat was in the Spanish province of Florida, he notified our government that if it was signified to him that the possession of the Floridas would be desirable to the United States, it should be forthwith accomplished. He only believed he had the assent of his government, but in that belief, and because his word had been given, he never rested until his military occupation of the territory was complete.

The Democratic party has lately declared to the people that if it was trusted and invested with power, their burdens of taxation should be lightened, and that a better and more just distribution of benefits should be assured to them. There is no doubt concerning our commission from the people to do this work, and there is no doubt that we have received their trust and confidence on the faith of our promises. In these circumstances, there is no sign of Jacksonian determination and persistency in faltering or hesitating in the cause we have undertaken. If we accepted the trust and confidence of the people with any other design than to respond fully to them, we have been dishonored from the beginning. If we accepted them in good faith, disgrace and humiliation await us if we relax our efforts before the promised end is reached.

At New Orleans General Jackson attacked the enemy as soon as they landed, and fought against their making the least advance. It never occurred to him that by yielding to them a foot of ground, or giving them a moment's rest, his opportunity to defeat them would be promoted.

We, who are proud to call ourselves Jacksonian Democrats, have boldly and aggressively attacked a political heresy opposed to the best interests of the people and defended by an arrogant and unscrupulous party. The fight is still on. Who has the hardihood to say that we can lay claim to the least

Jacksonian spirit if in the struggle we turn our backs to the enemy, or lower in the least our colors?

President Jackson believed the United States Bank was an institution dangerous to the liberties and prosperity of the people. Once convinced of this, his determination to destroy it closely followed. He early began the attack, utterly regardless of any considerations of political expediency or personal advancement except as they grew out of his faith in the people, and giving no place in his calculations for any estimate of the difficulty of the undertaking. From the time the first blow was struck until the contest ended in his complete triumph, he allowed nothing to divert him from his purpose, and permitted no other issue to divide his energy or to be substituted for that on which he was intent.

The Democratic party of to-day, which conjures with the name of Jackson, has also attacked a monstrous evil, intrenched behind a perversion of governmental power and guarded by its selfish beneficiaries. On behalf of those among our people long neglected, we have insisted on tariff reform and an abandonment of unjust favoritism. We have thus adopted an issue great enough to deserve the undivided efforts of our party, involving considerations which, we profess to believe, lie at the foundation of the justice and fairness of popular rule.

If we are to act upon our declared belief in the power of that Jacksonian spirit which was the inspiration of our party in the days of our great leader, we shall be steadfast to the issue we have raised until it is settled and rightly settled. The steadfastness we need will not permit a premature and distracting search for other and perplexing questions, nor will it allow us to be tempted or driven by the enemy into new and tangled paths.

We have given pledges to the people, and they have trusted us. Unless we have outgrown the Democratic spirit of Jackson's time, our duty is plain. Our promise was not merely to labor in the people's cause until we should tire of the effort, or should discover a way which seemed to promise easier and quicker party ascendency. The service we undertook was not to advise those waiting for better days that their cause was hopeless, nor under any pretext to suggest a cessation of effort. Our engagement was to labor incessantly, bravely, and stubbornly, seeing nothing and considering nothing but ultimate success. These pledges and promises should be faithfully and honestly kept. Party faithlessness is party dishonor.

Nor is the sacredness of our pledges, and the party dishonor that would follow their violation, all we have to consider. We cannot trifle with our obligations to the people without exposure and disaster. We ourselves have aroused a spirit of jealous inquiry and discrimination touching political conduct which cannot be blinded; and the people will visit with quick revenge the party which betrays them.

I hope, then, I may venture to claim in this assemblage that, even if there had been but slight encouragement for the cause we have espoused, there would still be no justification for timidity and faint-heartedness. But with the success we have already achieved, amounting to a political revolution, it seems to me that it would be the height of folly, considered purely as a question of party management, to relax in the least our determination and persistency. If we suspect, anywhere in our counsels, compromising hesitation or a disposition to divert the unity of party efforts, let us be watchful. The least retreat bodes disaster; cowardice is often called conservatism, and an army scattered into sections invites defeat.

We have preached the doctrine that honesty and sincerity should be exacted from political parties. Let us not fall under the condemnation which awaits on shifty schemes and insincere professions.

I believe our countrymen are prepared to act on principle, and in no mood for political maneuvering. They will not waste time in studying conundrums, guessing riddles, or trying to interpret doubtful phrases. They demand a plain and simple statement of political purpose.

Above all things, political finesse should not lead us to forget that, at the end of our plans, we must meet face to face at the polls the voters of the land, with ballots in their hands, demanding as a condition of their support of our party fidelity and undivided devotion to the cause in which we have enlisted them.

If, inspired by the true Jacksonian spirit, we hold to the doctrine that party honesty is party duty and party courage is party expediency, we shall win a sure and lasting success through the deserved support of a discriminating, intelligent, and thoughtful people.

IX.

To a Political Rally, in Columbus, O.

EXECUTIVE MANSION,
ALBANY, September 24, 1884.

MY DEAR SIR:

I very much regret that the pressure of official duties will prevent my joining you at the meeting to be held in Columbus on the 25th inst. I hope the meeting will be a complete success, and that it will be the means of increasing the enthusiasm already aroused for the cause of good government.

I believe that the voters of the country are fully alive to the necessity of installing an administration of public affairs which shall be truly their own, not only because it is the result of their choice, but because its selected instrumentalities are directly from the body of the people and impressed with the people's thoughts and sentiments. They are tired, I think, of a rule so long continued that it has bred and fostered a class standing between them and their political action, and whose interest in affairs ends with partisan zeal and the advancement of personal advantage.

Let me remind the people that if they seek to make their public servants feel their direct responsibility to them, and be careful of their interests, their objects will not be accomplished by blind adherence to the party which has grown arrogant with long-continued power. Let me impress upon the people that the issue involved in the pending canvass is the establishment of a pure and honest administration of their government. Let me show them the way to this and warn them against any cunningly designed effort to lead them into other paths of irrelevant discussion.

With these considerations before them, and with an earnest presentation of our claims to the confidence of the people and of their responsibility, we need not fear the result of their intelligent action.

Yours very truly,

GROVER CLEVELAND.

ALLEN G. THURMAN,
  COLUMBUS, O.

X.

To the " Cleveland Democracy," Buffalo, N. Y.

EXECUTIVE MANSION,
WASHINGTON, D. C., September 30, 1885.

MY DEAR SIR:

Please accept my thanks for the pamphlet you sent me containing papers read before the Cleveland Democracy of Buffalo. The collection gives excellent proof of the amount and value of the work already done by the organization. I know of nothing which could better engage the endeavor of such an association than its declared objects—"to foster and disseminate Democratic principles" and "to promote and secure the political education and Democratic fellowship of its members."

A marked improvement in our politics must follow, I think, a better understanding of the reasons for the existence of parties, and a clearer apprehension of their relations to the welfare of the country and the prosperity of our people. Membership in a party might well rest less upon a blind, unreflecting enthusiasm for a certain continued partisan companionship and the hope of personal reward and advantage, and more upon a deliberate attachment to well-defined and understood party principles. And this better condition is to be realized largely as the result of such work as the Cleveland Democracy has undertaken.

The Democratic cause need have no fear of the most complete discussion of its principles; and the history of its great leaders and their achievements cannot fail to inspire the members of the party with pride and veneration. It is well in these latter days to turn back often and read of the faith which the founders of our party had in the people—how exactly they apprehended their needs and with what lofty aims and purposes they sought the public good.

The object of your organization should arouse the zeal and continuous effort of every member; and its usefulness should insure its encouragement and prosperity.

Yours sincerely,
GROVER CLEVELAND.

HERBERT P. BISSELL, ESQ., *President.*

XI.

To the President of the National Association of Clubs.

EXECUTIVE MANSION,
WASHINGTON, September 14, 1888.

CHAUNCEY F. BLACK, *President, etc.*

MY DEAR SIR : The papers which you kindly sent for my perusal, touching the scope, method, and purpose of the Association of Democratic Clubs, have strengthened my belief in the extreme importance of such organizations as have been thus associated.

The struggle upon which we have entered is in behalf of the people—the plain people of the land—and they must be reached. We do not proceed upon the theory that they are to be led by others who may or may not be in sympathy with their interests. We have undertaken to teach the voters as free, independent citizens, intelligent enough to insist upon their rights, interested enough to insist upon being treated justly, and patriotic enough to desire their country's welfare.

Thus this campaign is one of information and organization. Every citizen should be regarded as a thoughtful, responsible voter, and he should be furnished the means of examining the issues involved in the pending canvass for himself.

I am convinced that no agency is so effective to this end as the clubs which have been formed, permeating all parts of the country and making their influence felt in every neighborhood. By a systematic effort they make the objects of the Democratic party understood, by the fair and calm discussion of the Democratic position in this contest, among those with whom their members daily come in contact; and by preventing a neglect of the duty of suffrage on election day, these clubs will become, in my opinion, the most important instrumentality yet devised for promoting the success of our party.

Yours very truly,

GROVER CLEVELAND.

XII.

To the Democratic Societies of Pennsylvania.

NEW YORK, October 11, 1889.

MY DEAR SIR:

I am sorry that I shall not be able to be in Philadelphia at the General Assembly of the Democratic Societies of Pennsylvania on the 15th inst., and cannot, therefore, attend the meeting which will follow that assembly.

My estimate of the value of these Democratic Societies as agencies for the instruction of the people upon political topics and for the accomplishment of legitimate political work is well known, and there never was a time when, in the interests of good government and national prosperity, they were more needed.

The condition of political affairs is such that the attention of all true Democrats should be directed to the enforcement of the distinctive principles of the party; and in my opinion this is no time for the search after makeshifts and temporary expedients.

We, as a party, are fairly enlisted in the cause of the people, and patriotism, duty, and party success require that we should be constant and steadfast. All personal and selfish aims should be subordinated.

I confidently expect that in the work we have in hand our Democratic societies will exhibit an efficiency which will be gratefully acknowledged by all who have at heart the welfare and prosperity of the American people.

Yours very sincerely,
GROVER CLEVELAND.

CHAUNCEY F. BLACK.

XIII.

To the New York Convention of Democratic Clubs.

NEW YORK, October 21, 1889.

DEAR SIR:

I am in receipt of your invitation to attend the Convention of New York State Democratic Clubs to be held at the Hoffman House on the 22d inst.

I am glad that you were considerate enough of my situation and feelings to give me an opportunity to infer from your note that my failure to accept your invitation would neither cause great disappointment nor be construed as indicating any lack of interest in the work which the clubs represented in the league have undertaken.

These organizations had their origin in the heat and activity of a Presidential election, which furnishes plenty of that enthusiasm upon which political organizations easily subsist. While they are certainly very useful at such a time, it must be conceded that the noise and excitement of a campaign are not conducive to the accomplishment of missionary work or the effective dissemination of political truth. This most important work can better be done in more quiet surroundings, though usually it is not then so easy to maintain political associations.

It has been too often the case, if it may not be said to be the rule, that political clubs, whatever their declarations of perpetuity may have been, have only lived during the campaign in which they had their birth, and only performed temporary campaign work. I am very much pleased to learn that the League of New York Democratic Clubs intends to make the organizations of which it is composed permanent agencies for spreading and illustrating the doctrines of the Democratic party at all times and in all circumstances.

In making this effort the league is to be congratulated upon the fact that the principles of Democracy occupy at this time a larger place than they lately have in the consideration of the party. The study and propagation of these principles afford strong inducements to associated effort, and, what is better, these efforts are invested with a value and importance as great as the prosperity of our land, and as broad in their beneficence as the welfare of all our people.

I look to the ascendency of the principles upon which true Democracy rests, which will be greatly aided by the activity of leagues such as yours to secure us from wasting extravagance, from demagogic pretense, from sectional bitterness, and from the widespread corruption of our suffrage. Could labor and effort have greater or higher incentives than the accomplishment of these results ?   Yours very truly,

                                        GROVER CLEVELAND.

XIV.

To the Democracy of Kings County, N. Y.

                                        45 WILLIAM STREET,
                                NEW YORK, October 30, 1889.
DEAR SIR :

I have received your invitation, tendered on behalf of the Democratic organization of Kings County, to attend and address a mass meeting of the Democracy of the county on the evening of Friday, the 1st day of November.

You are quite right in suggesting that I am too well acquainted with the Democracy of Kings County to make necessary any assurance of the sincerity and earnestness of this invitation ; and I confess that it is difficult for me to decline the courtesy or disappoint the wishes of such kind party friends.

I cannot, however, quite satisfy myself that I ought, by accepting your invitation, to depart from the course which I have followed in all similar cases.

I know how ably the speakers who address the meeting will present the topics which are prominent in the canvass, and how well the claims of our candidates to public confidence will be advocated.

The thought which is uppermost in my mind leads me to suggest that this is a time for the Democrats of our State to guard against the indifference and lack of activity which are apt to result from the reaction of a recent Presidential campaign, and which, also, too often exist when the grade and character of the offices to be filled are not such as inspire the greatest party enthusiasm.

We should constantly bear in mind that every election involving Democratic principles is important to our party, and that indifference should not be permitted to invite defeat when fit and worthy men and true Democrats are presented as candidates for public office.

In the pending campaign, though the canvass has to do with State policy and State offices, it cannot be denied that it is also related in an important way to fundamental party principles ; and it should be our pleasure, as it is our duty, to give active and earnest support to the worthy and honest men, and the tried and true members of the Democratic party who are our candidates.

I hope that your mass meeting may be the means of arousing that Democratic activity, watchfulness, and enthusiasm which will insure Democratic success.

Yours very truly,

GROVER CLEVELAND.

JOHN P. ADAMS, Esq., *President, etc.*

XV.

To the Young Men's Democratic Club at Canton, O.

NEW YORK, November 22, 1889.

DEAR SIR:

I am pleased with the invitation you extend to Mrs. Cleveland and myself to be present at the anniversary meeting of the Young Men's Democratic Club on the 5th day of December. If the exercises you contemplate and outline in your letter are carried out, all who attend them are certainly promised a rare exposition of sound doctrine from the eloquent and able speakers you have secured. I am sorry that, owing to other engagements, we must be among the absent ones.

The spirit and tone of your letter, so far as it relates to the purposes of your club, are very gratifying. The constantly growing interest manifested by our young men in the principles of the Democratic party constitute, in my opinion, the most reliable hope of their ascendency. If, at any time in the past, it has with any truth been said that our party did not invite to its standard the enterprising and thoughtful young men of the country, to-day such an allegation shall be disputed.

And these men, keenly alive to their country's welfare, quick to discover the needs of the present, and ready, in the freedom of untrammeled thought, to follow in the pathway of good citizenship, can be safely trusted with political responsibilities. Hoping your meeting will be very successful, I am

Yours truly,

GROVER CLEVELAND,

XVI.

To the Tammany Society's Fourth of July Celebrations.

I.

MARION, MASS., June 30, 1890.

DEAR SIR:

My absence from the city of New York, and plans which I have already made, prevent my acceptance of the courteous invitation which I have received to attend the celebration by the Tammany Society of the one hundred and fourteenth anniversary of American independence.

The celebration contemplated by your ancient and time-honored organization will, it seems to me, fall short in the impressiveness due to the occasion if it does not persistently present and emphasize the idea that the Declaration of Independence was the protest of honest and sturdy men against the wrongs and oppressions of misgovernment. The reasons and justification for their revolt are exhibited in their recital of a long list of grievous instances of maladministration. They complained that their interests had been so neglected, and their rights as lawful subjects so violated, under British rule, that they were absolved from further fealty.

Our fathers, in establishing a new government upon the will of the people and consecrated to their care and just protection, could not prescribe limitations which would deny to political parties its conduct and administration. The opportunities and the temptations, thus necessarily presented to partisanship, have brought us to a time when party control is far too arrogant and bitter, and when, in public place, the true interests of the country are too lightly considered.

In this predicament, those who love their country may well remember, with comfort and satisfaction, on Independence Day, that the disposition of the American people to revolt against maladministration still remains to them, and is the badge of their freedom and independence, as well as their security for continued prosperity and happiness.

They will not revolt against their plan of government, for its protection and preservation supply every inspiration of true Americanism. But because they are free and independent American citizens, they will, as long as their love and veneration for their government shall last, revolt against the domination of any political party which, intrusted with power, sordidly seeks only its continuance, and which, faithlessly violating its plain and simple duty to the people, insults them with professions of disinterested solicitude while it eats out their substance.

And yet, with all this, we should not in blind security deny the existence of danger. The masses of our countrymen are brave and therefore generous; they are strong and therefore confident, and they are honest and therefore unsuspecting. Our peril lies in the ease with which they may be deluded and cajoled by those who would traffic with their interests.

No occasion is more opportune than the celebration of the one hundred and fourteenth anniversary of American independence to warn the American people of the present necessity on their part of a vigilant watchfulness of their rights and a jealous exaction of honest and unselfish performance of public duty.   Yours very truly,

GROVER CLEVELAND.

ABRAM B. TAPPEN, *Grand Sachem.*

2.

BUZZARD'S BAY, MASS., July 1, 1891.

DEAR SIR:

I am unable to accept your courteous invitation to be present at the celebration, by the Tammany Society, of the one hundred and fifteenth anniversary of American independence.

I should be glad to participate in the celebration which your society contemplates, and I hope the design of its promoters to make the occasion one "of exceptional significance and extended effects," will be fully realized.

Our American holiday cannot be appropriately celebrated without recalling the immense cost and the transcendent value of our national independence, and awakening and reserving in our hearts that spirit of patriotism which is the foundation of our independence and the security of our life as a nation.

Every American citizen should, on that day, consecrate himself anew to an unqualified allegiance to his government, and should soberly realize that no social or political relation in life can be worthily maintained unless it embraces an unselfish love of country.

Your time-honored association justly claims a proud history of devotion to a political party which has always insisted upon the integrity of our free institutions, and which has at all times professed to champion the rights of the people. I am, therefore, certain that the Tammany Society, in its celebration of Independence Day, will not fail to emphasize the truth that political organizations can only be valuable, and party efforts can only promise success, when they have for their purpose and inspiration the broadest and purest patriotism.

Yours very truly,

GROVER CLEVELAND.

THOMAS F. GILROY, *Grand Sachem.*

XVII.

To the Young Men's Democratic Association, Canton, O.

NEW YORK, November 25, 1890.

I thank you for the invitation I have just received to meet with the members of the Young Men's Democratic Club at Canton to rejoice over the late Democratic victory. I am sorry to say that it will be impossible for me to be present on the occasion you contemplate, but I hope that it will be full of enthusiasm and congratulation.

And yet may I not suggest one sober thought which should constantly be in our minds? Our late success is, of course, the triumph of Democratic principles, but that success was made possible by the co-operation of many who are not to be considered as irrevocably and under all circumstances members of our party.   They trusted us and allied themselves with us in the late struggle because they saw that those with whom they had acted politically were heedless of the interests of the country and untrue to the people.

We have still to convince them that Democracy means something more than mere management for party success and a partisan distribution of benefits after success.   This can only be done by insisting that in the conduct of our party, principles touching the public welfare shall be placed above spoils, and this is the sentiment of the masses of the Democratic party to-day.   They are disinterested and patriotic, and they should not be misrepresented by the tricks of those who would not scruple to use the party name for selfish purposes.

I do not say that there is danger of this; but I am convinced that our duty to those who have trusted us consists in pushing on, continually and vigorously, the principles in the advocacy of which we have triumphed, and thus superseding all that is ignoble and unworthy.   In this way we shall place our party on solid ground and confirm the people in the hope that we strive for their welfare, and, following this course, we shall deserve and achieve further success.

Yours very truly,
Grover Cleveland.

XVIII.

To the Cleveland Club, Atlanta, Ga.

New York, February 29, 1892.

My Dear Sir:

I will not attempt to conceal the gratification afforded me by the message you transmit from the Cleveland Club of Atlanta. I have received so many manifestations of friendliness from the people of Atlanta that I cherish toward them the warmest gratitude and liveliest affection.

I cannot say that I am certain I deserve all the laudation contained in the resolutions of your club.   I can say, however, that I find a sense of great satisfaction in the reflection that I have been permitted to aid somewhat in restoring to the people, in a large section of our country, their standing and position in our common American citizenship, not nominally and barrenly, but substantially and potentially.

For whatever I have done in this direction I have abundant reward in the prosperity of your people, which doubles our national prosperity; in the cheerful co-operation of your people, which insures a lasting national brotherhood; and in the appreciation by your people of all that has been done in their behalf.

After all, I look upon these beneficent accomplishments as resulting from the appreciation of true Democratic doctrines, and I believe that one who in public place submits himself to their guidance will find it easy to do justice and to subserve the interests of all his fellow-countrymen.

Yours very truly,
GROVER CLEVELAND.

CHAPTER XII.

I.

Serenade Speech from Balcony of Buffalo Democratic Club upon his Nomination for Governor, September 22, 1882.

MY FRIENDS:

I am sure there will be nothing for me to do in the campaign upon which we have just entered that will so appeal to my feelings, and about which I will have to take so much care, as in addressing you this evening. I must be careful what I say, or the recollections of the past and the appreciation of your esteem will quite overcome me.

I can but remember to-night the time when I came among you, friendless, unknown, and poor. I can but remember how, step by step, by the encouragement of my good fellow-citizens, I have gone on to receive more of their appreciation than is my due, until I have been honored with more distinction, perhaps, than I deserve. The position of Mayor of this great and proud city ought to be enough to satisfy the most ambitious. The position of Mayor, backed and supported as it is by every good citizen, I am sure, should satisfy any man, and it would seem almost grasping to wish for a higher honor. The promise of the future that is before me is somewhat saddened and dimmed by the reflection that, if carried out, I should have to leave my good friends of Buffalo to enter upon another sphere of activity.

Bear in mind, gentlemen, that whatever may come in the future, the people of Buffalo and all their kindnesses to me will ever have the warmest place in a grateful heart.

The event of to-day is an event which appeals to the local pride of us all, and I should be too vain to live with—too vain to be of any comfort to my friends—if I did not fully appreciate the fact that this splendid ovation is not altogether on account of personal preference. You are here to support a cause—a great cause, and while you may fully appreciate that a fellow-citizen is to bear aloft the banner of Democracy in this campaign, you are to remember that he is the standard-bearer in a cause that is dear to the people and in which all their interests are involved. You are to support it because you struggle for principles the ascendency of which will bring happiness, peace, and prosperity to the people.

It is fitting that the campaign should begin here at these club rooms, where, perhaps, more than in any other place, my candidacy was started and has been fostered. I wish that those valiant old soldiers—call them old men and old boys, if you will—were here to-night to enjoy with us the fruit of our labors.

Here we begin! Let us not believe that because local pride and preference urge us on and the prospect looks bright—let us not think that the battle is to be won without a great struggle. On the one side we are to fight in the interest of the people against a power upheld by a National Administration, and it will take the strongest effort to shake off its vise-like grip.

Remember that all the means and money at the command of the Administration are to be put into play against us.

Remember that New York is the battle ground of 1884.

Do not be cajoled into the belief that because we are confident here—because my neighbors are enthusiastic in my support—that this is going to win the day. Remember that this is a large State and one which is regarded as the key to an important position.

Off then with our coats! We must labor as we never did before, and not for personal preferences but for the great cause in which we are enlisted.

II.

Serenade Speech at Albany, October 12, 1883.

FELLOW-CITIZENS :

I am very much gratified by this remembrance of me in the middle of the rejoicing which to-night gladdens the hearts of the members of the party to which I am glad to belong. I do not for a moment attribute this demonstration and the compliment of the serenade to any other cause than the inclination of my party friends, at such a time as this, to congratulate each other on this occasion. Official place and public position may be laid aside, for a moment, while, as fellow-members of a party which has achieved a victory, we mingle our joy and exultation. We celebrate to-night a victory in a most important field, and a victory which gives us an earnest of a much greater yet to come. We look with pride and joy to the achievement of our brethren in a sister State, and yield to them all the praise and admiration which their gallantry and courage claim.

The first battle in the great campaign of 1884 has been fought and won. Ohio in the van calls on us to follow. What shall the answer be? The Democracy of New York sends back the ringing assurance that we are on the way, and in a few short days will be at her side, bearing glorious trophies. This is not an idle boast, full of temporary enthusiasm, nor the voice of blind partisan zeal. We shall succeed because we deserve success, because the people are just, and because we bear high aloft the banner of their rights. We know full well the need of watchfulness and effort, and we shall not fail to appreciate that neglect and slothfulness are a betrayal of our trust.

I congratulate most sincerely every true Democrat in the State of New York that the cause in which he is enlisted is so worthy of his best efforts, and that the candidates chosen to lead in the contest so well represent his cause. The convention which selected, for the Democratic party, the men now

presented to the people of the State for their suffrages had before it other men, any of whom the party would have delighted
to honor ; but a choice was to be made, and that it was well
and fairly made I fully believe. The charge or insinuation in
any quarter that the choice was influenced improperly, or determined otherwise than by the judgment of those upon whom
the responsibility was cast, will not deceive and may be safely
left to the intelligence of the people of the State.

For myself, I shall claim the privilege of aiding in the cause.
This cannot be done by fault-finding and cavil. I know I can
aid by performing the duties of my public trust for the benefit
of the people, for I am sure that the party which does not keep
near to them, and the party representatives who are not careful of their interests, they will repudiate. We seek to put the
affairs of the State in the hands of men having the full confidence of the party. We seek to put in higher places those who
have shown fidelity to every private and public trust. We
present to the people of the State candidates all of whom
come accredited with the confidence and affection of their
neighbors, which are the best credentials. Their ability to
perform the duties of the offices is unquestioned, and, fresh
from the people, they understand and will care for their
wants.

Believing these things, I am enlisted in their success, and I
hope that, through the hearty efforts of their party friends and
by the intelligent action of the voters of the State, I may welcome them to share in the administration of our State government.

III.

At Newark, N. J., October 26, 1884.

I am here to visit the county and State where I was born, in
response to the invitation of many political friends and a
number of those who, as neighbors, remember my family, if

not me. I do not wish to attempt any false pretense by declaring that ever since the day when, a very small boy, I left the State, I have languished in an enforced absence and longed to tread again its soil; and yet I may say, without affectation, that, though the way of life has led me far from the place of my birth, the names of Caldwell and Newark and the memories connected with these places are as fresh as ever. I have never been disloyal to my native State, but have ever kept a place warm in my heart for the love I cherish for my birthplace. I hope, then, that I shall not be regarded as a recreant son, but that I may, without challenge, lay claim to my place as a born Jerseyman.

If you will grant me this I shall not be too modest to assume to share the pride which you all must feel in the position the State of New Jersey and the county of Essex hold in the country to-day. The history of the State dates beyond the time when our Union was formed. Its farm-lands exceed in average value per acre those of any other State, and it easily leads all the States in a number of important industries. When we consider the city of Newark, we find a municipality ranking as the fourteenth in point of population among the cities of the land. It leads every other city in three important industries; it is second in another, and third in still another.

Of course, all these industries necessitate the existence of a large laboring population. This force, in my opinion, is a further element of strength and greatness in the State; no part of the community should be more interested in a wise and just administration of their government, none should be better informed as to their needs and rights, and none should guard more vigilantly against the smooth pretenses of false friends.

In common with other citizens they should desire an honest and economical administration of public affairs. It is quite plain, too, that the people have a right to demand that no more money shall be taken from them, directly or indirectly, for public use, than is necessary for this purpose. Indeed, the right of the government to exact tribute from the citizen is limited to its actual necessities, and every cent taken from the people beyond that required for their protection by the government is no better than robbery. We surely must condemn, then, a system which takes from the pockets of the people millions of dollars not needed for the support of the government, and which tends to the inauguration of corrupt schemes and extravagant expenditures.

The Democratic party has declared that all taxation shall be limited by the requirements of an economical government. This is plain and direct, and it distinctly recognized the value of labor, and its right to governmental care, when it declared that the necessary reduction in taxation, and the limitation thereof to the country's needs, should be effected without depriving American labor of the ability to compete successfully with foreign labor and without injuring the interests of our laboring population. At this time, when the suffrages of the laboring men are so industriously sought, they should, by careful inquiry, discover the party pledged to the protection of their interests, and which recognizes in their labor something most valuable to the prosperity of the country and primarily entitled to its care and protection. An intelligent examination will lead them to the exercise of their privileges as citizens in furtherance of their interests and the welfare of the country. An unthinking performance of their duty at the ballot-box will result in their injury and betrayal.

No party and no candidate can have cause to complain of the free and intelligent expression of the people's will. This expression will be free when uninfluenced by appeals to prejudice, or the senseless cry of danger selfishly raised by a party that seeks the retention of power and patronage ; and it will be intelligent when based upon calm deliberation and a full appreciation of the duty of good citizenship. In a government of the people no party gains to itself all the patriotism which the country contains. The perpetuity of our institutions and the public welfare surely do not depend upon unchanging party

ascendency, but upon a simple businesslike administration of
the affairs of government and the appreciation by public officers
that they are the people's servants, not their masters.

IV.

At Bridgeport, Conn., October 30, 1884.

I cannot forbear, at such a time as this, to express the pleasure I experience in the sincere and heartfelt welcome that the
people of New Haven, Bridgeport, and the State of Connecticut have accorded me.   If this welcome was a tribute to me as
an individual, I could only express my gratitude ; but when I
find I represent an idea that is the same with you as with me,
it is with a sense of responsibility that I stand before you.

The world has not produced so grand a spectacle as a nation
of freemen determining its own cause.   In that position you
stand to-night.   At such a time a leader stands in a solemn
position, and the plaudits of his hearers can only serve to increase the feeling of responsibility—that is, if he is a man true
to his country and to the best interests of her people—which
pervades the contest.

Survey the field of the coming contest.   See the forces
drawn up in array against you from a party strong in numbers,
flanked by a vast army of office-holders, long in power, rich in
resources, both of money and influence, but corrupt to the
core.   To-day, they seek to control the religious element of
your country ; to-morrow, they will endeavor to gain the interest of your millionaire magnates for the purpose of raising
money to carry on their campaign.

There should be no mistake about this contest.   It is an
attempt to break down the barrier between the people of the
United States and those that rule them.   The people are
bound down by a class of office-holders whose business it is to
make money out of their positions.   If you are to go on forever choosing your rulers from this class, what will be the

end ? This is a question every one of you can answer for himself. Because it is the party of the people thousands are flocking to our standard, for they love their fellow-countrymen and their country more than they do their party.

Let us feel that the people are the rulers of the nation, and not the office-holders, whose sole ambition and purpose is private gain. Let us also feel that if the people give us the power of government we hold from the people a sacred trust.

V.

As Chairman of the Democratic Ratification Meeting in the Cooper Union, New York, October 9, 1891.

My Fellow-Citizens:

I acknowledge with much satisfaction the compliment paid me by my selection as your presiding officer to-night. I am glad to meet an assemblage of my fellow-townsmen on an occasion when their thoughts turn to the political situation which confronts them and at a time when their duty as citizens, as well as members of a grand political organization, should be subject to their serious consideration.

If I may be indulged a few moments I shall occupy that much of your time in presenting some suggestions touching the condition and responsibilities of the Democracy to the people of the country, and the obligations and duty at this particular time of the Democracy of our State.

The Democratic party has been at all times, by profession and by tradition, the party of the people. I say by profession and tradition, but I by no means intend to hint, in the use of this expression, that, in its conduct and action, it has failed to justify its profession or been recreant to its traditions. It must, however, be admitted that we have had our seasons of revival, when the consciousness of what true Democracy really means has been especially awakened, and when we have been unusually aroused to a lively appreciation of the aggressiveness and activity which conscience exacts of those who profess the Democratic faith, and who are thus enlisted in the people's cause.

We contemplate to-night such a revival and the stupendous results which have thus far attended it. In view of these things we cannot be honest and sincere and fail to see that a stern and inexorable duty is now at our door.

We saw the money of the people unnecessarily extorted from them under the guise of taxation.

We saw that this was the result of a scheme perpetuated for the purpose of exacting tribute from the poor for the benefit of the rich.

We saw, growing out of this scheme, the wholesale debauchery and corruption of the people whom it impoverished.

We saw a party, which advocated and defended this wrong, gaining and holding power in the government by the shameless appeal to selfishness which it invited.

We saw the people actually burnishing the bonds of misrepresentation and misconception which held them, and we saw sordidness and the perversion of all that constitutes good citizenship on every hand, and sturdy Americanism in jeopardy.

We saw a party planning to retain partisan ascendency by throttling and destroying the freedom and integrity of the suffrage through the most radical and reckless legislation.

We saw waste and extravagance raiding the public treasury, and justified in official places, while economy in government expenditures was ridiculed by those who held in trust the people's money.

We saw the national assemblage of the people's representatives transformed to the mere semblance of a legislative assembly, by the brute force of a violently-created majority and by unprecedented arbitrary rulings, while it was jeeringly declared, by those who usurped its functions, to be no longer a deliberative body.

Then it was that the Democratic party, standing forth to do

determined battle against these abuses, which threatened the welfare and happiness of the people, called upon them to trust it, and promised them that the warfare should be relentless and uncompromising.

As results of the struggle then entered upon, never has the resistless force of the awakened thought of our countrymen been more completely demonstrated, and never has the irresistible strength of the principles of Democracy been more fully exemplified. From the West and from the East came tidings of victory. In the popular branch of the next Congress the party which lately impudently arrogated to itself the domination of that body, will fill hardly more than one-fourth of its seats. Democratic Governors occupy the enemy's strongholds in Iowa, Massachusetts, Ohio, Wisconsin, and Michigan. In Pennsylvania, the election of a Democratic Governor presented conclusive proof of Republican corruption exposed and Republican dishonesty detected.

But with all these results of a just and fearless Democratic policy, our work is not yet completely done ; and I want to suggest to you that any relaxation of effort within the lines established by the National Democracy will be a violation of the pledges we gave the people when we invited their co-operation and undertook their cause.

I do not forget that we are gathered together to ratify State nominations, and that we are immediately concerned with a State campaign. It seems to me, however, that, while national questions of the greatest import are yet unsettled, and when we are on the eve of a national campaign in which they must be again pressed upon the attention of the voters of the country, the Democracy of the great State of New York cannot and will not entirely ignore them. If we fail to retain ascendency in the Empire State, no matter upon what issue it is lost, and no matter how much our opponents may seek to avoid great and important topics, it will be claimed as the verdict of our people against the principles and platform of the National Democracy.

It is evident that if our opponents are permitted to choose the line of battle they will avoid all national issues. Thus far this is plainly their policy. There is nothing strange in this, for they may well calculate that, whatever may be their fate in other fields, they have been decisively beaten in the discussion of national questions. It can hardly be expected that they will come to the field of Waterloo again, unless forced to do so.

I am very far from having any fear of the result of a full discussion of the subjects which pertain to State affairs. We have an abundance of reasons to furnish why on these issues alone we should be further trusted with the State government; but it does not follow that it is wise to regard matters of national concern as entirely foreign to the pending canvass, and especially to follow the enemy in their lead entirely away from the issues they most fear and which they have the best of reasons to dread. This very fear and dread give in this particular case strength and pertinency to the doctrine that a party should at all times and in all places be made to feel the consequences of their misdeeds as long as they have remaining any power for harm and as long as they justify and defend their wrong-doing.

Those who act with us merely because they approve the present position of the National Democracy and the reforms we have undertaken, and who oppose in national affairs Republican policy and methods, and who still think the State campaign we have in hand has no relation to the principles and policy which they approve, are in danger of falling into a grave error. Our opponents in the pending canvass, though now striving hard to hide their identity in a cloud of dust raised by their iteration of irrelevant things, constitute a large factor in the party which, still far from harmless, seeks to perpetuate all the wrongs and abuses of Republican rule in national affairs. Though they may strive to appear tame and tractable in a State campaign, they but dissemble to gain a new opportunity for harm.

In the present condition of affairs it is not to be supposed that any consistent and thoughtful member of the Democratic organization can fail to see it his duty to engage enthusiastically and zealously in the support of the ticket and platform which represent our party in this campaign. They are abundantly worthy and deserving of support on their own merits and for their own sake. We seek to place at the head of our State government a man of affairs, who, in a long business career, has earned the good opinion and respect of all his fellows, whose honesty and trustworthiness have never been impeached, and who, I am sure, will administer the great office, to which he will be called, independently, fearlessly, and for the good of all the people of the State. We seek further to secure the Empire State in her Democratic steadfastness, and we seek to win a victory which shall redeem the pledges we have made to regard constantly the interests of the people of the land, and which shall give hope and confidence to the National Democracy in the struggles yet to come.

With these incentives and with these purposes in view, I cannot believe that any Democrat can be guilty of lukewarmness or slothfulness.

With a party united and zealous ; with no avoidance of any legitimate issue ; with a refusal to be diverted from the consideration of great national and State questions to the discussion of misleading things; and, with such a presentation of the issues involved as will prove our faith in the intelligence of the people of the State, the result cannot be doubtful.

VI.

At the Brooklyn Ratification Meeting, October 14, 1891.

My Fellow-Citizens:

It does not need the cordial welcome you give me to-night to convince me that I am among friends. The good will and attachment of the people and the Democracy of Kings County have been in times past repeatedly manifested toward me and are remembered with constant gratitude. There was, therefore, a potent and palpable reason why I should not decline an invitation to be with you to-night.

Another reason not less strong why I am here is found in the fact that this is a gathering of my political friends in the interest of the Democratic cause and in token of their hearty support of Democratic principles and candidates. In such an assemblage I always feel at home.

My extreme interest in the State campaign now pending arises from a conception of its importance, which I do not believe is at all exaggerated. The fact that it immediately precedes a national campaign in which the vote of New York may be a controlling factor, is, of itself, sufficient to enlist the activity of every man entitled to claim a place in Democratic councils. Besides this, the failure on the part of the Democracy of the State to emphasize further its support of the reforms to which the National Democracy is pledged, we must all confess would be a party humiliation.

There are, however, reasons beyond these, which are close at home and have relation to State interests, quite sufficient to arouse supreme Democratic efforts. There are dangers clearly imminent, and schemes almost unconcealed, which affect our State and which can only be avoided and defeated by the strong and determined protest of the united Democracy of New York.

The party we oppose, resting upon no fundamental principles, sustaining a precarious existence upon distorted sentiment, and depending for success upon the varying currents of selfish interests and popular misconception, cannot endure the sight of a community which is inclined to withstand its blandishments and which refuses to be led away by its misrepresentations. Thus, in its national management and methods it boldly seeks to thwart the intention of voters, if they are Democratic, and to stifle the voice of the people, if they speak in Democratic tones. I am sure it is not necessary to remind

you in proof of this of the latest effort of our opponents at
Washington in this direction, nor to speak of the Democratic
congratulation which spread throughout the land when, by the
defeat of the Force Bill, our boasted American freedom of
suffrage was saved and constitutional rights preserved through
the combined efforts of a Democratic Senatorial minority
splendidly led and grandly sustained.

Is there a Democrat—nay, is there any man—so dull as to
suppose that the Republican party in this State is not of the
same disposition as the party in the nation ? Do not the attitude and conduct of its representatives from this State in
national affairs abundantly prove that the party in New York
can be implicitly trusted to aid any scheme of this sort that
promises partisan advantage ? If further proof is desired that
New York Republicans are thoroughly imbued with the proclivities that characterize the party in national affairs, it is
readily found.   Under the positive requirements of our State
Constitution an enumeration of the inhabitants of the State
should have been made in 1885, and the Senatorial and Assembly districts newly adjusted in accordance with such an enumeration.   This has not yet been done, though our opponents
have had a majority in both branches of the legislature ever
since that year, except that in the last session a Democratic
majority appeared in the assembly.   A Republican reason for the
neglect of a plain duty in the matter of this enumeration is found
in the fact that, under such a new arrangement, localities which
have increased in population and at the same time in Democratic voters, would be entitled to a larger representation in the
legislature than they now have, while the existing adjustment is
a very comfortable one from a Republican standpoint.   In the
present condition, it is calculated that a Democratic majority in
the State must reach at least 50,000 in order to give us a majority in the assembly.   In 1885 we elected our State ticket by more
than 11,000 majority, and yet but 50 Democratic members of
assembly were elected, while the defeated party elected 78.
In 1886 our majority was nearly 8000, but only 54 Democratic

assemblymen were elected, to 74 Republicans. In 1887 a Democratic majority on our State ticket of more than 17,000 yielded only 56 Democratic assemblymen to 72 Republican. In 1888, though the State ticket was carried by a majority not much less, we had but 49 assemblymen to 79 for the defeated opposition. In 1889 with a majority of over 20,000 on our State ticket we elected but 57 assemblymen, while the defeated party secured 71. In 1890 we carried the State on the congressional vote by more than 75,000 majority, and yet elected but 68 members of assembly to 60 elected by the party so largely in the minority.

Whatever may be said about the quarrels between a Democratic Governor and a Republican Legislature over the manner in which a new enumeration should be made, there is no difficulty in finding enough, in Republican disposition and practices, to justify the suspicion that any pretext was welcome, to the representatives of that party in the State, that would serve to perpetuate the present condition. There is no reason to hope for a better and more just representation of the political sentiments of the people of the State. except through a complete dislodgment of those who have long profited by this injustice. Its continuance is directly involved in the present campaign, for not only a Governor, but a new senate and assembly are to be elected. No election will soon occur that will afford so good an opportunity to secure to our party the share in State legislation to which it is entitled, nor will the Democratic party soon have so good a chance to rectify a political wrong.

By way of further suggesting the importance of this campaign, I ask you not to forget that a new apportionment of representatives in Congress is to be made on the basis of the census just completed, and that it may devolve upon the next legislature to readjust the congressional districts of the State. Previous to 1883 these districts were so arranged that, though in 1880 our opponents carried the State by only about twenty-one thousand, they secured twenty congressman to thirteen elected by the Democrats, while in 1882, though the Democratic candidate for Governor had a majority of more than one hundred and ninety thousand, there were elected but twenty-one Democratic congressmen, one being a citizen of Brooklyn, elected at large, while the party in the minority elected thirteen representatives. The change of congressional districts made in 1883, by a Democratic legislature and approved by a Democratic Governor, may well be referred to as an illustration of Democratic fairness. In the election of 1884, the first held under the new arrangement, our national ticket carried the State by a small majority, but the congressional delegation was equally divided between the parties. In both the elections of 1886 and 1888, though the Democratic State ticket was elected by moderate majorities, our opponents elected nineteen congressmen, while only fifteen were secured by the party having a majority of votes in the State. It required a Democratic majority in the State of 75,000 to secure at the last election only three congressmen above the number elected by our opponents under the former adjustment, when their State ticket had not much more than one-fourth of that majority.

I am far from complaining of the present congressional adjustment. On the contrary, I am glad that my party was more than just and fair when it had the opportunity. But I want to put the inquiry whether, judging from the past conduct of our opponents in such matters, and from what seems to be their natural disposition, there is the least chance of their dealing fairly by the Democracy of the State if they have the control of the next arrangement of congressional districts.

I purposely refrain from detaining you with the presentation of other considerations which impress me with the importance at this time of Democratic activity, but I cannot avoid recalling the fact that I am in an atmosphere where the doctrine of home rule has especially flourished, and among a community where this Democratic doctrine has been unusually exemplified. Let me remind you that no Democratic locality can exist without attracting to it the wistful gaze of those who find an adherence to the doctrine of home rule and an attachment to the Democratic faith, obstacles to the political advantage they seek to gain without scruple as to their method of procedure.

I need not say that the safety of Democracy, in the State and here at your home, is only to be preserved by Democratic steadfastness. I do not forget how often and how effectively you have displayed that steadfastness in the past, nor do I forget your service to the State when you contributed to places of trust in its government and administration the intelligence, fidelity, and ability of your fellow-townsman who soon retires from the chief magistracy of your city ; and I will stifle my complaint that, in selecting his successor, you have recalled a recent and most valuable contribution to the cause of Democracy in national councils.

In your relation to the pending canvass, every Democrat who loves his country and his party must acknowledge the important service rendered by representatives of Kings County in aiding the formulation of a declaration of financial principles in the platform which the Democracy presents to the voters of the State, which leaves no room to doubt our insistance upon sound and honest money for all the people.

In conclusion, let me assure you that I have absolute confidence, based upon what you are and what you have done in the past, that in the campaign upon which we have entered, the Democrats of Kings County will more than ever exhibit their devotion to the Democratic cause.

VII.

Before the Business Men's Democratic Association in Madison Square Garden, New York, October 27, 1891.

FELLOW-CITIZENS:

I am glad to have the opportunity to be present on this occasion, even though I am able to do but little more than speak a word of greeting to the representatives of our business interests who are here assembled.

You have heard much, and have doubtless reflected much, concerning the important results which depend upon the political action of the people of our State at the coming election, and I am glad to believe that the business men of the city of New York understand that this political campaign is not only important to them in common with all their fellow-citizens, but that there are features in it which especially concern them.

It must be confessed that both here and in other parts of the country, those engaged in business pursuits have kept too much aloof from public affairs and have too generally acted upon the theory that neither their duty as citizens nor their personal interests required of them any habitual participation in political movements. This indifference and inactivity have resulted in a loss to our public service. I am firmly of the belief that, if a few business men could be substituted for professional men in official places, the people would positively gain by the exchange. And it is strange to me that our business men have not been quicker to see that their neglect of political duty is a constant danger to their personal and especial interests. They may labor and plan, in their counting houses or in their Exchanges, but, in the meantime, laws may be passed by those ignorant of their business bearings, which, in their operation, will counteract all this labor and defeat all this planning.

I have expressed the belief that the business men of our city are aroused to the fact that there are questions involved in the campaign in this State which concern them and their welfare in an unusual way. This is indicated by awakened interest on every side and by this immense demonstration. And it is difficult to see how it could be otherwise.

The city of New York as the center of all that makes ours the Empire State, and as the great heart from which life-giving currents flow to all parts of the country, cannot be indifferent to the questions, both State and national, which have relation to the State campaign now nearly closed.

Much has been said about the topics which should be discussed in the prosecution of this campaign. It has been contended that the canvass should be confined to State issues, and it has been claimed that national issues should be most prominently considered. I conceive the truth to be that both are proper subjects of discussion at this time ; and, in the presence of this assemblage, called together to consider the business features of the contest, I am impressed with the fact that the best test to employ, by way of discovering the legitimacy of any topic in the pending campaign, is to inquire whether it is connected with the good of the country and with the business of the city and State, and whether it will be at all influenced by the results of the canvass.

Can anyone doubt that the political verdict which the people of New York will give in November next, will affect her position in the general national engagement which will take place one year hence ? In this view, the proper adjustment of the tariff, which concerns so materially not only all our people, but the commerce and the business of our city, should be discussed. This, and the question of sound currency, cannot be separated from the business interests of our State ; and they should be put before our people now for the purpose of inviting their thought and settling their opinions.

Applying this same test, it is entirely plain that an economical administration of State affairs and the numerous other subjects having reference to a just, honest, and beneficent State government are, in a business sense, important and legitimate.

On all these questions the New York Democracy is right ; and we are willing and anxious to discuss them in any place and at any time.

But our opponents, apparently seeking to avoid the discussion of subjects legitimate to the canvass and affecting the business of our city and State, and exhibiting such weakness and fear as certainly ought not to escape notice, are shrieking throughout the State the demerits and dangerous proclivities of a certain political organization whose members support the principles and candidates of the Democratic party. It would be quite easy to show that, even if all they allege against this organization were true, the perils our opponents present to the people are baseless and absurd. But it seems to me the argument of such a question belittles an important situation.

Every man knows, or ought to satisfy himself whether the principles and policy presented to the people by the Democratic party are such as he approves. If they are, certainly his duty as a citizen obliges him to indorse them. Every man ought to satisfy himself whether the candidates of the Democratic party are men of such character and ability that he is willing to trust them in the administration of his State government. If he believes they are, he should not withhold his support from them upon any frivolous and irrelevant pretext.

The exercise of the right of suffrage is a serious business ; and a man's vote ought to express his opinion on the questions at issue. This it utterly fails to do if the voter listens to the ravings of our opponents, and allows his vote merely to record the extent to which he has yielded to the misleading and cunningly devised appeals to his prejudices, made in behalf of a desperate and discredited minority. Such a vote does not influence, in the least, the real settlement of any of the weighty matters of policy and principle upon which the people are called to pronounce judgment.

If enough such votes should be given to cause a false verdict in the State, those who should contribute to that result, and thus become disloyal to their beliefs, would find everything but satisfaction in their self-reproach, and in their sense of degradation which would follow the unconcealed contempt of those partisans who had duped them for the purpose of thus gaining a party advantage not otherwise possible.

In conclusion, I desire to disclaim any fear that the business men of New York can be thus deluded. They will not only apprehend the questions at issue, and see their duty and interest, in soberly passing upon them without prejudice or passion, but they will also appreciate the fact that the ticket they are asked by the Democratic party to support expressly recognizes them. It is headed by a man of business, who is certainly entitled to their confidence, and who is so creditable as their representative, that I believe his business character has escaped attack during a campaign in which every attack having any pretext whatever has been made. I will not especially refer by name to the remainder of our candidates—some of whom are my old and near friends—because I think I ought not to detain you longer than to say that they are all entirely worthy of support, and that by the triumphant election of every one of them the verdict of the people of the State ought to be recorded in favor of good government and the advancement of business interests.

VIII.

In Tremont Temple, Boston, October 31, 1891.

My Fellow-Citizens :

I should be quite uncomfortable at this moment if I supposed you regarded me as a stranger in your State, and only concerned as a Democratic spectator of the political campaign which stirs the people of this commonwealth. I hope it is not necessary to remind you that, by virtue of a sort of initiation which I have recently undergone, I have a right to claim a modified membership in the citizenship of Massachusetts ; and though I am obliged to confess a limitation in the extent of this citizenship I am somewhat compensated by what seems to me to be its quality. So far as I have a residence among you, it is the place where, amid quiet and peaceful surroundings, I enjoy that home life I so much love, where relaxation from labor and from care restores health and vigor, and where recreation, in pleasing variety, teaches me the lesson that man's

duty and mission are not only to do the work which his relations to his fellow-men impose upon him, but to appreciate the
things which the goodness of God supplies in nature for man's
delight. While, therefore, no conditions could cause the least
abatement in the pride I feel as a fully qualified citizen of the
great State of New York, I cannot be insensible to the fact
that my relationship to Massachusetts connects your State
with the elements in my life which are full of delightful sentiment and with those enjoyments which enlarge and cultivate
the heart and soul.

I have spent to-day at my Massachusetts home, and meet
you here pursuant to a promise that, on my way out of the
State, I would look in on this assemblage of those who are
enlisted in a grand and noble cause.

It is but natural that my errand to your State, and the inspection of that part of its soil of which I am the self-satisfied
owner, should arouse all the Massachusetts feeling to which
this ownership entitles me, and should intensify that interest
in the political behavior of the State which rightfully belongs
to my semi-citizenship.

My relations to you are, perhaps, too new-fledged to shield
me from an accusation of affectation if I should dwell, with the
rapture others might more properly exhibit, upon the history,
traditions, and achievements of Massachusetts. I am sure,
however, that I may, with perfect propriety, remind you that
the people of Massachusetts have in their keeping certain
precious things which they hold in trust for all their countrymen. They can no more appropriate Plymouth Rock and
Bunker Hill than they can confine within the limits of their
State the deeds, the example, and the fame of the men whom
Massachusetts contributed to the public service of the Nation
in the days when giants lived.

The influence of your State upon the politics of the country
has by no means been limited to the actual share she and her
representative men have taken in governmental management.
Her stake in the creation and the development of our country

took form in its embryonic days ; and this has given rise from
the beginning to the interested discussion among her people
of every public question, while the education and general information of her population have made such discussion intelligent and forceful.   Her schools and her institutions of learning have sent to all parts of the land young and thoughtful
men, imbued with sentiments and opinions not learned in their
books.   When her feeling has been most aroused she has
challenged the respect of the country because, though uncompromising, she has been habitually just, and, though radical,
she has been always great.

I cannot help recalling at this moment that you gave to the
Senate of the United States the man who is remembered by
all his countrymen as the best modern embodiment of American greatness ; that Webster, though he loved freedom and
hated slavery, never consented to the infringement of constitutional rights, even for the sake of freedom ; that, though his
love for Massachusetts was his consuming sentiment, he
emphatically declared that in the discharge of public duty he
would neither regard her especial interests nor her desires as
against his conception of the general interests of the country,
and that his patriotism and his love for the Union were so
great that he constantly sought to check the first sign of
estrangement among our people.

I recall the love of Massachusetts for the memory of Sum-
ner—the great Senator who unhesitatingly braved Executive
displeasure and party ostracism in loyalty to his sense of right;
who surprised and alienated a sentiment, born of patriotic
warmth, by advocating the obliteration of the reminders of the
triumphs of American soldiers over American soldiers ; and
who, throughout a long public career, illustrated his belief that
politics is but the application of moral principle to public
affairs.

If, from the contemplation of these lofty precedents, you turn
to the manner in which the sentiment and feeling of Massachusetts have of late been represented in both houses of Congress,

and if you thus find an unpleasing contrast, it is for you to say whether you are satisfied ; but, if this feeling and sentiment, genuine and unperverted, ought to bear the fruits of conciliation and trust among our countrymen, the avoidance of unnecessary irritation, and the abandonment of schemes which promise no better result than party supremacy through forced and unnatural suffrage, there certainly seems to be ground for apprehension that there has lately been something awry in your Federal representation. At any rate, it seems to me that the people themselves, in the State of Massachusetts, are constantly giving proof that they are ready and willing, obedient to a generous instinct and for the good of the entire country, to aid in building up American fraternity based upon mutual faith and confidence, and in restoring and reviving that unity and heartiness of aim and purpose upon which alone our national hope can securely rest.

We have fallen upon a time when especial interest is aroused among our people in subjects which seem to be vital to the welfare of the country. Our consumers, those of moderate means and the poor of the land, are too much neglected in our national policy; their life is made too hard for them, and too much favor is shown to pampered manufactures and rich monopolies. A condition of restlessness and irritation has grown up throughout the country, born of prevailing inequality and unfairness, which threatens an attack upon sound currency, and which awakens the fear and anxious solicitude of thoughtful and patriotic men ; economy in public expenditure has almost become a byword and jest; and partisanship in power executes its will by methods unprecedented and ruthless.

I have believed that the Democratic party was right in its position on all these subjects ; and I am willing to confess that my belief is confirmed by the verdict of the people of Massachusetts. When I see the old Commonwealth break away from party trammels in aid of right and honesty, when I see a majority of her last elected representatives in Congress chosen to enforce the principles we profess, and when I see her put at the head of her State government one of her young sons, who stands for these principles in the truest, cleanest, and most vigorous way, I am prepared to see, following the lead of Massachusetts, such a revival of moral sentiment in politics as will insure the general acceptance, by our countrymen, of the truths we preach.

Any man who fails to appreciate the immense motive power of the conscience of Massachusetts has viewed to little purpose the movements which have made their impress on our country's history, and which have led our national destiny. On the splendid roster of those here enlisted in our cause, and among the thousands recorded there who have seen beyond party lines the morals of political questions, are found the names of Adams and Everett and Andrew and Quincy and Garrison and Higginson and Pierce and Eliot and Hoar and Codman and Williams—giving proof that the people's cause has touched the conscience of Massachusetts.

The hearts of patriotic men in many States are warmed with gratitude for the strong and able young men your Commonwealth has contributed to our public life in this time of her awakening.

Again, their eyes are turned to Massachusetts. Young and vigorous Americanism has watched with pride and enthusiasm its best representative at the head of your State government, and those who love true Democracy have rejoiced far and wide that one who embodies their principles so truly, and exemplifies them so wisely, has borne himself so nobly. They look to the people of Massachusetts to recognize the faithful services of their young Governor and the manner in which he has upheld the dignity and honor of their State before their countrymen everywhere. They look to you, by his election and by the election of all the good men and true who, with him, bear the standard of your State Democracy, to demonstrate your steadfastness in the Democratic cause. They look to you to give to the national Democracy and the cause of the people, which it has in charge, the powerful aid of the still awakened conscience of Massachusetts.

Democrats of Massachusetts—men of Massachusetts—which shall your response be ?

IX.

In the Opera House at Providence, R. I., April 2, 1892.

MY FELLOW-CITIZENS :

I have found it impossible to decline the invitation you sent me to meet here to-day the Democracy of Rhode Island. I have come to look in the faces of the men who have been given the place of honor in the advance of the vast army which moves toward the decisive battlefield of next November. I have not come to point the way to consolation in case of your defeat, but I have come to share the enthusiasm which presages victory. I have not come to condole with you upon the difficulties which confront you, but to suggest that they will only add to the glory of your triumph. I have come to remind you that the intrenchments of spoils and patronage cannot avail against the valor and determination of right ; that corruption and bribery cannot smother and destroy the aroused conscience of our countrymen, and that splendid achievements await those who bravely, honestly, and stubbornly fight in the people's cause.

Let us not for a moment miss the inspiration of those words, " The People's Cause." They signify the defense of the rights of every man, rich or poor, in every corner of our land, who, by virtue of simple American manhood, lays claim to the promises of our free government, and they mean the promotion of the welfare and happiness of the humblest American citizen who confidingly invokes the protection of just and equal laws.

The covenant of our Democratic faith, as I understand it,

exacts constant effort in this cause, and its betrayal I conceive to be a crime against the creed of true Democracy.

The struggle in which you are engaged arrests the attention of your party brethren in every State ; and they pause in their preparation for the general engagement, near at hand, in which all will be in the field, and look toward Rhode Island with hope and trust. They read the legends on your banners and they hear your rallying cries, and know that your fight is in the people's cause.

If you should be defeated there will be no discouragement in this vast waiting army ; but you will earn their plaudits and cover yourselves with glory by winning success.

Large and bright upon your banners are blazoned the words " Tariff Reform "—the shibboleth of true Democracy and the test of loyalty to the people's cause.

Those who oppose tariff reform delude themselves if they suppose that it rests wholly upon appeals to selfish considerations and the promise of advantage, right or wrong ; or that our only hope of winning depends upon arousing animosity between different interests among our people. While we do not propose that those whose welfare we champion shall be blind to the advantages accruing to them from our plan of tariff reform, and while we are determined that these advantages shall not be surrendered to the blandishments of greed and avarice, we still claim nothing that has not underlying it moral sentiment and considerations of equity and good conscience.

Because our case rests upon such foundations, sordidness and selfishness cannot destroy it. The fight for justice and right is a clean and comforting one ; and because the American people love justice and right, ours must be a winning fight.

" The government of the Union is a government of the people ; it emanates from them ; its powers are granted by them, and are to be exercised directly on them and for their benefit."

This is not the language of a political platform. It is a

declaration of the highest court in the land, whose mandates all must obey, and whose definitions all partisans must accept.

In the light of this exposition of the duty the government owes to the people, the Democratic party claims that when, through Federal taxation, burdens are laid upon the daily life of the people, not necessary for the government's economical administration, and intended, whatever be the pretext, to enrich a few at the expense of the many, the governmental compact is violated.

A distinguished Justice of the Supreme Court, with no Democratic affiliations, but loved and respected when living by every American, and since his death universally lamented, has characterized such a proceeding as "none the less a robbery because it is done under the forms of law and is called taxation."

Let us then appreciate the fact that we not only stand upon sure and safe ground when we appeal to honesty and morality in our championship of the interests of the masses of our people as they are related to tariff taxation, but that our mission is invested with the highest patriotism when we attempt to preserve from perversion, distortion, and decay the justice, equality, and moral integrity which are the constituent elements of our scheme of popular government.

Those who believe in tariff reform, for the substantial good it will bring to the multitude who are neglected when selfish greed is in the ascendency ; those who believe that the legitimate motive of our government is to do equal and exact justice to all our people, and grant especial privileges to none ; those who believe that a nation, boasting that its foundation is in honesty and conscience, cannot afford to discard moral sentiment ; and those who would save our institutions from the undermining decay of sordidness and selfishness, can hardly excuse themselves if they fail to join us in the crusade we have undertaken. Certainly our sincerity cannot be questioned. In the beginning of the struggle we were not only bitterly opposed by a great party of avowed enemies, but were embar-

rassed by those in our own ranks who had become infected
with the unwholesome atmosphere our enemies had created.
We hesitated not a moment boldly to encounter both. We
unified our party, not by any surrender to the half-hearted
among our members, but by an honest appeal to Democratic
sentiment and conscience. We have never lowered our standard. It surely was not policy nor expediency that induced us
defiantly to carry the banner of tariff reform as we went forth
to meet a well-organized and desperately determined army in
the disastrous field of 1888. A time-serving or expediency-
hunting party would hardly have been found, the day after
such a crushing defeat, undismayed, defiant, and determined ;
still shouting the old war cry, and anxious to encounter again
in the people's cause our exultant enemy. We had not long
to wait. At the Waterloo of 1890, tariff reform had its vindication, and principle and steadfast devotion to American fairness and good faith gloriously triumphed over plausible shiftiness and attempted popular deception.

The Democratic party still champions the cause which defeat could not induce it to surrender, which no success, short
of complete accomplishment, can tempt it to neglect. Its position has been from the first frankly and fairly stated, and no
one can honestly be misled concerning it. We invite the
strictest scrutiny of our conduct in dealing with this subject,
and we insist that our cause has been open, fair, and consistent. I believe this is not now soberly denied in any quarter.

Our opponents, too, have a record on this question. Those
who still adhere to the doctrine that an important function of
the government is especially to aid them in their business ;
those who only see in the consumers of our land forced contributors to artificial benefits permitted by governmental
favoritism ; those who see in our workingmen only the tools
with which their shops and manufactories are to be supplied
at the cheapest possible cost, and those who believe there is no
moral question involved in the tariff taxation of the people, are

probably familiar with this record and abundantly satisfied with it.

It may, however, be profitably reviewed by those who believe that integrity and good faith have to do with governmental operations, and who honestly confess that present tariff burdens are not justly and fairly distributed. Such a review may also be of interest to those who believe that our consumers are entitled to be treated justly and honestly by the government, and that the workingman should be allowed to feel in his humble home, as he supplies his family's daily needs, that his earnings are not unjustly extorted from him for the benefit of the favored beneficiaries of unfair tariff laws.

This, then, is the record : When we began the contest for tariff reform it was said by our Republican opponents, in the face of our avowals and acts, that we were determined on free trade. A long advance was made, in their insincerity and impudence, when they accused us of acting in the interests of foreigners, and when they more than hinted that we had been bought with British gold. Those who distrusted the effectiveness of these senseless appeals insulted the intelligence of our people by claiming that an increase in the cost of articles to the consumer caused by the tariff was not a tax paid by him, but that it was paid by foreigners who sent their goods to our markets. Sectional prejudice was invoked in the most outrageous manner, and the people of the North were asked to condemn the measure of tariff reform proposed by us because members of Congress from the South had supported it.

These are fair samples of the arguments submitted to the American people in the Presidential campaign of 1888.

It will be observed that the purpose of these amazing deliverances was to defeat entirely any reform in the tariff—though it had been enacted at a time when the expense of a tremendous war justified the exaction of tribute from the people which in time of peace became a grievous burden ; though it had congested the Federal Treasury with a worse than useless surplus, inviting reckless public waste and extravagance ; and though, in many of its features, the only purpose of its continuation was the bargaining it permitted for party support.

There were those, however, in the ranks of our opponents who recognized the fact that we had so aroused popular attention to the evils and injustice of such a tariff that it might not be safe to rely for success upon a bald opposition to its reform. These were the grave and sedate Republican statesmen who declared that they never, *never*, could consent to subserve the interests of England at the expense of their own country, as the wicked Democrats proposed to do, and that they felt constrained to insist upon a tariff, protective to the point of prohibition, because they devotedly loved our workingmen and were determined that their employment should be constant and that their wages should never sink to the disgusting level of the pauper labor of Europe, but that, in view of the fact that the war in which the tariff then existing originated had been closed for more than twenty years, and in view of the further fact that the public Treasury was overburdened, they were willing to readjust the tariff, if it could only be done by its friends instead of " rebel Brigadiers."

I will not refer to all the means by which our opponents succeeded in that contest. Suffice it to say, they gained complete possession of the government in every branch, and the tariff was reformed by its alleged friends. All must admit, however, that either this was not done by the people's friends, or that the effort in their behalf sadly miscarried or was ungratefully remembered ; for a few weeks thereafter, a relegation to private life among those occupying seats in Congress who had been active in reforming the tariff occurred, which amounted to a political revolution. These victims claimed that our voters failed to indorse their reform of the tariff because they did not understand it. It is quite probable, however, that if they did not understand it they felt it, and that, because it made them uncomfortable, they emphatically said such a reform was not what they wanted. At any rate, the consumer has found life harder since this reform than before, and if there is a workingman anywhere who has had his wages increased by virtue of its operation he has not yet made himself known. Plenty of mills and factories have been closed, thousands of men have thus lost employment, and we daily hear of reduced wages ; but the benefits promised from this reform, and its advantage to the people, who really need relief, are not apparent. The provision it contains permitting reciprocity of trade in certain cases, depending on the action of the President, is an admission, as far as it goes, against the theory upon which this reform is predicated, and it lamely limps in the direction of freer commercial exchanges. If " hypocrisy is the homage vice pays to virtue," reciprocity may be called the homage prohibitory protection pays to genuine tariff reform.

The demand in your platform for free raw materials ought, it seems to me, to be warmly seconded by the citizens of your State. The advantages to the people of Rhode Island of such a policy do not seem to be questionable, and I am not here to discuss them in detail ; but all I have said, touching the conduct and record of the Democratic party and its opponents in regard to tariff legislation, is in support of the proposition that all who desire the special relief referred to in your platform, or any other improvement in our tariff laws in the general interest of the people, must look to the Democratic party for it. The manufacturer who sees in free raw materials a reduced cost of his products, resulting in an increased consumption and an extension of his markets, and a constant activity and return for his invested capital, can hardly trust the party which first resisted any reform in the tariff, then juggled with it, and at last flatly refused him the relief he still needs. The workingman who has been deceived by the promise of higher wages and better employment, and who now constantly fears the closing of manufactories and the loss of work, ought certainly to be no longer cajoled by a party whose performance has so clearly given the lie to its professions. The consumer who has trusted to a reformation of the tariff by its friends, now that he feels the increased burden of taxation in his home, ought to look in another direction for relief.

If the Democratic party does not give to the State of Rhode Island, during the present session of Congress, the free raw materials she needs, it will be because a Republican Senate or Executive thwarts its design. At any rate, nothing shall divert us from our purpose to reform the tariff in this regard, as well as many others, be the time of its accomplishment near or remote.

It doubtless would please our adversaries if we could be allured from our watch and guard over the cause of tariff reform to certain other objects, thus forfeiting the people's trust and confidence. The national Democracy will hardly gratify this wish and turn its back upon the people's cause, to wander after false and unsteady lights in the wilderness of doubt and danger.

Our opponents must, in the coming national canvass, settle accounts with us on the issue of tariff reform. It will not do for them to say to us that this is an old and determined contention. The Ten Commandments are thousands of years old ; but they and the doctrine of tariff reform will be taught and preached until mankind and the Republican party shall heed the injunction, " Thou shalt not steal."

As I leave you, let me say to you that your cause deserves success ; and let me express the hope that the close of your canvass will bring you no regrets on account of activity relaxed or opportunities lost. Demonstrate to your people the merits of your cause, and trust them. Above all things, banish every personal feeling of discontent, and let every personal consideration be merged in a determination, pervading your ranks everywhere, to win a victory. With a cause so just, and with activity, vigilance, harmony, and determination on the part of Rhode Island's stanch Democracy, I believe you will not fail.

CHAPTER XIII.

ON SOME SOCIAL AND ECONOMIC QUESTIONS.

I.

THE PUBLICITY OF CORPORATIONS.

(From the First Message to the New York Legislature, January, 1884.)

THE action of the Board of Railroad Commissioners in requiring the filing of quarterly reports by the railroad companies, exhibiting their financial condition, is a most important step in advance, and should be abundantly sustained. It would, in my opinion, be a most valuable protection to the people if other large corporations were obliged to report to some department their transactions and financial condition.

The State creates these corporations upon the theory that some proper thing of benefit can be better done by them than by private enterprise, and that the aggregation of the funds of many individuals may be thus profitably employed. They are launched upon the public with the seal of the State, in some sense, upon them. They are permitted to represent the advantages they possess and the wealth sure to follow from admission to membership. In one hand is held a charter from the State, and in the other is held their preferred stock.

It is a fact, singular, though well-established, that people will pay their money for stock in a corporation engaged in enterprises in which they would refuse to invest if in private hands.

It is a grave question whether the formation of these artificial bodies ought not to be checked, or better regulated, and in some way supervised.

At any rate, they should always be kept well in hand, and the funds of its citizens should be protected by the State which has invited their investment. While the stockholders are the owners of the corporate property, notoriously they are oftentimes completely in the power of the directors and managers who acquire a majority of the stock and by this means perpetuate their control, using the corporate property and franchises for their benefit and profit, regardless of the interests and rights of the minority of stockholders. Immense salaries are paid to officers ; transactions are consummated by which the directors make money, while the rank and file among the stockholders lose it ; the honest investor waits for dividends and the directors grow rich. It is suspected, too, that large sums are spent under various disguises in efforts to influence legislation.

It is not consistent to claim that the citizen must protect himself by refusing to purchase stock. The law constantly recognizes the fact that people should be defended from false representations and from their own folly and cupidity. It punishes obtaining goods by false pretenses, gambling, and lotteries.

It is a hollow mockery to direct the owner of a small amount of stock in one of these institutions to the courts. Under existing statutes, the law's delay, perplexity and uncertainty lead but to despair.

The State should either refuse to allow these corporations to exist under its authority or patronage, or acknowledging their paternity and its responsibility, should provide a simple, easy way for its people whose money is invested, and the public generally, to discover how the funds of these institutions are spent, and how their affairs are conducted. It should, at the same time, provide a way by which the squandering or misuse of corporate funds would be made good to the parties injured thereby.

This might well be accomplished by requiring corporations to file reports frequently, made out with the utmost detail, and which would not allow lobby expenses to be hidden under the pretext of legal services and counsel fees, accompanied by vouchers and sworn to by the officers making them, showing particularly the debts, liabilities, expenditures, and property of the corporation. Let this report be delivered to some appropriate department or officer, who shall audit and examine the same ; provide that a false oath to such account shall be perjury and make the directors liable to refund to the injured stockholders any expenditure which shall be determined improper by the auditing authority.

Such requirements might not be favorable to stock speculation, but they would protect the innocent investors ; they might make the management of corporations more troublesome, but this ought not to be considered when the protection of the people is the matter in hand. It would prevent corporate efforts to influence legislation ; the honestly conducted and strong corporations would have nothing to fear ; the badly managed and weak ought to be exposed.

II.

LEGISLATIVE BILLS OF A PURELY LOCAL CHARACTER.

(From the Second Message to the New York Legislature, January, 1884.)

Another evil which has a most pernicious influence in legislation is the introduction and consideration of bills, purely local in their character, affecting only special interests, which ought not upon any pretext to be permitted to encumber the statutes of the State. Every consideration of expediency, as well as the language and evident intent of the Constitution, dictate the exclusion of such matters from legislative consideration. The powers of Boards of Supervisors and other local authorities have been enlarged, for the express purpose of permitting them to deal intelligently and properly with such subjects. But, notwithstanding this, bills are introduced authorizing the building and repairing of bridges and highways, the erection of engine houses and soldiers' monuments, the establishment of libraries, the regulation or purchase of cemeteries, and other things of a like nature.

In many cases no better excuse exists for the presentation of such bills than the dignity and force which are supposed to be gained for their objects by legal enactment, the saving of expense and trouble to those interested in their purposes, and the local notoriety and popularity sought by the legislators having them in charge. Their consideration retards the business of the session and occupies time which should be devoted to better purposes. And this is not the worst result that may follow in their train. Such measures, there are grounds to suspect, are frequently made the means of securing, by a promise of aid in their passage, the votes of those who introduce them, in favor of other and more vicious legislation.

III.

THE ARBITRATION OF LABOR DISPUTES.

I.

To the Senate and House of Representatives:

The Constitution imposes upon the President the duty of recommending to the consideration of Congress from time to time such measures as he shall judge necessary and expedient.

I am so deeply impressed with the importance of immediately and thoughtfully meeting the problem which recent events and a present condition have thrust upon us, involving the settlement by arbitration of disputes arising between our laboring men and their employers, that I am constrained to recommend to Congress legislation upon this serious and pressing subject.

Under our form of government, the value of labor as an element of national prosperity should be distinctly recognized, and the welfare of the laboring man should be regarded as especially entitled to legislative care. In a country which offers to all its citizens the highest attainment of social and political distinction, its workingmen cannot justly or safely be considered as irrevocably consigned to the limits of a class and entitled to no attention and allowed no protest against neglect.

The laboring man, bearing in his hand an indispensable contribution to our growth and progress, may well insist, with manly courage and as a right, upon the same recognition from those who make our laws as is accorded to any other citizen having a valuable interest in charge ; and his reasonable demands should be met in such a spirit of appreciation and fairness as to induce a contented and patriotic co-operation in the achievement of a grand national destiny.

While the real interests of labor are not promoted by a resort to threats and violent manifestations, and while those who, under the pretext of an advocacy of the claims of labor, wantonly attack the rights of capital, and for selfish purposes or the love of disorder sow seeds of violence and discontent, should neither be encouraged nor conciliated, all legislation on the subject should be calmly and deliberately undertaken, with no purpose of satisfying unreasonable demands or gaining partisan advantage.

The present condition of the relations between labor and capital is far from satisfactory. The discontent of the employed is due, in a large degree, to the grasping and heedless exactions of employers, and the alleged discrimination in favor of capital as an object of governmental attention. It must also be conceded that the laboring men are not always careful to avoid causeless and unjustifiable disturbance.

Though the importance of a better accord between these interests is apparent, it must be borne in mind that any effort in that direction, by the Federal government, must be greatly

limited by constitutional restrictions. There are many grievances which legislation by Congress cannot redress, and many
conditions which cannot by such means be reformed.

I am satisfied, however, that something may be done under
Federal authority to prevent the disturbances which so often
arise from disputes between employers and the employed, and
which at times seriously threaten the business interests of the
country ; and in my opinion the proper theory upon which to
proceed is that of voluntary arbitration as the means of settling these difficulties.

But I suggest that instead of arbitrators chosen in the heat
of conflicting claims, and after each dispute shall arise, for the
purpose of determining the same, there be created a Commission of Labor, consisting of three members, who shall be reg-
ular officers of the government, charged among other duties
with the consideration and settlement, when possible, of all
controversies between labor and capital.

A commission thus organized would have the advantage of
being a stable body, and its members, as they gained experience, would constantly improve in their ability to deal intelligently and usefully with the questions which might be submitted to them. If arbitrators are chosen for temporary
service as each case of dispute arises, experience and familiarity with much that is involved in the question will be lacking, extreme partisanship and bias will be the qualifications
sought on either side, and frequent complaints of unfairness
and partiality will be inevitable. The imposition upon a
Federal court of a duty so foreign to the judicial function as
the selection of an arbitrator in such cases, is at least of
doubtful propriety.

The establishment by Federal authority of such a bureau
would be a just and sensible recognition of the value of labor,
and of its right to be represented in the departments of the
government. So far as its conciliatory offices shall have relation to disturbance which interfered with transit and commerce between the States, its existence would be justified,

under the provision of the Constitution which gives to Congress the power " to regulate commerce with foreign nations and among the several States." And in the frequent disputes between the laboring men and their employers of less extent, and the consequences of which are confined within State limits and threaten domestic violence, the interposition of such a commission might be tendered upon the application of the legislature or executive of a State, under the constitutional provision which requires the general government to " protect" each of the States "against domestic violence."

If such a commission were fairly organized, the risk of a loss of popular support and sympathy, resulting from a refusal to submit to so peaceful an instrumentality, would constrain both parties to such disputes to invoke its interference and abide by its decisions. There would also be good reason to hope that the very existence of such an agency would invite application to it for advice and counsel, frequently resulting in the avoidance of contention and misunderstanding.

If the usefulness of such a commission is doubted because it might lack power to enforce its decisions, much encouragement is derived from the conceded good that has been accomplished by the railroad commissions which have been organized in many of the States, which, having little more than advisory power, have exerted a most salutary influence in the settlement of disputes between conflicting interests.

In July, 1884, by a law of Congress, a Bureau of Labor was established and placed in charge of a Commissioner of Labor, who is required to " collect information upon the subject of labor, its relations to capital, the hours of labor and the earnings of laboring men and women, and the means of promoting their material, social, intellectual, and moral prosperity."

The commission which I suggest could easily be engrafted upon the bureau thus already organized, by the addition of two more commissioners and by supplementing the duties now imposed upon it by such other powers and functions as would permit the commissioners to act as arbitrators, when necessary, between labor and capital, under such limitations and upon such occasions as should be deemed proper and useful.

Power should also be distinctly conferred upon this bureau to investigate the causes of all disputes as they occur, whether submitted for arbitration or not, so that information may always be at hand to aid legislation on the subject when necessary and desirable.

GROVER CLEVELAND.

EXECUTIVE MANSION,
April 22, 1886.

————

2.

(From the Second Annual Message to Congress, December, 1886.)

The relations of labor to capital and of laboring men to their employers are of the utmost concern to every patriotic citizen. When these are strained and distorted, unjustifiable claims are apt to be insisted upon by both interests, and in the controversy which results the welfare of all and the prosperity of the country are jeopardized. Any intervention of the general government, within the limits of its constitutional authority, to avert such a condition should be willingly accorded.

In a special message transmitted to the Congress at its last session I suggested the enlargement of our present Labor Bureau and adding to its present functions the power of arbitration in cases where differences arise between employer and employed. When these differences reach such a stage as to result in the interruption of commerce between the States, the application of this remedy by the general government might be regarded as entirely within its constitutional powers. And I think we might reasonably hope that such arbitrators, if carefully selected, and if entitled to the confidence of the parties to be affected, would be voluntarily called to the settlement of controversies of less extent and not necessarily within the domain of Federal regulation.

I am of the opinion that this suggestion is worthy the attention of the Congress.

But, after all has been done by the passage of laws, either Federal or State, to relieve a situation full of solicitude, much more remains to be accomplished by the reinstatement and cultivation of a true American sentiment which recognizes the equality of American citizenship. This, in the light of our traditions and in loyalty to the spirit of our institutions, would teach that a hearty co-operation on the part of all interests is the surest path to national greatness and the happiness of all our people, that capital should, in recognition of the brotherhood of our citizenship and in a spirit of American fairness, generously accord to labor its just compensation and consideration, and that contented labor is capital's best protection and faithful ally. It would teach, too, that the diverse situations of our people are inseparable from our civilization, that every citizen should, in his sphere, be a contributor to the general good, that capital does not necessarily tend to the oppression of labor, and that violent disturbances and disorders alienate from their promoters true American sympathy and kindly feeling.

IV.

PLACE-HOLDING AS A BUSINESS.

EXECUTIVE MANSION,
ALBANY, February 4, 1885.

MY DEAR YOUNG FRIEND:

I cannot attempt to answer all the letters addressed to me by those, both old and young, who ask for places. But, if you are the boy I think you are, your letter is based upon a claim to help your mother and others who are partly dependent upon your exertions. I judge from what you write that you now have a situation in a reputable business house. I cannot urge you too strongly to give up all idea of employment in a public office, and to determine to win advancement and promotion where you are.

There are no persons so forlorn and so much to be pitied as those who have learned, in early life, to look to public positions for a livelihood. It unfits a man or boy for any other business, and is apt to make a kind of respectable vagrant of him. If you do well in other occupations, and thus become valuable to the people, they will find you out when they want a good man for public service.

You may be sure that I am, as you say, the friend of every boy willing to help himself; but my experience teaches me that I cannot do you a better service than to advise you not to join the great army of office-seekers.

I never sought an office of any kind in my life; and, if you live and follow my advice, I am certain that you will thank me for it some day.

> Yours truly,
> GROVER CLEVELAND.

V.

THE HOMES OF POLYGAMY.

(First Annual Message to Congress, December 8, 1885.)

In the Territory of Utah the law of the United States passed for the suppression of polygamy has been energetically and faithfully executed during the past year, with measurably good results. A number of convictions have been secured for unlawful cohabitation, and in some cases pleas of guilty have been entered and a slight punishment imposed, upon a promise by the accused that they would not again offend against the law, nor advise, counsel, aid, or abet, in any way, its violation by others.

The Utah commissioners express the opinion, based upon such information as they are able to obtain, that but few polygamous marriages have taken place in the Territory during the last year. They further report that while there cannot be found upon the registration lists of voters the name of a man actually guilty of polygamy, and while none of that class is holding office, yet at the last election in the Territory, all the officers elected, except in one county, were men who, though not actually living in the practice of polygamy, subscribe to the doctrine of polygamous marriages as a divine revelation and a law unto all, higher and more binding upon the conscience than any human law, local or national. Thus is the strange spectacle presented of a community protected by a republican form of government, to which they all owe allegiance, sustaining by their suffrages a principle and a belief which set at naught that obligation of absolute obedience to the law of the land which lies at the foundation of republican institutions.

The strength, the perpetuity, and the destiny of the nation rest upon our homes, established by the law of God, guarded by parental care, regulated by parental authority, and sanctified by parental love. These are not the homes of polygamy.

The mothers of our land, who rule the nation as they mold the characters and guide the actions of their sons, live according to God's holy ordinances, and each, secure and happy in the exclusive love of the father of her children, sheds the warm light of true womanhood, unperverted and unpolluted, upon all within her pure and wholesome family circle. These are not the cheerless, crushed, and unwomanly mothers of polygamy.

The fathers of our families are the best citizens of the republic. Wife and children are the sources of patriotism, and conjugal and parental affection beget devotion to the country. The man who, undefiled with plural marriage, is surrounded in his single home with his wife and children, has a stake in the country which inspires him with respect for its laws and courage for its defense. These are not the fathers of polygamous families.

There is no feature of this practice, or the system which sanctions it, which is not opposed to all that is of value in our institutions.

There should be no relaxation in the firm but just execution of the law now in operation, and I should be glad to approve such further discreet legislation as will rid the country of this blot upon its fair fame.

Since the people upholding polygamy in our Territories are re-enforced by immigration from other lands, I recommend that a law be passed to prevent the importation of Mormons into the country.

VI.

RECIPROCITY TREATIES AND THE REVENUE.

(From the First Annual Message, December, 1885.)

On taking office, I withdrew for re-examination the treaties signed with Spain and Santo Domingo, then pending before the Senate. The result has been to satisfy me of the inexpediency of entering into engagements of this character not covering the entire traffic.

These treaties contemplated the surrender by the United States of large revenues for inadequate considerations. Upon sugar alone duties were surrendered to an amount far exceeding all the advantages offered in exchange. Even were it intended to relieve our consumers, it was evident that, so long as the exemption but partially covered our importation, such relief would be illusory. To relinquish a revenue so essential seemed highly improvident at a time when new and large drains upon the Treasury were contemplated. Moreover, embarrassing questions would have arisen under the favored-nation clauses of treaties with other nations.

As a further objection, it is evident that tariff regulation by treaty diminishes that independent control over its own revenues which is essential for the safety and welfare of any government. Emergency calling for an increase of taxation may at any time arise, and no engagement with a foreign power should exist to hamper the action of the government.

VII.

INTERNATIONAL COPYRIGHT AND THE DUTY ON ART WORKS.

I.

(From the First Annual Message to Congress, December, 1885.)

An international copyright conference was held at Berne in September, on the invitation of the Swiss Government. The envoy of the United States attended as a delegate, but refrained from committing this government to the results, even by signing the recommendatory protocol adopted. The interesting and important subject of international copyright has been before you for several years. Action is certainly desirable to effect the object in view. And while there may be question as to the relative advantage of treating it by legislation or by specific treaty, the matured views of the Berne conference cannot fail to aid your consideration of the subject.

Past Congresses have had under consideration the advisability of abolishing the discrimination made by the tariff laws in favor of the works of American artists. The odium of the policy which subjects to a high rate of duty the paintings of foreign artists, and exempts the productions of American artists residing abroad, and who receive gratuitously advantages and instruction, is visited upon our citizens engaged in art culture in Europe, and has caused them, with practical unanimity, to favor the abolition of such an ungracious distinction ; and in their interest, and for other obvious reasons, I strongly recommend it.

———

2.

(From the Second Annual Message to Congress, December, 1886.)

The drift of sentiment in civilized communities toward full recognition of the rights of property in the creations of the human intellect has brought about the adoption, by many important nations, of an international Copyright Convention, which was signed at Berne on the 18th of September, 1885.

Inasmuch as the Constitution gives to Congress the power "to promote the progress of science and useful arts by securing for limited times to authors and inventors the exclusive right to their respective writings and discoveries," this government did not feel warranted in becoming a signatory, pending the action of Congress upon measures of international copyright now before it; but the right of adhesion to the Berne Convention hereafter has been reserved. I trust the subject will receive at your hands the attention it deserves, and that the just claims of authors, so urgently pressed, will be duly heeded.

Representations continue to be made to me of the injurious effect upon American artists studying abroad and having free access to the art collections of foreign countries, of maintaining a discriminating duty against the introduction of the works of their brother artists of other countries; and I am induced to repeat my recommendation for the abolition of that tax.

3.

(To the American Copyright League.)

NEW YORK, December 6, 1889.

MY DEAR MR. JOHNSON:

I hope that I need not assure you how much I regret my inability to be with you and other friends and advocates of international copyright in this hour. It seems to me very strange that a movement having so much to recommend it to the favor of just and honest men should languish in the hands of our lawmakers.

It is not pleasant to have forced upon one the reflection that perhaps the fact that it is simply just and fair is to its present disadvantage. And yet I believe, and I know you and the others engaged in the cause believe, that ultimately and with continued effort the friends of this reform will see their hopes realized. Then it will be great satisfaction to know and feel that success was achieved by force of fairness, justice, and morality.　　　Yours very truly,

　　　　　　　　　　　　GROVER CLEVELAND.

MR. R. U. JOHNSON, *Secretary*.

VIII.

MORAL ISSUES IN POLITICS.

(Interview in the New York *Commercial Advertiser*, September 19, 1889.)

I am very much pleased, as every other true Democrat should be, both with the utterances of their conventions in Ohio and New Jersey, on national questions, and with the nominees. The platforms and the candidates stand for sturdy Democracy and for honest, wholesome tariff reform ; and they indicate that the Democratic party is in no mood for time-serving, hand-to-mouth evasion.

The Democracy, believing in certain principles and satisfied that the triumph of these principles involves the prosperity and well-being of the people, boldly announce them in full reliance on the sober thought and the intelligence of our countrymen. Here is found the very essence of Democratic faith. This undaunted courage, not born of expediency, and this devotion to the people's cause, manifested not only in the action of party organizations in certain States, but in Democratic utterances all over the land, are sufficient to make us all proud of our party.

Nor do we fight a losing battle, with only the consciousness of being right as our consolation in defeat. It seems to me that there never has been such an advance in any political question as there has lately been in favor of tariff reform. A fair examination of the subject by the people is bearing fruit and gives assurance that its triumph is at hand. So, if among those counted as Democrats, there are found timid souls, not well-grounded in the faith, who long for the fleshpots of vacillating shifts and evasions, the answer to their fears should be : " Party honesty is party expediency."

IX.

BALLOT REFORM—HOW THE SUFFRAGE IS DEBAUCHED.

(Interview in the Nashville *American*, February 1, 1890.)

Honest government would profit by ballot reform, and so would every worthy cause which depends upon honest and not upon corrupt methods for success.

The franchise is not debauched in the interest of good laws and honest government. It is by those who have special interests to subserve at the people's expense, and not by those whose interests are in common with the masses, that the ballot is corrupted. There are no rich and powerful corporations interested in buying " floaters " or coercing employees to vote for a reformation of our tariff laws.

The powers of corruption are employed upon the other side, and tariff reform, as all other reforms, must depend upon the unbought suffrage of the people. If the people are capable of self-government, and are to remain so, there cannot be too many safeguards about the expression of their will.

X.

THE EDUCATION OF THE COLORED PEOPLE.

816 MADISON AVENUE,
NEW YORK, January 14, 1891.

ISAIAH T. MONTGOMERY, ESQ.

Mr. Henry F. Downing has put in my hands your letter to him in relation to the school for the instruction of colored children at your home. The condition you describe has arrested my attention, and the projects you have in hand for the improvement of your people interest me so much that I feel like aiding you, though it be but to a slight extent.

I have an idea that opportunities for education and practical information among the colored population are most necessary to the proper solution of the race question in the South. At any rate, it seems to me to be of the utmost importance. If our colored boys are to exercise in their mature years the right of citizenship, they should be fitted to perform their duties intelligently and thoroughly. I hope that, in the school you seek to establish, the course of teaching will be directed to this end.

Inclosed please find my check for $25, which I contribute with hearty wishes for the success of your patriotic and praiseworthy undertaking.

Yours very truly,

GROVER CLEVELAND.

XI.

THE CHARACTER OF REPORTERS.

(Interview in *Daily Continent*, New York, April 12, 1891.)

I believe a large majority of reporters are decent and honorable men, who would prefer to do clean and respectable work. Of course there are some among them who are mentally and morally cracked, and who never ought to be trusted to report for the public anything they claim to have seen or heard. Eliminate these, and I do not think any of the remainder would deliberately indulge in downright barefaced falsehood; but there is something connected with their work that they appear to think is necessary to its complete finish, which, for want of a better word, may be called embellishing. This proceeds so far, sometimes, that, almost unknown to himself, the reporter falls into mischievous and exasperating falsehood—sometimes lacking the intent to annoy and injure and sometimes not. There ought to be much less of this. The reporter who sends in these extravagant embellishments can never know when they may constitute the most outrageous injury to the feelings of the innocent and defenseless.

But, as a general rule, the responsibility for all that is objectionable in the reportorial occupation should be laid at the doors of the managers and owners of newspapers. If they wanted fair and truthful reports, they would be furnished them with more alacrity than they are now supplied with the trash so often demanded as a test of the reporter's skill and ability.

Good, clean journalism and a proper sense of newspaper responsibility, prevailing at headquarters, would soon weed out the bad among reporters, and would so raise the standard of the duties of those remaining that they would not only be gladly welcomed by all who have information interesting to the public to impart, but would be received, without the suspicion of intrusion, at any place where legitimate news could be collected.

XII.

TRIBUTE TO DR. OLIVER WENDELL HOLMES.

UPPER SARANAC LAKE,
August 23, 1884.

To the Editors of "The Critic":

Your note suggesting a contribution to the Holmes number of *The Critic* has just been forwarded to me. Though I am not able to send you a word in time for its insertion in the forthcoming number, and though I should almost fear to place anything I might write in a collection which I know will be so rich in precious tributes, yet I cannot refrain from the expression of my hearty appreciation and admiration of your undertaking.

Not only the works of such a man as Dr. Holmes, but his life and years, belong to the country which they enrich and make more illustrious. God is good in that he has spared him thus long to his fellow-Americans; but in a totally unthinking and instinctive way, and as if our friend himself willed his stay with us, we find ourselves cherishing a sense of gratitude to him for continuing to shed so kindly and benign an influence upon our Nation's life.

The seventy-fifth birthday anniversary, which the Holmes number of *The Critic* commemorates, should be the occasion of hearty congratulation, not only to the man who has been spared so long, but to every American citizen.

GROVER CLEVELAND.

CHAPTER XIV.

THE CHARACTER OF GEORGE WASHINGTON.*

I.

Mr. President and Gentlemen :

It is sometimes said of us that we have too few holidays, and this perhaps is true. We do not boast the antiquity nor the long history which accumulates numerous days of national civic observance; and the rush and activity of our people's life are not favorable to that conservative and deliberate sentiment which creates and establishes holidays. So far as such days might commemorate the existence or achievements of some conspicuous personage, their infrequency may be largely attributed to our democratic spirit and the presumption arising from our institutions. In this land of ours—owned, possessed, and governed by the people—we, in theory at least, demand and expect that every man will, in his sphere, be a patriot, and that every faculty of greatness and usefulness with which he is endowed will be devoted to his country and his fellow-men. We have had no dearth of distinguished men, and no better heroism has anywhere been seen than here. But they belong so naturally to us, that we usually deem them sufficiently noticed and commemorated when they are acknowledged as contributions to the common fund of our national pride and glory.

Thus it happens that in this country but two birthdays are publicly celebrated. We reverently speak of one as the day when the Redeemer of Mankind appeared among men. On

* An address before the Southern Society of New York, on Washington's birthday, February 22, 1890, in response to the toast "The Birthday of George Washington."

the other the man was born whose mission it was to redeem the American people from bondage and dependence and to display to the world the possibility of popular self-government.

It would be strange, indeed, if this day should ever be neglected by our fellow-countrymen. It would be like a nation's blotting out the history which cements its governmental edifice, or expunging its traditions from which flow that patriotic love and devotion of its people which are the best guarantees of peaceful rule and popular contentment.

We certainly need at least one day which shall recall to our minds the truth that the price of our country was unselfish labor and sacrifice, that men fought and suffered that we might be free, and that love and American brotherhood are necessary elements to the full and continued enjoyment of American freedom, prosperity, and happiness.

We are apt to forget these things in our engrossment with the activities which attend the development of our country and in the impetuous race after wealth which has become a characteristic of our people. There is danger that we may grow heedless of the fact that our institutions are a precious legacy which, for their own sake, should be jealously watched and guarded, and there is danger that this condition may induce selfishness and sordidness, followed by the idea that patriotism and morality have no place in statecraft, and that a political career may be entered upon like any other trade for private profit and advantage

This is a frightful departure from the doctrines upon which our institutions rest; and surely it is the extreme of folly to hope that our scheme of government will effect its purpose and intent when every condition of its birth and life is neglected.

Point to your immense fortunes, if you will; point to your national growth and prosperity; boast of the day of practical politics, and discard as obsolete all sentiment and all conception of morality and patriotism in public life, but do not for a moment delude yourselves into the belief that you are navigating in the safe course marked out by those who launched and blessed the Ship of State.

Is Washington accused even in these days of being a sentimentalist? Listen to the admonition he addressed "as an old and affectionate friend" to his fellow-countrymen, whom he loved so well and for whom he had labored so long, as he retired from their service:

> Of all the dispositions and habits which lead to political prosperity, religion and morality are indispensable supports. In vain would that man claim the tribute of patriotism who should labor to subvert these great pillars of human happiness, these firmest props of the duties of men and citizens. The mere politician, equally with the pious man, ought to respect and cherish them.

And all is summed up and applied directly to our situation when he adds:

> It is substantially true that virtue or morality is a necessary spring of popular government.

When did we outgrow these sentiments? When did we advance so far in knowledge above our fathers as safely to cast aside these beliefs? Let us be sober and thoughtful, and if we find that these things have lost their hold on our minds and hearts, let us take soundings, for the rocks are near.

We need in our public and private life such pure and chastened sentiments as result from the sincere and heartfelt observance of days like this, and we need such quickening of our patriotism as the sedate contemplation of the life and character of Washington creates.

Most of all, because it includes all, we need a better appreciation of true American citizenship. I do not mean by this, that thoughtless pride of country which is everywhere assumed sometimes without sincerity, nor the sordid attachment born of benefits received or favors expected, but that deep and sentimental love for our citizenship which flows from the consciousness that the blessing of Heaven was invoked at its birth; that it was nurtured in the faith of God; and that it grew strong in the self-denying patriotism of our fathers and in their love of mankind.

Such an apprehension of American citizenship will consecrate us all to the disinterested service of our country and incite us to drive from the temple of our liberties the money changers and they who buy and sell.

Washington was the most thorough American that ever lived. His sword was drawn to carve out American citizenship, and his every act and public service was directed to its establishment. He contemptuously spurned the offer of kingly power, and never faltered in his hope to make most honorable the man who could justly call himself an American.

In the most solemn manner he warned his countrymen against any attack upon the unity of the government, and called upon them to frown indignantly upon any attempt to alienate any portion of the country from the rest, or to enfeeble the sacred ties that linked together the various parts.

His admonition reached the climax of its power and force when he said:

Citizens by birth or choice of a common country, that country has a right to concentrate your affections. The name of " American," which belongs to you in your national capacity, must always exalt the just pride of patriotism more than any appellation derived from any local discriminations.

In an evil hour, and amid rage and resentment, the warning of Washington was disregarded and the unity of our government was attacked. In blood and devastation it was saved, and the name of "American," which belonged to all of us, was rescued. From the gloom of desolation and estrangement all our countrymen were drawn again to their places by the mystic bond of American citizenship which, for all time to come, shall hold and ennoble them as hearty co-workers in accomplishing the national destiny which to the day of his death inspired the faith and hope of Washington.

As we commemorate his birth to-night, we will invoke his precious influence and renew our patriotic and disinterested love of country. Let us thank God that he has lived, and that he has given to us the highest and best example of American citizenship. And let us especially be grateful that we have this sacred memory, which spanning time, vicissitude, and unhappy alienation, calls us together in sincere fellowship and brotherly love on "The birthday of George Washington."

II.

SENTIMENT IN OUR NATIONAL LIFE.*

MR. PRESIDENT, LADIES AND GENTLEMEN:

Among the few holidays which the rush and hurry of American life concede to us, surely no one of a secular character is so suggestive and impressive as the day we celebrate on this occasion. We not only commemorate the birth of the greatest American who ever lived, but we recall, as inseparably con-- nected with his career, all the events and incidents which led up to the establishment of free institutions in this land of ours, and culminated in the erection of our wondrous nation.

The University of Michigan, therefore, most appropriately honors herself and does a fitting public service by especially providing for such an observance of the day as is calculated to turn to the contemplation of patriotic duty the thoughts of the young men whom she is soon to send out to take places in the ranks of American citizenship.

I hope it may not be out of place for me to express the gratification it affords me as a member of the legal profession, to know that the conduct of these exercises has been committed to the classes of the Law Department of the University. There seems to me to be a propriety in this, for I have always thought the influences surrounding the practice and study of the law should especially induce a patriotic feeling. The business of the profession is related to the enforcement and operation of the laws which govern our people; and its mem-

* An address before the students of the University of Michigan, at Ann Arbor, February 22, 1892.

bers, more often than those engaged in other occupations, are called to a participation in making these laws. Besides, they are constantly brought to the study of the fundamental law of the land, and a familiarity with its history. Such study and familiarity should be sufficient of themselves to increase a man's love of country; and they certainly cannot fail to arouse his veneration for the men who laid the foundations of our nation sure and steadfast in a written constitution, which has been declared, by the greatest living English statesman, to be "the most wonderful work ever struck off at a given time by the brain and purpose of man."

Washington had more to do with the formation of the constitution than our enthusiasm for other phases of the great work he did for his country usually makes prominent. He fought the battles which cleared the way for it. He best knew the need of consolidating under one government the colonies he had made free, and he best knew that without this consolidation, a wasting war, the long and severe privations and sufferings his countrymen had undergone and his own devoted labor in the cause of freedom, were practically in vain. The beginning of anything like a public sentiment looking to the formation of our nation is traceable to his efforts. The circular letter he sent to the governors of the States, as early as the close of the War of the Revolution, contained the germ of the constitution; and all this was recognized by his unanimous choice to preside over the convention that framed it. His spirit was in and through it all.

But whatever may be said of the argument presented in support of the propriety of giving the law classes the management of this celebration, it is entirely clear that the University herself furnishes to all her students a most useful lesson when, by decreeing the observance of this day, she recognizes the fact that the knowledge of books she imparts is not a complete fulfillment of her duty, and concedes that the education with which she so well equips her graduates for individual success in life and for business and professional usefulness, may profitably be supplemented by the stimulation of their patriotism, and by the direction of their thoughts to subjects relating to their country's welfare.   I do not know how generally such an observance of Washington's birthday, as has been here established, prevails in our other universities and colleges; but I am convinced that any institution of learning in our land which neglects to provide for the instructive and improving observance of this day within its walls, falls short of its attainable measure of usefulness and omits a just and valuable contribution to the general good.   There is great need of educated men in our public life, but it is the need of educated men with patriotism. The college graduate may be, and frequently is, more unpatriotic and less useful in public affairs than the man who, with limited education, has spent the years when opinions are formed in improving contact with the world instead of being within college walls and confined to the study of books.   If it be true, as is often claimed, that the scholar in politics is generally a failure, it may well be due to the fact that, during his formative period when lasting impressions are easily received, his intellect alone has been cultivated at the expense of wholesome and well-regulated sentiment.

I speak to-day in advocacy of this sentiment.   If it is not found in extreme and exclusive mental culture, neither is it found in the busy marts of trade, nor in the confusion of bargaining, nor in the mad rush after wealth.   Its home is in the soul and memory of man.   It has to do with the moral sense. It reverences traditions, it loves ideas, it cherishes the names and the deeds of heroes, and it worships at the shrine of patriotism.   I plead for it because there is a sentiment, which in some features is distinctively American, that we should never allow to languish.

When we are told that we are a practical and common sense people, we are apt to receive the statement with approval and applause.   We are proud of its truth and naturally proud because its truth is attributable to the hard work we have had to do ever since our birth as a nation, and because of the stern labor we still see in our way before we reach our determined destiny. There is cause to suspect, however, that another and less creditable reason for our gratification arises from a feeling that there is something heroically American in treating with indifference or derision all those things which, in our view, do not directly and palpably pertain to what we call, with much satisfaction, practical affairs, but which, if we were entirely frank, we should confess might be called money-getting and the betterment of individual condition. Growing out of this feeling, an increasing disposition is discernible among our people, which begrudges to sentiment any time or attention that might be given to business and which is apt to crowd out of mind any thought not directly related to selfish plans and purposes.

A little reflection ought to convince us that this may be carried much too far. It is a mistake to regard sentiment as merely something which, if indulged, has a tendency to tempt to idle and useless contemplation or retrospection, thus weakening in a people the sturdiness of necessary endeavor and diluting the capacity for national achievement.

The elements which make up the sentiment of a people should not be counted as amiable weaknesses because they are not at all times noisy and turbulent. The gentleness and loveliness of woman do not cause us to forget that she can inspire man to deeds of greatness and heroism; that as wife she often makes man's career noble and grand, and that as mother she builds and fashions in her son the strong pillars of a State. So the sentiment of a people which, in peace and contentment, decks with flowers the temple of their rule, may, in rage and fury, thunder at its foundations. Sentiment is the cement which keeps in place the granite blocks of governmental power, or the destructive agency whose explosion heaps in ruins their scattered fragments. The monarch who cares only for his sovereignty and safety, leads his subjects to forgetfulness of oppression by a pretense of love for their traditions; and the ruler who plans encroachments upon the liberties of his people, shrewdly proceeds under the apparent sanction of their sentiment. Appeals to sentiment have led nations to bloody wars which have destroyed dynasties and changed the lines of imperial territory. Such an appeal summoned our fathers to the battlefields where American independence was won, and such an appeal has scattered soldiers' graves all over our land, which mutely give evidence of the power of our government and the perpetuity of our free institutions.

I have thus far spoken of a people's sentiment as something which may exist and be effective under any form of government, and in any national condition. But the thought naturally follows, that, if this sentiment may be so potent in countries ruled by a power originating outside of popular will, how vital must its existence and regulation be among our countrymen, who rule themselves and make and administer their own laws. In lands less free than ours, the control of the governed may be more easily maintained if those who are set over them see fit to make concession to their sentiment; yet, with or without such concession, the strong hand of force may still support the power to govern. But sentiment is the very life blood of our nation. Our government was conceived amid the thunders that echoed "All men are created equal," and it was brought forth while free men shouted "We, the people of the United States." The sentiment of our fathers, made up of their patriotic intentions, their sincere beliefs, their homely impulses and their noble aspirations, entered into the government they established; and, unless it is constantly supported and guarded by a sentiment as pure as theirs, our scheme of popular rule will fail. Another and a different plan may take its place; but this which we hold in sacred trust, as it originated in patriotism, is only fitted for patriotic and honest uses and purposes, and can only be administered in its integrity and intended beneficence, by honest and patriotic men. It can no more be saved nor faithfully conducted by a selfish, dishonest, and corrupt people, than a stream can rise above its source or be better and purer than its fountain head.

None of us can be ignorant of the ideas which constitute the sentiment underlying our national structure. We know they are a reverent belief in God, a sincere recognition of the value and power of moral principle and those qualities of heart which make a noble manhood, devotion to unreserved patriotism, love for man's equality, unquestioning trust in popular rule, the exaction of civic virtue and honesty, faith in the saving quality of universal education, protection of a free and unperverted expression of the popular will, and an insistence upon a strict accountability of public officers as servants of the people.

These are the elements of American sentiment; and all these should be found deeply imbedded in the minds and hearts of our countrymen. When anyone of them is displaced, the time has come when a danger signal should be raised. Their lack among the people of other nations—however great and powerful they may be—can afford us no comfort nor reassurance. We must work out our destiny unaided and alone in full view of the truth that nowhere, so directly and surely as here, does the destruction or degeneracy of the people's sentiment undermine the foundations of governmental rule.

Let us not for a moment suppose that we can outgrow our dependence upon this sentiment, nor that in any stage of national advance and development it will be less important. As the love of family and kindred remains to bless and strengthen a man in all the vicissitudes of his mature and busy life, so must our American sentiment remain with us as a people—a sure hope and reliance in every phase of our country's growth. Nor will it suffice that the factors which compose this sentiment have a sluggish existence in our minds, as articles of an idle faith which we are willing perfunctorily to profess. They must be cultivated as motive principles, stimulating us to effort in the cause of good government, and constantly warning us against the danger and dishonor of faithlessness to the sacred cause we have in charge and heed-

lessness of the blessings vouchsafed to us and future generations, under our free institutions.

These considerations emphasize the value which should be
placed upon every opportunity afforded us for the contemplation of the pure lives and patriotic services of those who have
been connected with the controlling incidents of our country's
history.   Such contemplation cannot fail to re-enforce and
revive the sentiment absolutely essential to useful American
citizenship, nor fail to arouse within us a determinaton that
during our stewardship no harm shall come to the political
gifts we hold in trust from the fathers of the Republic.

It is because George Washington completely represented all
the elements of American sentiment that every incident of his
life, from his childhood to his death, is worth recalling—
whether it impresses the young with the beauty and value of
moral traits, or whether it exhibits to the wisest and oldest an
example of sublime accomplishment and the highest possible
public service.   Even the anecdotes told of his boyhood have
their value.   I have no sympathy with those who, in these latter
days, attempt to shake our faith in the authenticity of these
stories, because they are not satisfied with the evidence in their
support, or because they do not seem to accord with the conduct of boys in this generation.   It may well be, that the
stories should stand and the boys of the present day be pitied.

At any rate, these anecdotes have answered an important
purpose; and in the present state of the proofs, they should,
in my opinion, be believed.   The cherry tree and hatchet
incident and its companion declaration that the Father of his
Country never told a lie, have indelibly fixed upon the mind
of many a boy the importance of truthfulness.   Of all the
legends containing words of advice and encouragement which
hung upon the walls of the little district schoolhouse where a
large share of my education was gained, I remember but one,
which was in these words: "George Washington had only a
common school education."

I will not plead guilty to the charge of dwelling upon the

little features of a great subject. I hope the day will never come when American boys cannot know of some trait or some condition in which they may feel that they ought to be or are like Washington. I am not afraid to assert that a multitude of men can be found in every part of our land, respected for their probity and worth, and most useful to the country and to their fellow-men, who will confess their indebtedness to the story of Washington and his hatchet; and many a man has won his way to honor and fame, notwithstanding limited school advantages, because he found hope and incentive in the high mission Washington accomplished with only a common school education. These are not little and trivial things. They guide and influence the forces which make the character and sentiment of a great people.

I should be ashamed of my country, if, in further speaking of what Washington has done for the sentiment of his country-men, it was necessary to make any excuse for a reference to his constant love and fond reverence, as boy and man, for his mother. This filial love is an attribute of American man-hood, a badge which invites our trust and confidence, and an indispensable element of American greatness. A man may compass important enterprises, he may become famous, he may win the applause of his fellows, he may even do public service and deserve a measure of popular approval, but he is not right at heart, and can never be truly great, if he forgets his mother.

In the latest biography of Washington we find the follow-ing statement concerning his mother: "That she was affec-tionate and loving cannot be doubted, for she retained to the last a profound hold upon the reverential devotion of her son; and yet as he rose steadily to the pinnacle of human greatness, she could only say that 'George had been a good boy, and she was sure he would do his duty.'"

I cannot believe that the American people will consider themselves called upon to share the deprecatory feeling of the biographer, when he writes that the mother of Washington could *only* say of her son that she believed he would be faithful to the highest earthly trusts, because he had been good; nor that they will regard her words merely as an amiably tolerated expression of a fond mother. If they are true to American sentiment, they will recognize in this language the announcement of the important truth that, under our institutions and scheme of government, goodness, such as Washington's, is the best guarantee for the faithful discharge of public duty. They will certainly do well for the country and for themselves, if they adopt the standard the intuition of this noble woman suggests, as the measure of their trust and confidence. It means the exaction of moral principle and personal honor and honesty and goodness as indispensable credentials to political preferment.

I have referred only incidentally to the immense influence and service of Washington in forming our Constitution. I shall not dwell upon his lofty patriotism, his skill and fortitude as the military commander who gained our independence, his inspired wisdom, patriotism, and statesmanship as first President of the republic, his constant love for his countrymen, and his solicitude for their welfare at all times. The story has been often told, and is familiar to all. If I should repeat it, I should only seek to present further and probably unnecessary proof of the fact that Washington embodied in his character, and exemplified in his career, that American sentiment in which our government had its origin, and which I believe to be a condition necessary to our healthful national life.

I have not assumed to instruct you. I have merely yielded to the influence of the occasion; and attempted to impress upon you the importance of cultivating and maintaining true American sentiment, suggesting that, as it has been planted and rooted in the moral faculties of our countrymen, it can only flourish in their love of truth and honesty and virtue and goodness. I believe that God has so ordained it for the people he has selected for his special favor; and I know that the decrees of God are never obsolete.

I beg you, therefore, to take with you, when you go forth to assume the obligations of American citizenship, as one of the best gifts of your Alma Mater, a strong and abiding faith in the value and potency of a good conscience and a pure heart. Never yield one iota to those who teach that these are weak and childish things, not needed in the struggle of manhood with the stern realities of life. Interest yourselves in public affairs as a duty of citizenship; but do not surrender your faith to those who discredit and debase politics by scoffing at sentiment and principle, and whose political activity consists in attempts to gain popular support by cunning devices and shrewd manipulation. You will find plenty of these who will smile at your profession of faith, and tell you that truth and virtue and honesty and goodness were well enough in the old days when Washington lived, but are not suited to the present size and development of our country and the progress we have made in the art of political management. Be steadfast. The strong and sturdy oak still needs the support of its native earth, and, as it grows in size and spreading branches, its roots must strike deeper in the soil which warmed and fed its first tender sprout. You will be told that the people have no longer any desire for the things you profess. Be not deceived. The people are not dead but sleeping. They will awaken in good time, and scourge the money-changers from their sacred temple.

You may be chosen to public office. Do not shrink from it, for holding office is also a duty of citizenship. But do not leave your faith behind you. Every public office, small or great, is held in trust for your fellow-citizens. They differ in importance, in responsibility, and in the labor they impose; but the duties of none of them can be well performed if the mentorship of a good conscience and pure heart be discarded. Of course, other equipment is necessary, but without this mentorship all else is insufficient. In times of gravest responsibility it will solve your difficulties; in the most trying hour it will lead you out of perplexities, and it will, at all times, deliver you from temptation.

In conclusion, let me remind you that we may all properly learn the lesson appropriate to Washington's birthday, if we will; and that we shall fortify ourselves against the danger of falling short in the discharge of any duty pertaining to citizenship, if, being thoroughly imbued with true American sentiment and the moral ideas which support it, we are honestly true to ourselves.

> To thine own self be true,
> And it must follow as the night the day :
> Thou can'st not then be false to any man.

CHAPTER XV.

I.

ALBANY, February 24, 1885.

To the Hon. A. J. WARNER AND OTHERS, *Members of the Forty-eighth Congress:*

GENTLEMEN :

THE letter which I have had the honor to receive from you invites, and, indeed, obliges me to give expression to some grave public necessities, although in advance of the moment when they would become the objects of my official care and partial responsibility. Your solicitude that my judgment shall have been carefully and deliberately formed is entirely just, and I accept the suggestion in the same friendly spirit in which it has been made. It is also fully justified by the nature of the financial crisis, which, under the operation of the act of Congress of February 28, 1878, is now close at hand. By a compliance with the requirements of that law all the vaults of the Federal Treasury have been and are heaped full of silver coins, which are now worth less than 85 per cent. of the gold dollar prescribed as "the unit of value" in section 14 of the act of February 12, 1873, and which, with the silver certificates representing such coin, are receivable for all public dues. Being thus receivable, while also constantly increasing in quantity at the rate of $28,000,000 a year, it has followed, of necessity, that the flow of gold into the Treasury has been steadily diminished. Silver and silver certificates have displaced and are now displacing gold, and the sum of gold in the Federal Treasury now available for the payment of the gold obligations of the United States, and for the redemption of the United States notes called " greenbacks," if not already encroached upon, is perilously near such encroachment.

These are facts which, as they do not admit of difference of opinion, call for no argument. They have been forewarned to us in the official reports of every Secretary of the Treasury from 1878 till now. They are plainly affirmed in the last December report of the present Secretary of the Treasury to the Speaker of the present House of Representatives. They appear in the official documents of this Congress and in the records of the New York Clearing-house, of which the Treasury is a member, and through which the bulk of the receipts and payments of the Federal Government and of the country pass.

These being the facts of our present condition, our danger, and our duty to avert that danger, would seem to be plain. I hope that you concur with me, and with the great majority of our fellow-citizens, in deeming it most desirable at the present juncture to maintain and continue in use the mass of our gold coin as well as the mass of silver already coined. This is possible by a present suspension of the purchase and coinage of silver. I am not aware that by any other method it is possible. It is of momentous importance to prevent the two metals from parting company ; to prevent the increasing displacement of gold by the increasing coinage of silver ; to prevent the disuse of gold in the custom-houses of the United States in the daily business of the people ; to prevent the ultimate expulsion of gold by silver.

Such a financial crisis as these events would certainly precipitate, were it now to follow upon so long a period of commercial depression, would involve the people of every city and every State in the Union in a prolonged and disastrous trouble. The revival of business enterprise and prosperity, so ardently desired and apparently so near, would be hopelessly postponed. Gold would be withdrawn to its hoarding-places, and an unprecedented contraction in the actual volume of our currency would speedily take place. Saddest of all, in every workshop, mill, factory, store, and on every railroad and farm, the wages of labor, already depressed, would suffer still further depression by a scaling down of the purchasing power of every so-called dollar paid into the hand of toil. From these impending calamities it is surely a most patriotic and grateful duty of the representatives of the people to deliver them.

I am, gentlemen, with sincere respect, your fellow-citizen,

GROVER CLEVELAND.

II.

From the First Annual Message to Congress, December 8, 1885.

The very limited amount of circulating notes issued by our national banks compared with the amount the law permits them to issue, upon a deposit of bonds for their redemption, indicates that the volume of our circulating medium may be largely increased through this instrumentality.

Nothing more important than the present condition of our currency and coinage can claim your attention.

Since February, 1878, the government has, under the compulsory provisions of law, purchased silver bullion and coined the same at the rate of more than two millions of dollars every month. By this process, up to the present date, 215,759,431 silver dollars have been coined.

A reasonable appreciation of a delegation of power to the general government would limit its exercise, without express restrictive words, to the people's needs and the requirements of the public welfare.

Upon this theory, the authority to " coin money " given to Congress by the Constitution, if it permits the purchase by the government of bullion for coinage in any event, does not justify such purchase and coinage to an extent beyond the amount needed for a sufficient circulating medium.

The desire to utilize the silver product of the country should not lead to a misuse or the perversion of this power.

The necessity for such an addition to the silver currency of

the nation as is compelled by the silver coinage act, is nega-
tived by the fact that up to the present time only about fifty
millions of the silver dollars so coined have actually found
their way into circulation, leaving more than one hundred and
sixty-five millions in the possession of the government, the
custody of which has entailed a considerable expense for the
construction of vaults for its deposit. Against this latter
amount there are outstanding silver certificates amounting to
about ninety-three millions of dollars.

Every month two millions of gold in the public Treasury
are paid out for two millions or more of silver dollars, to be
added to the idle mass already accumulated.

If continued long enough, this operation will result in the
substitution of silver for all the gold the government owns
applicable to its general purposes. It will not do to rely upon
the customs receipts of the government to make good this
drain of gold, because—the silver thus coined having been
made legal tender for all debts and dues, public and private,
at times during the last six months fifty-eight per cent. of the
receipts for duties has been in silver or silver certificates, while
the average within that period has been twenty per cent. The
proportion of silver and its certificates received by the government will probably increase as time goes on, for the reason
that, the nearer the period approaches when it will be obliged
to offer silver in payment of its obligations, the greater
inducement there will be to hoard gold against depreciation in
the value of silver, or for the purpose of speculating.

This hoarding of gold has already begun.

When the time comes that gold has been withdrawn from
circulation, then will be apparent the difference between the
real value of the silver dollar and a dollar in gold, and the two
coins will part company. Gold, still the standard of value,
and necessary in our dealings with other countries, will be at a
premium over silver ; banks, which have substituted gold for
the deposits of their customers, may pay them with silver
bought with such gold, thus making a handsome profit ; rich

speculators will sell their hoarded gold to their neighbors who need it to liquidate their foreign debts, at a ruinous premium over silver, and the laboring men and women of the land, most defenseless of all, will find that the dollar, received for the wage of their toil, has sadly shrunk in its purchasing power.   It may be said that the latter result will be but temporary, and that ultimately the price of labor will be adjusted to the change ; but even if this takes place the wage worker cannot possibly gain, but must inevitably lose, since the price he is compelled to pay for his living will not only be measured in a coin heavily depreciated, and fluctuating and uncertain in its value, but this uncertainty in the value of the purchasing medium will be made the pretext for an advance in prices beyond that justified by actual depreciation.

The words uttered in 1834 by Daniel Webster, in the Senate of the United States, are true to-day : " The very man of all others who has the deepest interest in a sound currency, and who suffers most by mischievous legislation in money matters, is the man who earns his daily bread by his daily toil."

The most distinguished advocate of bi-metallism, discussing our silver coinage, has lately written : " No American citizen's hand has yet felt the sensation of cheapness, either in receiving or expending the Silver Act dollars."

And those who live by labor or legitimate trade never will feel that sensation of cheapness.   However plenty silver dollars may become, they will not be distributed as gifts among the people ; and if the laboring man should receive four depreciated dollars where he now receives but two, he will pay in the depreciated coin more than double the price he now pays for all the necessaries and comforts of life.

Those who do not fear any disastrous consequences arising from the continued compulsory coinage of silver as now directed by law, and who suppose that the addition to the currency of the country intended as its result will be a public benefit, are reminded that history demonstrates that the point is easily reached in the attempt to float at the same time two sorts of money of different excellence, when the better will cease to be in general circulation. The hoarding of gold, which has already taken place, indicates that we shall not escape the usual experience in such cases. So, if this silver coinage be continued, we may reasonably expect that gold and its equivalent will abandon the field of circulation to silver alone. This, of course, must produce a severe contraction of our circulating medium, instead of adding to it.

It will not be disputed that any attempt on the part of the government to cause the circulation of silver dollars worth eighty cents, side by side with gold dollars worth one hundred cents, even within the limit that legislation does not run counter to the laws of trade, to be successful must be seconded by the confidence of the people that both coins will retain the same purchasing power and be interchangeable at will. A special effort has been made by the Secretary of the Treasury to increase the amount of our silver coin in circulation ; but the fact that a large share of the limited amount thus put out has soon returned to the public treasury in payment of duties, leads to the belief that the people do not now desire to keep it in hand ; and this, with the evident disposition to hoard gold, gives rise to the suspicion that there already exists a lack of confidence among the people touching our financial proc-esses. There is certainly not enough silver now in circula-tion to cause uneasiness ; and the whole amount coined and now on hand might, after a time, be absorbed by the people without apprehension ; but it is the ceaseless stream that threatens to overflow the land which causes fear and uncer-tainty.

What has been thus far submitted upon this subject relates almost entirely to considerations of a home nature, uncon-nected with the bearing which the policies of other nations have upon the question. But it is perfectly apparent that a line of action in regard to our currency cannot wisely be settled upon or persisted in, without considering the attitude, on the subject, of other countries with whom we maintain intercourse through commerce, trade, and travel. An acknowledgment of this fact is found in the Act by virtue of which our silver is compulsorily coined. It provides that " the President shall invite the governments of the countries composing the Latin Union, so called, and of such other European nations as he may deem advisable, to join the United States in a conference to adopt a common ratio between gold and silver for the purpose of establishing internationally the use of bi-metallic money and securing fixity of relative value between these metals."

This conference absolutely failed, and a similar fate has awaited all subsequent efforts in the same direction. And still we continue our coinage of silver at a ratio different from that of any other nation. The most vital part of the silver-coinage Act remains inoperative and unexecuted, and without an ally or friend, we battle upon the silver field in an illogical and losing contest.

To give full effect to the design of Congress on this subject I have made careful and earnest endeavor since the adjournment of the last Congress.

To this end I delegated a gentleman, well instructed in fiscal science, to proceed to the financial centers of Europe, and, in conjunction with our Ministers to England, France, and Germany, to obtain a full knowledge of the attitude and intent of those governments in respect of the establishment of such an international ratio as would procure free coinage of both metals at the mints of those countries and our own. By my direction our Consul General at Paris has given close attention to the proceedings of the congress of the Latin Union, in order to indicate our interest in its object and report its action.

It may be said, in brief, as the result of these efforts, that the attitude of the leading powers remains substantially unchanged since the monetary conference of 1881, nor is it to be questioned that the views of these governments are, in each instance, supported by the weight of public opinion.

The steps thus taken have therefore only more fully demonstrated the uselessness of further attempts, at present, to arrive at any agreement on the subject with other nations.

In the meantime we are accumulating silver coin, based upon our own peculiar ratio, to such an extent, and assuming so heavy a burden to be provided for in any international negotiations, as will render us an undesirable party to any future monetary conference of nations.

It is a significant fact that four of the five countries composing the Latin Union, mentioned in our coinage Act, embarrassed with their silver currency, have just completed an agreement among themselves that no more silver shall be coined by their respective governments, and that such as has been already coined, and in circulation, shall be redeemed in gold by the country of its coinage. The resort to this expedient by these countries may well arrest the attention of those who suppose that we can succeed, without shock or injury, in the attempt to circulate, upon its merits, all the silver we may coin under the provisions of our silver coinage Act.

The condition in which our Treasury may be placed by a persistence in our present course, is a matter of concern to every patriotic citizen who does not desire his government to pay in silver such of its obligations as should be paid in gold. Nor should our condition be such as to oblige us, in a prudent management of our affairs, to discontinue the calling in and payment of interest-bearing obligations, which we have the right now to discharge, and thus avoid the payment of further interest thereon.

The so-called debtor class, for whose benefit the continued compulsory coinage of silver is insisted upon, are not dishonest because they are in debt ; and they should not be suspected of a desire to jeopardize the financial safety of the country, in order that they may cancel their present debts by paying the same in depreciated dollars. Nor should it be forgotten that it is not the rich nor the money-lender alone that must submit to such a readjustment enforced by the government and their debtors. The pittance of the widow and the orphan, and the income of helpless beneficiaries of all kinds, would be disastrously reduced. The depositors in savings banks and in other institutions which hold in trust the savings of the poor, when their little accumulations are scaled down to meet the new order of things, would, in their distress, painfully realize the delusion of the promise made to them that plentiful money would improve their condition.

We have now on hand all the silver dollars necessary to supply the present needs of the people and to satisfy those who from sentiment wish to see them in circulation ; and if their coinage is suspended they can be readily obtained by all who desire them. If the need of more is at any time apparent their coinage may be renewed.

That disaster has not already overtaken us furnishes no proof that danger does not wait upon a continuation of the present silver coinage. We have been saved by the most careful management and unusual expedients, by a combination of fortunate conditions, and by a confident expectation that the course of the government in regard to silver coinage would be speedily changed by the action of Congress.

Prosperity hesitates upon the threshold because of the dangers and uncertainties surrounding this question. Capital timidly shrinks from trade, and investors are unwilling to take the chance of the questionable shape in which their money will be returned to them, while enterprise halts at a risk against which care and sagacious management do not protect.

As a necessary consequence labor lacks employment, and suffering and distress are visited upon a portion of our fellow-citizens especially entitled to the careful consideration of those charged with the duties of legislation. No interest appeals to us so strongly for a safe and stable currency as the vast army of the unemployed.

I recommend the suspension of the compulsory coinage of silver dollars, directed by the law passed in February, 1878.

III.

From the Second Annual Message to Congress, December 6, 1886.

During the fiscal year ended June 30, 1886, there were coined, under the compulsory silver-coinage Act of 1878, 29,-838,905 silver dollars, and the cost of the silver used in such coinage was $23,448,960.01. There had been coined up to the close of the previous fiscal year, under the provisions of the law, 203,882,554 silver dollars, and on the 1st day of December, 1886, the total amount of such coinage was $247,131,549.

The Director of the Mint reports that at the time of the passage of the law of 1878 directing this coinage, the intrinsic value of the dollars thus coined was ninety-four and one-fourth cents each, and that on the 31st day of July, 1886, the price of silver reached the lowest stage ever known, so that the intrinsic or bullion price of our standard silver dollar at that date was less than seventy-two cents. The price of silver on the 30th day of November last was such as to make these dollars intrinsically worth seventy-eight cents each.

These differences in value of the coins represent the fluctuations in the price of silver, and they certainly do not indicate that compulsory coinage by the government enhances the price of that commodity or secures uniformity in its value.

Every fair and legal effort has been made by the Treasury Department to distribute this currency among the people. The withdrawal of the United States Treasury notes of small denominations, and the issuing of small silver certificates, have been resorted to in the endeavor to accomplish this result, in obedience to the will and sentiments of the representatives of the people in the Congress. On the 27th day of November, 1886, the people held of these coins, or certificates representing them, the nominal sum of $166,873,041, and we still had $79,464,345 in the Treasury, as against about $142,894,055 in the hands of the people, and $72,865,376 remaining in the Treasury one year ago. The Director of the Mint again urges the necessity of more vault room for the purpose of storing these silver dollars, which are not needed for circulation by the people.

I have seen no reason to change the views expressed in my last annual message on the subject of this compulsory coinage; and I again urge its suspension on all the grounds contained in my former recommendation, re-enforced by the significant increase of our gold exportations during the last year, as appears by the comparative statement herewith presented, and for the further reasons that the more this currency is distributed among the people the greater becomes our duty to protect it from disaster ; that we now have abundance for all our needs ; and that there seems but little propriety in building vaults to store such currency when the only pretense for its coinage is the necessity of its use by the people as a circulating medium.

IV.

From Fourth Annual Message to Congress, December 3, 1888.

At the close of the fiscal year ended June 30, 1887, there had been coined under the compulsory silver-coinage Act $266,988,280 in silver dollars, $55,504,310 of which were in the hands of the people.

On the 30th day of June, 1888, there had been coined $299,708,790 ; and of this $55,829,303 was in circulation in coin, and $200,387,376 in silver certificates, for the redemption of which silver dollars to that amount were held by the government.

On the 30th day of November, 1888, $312,570,990 had been coined, $60,970,990 of the silver dollars were actually in circulation, and $237,418,346 in certificates.

The Secretary recommends the suspension of the further coinage of silver, and in such recommendation I earnestly concur.

V.

Letter to the Reform Club Meeting, February 10, 1891.

E. ELLERY ANDERSON, *Chairman :*

DEAR SIR : I have this afternoon received your note inviting me to attend to-morrow evening the meeting called for the purpose of voicing the opposition of the business men of our city to " the free coinage of silver in the United States."

I shall not be able to attend and address the meeting as you request, but I am glad that the business interests of New York are at last to be heard on this subject. It surely cannot be necessary for me to make a formal expression of my agreement with those who believe that the greatest peril would be invited by the adoption of the scheme, embraced in the measure now pending in Congress, for the unlimited coinage of silver at our mints.

If we have developed an unexpected capacity for the assimilation of a largely increased volume of this currency, and even if we have demonstrated the usefulness of such an increase, these conditions fall far short of insuring us against disaster if, in the present situation, we enter upon the dangerous and reckless experiment of free, unlimited, and independent silver coinage.

Yours very truly,
GROVER CLEVELAND.

CHAPTER XVI.

ON PENSIONS AND TO SOLDIERS' ORGANIZATIONS.

I.

At the G. A. R. Banquet, in Buffalo, July 4, 1884.

I AM almost inclined to complain because the sentiment to which I am requested to respond is not one which permits me to speak at length of the city which, for more than twenty-nine years, has been my home. You bid me speak of the State, while everything that surrounds me, and all that has been done to-day, remind me of other things. I cannot fail to remember most vividly, to-night, that exactly two years ago I felt that much of the responsibility of a certain celebration rested on my shoulders. I suppose there were others who did more than I to make the occasion a success, but I know that I considered myself an important factor, and that when, after weeks of planning and preparation, the day came and finally passed, I felt as much relieved as if the greatest effort of my life had been a complete success.

On that day we laid the corner stone of the monument which has to-day been unveiled in token of its completion. We celebrated, too, the semi-centennial of our city's life. I was proud then to be its chief executive, and everything connected with its interests and prosperity was dear to me. To-night I am still proud to be a citizen of Buffalo, and my fellow-townsmen cannot, if they will, prevent the affection I feel for my city and its people. But my theme is a broader one, and one that stirs the heart of every citizen of the State.

The State of New York, in all that is great, is easily the leader of all the States. Its history is filled with glorious deeds, and its life is bound up with all that makes the nation great. From the first of the nation's existence our State has been the constant and generous contributor to its life and growth and vigor.

But to the exclusion of every other thought to-night, there is one passage in the history of the State that crowds upon my mind.

There came a time when discord reached the family circle of States, threatening the nation's life. Can we forget how wildly New York sprang forward to protect and preserve what she had done so much to create and build up. Four hundred and fifty thousand men left her borders to stay the tide of destruction.

During the bloody affray which followed, nearly fourteen thousand and five hundred of her sons were killed in battle or died of wounds. Their bones lie in every State where the war for the Union was waged. Add to these nearly seventeen thousand and five hundred of her soldiers, who, within that sad time, died of disease, and then contemplate the pledges of New York's devotion to a united country, and the proofs of her faith in the supreme destiny of the sisterhood of States.

And there returned to her thousands of her sons who fought and came home laden with the honors of patriotism, many of whom still survive, and, like the minstrels of old, tell us of heroic deeds and battles won which saved the nation's life.

When our monument, which should commemorate the sufferings and death of their comrades, was begun, the veterans of New York were here. To-day they come again and view complete its fair proportions, which in the years to come shall be a token that the patriotic dead are not forgotten.

The State of New York is rich in her soldier dead, and she is rich in her veterans of the war. Those who still survive, and the members of the Grand Army of the Republic, hold in trust for the State the blessed memories which connect her with her dead ; and these memories we know will be kept alive and green.

Long may the State have her veterans of the war : and long may she hold them in grateful and chastened remembrance. And as often as her greatness and her grandeur are told, let these be called the chief jewels in her crown.

II.

From the First Annual Message to Congress, December, 1885.

While there is no expenditure of the public funds which the people more cheerfully approve than that made in recognition of the services of our soldiers, living and dead, the sentiment underlying the subject should not be vitiated by the introduction of any fraudulent practices. Therefore, it is fully as important that the rolls should be cleansed of all those who by fraud have secured a place thereon, as that meritorious claims should be speedily examined and adjusted. The reforms in the methods of doing the business of this bureau which have lately been inaugurated promise better results in both these directions.

III.

From the Veto of the Andrew J. White Pension Bill,
May 8, 1886.

The policy of frequently reversing, by special enactment, the decisions of the bureau invested by law with the examination of pension claims, fully equipped for such examination, and which ought not to be suspected of any lack of liberality to our veteran soldiers, is exceedingly questionable. It may well be doubted if a committee of Congress has a better opportunity than such an agency to judge of the merits of these claims. If, however, there is any lack of power in the Pension

Bureau for a full investigation it should be supplied ; if the system adopted is inadequate to do full justice to claimants, it should be corrected ; and if there is a want of sympathy and consideration for the defenders of our government the bureau should be reorganized.

The disposition to concede the most generous treatment to the disabled, aged, and needy among our veterans ought not to be restrained ; and it must be admitted that, in some cases, justice and equity cannot be done nor the charitable tendencies of the government in favor of worthy objects of its care indulged under fixed rules. These conditions sometimes justify a resort to special legislation ; but I am convinced that the interposition by special enactment in the granting of pensions should be rare and exceptional. In the nature of things, if this is lightly done and upon slight occasion, an invitation is offered for the presentation of claims to Congress, which, upon their merits, could not survive the test of an examination by the Pension Bureau, and whose only hope of success depends upon sympathy, often misdirected, instead of right and justice. The instrumentality organized by law for the determination of pension claims is thus often overruled and discredited, and there is danger that in the end popular prejudice will be created against those who are worthily entitled to the bounty of the government.

There have lately been presented to me on the same day, for approval, nearly two hundred and forty special bills granting and increasing pensions, and restoring to the pension list the names of parties which for cause have been dropped. To aid Executive duty they were referred to the Pension Bureau for examination and report. After a delay absolutely necessary they have been returned to me within a few hours of the limit constitutionally permitted for Executive action. Two hundred and thirty-two of these bills are thus classified :

Eighty-one cover cases in which favorable action by the Pension Bureau was denied by reason of the insufficiency of the testimony filed to prove the facts alleged.

These bills I have approved on the assumption that the claims were meritorious, and that by the passage of the bills the government has waived full proof of the facts.

Twenty-six of the bills cover claims rejected by the Pension Bureau, because the evidence produced tended to prove that the alleged disability existed before the claimant's enlistment ; twenty-one cover claims which have been denied by such bureau, because the evidence tended to show that the disability, though contracted in the service, was not incurred in the line of duty ; thirty-three cover claims which have been denied, because the evidence tended to establish that the disability originated after the soldier's discharge from the army ; forty-seven cover claims which have been denied, because the general pension laws contain no provisions under which they could be allowed ; and twenty-four of the claims have never been presented to the Pension Bureau.

IV.

From the Message Vetoing the Elizabeth S. De Krafft Pension Bill, June 21, 1886.

I am so thoroughly tired of disapproving gifts of public money to individuals who, in my view, have no right or claim to the same, notwithstanding apparent Congressional sanction, that I interpose, with a feeling of relief, a veto in a case where I find it unnecessary to determine the merits of the application. In speaking of the promiscuous and ill-advised grants of pensions which have lately been presented to me for approval, I have spoken of their " apparent Congressional sanction " in recognition of the fact that a large proportion of these bills have never been submitted to a majority of either branch of Congress, but are the results of nominal sessions held for the express purpose of their consideration and attended by a small minority of the members of the respective houses of the legislative branch of government.

Thus, in considering these bills, I have not felt that I was aided by the deliberate judgment of the Congress ; and when I have deemed it my duty to disapprove many of the bills presented, I have hardly regarded my action as a dissent from the conclusions of the people's representatives.

I have not been insensible to the suggestions which should influence every citizen, either in private station or official place, to exhibit not only a just but a generous appreciation of the services of our country's defenders.   In reviewing the pension legislation presented to me, many bills have been approved upon the theory that every doubt should be resolved in favor of the proposed beneficiary.   I have not, however, been able to divest myself entirely of the idea that the public money appropriated for pensions is the soldiers' fund, which should be devoted to the indemnification of those who, in the defense of the Union and in the nation's service, have worthily suffered, and who, in the day of their dependence, resulting from such suffering, are entitled to the benefaction of their government. This reflection lends to the bestowal of pensions a kind of sacredness which invites the adoption of such principles and regulations as will exclude perversion as well as insure a liberal and generous application of grateful and benevolent designs. Heedlessness and a disregard of the principle which underlies the granting of pensions are unfair to the wounded, crippled soldier, who is honored in the just recognition of his government.   Such a man should never find himself side by side on the pension-roll with those who have been tempted to attribute the natural ills to which humanity is heir to service in the army.   Every relaxation of principle in the granting of pensions invites applications without merit, and encourages those who, for gain, urge honest men to become dishonest.   Thus is the demoralizing lesson taught the people that, as against the public Treasury, the most questionable expedients are allowable.

V.

From the Message Vetoing the Francis Deming Pension Bill, July 5, 1886.

None of us is entitled to credit for extreme tenderness and consideration toward those who fought their country's battles ; these are sentiments common to all good citizens ; they lead to the most benevolent care on the part of the government and deeds of charity and mercy in private life. The blatant and noisy self-assertion of those who, from motives that may well be suspected, declare themselves above all others friends of the soldier, cannot discredit or belittle the calm, steady, and affectionate regard of a grateful nation.

An appropriation has just been passed setting apart seventy-six millions of dollars of the public money for distribution as pensions, under laws liberally constructed, with a view of meeting every meritorious case ; more than a million of dollars was added to maintain the Pension Bureau, which is charged with the duty of a fair, just, and liberal apportionment of this fund.

Legislation has been at the present session of Congress perfected, considerably increasing the rate of pension in certain cases. Appropriations have also been made of large sums for the support of national homes where sick, disabled, or needy soldiers are cared for ; and within a few days a liberal sum has been appropriated for the enlargement and increased accommodation and convenience of these institutions.

All this is no more than should be done.

But with all this, and with the hundreds of special acts which have been passed, granting pensions in cases where, for my part, I am willing to confess that sympathy rather than judgment has often led to the discovery of a relation between injury or death and military service, I am constrained by a sense of public duty to interpose against establishing a principle and setting a precedent which must result in unregulated, partial,

and unjust gifts of public money under the pretext of indem-
nifying those who suffered in their means of support as an
incident of military service.

VI.

From the Second Annual Message, December, 1886.

The American people, with a patriotic and grateful regard
for our ex-soldiers—too broad and too sacred to be monopolized by any special advocates—are not only willing but
anxious that equal and exact justice should be done to all
honest claimants for pensions. In their sight the friendless
and destitute soldier, dependent on public charity, if otherwise
entitled, has precisely the same right to share in the provision
made for those who fought their country's battles as those
better able, through friends and influence, to push their claims.
Every pension that is granted under our present plan upon
any other grounds than actual service and injury or disease
incurred in such service, and every instance of the many in
which pensions are increased on other grounds than the merits
of the claim, work an injustice to the brave and crippled, but
poor and friendless soldier, who is entirely neglected or who
must be content with the smallest sum allowed under general
laws.

There are far too many neighborhoods in which are found
glaring cases of inequality of treatment in the matter of pensions ; and they are largely due to a yielding in the Pension
Bureau to importunity on the part of those, other than the
pensioner, who are especially interested, or they arise from
special acts passed for the benefit of individuals.

The men who fought side by side should stand side by side
when they participate in a grateful nation's kind remembrance.

Every consideration of fairness and justice to our ex-
soldiers, and the protection of the patriotic instinct of our citizens from perversion and violation, point to the adoption of a

pension system, broad and comprehensive enough to cover every contingency, and which shall make unnecessary an objectionable volume of special legislation.

As long as we adhere to the principle of granting pensions for service, and disability as the result of the service, the allowance of pensions should be restricted to cases presenting these features.

Every patriotic heart responds to a tender consideration for those who, having served their country long and well, are reduced to destitution and dependence, not as an incident of their service, but with advancing age or through sickness or misfortune. We are all tempted by the contemplation of such a condition to supply relief, and are often impatient of the limitations of public duty. Yielding to no one in the desire to indulge this feeling of consideration, I cannot rid myself of the conviction that if these ex-soldiers are to be relieved, they and their cause are entitled to the benefit of an enactment, under which relief may be claimed as a right, and that such relief should be granted under the sanction of law, not in evasion of it ; nor should such worthy objects of care, all equally entitled, be remitted to the unequal operation of sympathy, or the tender mercies of social and political influence with their unjust discriminations.

The discharged soldiers and sailors of the country are our fellow-citizens, and interested with us in the passage and faithful execution of wholesome laws. They cannot be swerved from their duty of citizenship by artful appeals to their spirit of brotherhood, born of common peril and suffering, nor will they exact, as a test of devotion to their welfare, a willingness to neglect public duty in their behalf.

VII.

Veto of the Dependent Pension Bill.

To the House of Representatives :

I herewith return without my approval House Bill No. 10,457, entitled " An act for the relief of dependent parents and honorably discharged soldiers and sailors who are now disabled and dependent upon their own labor for support."

This is the first general bill that has been sanctioned by the Congress, since the close of the late Civil War, permitting a pension to the soldiers and sailors who served in that war upon the ground of service and present disability alone, and in the entire absence of any injuries received by the casualties or incidents of such service.

While by almost constant legislation since the close of this war there has been compensation awarded for every possible injury received as a result of military service in the Union Army, and while a great number of laws passed for that purpose have been administered with great liberality, and have been supplemented by numerous private acts to reach special cases, there has not, until now, been an avowed departure from the principle, thus far adhered to respecting Union soldiers, that the bounty of the government, in the way of pensions, is generally bestowed, when granted, on those who, in their military service and in the line of military duty, have, to a greater or less extent, been disabled.

But it is a mistake to suppose that service pensions, such as are permitted by the second section of the bill under consideration, are new to our legislation. In 1818, thirty-five years after the close of the Revolutionary war, they were granted to the soldiers engaged in that struggle, conditional upon service until the end of the war, or for a term not less than nine months, and requiring every beneficiary under the act to be one " who is, or hereafter by reason of his reduced circumstances in life shall be, in need of assistance from his country for support." Another law of a like character was

passed in 1828, requiring service until the close of the Revolutionary war ; and still another, passed in 1832, provided
for those persons not included in the previous statute, but who
served two years at some time during the war, and giving a
proportionate sum to those who had served not less than six
months.

A service pension law was passed for the benefit of the
soldiers of 1812 in the year 1871—fifty-six years after the
close of that war—which required only sixty days' service ;
and another was passed in 1878—sixty-three years after the
war—requiring only fourteen days' service.

The service pension bill passed at this session of Congress,
thirty-nine years after the close of the Mexican war, for the
benefit of the soldiers of that war, requires either some degree
of disability or dependency, or that the claimant under its
provisions should be sixty-two years of age ; and in either
case that he should have served sixty days or been actually
engaged in a battle.

It will be seen that the bill of 1818 and the Mexican pension bill, being thus passed nearer the close of the wars in
which their beneficiaries were engaged than the others—one
thirty-five years and the other thirty-nine years after the termination of such wars—embraced persons who were quite advanced in age, assumed to be comparatively few in number,
and whose circumstances, dependence, and disabilities were
clearly defined and could be quite easily fixed.

The other laws referred to appear to have been passed at a
time so remote from the military service of the persons which
they embraced, that their extreme age alone was deemed to
supply a presumption of dependency and need.

The number of enlistments in the Revolutionary war is
stated to be 309,791, and in the war of 1812, 576,622 ; but it
is estimated that, on account of repeated re-enlistments, the
number of individuals engaged in these wars did not exceed
one-half of the number represented by these figures. In the
war with Mexico the number of enlistments is reported to be

112,230, which represents a greater proportion of individuals engaged than the reported enlistments in the two previous wars.

The number of pensions granted under all laws to soldiers of the Revolution is given at 62,069 ; to soldiers of the war of 1812 and their widows, 60,178 ; and to soldiers of the Mexican war and their widows, up to June 30, 1885, 7619. The latter pensions were granted to the soldiers of a war involving much hardship, for disabilities incurred as a result of such service ; and it was not till within the last month that the few remaining survivors were awarded a service pension.

The war of the rebellion terminated nearly twenty-two years ago ; the number of men furnished for its prosecution is stated to be 2,772,408. No corresponding number of statutes have ever been passed to cover every kind of injury or disability incurred in the military service of any war. Under these statutes 561,576 pensions have been granted from the year 1861 to June 30, 1886, and more than 2600 pensioners have been added to the rolls by private acts passed to meet cases, many of them of questionable merit, which the general laws did not cover.

On the 1st day of July, 1886, 365,763 pensioners of all classes were upon the pension rolls, of whom 305,605 were survivors of the war of the rebellion, and their widows and dependents. For the year ending June 30, 1887, $75,000,000 have been appropriated for the payment of pensions, and the amount expended for that purpose from 1861 to July 1, 1886, is $808,624,811.51.

While annually paying out such a vast sum for pensions already granted, it is now proposed, by the bill under consideration, to award a service pension to the soldiers of all wars in which the United States has been engaged, including, of course, the war of the rebellion, and to pay those entitled to the benefits of the act the sum of twelve dollars per month.

So far as it relates to the soldiers of the late Civil War, the bounty it affords them is given thirteen years earlier than it has been furnished to the soldiers of any other war, and before a large majority of its beneficiaries have advanced in age beyond the strength and vigor of the prime of life.

It exacts a military or naval service of only three months, without any requirement or actual engagement with an enemy in battle, and without a subjection to any of the actual dangers of war.

The pension it awards is allowed to enlisted men who have not suffered the least injury, disability, loss, or damage of any kind, incurred in or in any degree referable to their military service, including those who never reached the front at all, and those discharged from rendezvous at the close of the war, if discharged three months after enlistment. Under the last call of the President for troops, in December, 1864, 11,303 men were furnished who were thus discharged.

The section allowing this pension does, however, require, besides a service of three months and an honorable discharge, that those seeking the benefit of the act shall be such as " are now or may hereafter be suffering from mental or physical disability, not the result of their own vicious habits or gross carelessness, which incapacitates them for the performance of labor in such a degree as to render them unable to earn a support, and who are dependent upon their daily labor for support."

It provides further that such persons shall, upon making proof of the fact, " be placed on the list of invalid pensioners of the United States, and be entitled to receive, for such total inability to procure their subsistence by daily labor, twelve dollars per month ; and such pension shall commence from the date of the filing of the application in the Pension Office, upon proof that the disability then existed, and continue during the existence of the same in the degree herein provided ; provided that persons who are now receiving pensions under existing laws, or whose claims are pending in the Pension Office, may, by application to the Commissioner of Pensions, in such form as he may prescribe, receive the benefit of this act."

It is manifestly of the utmost importance that statutes which, like pension laws, should be liberally administered as measures of benevolence in behalf of worthy beneficiaries should admit of no uncertainty as to their general objects and consequences.

Upon a careful consideration of the language of the section of this bill above given, it seems to me to be so uncertain and liable to such conflicting constructions, and to be subject to such unjust and mischievous application, as to furnish alone sufficient ground for disapproving the proposed legislation.

Persons seeking to obtain the pension provided by this section must be now or hereafter :

1. "Suffering from mental or physical disability."

2. Such disability must not be "the result of their own vicious habits or gross carelessness."

3. Such disability must be such as " incapacitates them for the performance of labor in such a degree as to render them unable to earn a support."

4. They must be "dependent upon their daily labor for support."

5. Upon proof of these conditions they shall " be placed on the lists of invalid pensioners of the United States, and be entitled to receive, for such total inability to procure their subsistence by daily labor, twelve dollars per month."

It is not probable that the words last quoted, "such total inability to procure their subsistence by daily labor," at all qualify the conditions prescribed in the preceding language of the section. The "total inability " spoken of must be " such" inability—that is, the inability already described and constituted by the conditions already detailed in the previous parts of the section.

It thus becomes important to consider the meaning and the scope of these last mentioned conditions.

The mental and physical disability spoken of has a distinct meaning in the practice of the Pension Bureau, and includes every impairment of bodily or mental strength and vigor. For such disabilities there are now paid one hundred and thirty-one different rates of pension, ranging from $1 to $100 per month.

This disability must not be the result of the applicant's "vicious habits or gross carelessness." Practically, this division is not important. The attempt of the government to escape the payment of a pension, on such a plea, would, of course, in a very large majority of instances, and regardless of the merits of the case, prove a failure. There would be that strange but nearly universal willingness to help the individual as between him and the public Treasury which goes very far to insure a state of proof in favor of the claimant.

The disability of applicants must be such as to "incapacitate them for the performance of labor in such a degree as to render them unable to earn a support."

It will be observed that there is no limitation or definition of the incapacitating injury or ailment itself. It need only be such a degree of disability from any cause as renders the claimant unable to earn a support by labor. It seems to me that the "support" here mentioned as one which cannot be earned, is a complete and entire support, with no diminution on account of the least impairment of physical or mental condition. If it had been intended to embrace only those who by disease or injury were totally unable to labor, it would have been very easy to express that idea, instead of recognizing, as is done, a "degree" of such inability.

What is a support? Who is to determine whether a man earns it, or has it, or has it not? Is the government to enter the homes of claimants for pension, and after an examination of their surroundings and circumstances settle those questions? Shall the government say to one man that his manner of subsistence by his earnings is a support, and to another that the things his earnings furnish are not a support? Any attempt, however honest, to administer this law in such a manner would necessarily produce more unfairness and unjust discrimination and give more scope for partisan partiality, and would result in more perversion of the government's benevolent intentions, than the execution of any statute ought to permit.

If, in the effort to carry out the proposed law, the degree of disability, as related to earnings, be considered for the purpose of discovering if in any way it curtails the support which the applicant if entirely sound would earn, and to which he is entitled, we enter the broad field long occupied by the Pension Bureau, and we recognize as the only difference between the proposed legislation and previous laws passed for the benefit of the surviving soldiers of the civil war, the incurrence in one case of disabilities in military service, and in the other disabilities existing, but in no way connected with or resulting from such service.

It must be borne in mind that in no case is there any grading of this proposed pension.   Under the operation of the rule first suggested, if there is a lack in any degree, great or small, of the ability to earn such a support as the government determines the claimant should have, and by the application of the rule secondly suggested, if there is a reduction in any degree of the support which he might earn if sound, he is entitled to a pension of $12.

In the latter case, and under the proviso of the proposed bill, permitting persons now receiving pensions to be admitted to the benefits of the act, I do not see how those now on the pension roll for disabilities incurred in the service, and which diminish their earning capacity, can be denied the pension provided in this bill.

Of course none will apply who are now receiving $12 or more per month.   But on the 30th day of June, 1886, there were on the pension rolls 202,621 persons who were receiving fifty-eight different rates of pension from $1 to $11.75 per month.   Of these, 28,142 were receiving $2 per month; 63,116, $4 per month ; 37,254, $6 per month ; and 50,274, whose disabilities were rated as total, $8 per month.

As to the meaning of the section of the bill under consideration there appears to have been quite a difference of opinion among its advocates in the Congress. The chairman of the Committee on Pensions in the House of Representatives who reported the bill, declared that there was in it no provision for pensioning anyone who has a less disability than a total inability to labor, and that it was a charity measure. The chairman of the Committee on Pensions in the Senate, having charge of the bill in that body, dissented from the construction of the bill announced in the House of Representatives, and declared that it not only embraced all soldiers totally disabled, but in his judgment all who are disabled to any considerable extent; and such a construction was substantially given to the bill by another distinguished Senator who, as a former Secretary of the Interior, had imposed upon him the duty of executing pension laws and determining their intent and meaning.

Another condition, required of claimants under this act, is that they shall be " dependent upon their daily labor for support."

This language, which may be said to assume that there exists within the reach of the persons mentioned " labor," or the ability in some degree to work, is more aptly used in a statute describing those not wholly deprived of this ability, than in one which deals with those utterly unable to work.

I am of the opinion that it may fairly be contended that under the provisions of this section any soldier, whose faculties of mind or body have become impaired by accident, disease, or age, irrespective of his service in the army as a cause, and who, by his labor only, is left incapable of gaining the fair support he might with unimpaired powers have provided for himself, and who is not so well endowed with this world's goods as to live without work, may claim to participate in its bounty ; that it is not required that he should be without property, but only that labor should be necessary to his support in some degree ; nor is it required that he should be now receiving support from others.

Believing this to be the proper interpretation of the bill, I cannot but remember that the soldiers of our Civil War, in their pay and bounty, received such compensation for military service as had never been received by soldiers before, since mankind first went to war ; that never before, on behalf of any soldiery, have so many and such generous laws been passed to relieve against the incidents of war ; that statutes have been passed giving them a preference in all public employments ; that the really needy and homeless Union soldiers of the rebellion have been, to a large extent, provided for at soldiers' homes, instituted and supported by the government, where they are maintained together, free from the sense of degradation which attaches to the usual support of charity ; and that never before in the history of the country has it been proposed to render government aid toward the support of any of its soldiers based alone upon a military service so recent, and where age and circumstances appeared so little to demand such aid.   .

Hitherto such relief has been granted to surviving soldiers few in number, venerable in age, after a long lapse of time since their military service, and as a parting benefaction tendered by a grateful people.

I cannot believe that the vast peaceful army of Union soldiers, who, having contentedly resumed their places in the ordinary avocations of life, cherish as sacred the memory of patriotic service, or who, having been disabled by the casualties of war, justly regard the present pension-roll, on which appear their names, as a roll of honor, desire, at this time and in the present exigency, to be confounded with those who, through such a bill as this, are willing to be objects of simple charity and to gain a place upon the pension roll through alleged dependence.

Recent personal observation and experience constrain me to refer to another result which will inevitably follow the passage of this bill. It is sad, but nevertheless true, that already in the matter of procuring pensions there exists a widespread disregard of truth and good faith, stimulated by those who as agents undertake to establish claims for pensions, heedlessly entered upon by the expectant beneficiary, and encouraged or at least not condemned by those unwilling to obstruct a neighbor's plans.

In the execution of this proposed law, under any interpretation, a wide field of inquiry would be opened for the establishment of facts largely within the knowledge of the claimants alone ; and there can be no doubt that the race after the pensions offered by this bill would not only stimulate weakness and pretended incapacity for labor, but put a further premium on dishonesty and mendacity.

The effect of new invitations to apply for pensions, or of new advantages added to causes for pensions already existing, is sometimes startling.

Thus in March, 1879, large arrearages of pensions were allowed to be added to all claims filed prior to July 1, 1880. For the year from July 1, 1879, to July 1, 1880, there were filed 110,673 claims, though in the year immediately previous there were but 36,832 filed, and in the year following but 18,455.

While cost should not be set against a patriotic duty or the recognition of a right, still, when a measure proposed is based upon generosity or motives of charity, it is not amiss to meditate somewhat upon the expense which it involves. Experience has demonstrated, I believe, that all estimates concerning the probable future cost of a pension list are uncertain and unreliable, and always fall far below actual realization.

The chairman of the House Committee on Pensions calculates that the number of pensioners under this bill would be 33,105, and the increased cost $4,767,120 ; this is upon the theory that only those who are entirely unable to work would be its beneficiaries. Such was the principle of the Revolutionary pension law of 1818, much more clearly stated, it seems to me, than in this bill. When the law of 1818 was upon its passage in Congress the number of pensioners to be benefited thereby was thought to be 374 ; but the number of applicants under the act was 22,297, and the number of pensions actually allowed 20,485, costing, it is reported, for the first year, $1,847,900, instead of $40,000, the estimated expense for that period.

A law was passed in 1853 for the benefit of the surviving widows of Revolutionary soldiers who were married after January 1, 1800. It was estimated that they numbered 300 at the time of the passage of the act ; but the number of pensions allowed was 3742, and the amount paid for such pensions, during the first year of the operation of the act, was $180,000 instead of $24,000, as had been estimated.

I have made no search for other illustrations, and the above, being at hand, are given as tending to show that estimates cannot be relied upon in such cases.

If none should be pensioned under this bill except those utterly unable to work, I am satisfied that the cost stated in the estimate referred to would be many times multiplied, and with a constant increase from year to year ; and if those partially unable to earn their support should be admitted to the privileges of this bill, the probable increase of expense would be almost appalling.

I think it may be said that at the close of the War of the Rebellion, every Northern State and a great majority of Northern counties and cities were burdened with taxation on account of the large bounties paid our soldiers ; and the bonded debt, thereby created, still constitutes a large item in the account of the tax-gatherer against the people. Federal taxation, no less borne by the people than that directly levied upon their property, is still maintained at the rate made necessary by the exigencies of war. If this bill should become a law, with its tremendous addition to our pension obligation, I am thoroughly convinced that further efforts to reduce the Federal revenue and restore some part of it to our people, will and perhaps should be seriously questioned.

It has constantly been a cause of pride and congratulation

to the American citizen that his country is not put to the charge of maintaining a large standing army in time of peace. Yet we are now living under a war tax which has been tolerated in peaceful times to meet the obligations incurred in war. But for years past, in all parts of the country, the demand for the reduction of the burdens of taxation upon our labor and production has increased in volume and urgency.

I am not willing to approve a measure presenting the objections to which this bill is subject, and which, moreover, will have the effect of disappointing the expectation of the people and their desire and hope for relief from war taxation in time of peace.

In my last annual message the following language was used :

Every patriotic heart responds to a tender consideration for those who, having served their country long and well, are reduced to destitution and dependence, not as an incident of their service, but with advancing age or through sickness or misfortune. We are all tempted by the contemplation of such a condition to supply relief, and are often impatient of the limitation of public duty. Yielding to no one in the desire to indulge this feeling of consideration, I cannot rid myself of the conviction that if these ex-soldiers are to be relieved, they and their cause are entitled to the benefit of an enactment, under which relief may be claimed as a right, and that such relief should be granted under the sanction of law, not in evasion of it ; nor should such worthy objects of care, all equally entitled, be remitted to the unequal operation of sympathy, or the tender mercies of social and political influence with their unjust discriminations.

I do not think that the objects, the conditions, and the limitations thus suggested are contained in the bill under consideration.

I adhere to the sentiments thus heretofore expressed. But the evil threatened by this bill is, in my opinion, such that, charged with a great responsibility in behalf of the people, I cannot do otherwise than to bring to the consideration of this measure my best efforts of thought and judgment, and perform

my constitutional duty in relation thereto, regardless of all
consequences, except such as appear to me to be related to the
best and highest interests of the country.

GROVER CLEVELAND.

EXECUTIVE MANSION,
WASHINGTON, February 11, 1887.

VIII.

From the Message Vetoing the Loren Burritt Pension Bill, February 21, 1887.

This bill was reported upon adversely by the House Committee on Pensions ; and they, while fully acknowledging the
distressing circumstances surrounding the case, felt constrained
to adverse action, on the ground, as stated in the language of
their report, that " there are many cases just as helpless and
requiring as much attention as this one, and were the relief
asked for granted in this instance it might reasonably be
looked for in all."

No man can check, if he would, the feeling of sympathy and
pity aroused by the contemplation of utter helplessness as the
result of patriotic and faithful military service. But in the
midst of all this, I cannot put out of mind the soldiers in this
condition who were privates in the ranks, who sustained the
utmost hardships of war, but who, because they were privates,
and in the humble walks of life, are not so apt to share in
special favors of Congressional action. I find no reason why
this beneficiary should be singled out from his class, except it
be that he was a lieutenant-colonel instead of a private.

I am aware of a precedent for the legislation proposed,
which is furnished by an enactment of the last session of Congress, to which I assented, as I think improvidently; but I am
certain that exact equality and fairness in the treatment of our
veterans is after all more just, beneficent, and useful than unfair discrimination in favor of officers, or the special benefit,
born of sympathy, in individual cases.

IX.

Letter to the Reunion of Union and ex-Confederate Soldiers held at Gettysburg, July 2, 1887.

EXECUTIVE MANSION,
WASHINGTON, June 24, 1887.

MY DEAR SIR :

I have received your invitation to attend, as a guest of the Philadelphia Brigade, a reunion of ex-Confederate soldiers of Pickett's Division who survived their terrible charge at Gettysburg, and those of the Union Army still living, by whom it was heroically resisted.

The fraternal meeting of these soldiers upon the battlefield where twenty-four years ago, in deadly affray, they fiercely sought each other's lives, where they saw their comrades fall, and where all their thoughts were of vengeance and destruction, will illustrate the generous impulse of brave men and their honest desire for peace and reconciliation.

The friendly assault there to be made will be resistless, because inspired by American chivalry; and its results will be glorious, because conquered hearts will be its trophies of success. Thereafter this battlefield will be consecrated by a victory which shall presage the end of the bitterness of strife, the exposure of the insincerity which conceals hatred by professions of kindness, the condemnation of frenzied appeals to passion for unworthy purposes, and the beating down of all that stands in the way of the destiny of our united country.

While those who fought, and who have so much to forgive, lead in the pleasant ways of peace, how wicked appear the traffic in sectional hate and the betrayal of patriotic sentiment !

It surely cannot be wrong to desire the settled quiet which lights for our entire country the path to prosperity and greatness ; nor need the lessons of the war be forgotten and its results jeopardized in the wish for that genuine fraternity which insures national pride and glory.

I should be very glad to accept your invitation and be with you at that interesting reunion, but other arrangements already made and my official duties here will prevent my doing so.

Hoping that the occasion will be as successful and useful as its promoters can desire,

I am, yours very truly,

GROVER CLEVELAND.

MR. JOHN W. FRAZIER, *Secretary, etc.*

X.

Letter to the Mayor of St. Louis, Mo.

EXECUTIVE MANSION,
WASHINGTON, July 4, 1887.

HON. DAVID R. FRANCIS, *Mayor and Chairman.*

MY DEAR SIR : When I received the extremely cordial and gratifying invitation from the citizens of St. Louis, tendered by a number of her representative men, to visit that city during the national encampment of the Grand Army of the Republic, I had been contemplating for some time the acceptance of an invitation from that organization to the same effect, and had considered the pleasure which it would afford me, if it should be possible, to meet not only members of the Grand Army, but the people of St. Louis, and other cities in the West, which the occasion would give me an opportunity to visit. The exactions of my public duties I felt to be so uncertain, however, that, when first confronted by the delegation of which you were the head, I expected to do no more at that time than to promise the consideration of the double invitation tendered me, and express the pleasure it would give me to accept the same thereafter, if possible. But the cordiality and sincerity of your presentation, reinforced by the heartiness of the good people who surrounded you, so impressed me that I could not resist the feeling which prompted me to assure you on the spot that I would be with you and the Grand Army of the

Republic at the time designated, if nothing happened in the meantime absolutely to prevent my leaving Washington.

Immediately upon the public announcement of this conclusion, expressions emanating from certain important members of the Grand Army of the Republic, and increasing in volume and virulence, constrained me to review my acceptance of these invitations.

The expressions referred to go to the extent of declaring that I would be an unwelcome guest at the time and place of the national encampment. This statement is based, as well as I can judge, upon certain official acts of mine, involving important public interests, done under the restraints and obligations of my oath of office, which do not appear to accord with the wishes of some members of the Grand Army of the Republic.

I refuse to believe that this organization, founded upon patriotic ideas, composed very largely of men entitled to lasting honor and consideration, and whose crowning glory it should be that they are American citizens as well as veteran soldiers, deems it a part of its mission to compass any object or purpose by attempting to intimidate the Executive or coerce those charged with making and executing the laws. And yet the expressions to which I have referred indicate such a prevalence of unfriendly feeling and such a menace to an occasion which should be harmonious, peaceful, and cordial, that they cannot be ignored.

I beg you to understand that I am not conscious of any act of mine which should make me fear to meet the Grand Army of the Republic, or any other assemblage of my fellow-citizens. The account of my official stewardship is always ready for presentation to my countrymen.

I should not be frank if I failed to confess, while disclaiming all resentment, that I have been hurt by the unworthy and wanton attacks upon me growing out of this matter, and the reckless manner in which my actions and motives have been misrepresented both publicly and privately, for which, however, the Grand Army of the Republic, as a body, is by no means responsible.

The threats of personal violence and harm, in case I undertook the trip in question, which scores of misguided, unbalanced men under the stimulation of excited feeling have made, are not even considered.

Rather than abandon my visit to the West and disappoint your citizens, I might, if I alone were concerned, submit to the insults to which, it is quite openly asserted, I would be helplessly subjected if present at the encampment; but I should bear with me there the people's highest office, the dignity of which I must protect; and I believe that neither the Grand Army of the Republic as an organization, nor anything like a majority of its members, would ever encourage any scandalous attacks upon it.

If, however, among the membership of this body there are some, as certainly seems to be the case, determined to denounce me and my official acts at the national encampment, I believe they should be permitted to do so, unrestrained by my presence as a guest of their organization, or as a guest of the hospitable city in which their meeting is held.

A number of Grand Army posts have signified their intention, I am informed, to remain away from the encampment in case I visit the city at that time. Without considering the merits of such an excuse, I feel that I ought not to be the cause of such non-attendance. The time and place of the encampment were fixed long before my invitations were received. Those desiring to participate in its proceedings should be first regarded, and nothing should be permitted to interfere with their intentions.

Another consideration of more importance than all others remains to be noticed. The fact was referred to by you when you verbally presented the invitation of the citizens of St. Louis, that the coming encampment of the Grand Army of the Republic would be the first held in a Southern State. I suppose this fact was mentioned as a pleasing indication of the fraternal feeling fast gaining ground throughout the entire land and hailed by every patriotic citizen as an earnest that the Union has really and in fact been saved in sentiment and in spirit, with all the benefits it vouchsafes to a united people.

I cannot rid myself of the belief that the least discord on this propitious occasion might retard the progress of the sentiment of the common brotherhood which the Grand Army of the Republic has so good an opportunity to increase and foster. I certainly ought not to be the cause of such discord in any event or upon any pretext.

It seems to me that you and the citizens of St. Louis are entitled to this unreserved statement of the conditions which have constrained me to forego my contemplated visit, and to withdraw my acceptance of your invitation. My presence in your city, at the time you have indicated, can be of but little moment compared with the importance of a cordial and harmonious entertainment of your other guests.

I assure you that I abandon my plan without the least personal feeling, except regret, constrained thereto by a sense of duty, actuated by a desire to save any embarrassment to the people of St. Louis or their expected guests, and with a heart full of grateful appreciation of the sincere and unaffected kindness of your citizens.

Hoping the encampment may be an occasion of much usefulness, and that its proceedings may illustrate the highest patriotism of American citizenship,

I am,

Yours very sincerely,

GROVER CLEVELAND.

XI.

From the Message Vetoing the Mary Ann Dougherty Pension Bill, July 5, 1888.

I cannot spell out any principle upon which the bounty of the government is bestowed through the instrumentality of the flood of private pension bills that reach me. The theory seems to have been adopted that no man who served in the army can be the subject of death or impaired health except they are chargeable to his service. Medical theories are set at naught and the most startling relation is claimed between alleged incidents of military service and disability or death. Fatal apoplexy is admitted as the result of quite insignificant wounds, heart disease is attributed to chronic diarrhea, consumption to hernia, and suicide is traced to army service in a wonderfully devious and curious way.

Adjudications of the Pension Bureau are overruled in the most peremptory fashion by the special acts of Congress, since nearly all the beneficiaries named in these bills have unsuccessfully applied to that Bureau for relief.

This course of special legislation operates very unfairly.

Those with certain influence or friends to push their claims procure pensions, and those who have neither friends nor influence must be content with their fate under general laws. It operates unfairly by increasing, in numerous instances, the pensions of those already on the rolls, while many other more deserving cases, from the lack of fortunate advocacy, are obliged to be content with the sum provided by general laws.

The apprehension may well be entertained that the freedom with which these private pension bills are passed furnishes an inducement to fraud and imposition, while it certainly teaches the vicious lesson to our people that the treasury of the National Government invites the approach of private need.

None of us should be in the least wanting in regard for the veteran soldier, and I will yield to no man in a desire to see those who defended the government when it needed defenders liberally treated. Unfriendliness to our veterans is a charge easily and sometimes dishonestly made.

I insist that the true soldier is a good citizen, and that he will be satisfied with generous, fair, and equal consideration for those who are worthily entitled to help.

I have considered the pension list of the Republic a roll of honor, bearing names inscribed by national gratitude, and not by improvident and indiscriminate alms-giving.

I have conceived the prevention of the complete discredit which must ensue from the unreasonable, unfair, and reckless granting of pensions by special acts to be the best service I can render our veterans.

In the discharge of what has seemed to me my duty as related to legislation and in the interests of all the veterans of the Union Army, I have attempted to stem the tide of improvident pension enactments, though I confess to a full share of responsibility for some of these laws that should not have been passed.

I am far from denying that there are cases of merit which cannot be reached except by special enactment ; but I do not believe there is a member of either House of Congress who will not admit that this kind of legislation has been carried too far.

I have now before me more than one hundred special pension bills which can hardly be examined within the time allowed for that purpose.

My aim has been at all times, in dealing with bills of this character, to give the applicant for a pension the benefit of any doubt that might arise and which balanced the propriety of granting a pension, if there seemed any just foundation for the application ; but when it seemed entirely outside of every rule, in its nature or the proof supporting it, I have supposed I only did my duty in interposing an objection.

It seems to me that it would be well if our general pension laws should be revised with a view of meeting every meritorious case that can arise. Our experience and knowledge of any existing deficiencies ought to make the enactment of a complete pension code possible. In the absence of such a revision, and if pensions are to be granted upon equitable grounds and without regard to general laws, the present methods would be greatly improved by the establishment of some tribunal to examine the facts in every case and determine upon the merits of the application.

XII.

*From the Message Vetoing the Theresa Herbst Pension Bill,
July 17, 1888.*

John Herbst, the husband of the beneficiary named in this bill, enlisted August 26, 1862. He was wounded in the head at the battle of Gettysburg, July 2, 1863. He recovered from this wound, and on the 19th day of August, 1864, was captured by the enemy. After his capture he joined the Confederate forces, and in 1865 was captured by General Stoneman, while in arms against the United States Government. He was imprisoned and voluntarily made known the fact that he formerly belonged to the Union Army. Upon taking the oath of allegiance and explaining that he deserted to the enemy to escape the hardship and starvation of prison life, he was released and mustered out of the service on the 11th day of October, 1865.

He was regularly borne on the Confederate muster-rolls for probably nine or ten months. No record is furnished of the number of battles in which he fought against the soldiers of the Union, and we shall never know the death and the wounds which he inflicted upon his former comrades in arms. He never applied for a pension, though it is claimed now that at the time of his discharge he was suffering from rheumatism and dropsy, and that he died in 1868 of heart disease. If such disabilities were incurred in military service they were likely the result of exposure in the Confederate Army ; but it is not improbable that this soldier never asked a pension because he considered that the generosity of his government had been sufficiently taxed when the full forfeit of his desertion was not exacted.

The greatest possible sympathy and consideration are due to those who bravely fought, and, being captured, as bravely languished in rebel prisons. But I will take no part in putting a name upon our pension-roll which represents a Union soldier found fighting against a cause he swore he would uphold ;

nor should it be for a moment admitted that such desertion
and treachery are excused when they avoid the rigors of
honorable capture and confinement. It would have been a
sad condition of affairs if every captured Union soldier had
deemed himself justified in fighting against his government
rather than to undergo the privations of capture.

XIII.

From the Fourth Annual Message to Congress,
December, 1888.

I am thoroughly convinced that our general pension laws
should be revised and adjusted to meet, as far as possible in
the light of our experience, all meritorious cases. The fact
that one hundred and two different rates of pensions are paid
cannot, in my opinion, be made consistent with justice to the
pensioners or to the government ; and the numerous private
pension bills that are passed, predicated upon the imperfection
of general laws, while they increase in many cases existing
inequality and injustice, lend additional force to the recommendation for a revision of the general laws on this subject.

The laxity of ideas prevailing among a large number of our
people regarding pensions is becoming every day more marked.
The principles upon which they should be granted are in
danger of being altogether ignored, and already pensions are
often claimed because the applicants are as much entitled as
other successful applicants, rather than upon any disability
reasonably attributable to military service. If the establishment of vicious precedents be continued, if the granting of
pensions be not divorced from partisan and other unworthy
and irrelevant considerations, and if the honorable name of
veteran unfairly becomes by these means but another term
for one who constantly clamors for the aid of the Government,
there is danger that injury will be done to the fame and

patriotism of many whom our citizens all delight to honor, and that a prejudice will be aroused unjust to meritorious applicants for pensions.

XIV.

To a Pennsylvania Grand Army Post.

NEW YORK, October 24, 1889.

E. W. FOSNOT, ESQ.

DEAR SIR : Applications such as you make in your letter of the 22d instant are so numerous that it is impossible to comply with them all. You ask that Mrs. Cleveland or I shall contribute something to be " voted off " at the coming fair to be held by Post 176, of the Grand Army of the Republic, Department of Pennsylvania, and you state that the purpose of the fair is to increase the charity fund of the Post.

I do not know what your idea is as to the thing which we should send, and do not care to assume that anything which we might contribute to be " voted off " would be of especial value to the cause for which the fair is to be held. But it is so refreshing, in these days when the good that is in the Grand Army of the Republic is often prostituted to the worst purposes, to know that at least one Post proposes, by its efforts, to increase its efficiency as a charitable institution, that I gladly send a small money contribution in aid of this object.

No one can deny that the Grand Army of the Republic has been played upon by demagogues for partisan purposes, and has yielded to insidious blandishments to such an extent that it is regarded by many good citizens, whose patriotism and fairness cannot be questioned, as an organization which has wandered a long way from its avowed design. Whether this idea is absolutely correct or not, such a sentiment not only exists, but will grow and spread, unless within the organization, something is done to prove that its objects are not partisan, unjust and selfish.

In this country, where the success of our form of government depends upon the patriotism of all our people, the best soldier should be the best citizen.

Yours very truly,

GROVER CLEVELAND.

CHAPTER XVII.

THE INDIAN PROBLEM.

I.

From the First Annual Message to Congress, December, 1885.

IT is useless to dilate upon the wrongs of the Indians, and as useless to indulge in the heartless belief that, because their wrongs are revenged in their own atrocious manner, therefore they should be exterminated. They are within the care of our government, and their rights are, or should be, protected from invasion by the most solemn obligations. They are properly enough called the wards of the government; and it should be borne in mind that this guardianship involves, on our part, efforts for the improvement of their condition and the enforcement of their rights. There seems to be general concurrence in the proposition that the ultimate object of their treatment should be their civilization and citizenship. Fitted by these to keep pace in the march of progress with the advanced civilization about them, they will readily assimilate with the mass of our population, assuming the responsibilities and receiving the protection incident to this condition. The difficulty appears to be in the selection of the means to be at present employed toward the attainment of this result.

Our Indian population, exclusive of that in Alaska, is reported as numbering 260,000, nearly all being located on lands set apart for their use and occupation, aggregating over 134,000,000 of acres. These lands are included in the boundaries of 171 reservations of different dimensions, scattered in twenty-one States and Territories, presenting great variations in climate and in the kind and quality of their soils. Among the Indians upon these several reservations there exist the most marked differences in natural traits and disposition and in their progress toward civilization. While some are lazy, vicious, and stupid, others are industrious, peaceful, and intelligent; while a portion of them are self-supporting and independent, and have so far advanced in civilization that they make their own laws, administered through officers of their own choice, and educate their children in schools of their own establishment and maintenance, others still retain, in squalor and dependence, almost the savagery of their natural state.

In dealing with this question the desires manifested by the Indians should not be ignored. Here, again, we find a great diversity. With some the tribal relation is cherished with the utmost tenacity, while its hold upon others is considerably relaxed; the love of home is strong with all, and yet there are those whose attachment to a particular locality is by no means unyielding; the ownership of their lands in severalty is much desired by some, while by others, and sometimes among the most civilized, such a distribution would be bitterly opposed.

The variation of their wants, growing out of and connected with the character of their several locations, should be regarded. Some are upon reservations most fit for grazing, but without flocks or herds; and some, on arable land, have no agricultural implements; while some of the reservations are double the size necessary to maintain the number of Indians now upon them; in a few cases, perhaps, they should be enlarged.

Add to all this the difference in the administration of the agencies. While the same duties are devolved upon all, the disposition of the agents, and the manner of their contact with the Indians, have much to do with their condition and welfare. The agent who perfunctorily performs his duty and slothfully neglects all opportunity to advance their moral and physical improvement, and fails to inspire them with a desire for better things, will accomplish nothing in the direction of their civilization, while he who feels the burden of an important trust, and has an interest in his work, will, by consistent example, firm, yet considerate treatment, and well-directed aid and encouragement, constantly lead those under his charge toward the light of their enfranchisement.

The history of all the progress which has been made in the civilization of the Indian, I think will disclose the fact that the beginning has been religious teaching, followed by or accompanying secular education. While the self-sacrificing and pious men and women who have aided in this good work, by their independent endeavor, have for their reward the beneficent results of their labor and the consciousness of Christian duty well performed, their valuable services should be fully acknowledged by all who, under the law, are charged with the control and management of our Indian wards.

What has been said indicates that, in the present condition of the Indians, no attempt should be made to apply a fixed and unyielding plan of action to their varied and varying needs and circumstances.

The Indian Bureau, burdened as it is with their general oversight and with the details of the establishment, can hardly possess itself of the minute phases of the particular cases needing treatment; and thus the propriety of creating an instrumentality auxiliary to those already established for the care of the Indians suggests itself.

I recommend the passage of a law authorizing the appointment of six commissioners, three of whom shall be detailed from the Army, to be charged with the duty of a careful inspection from time to time of all the Indians upon our reservations or subject to the care and control of the government, with a view of discovering their exact condition and needs, and determining what steps shall be taken on behalf of the government to improve their situation in the direction of their self-support and complete civilization; that they ascertain from such inspection what, if any, of the reservations may be reduced in area, and in such cases what part, not needed for Indian occupation, may be purchased by the government from the Indians, and disposed of for their benefit; what, if any, Indians may, with their consent, be removed to other reservations, with a view of their concentration and the sale on their behalf of their abandoned reservations; what Indian lands now held in common should be allotted in severalty; in what manner and to what extent the Indians upon the reservations can be placed under the protection of our laws and subjected to their penalties; and which, if any, Indians should be invested with the right of citizenship. The powers and functions of the commissioners in regard to these subjects should be clearly defined, though they should, in conjunction with the Secretary of the Interior, be given all the authority to deal definitely with the questions presented, deemed safe and consistent.

They should be also charged with the duty of ascertaining the Indians who might properly be furnished with implements of agriculture, and of what kind; in what cases the support of the government should be withdrawn; where the present plan of distributing Indian supplies should be changed; where schools may be established and where discontinued; the conduct, methods, and fitness of agents in charge of reservations; the extent to which such reservations are occupied or intruded upon by unauthorized persons; and generally all matters related to the welfare and improvement of the Indian.

They should advise with the Secretary of the Interior concerning these matters of detail in management, and he should be given power to deal with them fully, if he is not now invested with such power.

This plan contemplates the selection of persons for commissioners who are interested in the Indian question, and who have practical ideas upon the subject of their treatment.

The expense of the Indian Bureau during the last fiscal year was more than $6,500,000. I believe much of this expenditure might be saved under the plan proposed; that its economical effects would be increased with its continuance; that the safety of our frontier settlers would be subserved under its operation, and that the nation would be saved through its results from the imputation of inhumanity, injustice, and mismanagement.

———

II.

From the Second Annual Message, December, 1886.

The present system of agencies, while absolutely necessary and well adapted for the management of our Indian affairs and for the ends in view when it was adopted, is, in the present stage of Indian management, inadequate, standing alone, for the accomplishment of an object which has become pressing in its importance—the more rapid transition from tribal organizations to citizenship of such portions of the Indians as are capable of civilized life.

When the existing system was adopted the Indian race was outside of the limits of organized States and Territories, and beyond the immediate reach and operation of civilization; and all efforts were mainly directed to the maintenance of friendly relations and the preservation of peace and quiet on the frontier. All this is now changed. There is no such thing as the Indian frontier. Civilization, with the busy hum of industry and the influences of Christianity, surrounds these people at every point. None of the tribes is outside of the bounds of organized government and society, except that the territorial system has not been extended over that portion of the country known as the Indian Territory. As a race the Indians are no longer hostile, but may be considered as submissive to the control of the government; few of them only are troublesome. Except the fragments of several bands, all are now gathered upon reservations.

It is no longer possible for them to subsist by the chase and the spontaneous productions of the earth. With an abundance of land, if furnished with the means and implements for profitable husbandry, their life of entire dependence upon government rations from day to day is no longer defensible. Their inclination, long fostered by a defective system of control, is to cling to the habits and customs of their ancestors and struggle with persistence against the change of life which their altered circumstances press upon them. But barbarism and civilization cannot live together. It is impossible that such incongruous conditions should coexist on the same soil.

They are a portion of our people, are under the authority of our government, and have a peculiar claim upon, and are entitled to, the fostering care and protection of the nation. The government cannot relieve itself of this responsibility until they are so far trained and civilized as to be able wholly to manage and care for themselves. The paths in which they should walk must be clearly marked out for them, and they must be led or guided until they are familiar with the way and competent to assume the duties and responsibilities of our citizenship.

Progress in this great work will continue only at the present slow pace and at great expense, unless the system and methods of management are improved to meet the changed conditions and urgent demands of the service.

The agents having general charge and supervision in many cases of more than 5000 Indians, scattered over large reservations, and burdened with the details of accountability for funds and supplies, have time to look after the industrial training and improvement of a few Indians only; the many are neglected and remain idle and dependent—conditions not favorable for progress in civilization.

The compensation allowed these agents and the conditions of the service are not calculated to secure for the work men who are fitted by ability and skill to plan properly and direct intelligently the methods best adapted to produce the most speedy results and permanent benefits. Hence the necessity for a supplemental agency or system, directed to the end of promoting the general and more rapid transition of the tribes from habits and customs of barbarism to the ways of civilization.

With an anxious desire to devise some plan of operation by which to secure the welfare of the Indians, and to relieve the Treasury as far as possible from the support of an idle and dependent population, I recommended in my previous annual message the passage of a law authorizing the appointment of a commission, as an instrumentality auxiliary to those already established, for the care of the Indians. It was designed that this commission should be composed of six intelligent and capable persons—three to be detailed from the Army—having practical ideas upon the subject of the treatment of Indians, and interested in their welfare; and that it should be charged, under the direction of the Secretary of the Interior, with the management of such matters of detail as cannot, with the present organization, be properly and successfully conducted, and which present different phases, as the Indians themselves differ, in their progress, needs, disposition, and capacity for improvement or immediate self-support.

By the aid of such a commission much unwise and useless expenditure of money, waste of materials, and unavailing effort might be avoided; and it is hoped that this, or some measure which the wisdom of Congress may better devise to supply the deficiency of the present system, may receive your consideration, and the appropriate legislation be provided.

The time is ripe for the work of such an agency. There is less opposition to the education and training of the Indian youth, as shown by the increased attendance upon the schools, and there is a yielding tendency for the individual holding of lands. Development and advancement in these directions are essential, and should have every encouragement. As the rising generation are taught the language of civilization and trained in habits of industry, they should assume the duties, privileges, and responsibilities of citizenship.

No obstacle should hinder the location and settlement of any Indian willing to take land in severalty; on the contrary, the inclination to do so should be stimulated at all times when proper and expedient. But there is no authority of law for making allotments on some of the reservations, and on others the allotments provided for are so small that the Indians, though ready and desiring to settle down, are not willing to accept such small areas when their reservations contain ample lands to afford them homesteads of sufficient size to meet their present and future needs.

These inequalities of existing special laws and treaties should be corrected, and some general legislation on the subject should be provided, so that the more progressive members of the different tribes may be settled upon homesteads, and by their example lead others to follow, breaking away from tribal customs and substituting therefor the love of home, the interest of the family, and the rule of the State.

The Indian character and nature are such that they are not easily led while brooding over unadjusted wrongs. This is especially so regarding their lands. Matters arising from the construction and operation of railroads across some of the reservations, and claims of title and right of occupancy set up by white persons to some of the best land within other reservations, require legislation for their final adjustment.

The settlement of these matters will remove many embarrassments to progress in the work of leading the Indians to the adoption of our institutions and bringing them under the operation, the influence, and the protection of the universal laws of our country.

III.

Text-books in Indian Schools.

EXECUTIVE MANSION,
WASHINGTON, March 29, 1888.

REV. JAMES MORROW, D. D.:

MY DEAR SIR: I have received from you certain resolutions passed at the Annual Conference of the Methodist Episcopal Church held at Philadelphia on the 20th instant. I am not informed how to address a response to the officers of the con-

ference who have signed these resolutions, and for that reason
I transmit my reply to you.

The action taken by this assemblage of Christian men has
greatly surprised and disappointed me. They declare "that
this conference earnestly protests against the recent action of
the government excluding the use of native languages in the
education of the Indians, and especially the exclusion of the
Dakota Bible among those tribes where it was formerly used.
That, while admitting that there are advantages in teaching
English to the Indians, to compel them to receive all religious
instruction in that language would practically hinder their receiving it in the most effective way, as the line of power travels
with the human heart, and the heart of the Indian is in his language. That it is in harmony with the genius of our country
—a free church in a free state—that the operations of all
missionary societies should be untrammeled by state interferences."

The rules of the Indian Bureau upon the subject referred
to are as follows :

First. No text-books in the vernacular will be allowed in
any school where children are placed under contract or where
the government contributes in any manner whatever to the
support of the school. No oral instruction in the vernacular
will be allowed at such schools. The entire curriculum must
be in the English language.

Second. The vernacular may be used in missionary schools
only for oral instruction in morals and religion, where it is
deemed to be an auxiliary to the English language in conveying such instruction ; and only native Indian teachers will be
permitted to teach otherwise in any Indian vernacular; and
these native teachers will only be allowed so to teach in
schools not supported in whole or in part by the government,
and at remote points, where there are no government or contract schools where the English language is taught. These
native teachers are only allowed to teach in the vernacular
with a view of reaching those Indians who cannot have the

advantages of instruction in English, and such instruction must give way to the English-teaching schools as soon as they are established where the Indians can have access to them.

Third. A limited theological class of Indian young men may be trained in the vernacular at any purely missionary school supported exclusively by missionary societies, the object being to prepare them for the ministry, whose subsequent work shall be confined to preaching, unless they are employed as teachers in remote settlements where English schools are inaccessible.

Fourth. These rules are not intended to prevent the possession or use by any Indian of the Bible published in the vernacular, but such possession or use shall not interfere with the teachers of the English language to the extent and in the manner herein before directed.

The government seeks, in its management of the Indians, to civilize them, and to prepare them for that contact with the world which necessarily accompanies civilization. Manifestly, nothing is more important to the Indian, from this point of view, than a knowledge of the English language. All the efforts of those having the matter in charge tend to the ultimate mixture of the Indians with our other people, thus making one community equal in all those things which pertain to American citizenship.

But this ought not to be done while the Indians are entirely ignorant of the English language. It seems to me it would be a cruel mockery to send them out into the world without this shield from imposition and without this weapon to force their way to self-support and independence.

Nothing can be more consistent, then, than to insist upon the teaching of English in our Indian schools. It will not do to permit these wards of the nation, in their preparation to become their own masters, to indulge in their barbarous language because it is easier for them or because it pleases them. The action of the conference, therefore, surprises me, if by it they mean to protest against such exclusion as is prescribed in

the order. It will be observed that "text-books in the vernacular" are what are prohibited, and "oral instruction"; the
"entire curriculum" must be in English. These are the terms
used to define the elements of an ordinary secular education
and do not refer to religious or moral teaching. Secular
teaching is the object of the ordinary government schools; but
surely there can be no objection to reading a chapter in the
Bible in English, or in Dakota if English could not be understood, at the daily opening of those schools, as is done in very
many other well-regulated secular schools. It may be, too,
that the use of words in the vernacular may be sometimes necessary to aid in communicating a knowledge of the English
language; but the use of the vernacular should not be encouraged or continued beyond the limit of such necessity; and the
"text-books," the "oral instruction" in a general sense, and
the "curriculum" certainly should be in English. In missionary schools moral and religious instruction may be given in the
vernacular as an auxiliary to English in conveying such
instruction. Here, while the desirability of some instruction
in morals and religion is recognized, the extreme value of
learning the English language is not lost sight of. And the
provision which follows, that only native teachers shall "otherwise"—that is, except for moral or religious instruction—
teach the vernacular, and only in remote places and until government or contract schools are established, is in exact keeping
with the purpose of the government to exclude the Indian
languages from the schools so far as is consistent with a due
regard for the continuance of moral and religious teaching in
the missionary schools, and except in such cases as the exclusion would result in the entire neglect of secular for other
instruction.

Provision is made in the rules for the theological training of
young men in missionary schools to fit them as Indian preach-
ers, and the possession and use of the Bible, so far as they do
not interfere with the secular English teaching insisted upon,
are especially secured.

I cannot believe that these rules of the Indian Bureau were at hand when the resolutions before me were adopted. If they were I think they were strangely misunderstood, though the mild admission that "there are advantages in teaching English to the Indians" indicates that there is a wide difference between those who appear cautiously to make such an admission and the many others interested in Indian improvement who deem such teaching the paramount object of immediate effort.

The rules referred to have been modified and changed in their phraseology, to meet the views of good men who seek to aid the government in its benevolent intentions, until it was supposed their meaning was quite plain and their purpose satisfactory. There need be no fear that in their execution they will at all interfere with the plans of those who sensibly desire the improvement and welfare of the Indians. At any rate, until it is demonstrated that these rules operate as impediments to Indian advancement they will be adhered to, while the government will continue to invoke the assistance of all Christian people and organizations in this very important and interesting part of labor intrusted to it.

Yours very truly,

GROVER CLEVELAND.

IV.

From the Fourth Annual Message, December, 1888.

The condition of our Indian population continues to improve, and the proofs multiply that the transforming change, so much to be desired, which shall substitute for barbarism enlightenment and civilizing education, is in favorable progress. Our relations with these people during the year have been disturbed by no serious disorders, but rather marked by a better realization of their true interests, and increasing confidence and good-will. These conditions testify to the value of the higher tone of consideration and humanity which has governed the later methods of dealing with them, and commend its continued observance.

Allotments in severalty have been made on some reservations until all those entitled to land thereon have had their shares assigned, and the work is still continued. In directing the execution of this duty I have not aimed so much at rapid dispatch as to secure just and fair arrangements which shall best conduce to the objects of the law, by producing satisfaction with the results of the allotments made. No measure of general effect has ever been entered on from which more may be fairly hoped, if it shall be discreetly administered. It proffers opportunity and inducement to that independence of spirit and life which the Indian peculiarly needs, while at the same time the inalienability of title affords security against the risks his inexperience of affairs or weakness of character may expose him to in dealing with others. Whenever begun upon any reservation it should be made complete, so that all are brought to the same condition, and, as soon as possible, community in lands should cease by opening such as remain unallotted to settlement. Contact with the ways of industrious and successful farmers will, perhaps, add a healthy emulation which will both instruct and stimulate.

But no agency for the amelioration of this people appears to me so promising as the extension, urged by the Secretary, of such complete facilities of education as shall, at the earliest possible day, embrace the teachable Indian youth, of both sexes, and retain them with a kindly and beneficent hold until their characters are formed and their faculties and dispositions trained to the sure pursuit of some form of useful industry. Capacity of the Indian no longer needs demonstration. It is established. It remains to make the most of it, and when that shall be done the curse will be lifted, the Indian race saved, and the sin of their oppression redeemed. The time of its accomplishment depends upon the spirit and justice with which it shall be prosecuted. It cannot be too soon for the Indian, nor for the interests and good name of the nation.

The average attendance of Indian pupils on the schools increased by over 900 during the year, and the total enrollment reached 15,212. The cost of maintenance was not materially raised. The number of teachable Indian youth is now estimated at 40,000, or nearly three times the enrollment of the schools. It is believed that the obstacles in the way of instructing are all surmountable, and that the necessary expenditure would be a measure of economy.

The Sioux tribes on the great reservation of Dakota refused to assent to the act passed by the Congress at its last session for opening a portion of their lands to settlement, notwithstanding modification of the terms was suggested which met most of their objections. Their demand is for immediate payment of the full price of $1.25 per acre for the entire body of land the occupancy of which they are asked to relinquish.

The manner of submission insured their fair understanding of the law, and their action was undoubtedly as thoroughly intelligent as their capacity admitted. It is at least gratifying that no reproach of overreaching can in any manner lie against the government, however advisable the favorable completion of the negotiation may have been esteemed.

I concur in the suggestions of the Secretary regarding the Turtle Mountain Indians, the two reservations in California, and the Crees. They should, in my opinion, receive immediate attention.

The Apache Indians, whose removal from their reservation in Arizona followed the capture of those of their number who engaged in a bloody and murderous raid during a part of the years 1885 and 1886, are now held as prisoners of war at Mount Vernon barracks, in the State of Alabama. They numbered, on the 31st day of October, the date of the last report, 83 men, 170 women, 70 boys, and 59 girls, in all 382 persons. The commanding officer states that they are in good health and contented, and that they are kept employed as fully as is possible in the circumstances. The children, as they arrive at a suitable age, are sent to the Indian schools at Carlisle and Hampton. Last summer some charitable and kind people asked permission to send two teachers to these Indians, for the purpose of instructing the adults as well as such children as should be found there. Such permission was readily granted, accommodations were provided for the teachers, and some portions of the buildings at the barracks were made available for school purposes. The good work contemplated has been commenced, and the teachers engaged are paid by the ladies with whom the plan originated.

I am not at all in sympathy with those benevolent but injudicious people who are constantly insisting that these Indians should be returned to their reservation. Their removal was an absolute necessity if the lives and property of citizens upon the frontier are to be at all regarded by the government. Their continued restraint, at a distance from the scene of their repeated and cruel murders and outrages, is still necessary. It is a mistaken philanthropy, every way injurious, which prompts the desire to see these savages returned to their old haunts. They are in their present location as the result of the best judgment of those having official responsibility in the matter, and who are by no means lacking in kind consideration for the Indians. A number of these prisoners have forfeited their lives to outraged law and humanity. Experience has proved that they are dangerous and cannot be trusted. This is true not only of those who, on the warpath, have heretofore actually been guilty of atrocious murder, but of their kindred and friends, who, while they remained upon their reservation, furnished aid and comfort to those absent with bloody intent ?

These prisoners should be treated kindly and kept in restraint far from the locality of their former reservation ; they should be subjected to efforts calculated to lead to their improvement and the softening of their savage and cruel instincts, but their return to their old home should be persistently restricted.

The Secretary in his report gives a graphic history of these Indians, and recites with painful vividness their bloody deeds and the unhappy failure of the government to manage them by peaceful means. It will be amazing if a perusal of this history will allow the survival of a desire for the return of these prisoners to their reservation upon sentimental or any other grounds.

CHAPTER XVIII.

THE PUBLIC DOMAIN.

I.

From the First Annual Message, December, 1885.

THE public domain had its origin in cessions of land by the States to the general government. The first cession was made by the State of New York, and the largest, which in area exceeded all the others, by the State of Virginia. The territory, the proprietorship of which became thus vested in the general government, extended from the western line of Pennsylvania to the Mississippi River. These patriotic donations of the States were encumbered with no condition, except that they should be held and used "for the common benefit of the United States." By purchase, with the common fund of all the people, additions were made to this domain until it extended to the northern line of Mexico, the Pacific Ocean, and the Polar Sea. The original trust, "for the common benefit of the United States," attached to all. In the execution of that trust the policy of many homes, rather than large estates, was adopted by the government. That these might be easily obtained, and be the abode of security and contentment, the laws for their acquisition were few, easily understood, and general in their character. But the pressure of local interests, combined with a speculative spirit, has in many instances procured the passage of laws which marred the harmony of the general plan, and encumbered the system with a multitude of general and special enactments, which render the land laws complicated, subject the titles to uncertainty, and the purchasers often to oppression and wrong. Laws which were intended for the "common benefit" have been perverted so that large quantities of land are vesting in single ownerships. From the multitude and character of the laws, this consequence seems incapable of correction by mere administration.

It is not for the "common benefit of the United States" that a large area of the public lands should be acquired, directly or through fraud, in the hands of a single individual. The nation's strength is in the people. The nation's prosperity is in their prosperity. The nation's glory is in the equality of her justice. The nation's perpetuity is in the patriotism of all her people. Hence, as far as practicable, the plan adopted in the disposal of the public lands should have in view the original policy, which encouraged many purchasers of these lands for homes and discouraged the massing of large areas. Exclusive of Alaska, about three-fifths of the national domain have been sold or subjected to contract or grant. Of the remaining two-fifths a considerable portion is either mountain or desert. A rapidly increasing population creates a growing demand for homes, and the accumulation of wealth inspires an eager competition to obtain the public land for speculative purposes. In the future this collision of interests will be more marked than in the past, and the execution of the nation's trust in behalf of our settlers will be more difficult.

II.

From the Second Annual Message, December, 1886.

The recommendations of the Secretary of the Interior and the Commissioner of the General Land Office looking to the better protection of public lands and of the public surveys, the preservation of national forests, the adjudication of grants to States and corporations and of private land claims, and the increased efficiency of the public-land service, are commended to the attention of Congress. To secure the widest distribution of public lands in limited quantities among settlers for residence and cultivation, and thus make the greatest number of individual homes, was the primary object of the public-land legislation in the early days of the republic. This system was a simple one. It commenced with an admirable scheme of public surveys, by which the humblest citizen could identify the tract upon which he wished to establish his home. The price of lands was placed within the reach of all the enterprising, industrious, and honest pioneer citizens of the country. It was soon, however, found that the object of the laws was perverted, under the system of cash sales, from a distribution of land among the people to an accumulation of land capital by wealthy and speculative persons. To check this tendency a preference right of purchase was given to settlers on the land, a plan which culminated in the general Pre-emption Act of 1841.

The foundation of this system was actual residence and cultivation. Twenty years later the homestead law was devised more surely to place actual homes in the possession of actual cultivators of the soil. The land was given without price, the sole conditions being residence, improvement, and cultivation. Other laws have followed, each designed to encourage the acquirement and use of land in limited individual quantities. But in later years these laws, through vicious administrative methods and under changed conditions of communication and transportation, have been so evaded and violated that their beneficent purpose is threatened with entire defeat. The methods of such evasions and violations are set forth in detail in the reports of the Secretary of the Interior and Commissioner of the General Land Office. The rapid appropriation of our public lands without *bona fide* settlement or cultivation, and not only without intention of residence, but for the purpose of their aggregation in large holdings, in many cases in the hands of foreigners, invites the serious and immediate attention of Congress.

The energies of the land department have been devoted, during the present administration, to remedy defects and correct abuses in the public-land service. The results of these efforts are so largely in the nature of reforms in the processes and methods of our land system as to prevent adequate estimate; but it appears, by a compilation from the reports of the Commissioner of the General Land Office, that the immediate effect in leading cases, which have come to a final termination, has been the restoration to the mass of public lands of 2,750,000 acres; that 2,370,000 acres are embraced in investigations now pending before the Departments or the courts, and that the action of Congress has been asked to effect the restoration of 2,790,000 acres additional; besides which four million acres have been withheld from reservation, and the rights of entry thereon maintained.

I recommend the repeal of the Pre-emption and Timber-culture Acts, and that the homestead laws be so amended as better to secure compliance with their requirements of residence, improvement, and cultivation for the period of five years from date of entry, without commutation or provision for speculative relinquishment. I also recommend the repeal of the desert-land laws unless it shall be the pleasure of the Congress so to amend these laws as to render them less liable to abuses. As the chief motive for an evasion of the laws, and the principal cause of their result in land accumulation instead of land distribution, is the facility with which transfers are made of the right intended to be secured to settlers, it may be deemed advisable to provide by legislation some guards and checks upon the alienation of homestead rights and lands covered thereby until patents issue.

III.

The Rights of Settlers.

EXECUTIVE MANSION,
WASHINGTON, D. C., April 25, 1887.

To the Secretary of the Interior:

DEAR SIR: I have examined with much care and interest the questions involved in the conflicting claims of Guilford

Miller and the Northern Pacific Railroad Company to certain public land in Washington Territory. The legal aspects of the case have been examined and passed upon by several officers of the government, who do not agree in their conclusions.

Miller claims to be a settler upon the land in question, whose possession dates from 1878. He alleges that he has made substantial improvements upon this land and cultivated the same, and it appears that he filed his claim to the same, under the homestead law, on the 29th day of December, 1884.

The railroad company contends that this land is within the territory or area from which it was entitled to select such a quantity of public land as might be necessary to supply any deficiency that should be found to exist in the specific land mentioned in a grant by the government to said company in aid of the construction of its road, such deficiency being contemplated as likely to arise from the paramount right of private parties and settlers within the territory embracing said granted lands, and that the land in dispute was thus selected by the company on the 19th day of December, 1883.

A large tract, including this land, was withdrawn, by an order of the Interior Department, from sale and from preemption and homestead entry in 1872, in anticipation of the construction of said railroad and a deficiency in its granted lands. In 1880, upon the filing of a map of definite location of the road, the land in controversy, and much more which had been so withdrawn, was found to lie outside of the limits which included the granted land ; but its withdrawal and reservation from settlement and entry under our land laws was continued upon the theory that it was within the limits of indemnity lands which might be selected by the company, as provided in the law making the grant.

The legal points in this controversy turned upon the validity and effect of the withdrawal and reservation of this land and the continuance thereof. The Attorney-General is of the opinion that such withdrawal and reservation were at all times effectual, and that they operated to prevent Miller from acquiring any interest in or right to the land claimed by him.

With this interpretation of the law and the former orders and action of the Interior Department, it will be seen that their effect has been the withdrawal and reservation since 1872 of thousands, if not millions, of acres of these lands from the operation of the land laws of the United States, thus placing them beyond the reach of our citizens desiring under such laws to settle and make homes upon the same, and that this has been done for the benefit of a railroad company having no fixed, certain, or definite interests in such lands. In this manner the beneficent policy and intention of the government in relation to the public domain have for all these years to that extent been thwarted.

There seems to be no evidence presented showing how much, if any, of this vast tract is necessary for the fulfillment of the grant to the railroad company, nor does there appear to be any limitation of the time within which this fact should be made known and the corporation obliged to make its selection. After a lapse of fifteen years this large body of the public domain is still held in reserve, to the exclusion of settlers, for the convenience of a corporate beneficiary of the government, and awaiting its selection, though it is entirely certain that much of this reserved land can never be honestly claimed by such corporation.

Such a condition of the public lands should no longer continue. So far as it is the result of executive rules and methods, these should be abandoned, and so far as it is a consequence of improvident laws, these should be repealed or amended.

Our public domain is our national wealth, the earnest of our growth and the heritage of our people. It should promise limitless development and riches, relief to a crowding population, and homes to thrift and industry.

These inestimable advantages should be jealously guarded,

and a careful and enlightened policy on the part of the government should secure them to the people.

In the case under consideration I assume that there is an abundance of land within the area which has been reserved for indemnity, in which no citizen or settler has a legal or equitable interest, for all purposes of such indemnification to this railroad company, if its grant has not already been satisfied. I understand, too, that selections made by such corporation are not complete and effectual until the same have been approved by the Secretary of the Interior, or unless they are made, in the words of the statute, under his direction.

You have thus far taken no action in this matter, and it seems to me that you are in a condition to deal with the subject in such a manner as to protect this settler from hardship and loss.

I transmit herewith the papers and documents relating to the case, which were submitted to me at my request.

I suggest that you exercise the power and authority you have in the premises, upon equitable considerations, with every presumption and intendment in favor of the settler; and in case you find this corporation is entitled to select any more of these lands than it has already acquired, that you direct it to select, in lieu of the land upon which Mr. Miller has settled, other land within the limits of this indemnity reservation, upon which neither he nor any other citizen has in good faith settled or made improvements.

I call your attention to sections 2450 and 2451 of the Revised Statutes of the United States, as pointing out a mode of procedure which may, perhaps, be resorted to, if necessary, for the purpose of reaching a just and equitable disposition of the case.

The suggestions herein contained can, I believe, be adopted without disregarding or calling in question the opinion of the Attorney-General upon the purely legal propositions which were submitted to him.

Yours very truly,

GROVER CLEVELAND.

IV.

From the Fourth Annual Message, December, 1888.

I cannot too strenuously insist upon the importance of proper measures to insure a right disposition of our public lands, not only as a matter of present justice, but in forecast of the consequences to future generations. The broad rich acres of our agricultural plains have been long preserved by nature to become her untrammeled gift to a people civilized and free, upon which should rest, in well-distributed owner- ship, the numerous homes of enlightened, equal, and frater- nal citizens. They came to national possession with the warning example in our eyes of the entail of iniquities in landed proprietorship which other countries have permitted and still suffer. We have no excuse for the violation of prin- ciples, cogently taught by reason and example, nor for the allowance of pretexts which have sometimes exposed our lands to colossal greed. Laws which open a door to fraudulent acquisition, or administration which permits favor to rapacious seizure by a favored few of expanded areas that many should enjoy, are accessory to offenses against our national welfare and humanity, not to be too severely condemned or punished.

It is gratifying to know that something has been done at last to redress the injuries to our people and check the perilous tendency of the reckless waste of the national domain. That over eighty million acres have been arrested from illegal usurpation, improvident grants, and fraudulent entries and claims, to be taken for the homesteads of honest industry— although less than the greater areas thus unjustly lost—must afford a profound gratification to right-feeling citizens as it is a recompense for the labors and struggles of the recovery. Our dear experience ought sufficiently to urge the speedy enact- ment of measures of legislation which will confine the future disposition of our remaining agricultural lands to the uses of actual husbandry and genuine homes.

Nor should our vast tracts of so-called desert lands be yielded up to the monopoly of corporations or grasping individuals, as appears to be much the tendency under the existing statute. These lands require but the supply of water to become fertile and productive. It is a problem of great moment how most wisely for the public good that factor shall be furnished. I cannot but think it perilous to suffer either these lands or the sources of their irrigation to fall into the hands of monopolies, which, by such means, may exercise lord-ship over the areas dependent on their treatment for pro-ductiveness. Already steps have been taken to secure accu-rate and scientific information of the conditions, which are the prime basis of intelligent action. Until this shall be gained, the course of wisdom appears clearly to lie in a suspension of further disposal, which only promises to create rights antago-nistic to the common interest. No harm can follow this cautionary conduct. The land will remain, and the public good presents no demand for hasty dispossession of national ownership and control.

CHAPTER XIX.

SOME NOTABLE VETOES.

I.

*Of an Appropriation for Celebrating Decoration Day.**

BUFFALO, May 8, 1882.

TO THE COMMON COUNCIL:

AT the last session of your honorable body a resolution was adopted directing the city clerk to draw a warrant for five hundred dollars in the favor of the Firemen's Benevolent Association.

This action is not only clearly unauthorized, but it is distinctly prohibited by the following clause of the State Constitution :

No county, city, town or village shall hereafter give any money or property, or loan its money or credit to, or in aid of any individual, association or corporation, or become directly or indirectly the owner of stock in or bonds of any association or corporation ; nor shall any such county, city, town, or

_____

* While the ordinance making this appropriation was still pending Mr. Cleveland wrote the following letter to the Chairman of the Committee having the matter in charge :

BUFFALO, May 7, 1882.

JOHN M. FARQUHAR, ESQ.

DEAR SIR : I have tried very hard, but failed to find a way, consistently to approve the resolution of the Common Council appropriating $500 for the observance of Decoration day.

If my action has the effect of stopping the payment of this sum for the purpose, and you attempt to raise the necessary sum by subscription, you may call on me for $50.

Yours very truly,

GROVER CLEVELAND.

village be allowed to incur any indebtedness, except for county, city, town, or village purposes.

At the same meeting of your honorable body the following resolution was passed :

> That the City Clerk be and is hereby directed to draw a warrant on the Fourth of July Fund for five hundred dollars, to the order of J. S. Edwards, Chairman of the Decoration Day Committee of the Grand Army of the Republic, for the purpose of defraying the expenses attending a proper observance of Decoration day.

I have taxed my ingenuity to discover a way consistently to approve of this resolution, but have been unable to do so.

It seems to me that it is not only obnoxious to the provisions of the Constitution above quoted, but that it also violates that section of the charter of the city which makes it a misdemeanor to appropriate money raised for one purpose to any other object. Under this section I think money raised "for the celebration of the Fourth of July, and the reception of distinguished persons," cannot be devoted to the observance of Decoration day.

I deem the object of this appropriation a most worthy one. The efforts of our veteran soldiers to keep alive the memory of their fallen comrades certainly deserve the aid and encouragement of their fellow-citizens. We should all, I think, feel it a duty and a privilege to contribute to the funds necessary to carry out such a purpose. And I should be much disappointed if an appeal to our citizens for voluntary subscription for this patriotic object should be in vain.

But the money so contributed should be a free gift of the citizens and taxpayers, and should not be extorted from them by taxation. This is so, because the purpose for which this money is asked does not involve their protection or interest as members of the community, and it may or may not be approved by them.

The people are forced to pay taxes into the city treasury only upon the theory that such money shall be expended for public purposes, or purposes in which they all have a direct and practical interest.

The logic of this position leads directly to the conclusion that, if the people are forced to pay their money into the public fund and it is spent by their servants and agents for purposes in which the people as taxpayers have no interest, the exaction of such taxes from them is oppressive and unjust.

I cannot rid myself of the idea that this city government, in its relation to the taxpayers, is a business establishment, and that it is put into our hands to be conducted on business principles.

This theory does not admit of our donating the public funds in the manner contemplated by the action of your honorable body.

I deem it my duty, therefore, to return both the resolutions referred to without my approval.

GROVER CLEVELAND.

II.

Of a Street Cleaning Contract, as Mayor of Buffalo, June 26, 1882.

TO THE COMMON COUNCIL :

I return without my approval the resolution of your honorable body, passed at its last meeting, awarding the contract for cleaning the paved streets and alleys of the city for the ensuing five years to George Talbot at his bid of four hundred and twenty-two thousand and five hundred dollars.

The bid thus accepted by your honorable body is more than one hundred thousand dollars higher than that of another perfectly responsible party for the same work ; and a worse and more suspicious feature in this transaction is that the bid now accepted is fifty thousand dollars more than that made by Talbot himself within a very few weeks, openly and publicly, to your honorable body, for performing precisely the same services. This latter circumstance is to my mind the manifestation on the part of the contractor of a reliance upon the forbearance and generosity of your honorable body, which would be more creditable if it were less expensive to the tax-payers.

I am not aware that any excuse is offered for the acceptance of this proposal, thus increased, except the very flimsy one that the lower bidders cannot afford to do the work for the sums they name.

This extreme tenderness and consideration for those who desire to contract with the city, and this touching and paternal solicitude lest they should be improvidently led into a bad bargain is, I am sure, an exception to general business rules, and seems to have no place in this selfish, sordid world, except as found in the administration of municipal affairs.

The charter of your city requires that the Mayor, when he disapproves any resolution of your honorable body, shall return the same with his objections.

This is a time for plain speech, and my objection to the action of your honorable body now under consideration shall be plainly stated. I withhold my assent from the same, because I regard it as the culmination of a most barefaced, impudent, and shameless scheme to betray the interests of the people and worse than to squander the public money.

I will not be misunderstood in this matter. There are those whose votes were given for this resolution whom I cannot and will not suspect of a willful neglect of the interests they are sworn to protect; but it has been fully demon-strated that there are influences, both in and about your honorable body, which it behooves every honest man to watch and avoid with the greatest care.

When cool judgment rules the hour, the people will, I hope and believe, have no reason to complain of the action of your honorable body. But clumsy appeals to prejudice or passion, insinuations, with a kind of a low, cheap cunning, as to the motives and purposes of others, and the mock heroism of brazen effrontery, which openly declare that a wholesome public sentiment is to be set at naught, sometimes deceive and lead honest men to aid in the consummation of schemes which, if exposed, they would look upon with abhorrence.

If the scandal in connection with this street cleaning contract, which has so aroused our citizens, shall cause them to select and watch with more care those to whom they intrust their interests, and if it serves to make all of us who are charged with official duties more careful in their performance, it will not be an unmitigated evil.

We are fast gaining positions in the grades of public stewardships. There is no middle ground. Those who are not for the people either in or out of your honorable body are against them and should be treated accordingly.

GROVER CLEVELAND,
Mayor.

III.

Of a Bill for the Purchase of Land by the Supervisors of Chautauqua County.

EXECUTIVE CHAMBER,
ALBANY, February 12, 1883.

TO THE ASSEMBLY :

Assembly bill No. 88, entitled " An Act authorizing the Board of Supervisors of Chautauqua County to appropriate money for the purchase " of land upon which to erect a soldiers' and sailors' monument, is herewith returned without approval.

It is not an agreeable duty to refuse to give sanction to the appropriation of money for such a worthy and patriotic object ; but I cannot forget that the money proposed to be appropriated is public money to be raised by taxation, and that all that justifies its exaction from the people is the necessity of its use for purposes connected with the safety and substantial welfare of the taxpayers.

The application of this principle furnishes, I think, a sufficient reason why this bill should not be approved.

I am of the opinion, too, that the appropriation of this money by the Board of Supervisors would constitute the incurring of an indebtedness by the county to be thereafter met by taxation. If this be true, the proposed legislation is forbidden by section eleven of article eight of the Constitution, which provides that no county, city, town, or village shall be allowed to incur any indebtedness except for county, city, town, or village purposes.

Before this prohibition became a part of the Constitution, a statute was passed permitting monuments to be erected to fallen soldiers at the expense of the inhabitants of the county within which they were located ; but the expenditure of money raised by taxation for such a purpose was only allowed when especially sanctioned by the vote of a majority of all the electors of the county. In the bill under consideration the taxpayers are not permitted to be heard on the subject.

It is thus evident that the legislation proposed guards less the rights and interests of the people than the statute passed before the Constitutional amendment prohibited all enactments of this description.

I may, perhaps, be permitted to express the hope that a due regard to fundamental principles, and a strict adherence to the letter and spirit of the Constitution, which furnish the limit as well as the guide to legislation, will prevent the passage of bills of this nature in the future.

GROVER CLEVELAND.

IV.

Of the Elevated Railroad Five Cent Fare Bill.

EXECUTIVE CHAMBER,
ALBANY, March 2, 1883.

To the Assembly :

Assembly bill No. 58, entitled " An Act to regulate the fare to be charged and collected by persons or corporations operating elevated railroads in the city of New York," is herewith returned without approval.

This bill prohibits the collection or receipt of more than five cents fare on any elevated railroad in the city of New York, for any distance between the Battery and Harlem River, and provides that, if any person or corporation operating such elevated railroads shall charge, demand, collect or receive any higher rate of fare, such person or corporation shall, in addition to all other penalties imposed by law, forfeit and pay to any person aggrieved fifty dollars for each offense, to be recovered by such person in any court of competent jurisdiction.

The importance of this measure and the interest which it has excited have impressed me with my responsibility, and led me to examine, with as much care as has been possible, the considerations involved.

I am convinced that in all cases the share which falls upon the Executive regarding the legislation of the State should be in no manner evaded, but fairly met by the expression of his carefully guarded and unbiased judgment. In this conclusion he may err, but, if he has fairly and honestly acted, he has performed his duty and given to the people of the State his best endeavor.

The elevated railroads in the city of New York are now operated by the Manhattan Railway Company, as the lessee of the New York Elevated Railway Company and the Metropolitan Elevated Railway Company.

Of course, whatever rights the lessee companies have in relation to the running and operation of their respective roads passed to the Manhattan Company under its lease.

The New York Elevated Railway Company is the successor of the West Side and Yonkers Patent Railway Company.

The latter company was formed under and in pursuance of an act passed on the 20th day of April, 1866.

The third section of that act provides that companies formed under its provisions " may fix and collect rates of fare on their respective roads, not exceeding five cents for each mile or any fraction of a mile for each passenger, and with right to a minimum fare of ten cents.

On the 22d day of April, 1867, an act was passed in relation
to this corporation, which provides for the manner of constructing its road, the eighth section of which act reads as follows :

The said company shall be authorized to demand and receive from each
passenger within the limits of the city of New York rates of fare not exceeding, for any distance less than two miles, five cents ; for every mile or fractional part of a mile in addition thereto, one cent.   Provided that when said
railway is completed and in operation between Battery Place and the vicinity
of Harlem River, the said company may, at its option, adopt a uniform rate not
exceeding ten cents for all distances upon Manhattan Island, and may also
collect said last named rate for a period of five years from and after the
passage of this act.

It was further provided by section 9 of this act that the
said company should pay a sum not exceeding five per cent. of
the net income of said railway from passenger traffic upon
Manhattan Island, into the treasury of the city of New York,
in such manner as the Legislature might thereafter direct, as a
compensation for the use of the streets of the city.

In 1868 a law was passed supplementary to the act last referred to, by which the said company was authorized to adopt
such form of motor as certain commissioners should, after due
experiment, recommend or approve.

Specific provision was made in the act to carry out section 9
of the law of 1867, in relation to the payment of the five per
cent. of the net income of the company into the treasury of the
city.

Section 3 of this act contains the following provision :

It shall be the duty of the constructing company aforesaid, before opening
its railway to public use, to file with the comptroller of the city of New York,
in form to be approved by the mayor of the city of New York, its bond in the
penal sum of $100,000, conditioned upon the true and faithful payment of the
revenue in amount and manner specified in the preceding section ; and the
payment thereof shall be the legal compensation in full for the use and occupancy of the streets by said railway as provided by law, and shall constitute an
agreement in the nature of a contract between said city and constructing company entitling the latter or its successors to the privileges and rates of fare
heretofore or herein legalized, which shall not be changed without the mutual

consent of the parties thereto as aforesaid ; and the mayor on behalf of said city may, in case of default in payments as aforesaid, sue for and collect at law any arrearages in such payment, and the claims of the city, therefore, shall constitute a lien on the railway of said company, having priority over all others.

The use of what are called dummy engines was afterward authorized in the operation of said road by the commissioners above referred to.

The New York Elevated Railroad Company was organized under the general railroad law passed in 1850, and the laws amendatory thereof and supplementary thereto.

Within a short time thereafter the last named company became the purchaser, under a foreclosure and by other transfers of the railway and all the rights, privileges, easements and franchises of the West Side and Yonkers Patent Railway Company (the name of which had in the meantime been changed to the West Side Elevated Patented Railway Company of New York City).

We have now reached a point where the New York Elevated Railway Company, one of the lessors of the Manhattan Railroad Company, has succeeded to all the rights and property of the West Side and Yonkers Patent Railway Company.

By a law passed on the 17th day of June, 1875 (the railway still being unfinished), it is declared that the New York Elevated Railroad Company having acquired, by purchase, under mortgage foreclosure and sale and other transfer, all the rights, powers, privileges, and franchises which were conferred upon the West Side and Yonkers Patent Railway Company by the acts above referred to, is " hereby confirmed in the possession and enjoyments of the said rights, powers, privileges, and franchises as fully and as large as they were so granted in and by the acts aforesaid to the said West Side and Yonkers Patent Railway Company.

The Court of Appeals, speaking of this law, uses the following language :

The effect of this act was to secure to the Elevated Railroad Company all the rights, privileges, and franchises of the West Side and Yonkers Patent Railway Company under the purchase by and transfer to it.

By the sixth section of this act, it is provided that the New York Elevated Railroad Company might demand and receive, from each passenger on its railroad, not exceeding ten cents for any distance of five miles or less, and with the assent required by section 3 of the act of 1868, hereinbefore referred to, not exceeding two cents for each additional mile or fractional part thereof.

Another act was passed in 1875, commonly called the Rapid Transit Act, which provided for the appointment of commissioners, who, among other things, were authorized to fix and determine the time within which roads subject to the provisions of the act should be completed, together with the maximum rates to be paid for transportation and conveyance over said railways, and the hours during which special cars should be run at reduced rates of fare.

Commissioners were duly appointed by the mayor of the city of New York, as provided by this act, who fixed and determined the route of the road of the New York Elevated Railroad Company, and prescribed with the utmost particularity the manner of its construction, and thereupon deliberately agreed with said company that it should charge as fare upon trains and cars other than what were called by the parties commission trains and cars, for all distances under five miles not to exceed ten cents, and not to exceed two cents for each mile or fraction of a mile over five miles, until the fare should amount to not exceeding fifteen cents for a through passenger from and between the Battery and intersection of Third avenue and One Hundred and Twenty-ninth street, and from and between the Battery and High Bridge not to exceed seventeen cents for a through passenger, and that for the entire distance from and between the Battery and Fifty-ninth street the fare should not exceed ten cents per passenger.

It was further agreed, between the said company and the commissioners, that commission trains should be run, during certain hours in the morning and evening, for the accommodation of the public and the laboring classes, upon which the fare should not exceed five cents from and between the Battery and Fifty-ninth street, nor any greater sum for any distance not exceeding five miles ; that it should not exceed seven cents for a through passenger from and between the Battery, or any point south thereof, and the Harlem River, and that such fare should not exceed eight cents on such commission cars and trains from and between the Battery and High Bridge.

And it was further agreed by said company that when the net income of the road, after all expenditures, taxes, and charges are paid, should amount to a sum sufficient to pay exceeding ten per cent. per annum on the capital stock of the company, that in such case and within six months thereafter, and so long as said net earnings amount to a sum sufficient to pay more than ten per cent. as aforesaid, the said company would run commission trains on its road at all hours during which it should be operated, at the rates of fare last mentioned.

Having thus completed an agreement with this company, the commissioners transmitted the same to the mayor of the City of New York, accompanied by a very congratulatory report of their proceedings, whereupon the mayor submitted the same to the Board of Aldermen, by whom it was approved. This was in the latter part of 1875.

Since that time the New York Elevated Railroad Company, upon the faith of the laws which have been recited, and its proceedings with the commissioners, at a very large expense, has completed its road from the Battery to the Harlem River, a distance of about ten miles.

The bill before me provides that, notwithstanding all the statutes that have been passed and all that has been done thereunder, passengers shall be carried the whole length of this road for five cents, a sum much less than is provided for in any of such statutes or stipulated in the proceedings of the commissioners.

I am of the opinion that, in the legislation and proceedings which I have detailed, and in the fact that pursuant thereto the road of the company was constructed and finished, there exists a contract in favor of this company, which is protected by that clause of the Constitution of the United States which prohibits the passage of a law by any State impairing the obligation of contracts.

But let it be supposed that this is not so, and that neither of these lessor companies is, in any way, protected from interference with their rates of fare, but that, on the contrary, they are subject to all the provisions of the general railroad act, under which they are both organized.

Section 33 of that act reads as follows :

The legislature may, when any such railroad shall be opened for use, from time to time alter or reduce the rate of freight, fare, or other profits upon said road ; but the same shall not, without the consent of the company, be so reduced as to produce with said profits less than ten per centum per annum on the capital actually expended ; nor unless on an examination of the amount received or expended, to be made by the State Engineer and Surveyor and the Comptroller, they shall ascertain that the net income derived by the company from all sources, for the year then last past, shall have exceeded an annual income of ten per cent. upon the capital of the corporation actually expended.

Even if the State has the power to reduce the fare on these roads, it has promised not to do so except under certain circumstances and after a certain examination.

I am not satisfied that these circumstances exist, and it is conceded that no such examination has been made.

The constitutional objections which I have suggested to the bill under consideration are not, I think, removed by the claim that the proposed legislation is in the nature of an alteration of the charters of these companies, and that this is permitted by the State Constitution and by the provisions of some of the laws to which I have referred.

I suppose that, while the charters of corporations may be altered or repealed, it must be done in subordination to the

Constitution of the United States, which is the supreme law of the land. This leads to the conclusion that the alteration of a charter cannot be made the pretext for the passage of a law which impairs the obligation of a contract.

If I am mistaken in supposing that there are legal objections to this bill, there is another consideration which furnishes to my mind a sufficient reason why I should not give it my approval.

It seems to me that to reduce these fares arbitrarily, at this time and under existing circumstances, involves a breach of faith on the part of the State, and a betrayal of confidence which the State has invited.

The fact is notorious that, for many years, rapid transit was the great need of the inhabitants of the city of New York, and was of direct importance to the citizens of the State. Projects which promised to answer the people's wants in this direction failed and were abandoned. The Legislature, appreciating the situation, willingly passed statute after statute calculated to aid and encourage a solution of the problem. Capital was timid, and hesitated to enter a new field full of risks and dangers. By the promise of liberal fares, as will be seen in all the acts passed on the subject, and through other concessions gladly made, capitalists were induced to invest their money in the enterprise, and rapid transit but lately became an accomplished fact. But much of the risk, expense, and burden attending the maintenance of these roads are yet unknown and threatening. In the meantime, the people of the city of New York are receiving the full benefit of their construction, a great enhancement of the value of the taxable property of the city has resulted, and, in addition to taxes, more than $120,000, being five per cent. in increase, pursuant to the law of 1868, has been paid by the companies into the city treasury, on the faith that the rate of fare agreed upon was secured to them. I am not aware that the corporations have, by any default, forfeited any of their rights ; and if they have, the remedy is at hand under existing laws. Their stock and their bonds are held by a large number of citizens, and the income of these roads depends entirely upon fares received from passengers. The reduction proposed is a large one, and it is claimed will permit no dividends to investors. This may not be true, but we should be satisfied it is not, before the proposed law takes effect.

It is manifestly important that invested capital should be protected, and that its necessity and usefulness in the development of enterprises valuable to the people should be recognized by conservative conduct on the part of the State government.

But we have especially in our keeping the honor and good faith of a great State, and we should see to it that no suspicion attaches, through any act of ours, to the fair fame of the commonwealth. The State should not only be strictly just, but scrupulously fair, and in its relations to the citizen every legal and moral obligation should be recognized. This can only be done by legislating without vindictiveness or prejudice, and with a firm determination to. deal justly and fairly with those from whom we exact obedience.

I am not unmindful of the fact that this bill originated in response to the demand of a large portion of the people of New York for cheaper rates of fare between their places of employment and their homes, and I realize fully the desirability of securing to them all the privileges possible, but the experience of other States teaches that we must keep within the limits of law and good faith, lest in the end we bring upon the very people whom we seek to benefit and protect, a hardship which must surely follow when these limits are ignored.

GROVER CLEVELAND,
Governor.

V.

Of the Amendments to the Charter of Buffalo.

EXECUTIVE CHAMBER,
ALBANY, April 9, 1883.

TO THE ASSEMBLY :

Assembly bill No. 553, entitled " An Act to amend chapter five hundred and nineteen of the laws of eighteen hundred and seventy, entitled ' An Act to amend the charter of the city of Buffalo,' passed April twenty-eight, eighteen hundred and seventy," is herewith returned without approval.

· The object of this bill is to reorganize entirely the fire department of the city of Buffalo.

The present department was established in 1880, under chapter 271 of the laws of that year, and its management and control are vested in three commissioners, who, pursuant to said law, were appointed by the mayor of the city.

The gentlemen thus appointed are citizens of unquestioned probity, intelligence, and executive ability, and enjoy and deserve the respect and confidence of all their fellow-townsmen.

Having very recently had official relations with this department, I cannot but testify to its efficiency and good management, and the economy with which its affairs are conducted. And yet, before it has been three years in operation, it is proposed, by the bill under consideration, to uproot and sweep away the present administration of this important department, and venture upon another experiment. This new scheme provides for the appointment, by the mayor, on the first Monday in May, 1883, of a chief of the fire department, one assistant chief, and two district chiefs ; the city is divided into two fire districts, and it is made the duty of the district chiefs to take the charge and management of all fires in their respective districts until the arrival of the chief or assistant chiefs.

I can see no reason for dividing, by law, the city into fire districts, unless it be to make new places to be filled by the city executive.

The provision that the district chief shall have charge and management of a fire in his district, until the arrival of his superior, gives excuse for the chief of another district, though first on the ground, to refrain from interference.

A fire department should be organized with a view to prompt and effective action upon a sudden emergency. Every member of the department should be, at all times, ready for service, and there should be no mischief invited, by rules too inflexible, as to who should have charge and management in time of danger to life and property.

Although the mayor of the city, under the provisions of the bill, has the absolute power of appointment to these offices, he may, in case of vacancy by death, resignation, removal, or otherwise, make special appointments, until permanent appointments are made. This was evidently copied from the charter of 1870, which allowed the mayor to appoint fire superintendents, by and with the advice and consent of the common council. It was intended to permit the filling of a vacancy by the mayor during the time which should elapse before a successor could be confirmed by the council. But in a case where no confirmation is necessary, such a provision is needless, incongruous, and mischievous. The mayor should be as well prepared to make a permanent appointment under this bill, in case of a vacancy, as a temporary one. This provision would seem to give him the power, by calling an appointment a temporary one, to retain the appointee as long as he sees fit, and, under the pretext of a permanent appointment, displace him by another without charges or an opportunity to be heard.

By section six of the bill an appeal is permitted from the decision of the mayor, upon the trial of any of these officers, to the Supreme Court of Buffalo. There is no such court in existence.

But waiving further criticism of details, my attention is directed to section twenty of the bill, which, to the promoters of this measure, is undoubtedly its most important feature.

It provides that immediately upon the appointment and qualification of the chief, the terms of the present commissioners
shall cease and determine, and that the terms of office of all
the other officers, firemen, and employees shall also cease and
determine ten days thereafter. Great care is exercised to
provide that the chiefs and all the firemen and employees, appointed under the new scheme, shall be discharged only for
cause, and after due hearing and an opportunity for defense ;
but to those now in the service, numbering about two hundred
drilled and experienced men, no such privileges are accorded.

The purpose of the bill is too apparent to be mistaken. A
tried, economical, and efficient administration of an important
department in a large city is to be destroyed, upon partisan
grounds or to satisfy personal animosities, in order that the
places and patronage attached thereto may be used for party
advancement.

I believe in an open and sturdy partisanship, which secures
the legitimate advantages of party supremacy ; but parties
were made for the people, and I am unwilling, knowingly, to
give my assent to measures purely partisan, which will sacrifice
or endanger their interests.

GROVER CLEVELAND.

VI.

Of the Texas Seed Bill.

EXECUTIVE MANSION,
WASHINGTON, February 16, 1887.

TO THE HOUSE OF REPRESENTATIVES :

I return without my approval House bill number ten thousand two hundred and three, entitled " An Act to enable the
Commissioner of Agriculture to make a special distribution of
seeds in drought-stricken counties of Texas, and making an
appropriation therefor."

It is represented that a long-continued and extensive drought has existed in certain portions of the State of Texas, resulting in a failure of crops and consequent distress and destitution.

Though there has been some difference in statements concerning the extent of the people's needs in the localities thus affected, there seems to be no doubt that there has existed a condition calling for relief ; and I am willing to believe that, notwithstanding the aid already furnished, a donation of seed-grain to the farmers located in this region, to enable them to put in new crops, would serve to avert a continuance or return of an unfortunate blight.

And yet I feel obliged to withhold my approval of the plan as proposed by this bill, to indulge a benevolent and charitable sentiment through the appropriation of public funds for that purpose.

I can find no warrant for such an appropriation in the Constitution, and I do not believe that the power and duty of the general government ought to be extended to the relief of individual suffering which is in no manner properly related to the public service or benefit. A prevalent tendency to disregard the limited mission of this power and duty should, I think, be steadfastly resisted, to the end that the lesson should be constantly enforced that, though the people support the government, the government should not support the people.

The friendliness and charity of our countrymen can always be relied upon to relieve their fellow-citizens in misfortune. This has been repeatedly and quite lately demonstrated. Federal aid in such cases encourages the expectation of paternal care on the part of the government and weakens the sturdiness of our national character, while it prevents the indulgence among our people of that kindly sentiment and conduct which strengthen the bonds of a common brotherhood.

It is within my personal knowledge that individual aid has, to some extent, already been extended to the sufferers mentioned in this bill. The failure of the proposed appropriation of ten thousand dollars additional, to meet their remaining wants, will not necessarily result in continued distress if the emergency is fully made known to the people of the country.

It is here suggested that the Commissioner of Agriculture is annually directed to expend a large sum of money for the purchase, propagation, and distribution of seeds and other things of this description, two-thirds of which are, upon the request of senators, representatives, and delegates in Congress, supplied to them for distribution among their constituents.

The appropriation of the current year for this purpose is one hundred thousand dollars, and it will probably be no less in the appropriation for the ensuing year. I understand that a large quantity of grain is furnished for such distribution, and it is supposed that this free apportionment among their neighbors is a privilege which may be waived by our senators and representatives.

If sufficient of them should request the Commissioner of Agriculture to send their shares of the grain thus allowed them, to the suffering farmers of Texas, they might be enabled to sow their crops; the constituents, for whom in theory this grain is intended, could well bear the temporary deprivation, and the donors would experience the satisfaction attending deeds of charity.

GROVER CLEVELAND.

VII.

Of the Direct Tax Bill.

EXECUTIVE MANSION,
WASHINGTON, March 2, 1889.

TO THE SENATE:

I herewith return without approval Senate bill number one hundred and thirty-nine, entitled "An Act to credit and pay to the several States and Territories and the District of Columbia all moneys collected under the direct tax levied by the Act of Congress approved August fifth, eighteen hundred and sixty-one."

The object of this bill is quite clearly indicated in its title. Its provisions have been much discussed in both branches of Congress and have received emphatic legislative sanction. I fully appreciate the interest which it has excited, and have by no means failed to recognize the persuasive presentation made in its favor. I know, too, that the interposition of Executive disapproval in this case is likely to arouse irritation and cause complaint and earnest criticism. Since, however, my judgment will not permit me to assent to the legislation proposed, I can find no way of turning aside from what appears to be the plain course of official duty.

On the 5th day of August, 1861, a Federal statute was passed entitled "An Act to provide increased revenue from imports, to pay interest on the public debt, and for other purposes."

This law was passed at a time when immense sums of money were needed by the government for the prosecution of a war for the Union ; and the purpose of the law was to increase in almost every possible way the Federal revenues. The first seven sections of the statute were devoted to advancing very largely the rates of duties on imports ; and to supplement this the eighth section provided that a direct tax of twenty millions of dollars should be annually laid, and that certain amounts therein specified should be apportioned to the respective States. The remainder of the law, consisting of fifty sections, contained the most particular and detailed provisions for the collection of the tax through Federal machinery.

It was declared, among other things, that the tax should be assessed and laid on all lands and lots of ground with their improvements and dwelling-houses ; that the annual amount of said taxes should be a lien upon all lands and real estate of the individuals assessed for the same, and that, in default of payment, the said taxes might be collected by distraint and sale of the goods, chattels, and effects of the delinquent persons.

This tax was laid in execution of the power conferred upon the general government for that purpose by the Constitution. It was an exercise of the right of the government to tax its citizens. It dealt with individuals, and the strong arm of Federal power was stretched out to exact from those who owed it support and allegiance their just share of the sum it had decreed should be raised by direct taxation for the general good. The lien created by this tax was upon the land and real estate of the "individuals assessed for the same," and for its collection the distraint and sale of personal property of the "persons delinquent" were permitted.

But, while the direct relationship and responsibility between the individuals taxed and the Federal government were thus created by the exercise of the highest attribute of sovereignty, it was provided in the statute that any State or Territory and the District of Columbia might lawfully "assume, assess, collect, and pay into the Treasury of the United States" its quota of said tax in its own way and manner, and by and through its own officers, assessors, and collectors; and it was further provided that such States or Territories as should give notice of their intention to thus assume and pay, or to assess, collect, and pay, into the Treasury of the United States such direct tax, should be entitled, in lieu of the compensation, pay, per diem, and percentage in said act prescribed and allowed to assessors, assistant assessors, and collectors of the United States, to a deduction of fifteen per centum of the quota of direct tax apportioned to such States or Territories and levied and collected through their officers.

It was also provided by this law and another passed the next year that certain claims of the States and Territories against the United States might be applied in payment of such quotas. Whatever may be said as to the effect of these provisions of the law, it can hardly be claimed that, by virtue thereof or any proceedings under them, the apportioned quotas of this tax became debts against the several States and Territories, or that they were liable to the general government therefor, in every event, and as principal debtors bound by an enforceable obligation.

In the forty-sixth section of the law it is provided that in case any State, Territory, or the District of Columbia, after notice given of its intention to assume and pay, or to levy, collect and pay said direct tax apportioned to it, should fail to pay the amount of said direct tax, or any part thereof, it should be lawful for the Secretary of the Treasury to appoint United States officers as in the act provided, whose duty it should be to proceed forthwith to collect all or any part of said direct tax, "the same as though said State, Territory, or District had not given notice nor assumed to levy, collect, and pay said taxes or any part thereof."

A majority of the States undertook the collection of their quotas and accounted for the amount thereof to the general government, by the payment of money or by setting off claims in their favor, against the tax. Fifteen per cent. of the amount of their respective quotas was retained as the allowance for collection and payment. In the Northern, or such as were then called the loyal States, nearly the entire quotas were collected and paid through the State agencies. The money necessary for this purpose was generally collected from the citizens of the States with their other taxes, and in whatever manner their quotas may have been cancelled, whether by the payment of money or setting off claims against the government, it is safe to say, as a general proposition, that the people of these States have individually been obliged to pay the assessments made upon them on account of this direct tax, and have intrusted it to their several States to be transmitted to the Federal Treasury.

In the Southern States, then in insurrection, whatever was actually realized in money upon this tax was collected directly by Federal officers without the interposition of State machinery ; and a part of its quota has been credited to each of these States.

The entire amount applied upon this tax, including the fifteen per cent. for collection, was credited to the several States and Territories upon the books of the Treasury, whether collected through their instrumentality or by Federal officers. The sum credited to all the States was $17,359,685.51, which includes more than two millions of dollars on account of the fifteen per cent. allowed for collecting. Of the amount credited, only about two millions and three hundred thousand dollars is credited to the insurrectionary States. The amount uncollected, of the twenty millions directed to be raised by this tax, was $2,646,314.49, and nearly this entire sum remained due upon the quotas apportioned to these States.

In this condition of affairs the bill under consideration directs the Secretary of the Treasury " to credit to each State and Territory of the United States and the District of Columbia a sum equal to all collections, by set-off or otherwise, made from said States and Territories and the District of Columbia, or from any of the citizens or inhabitants thereof or other persons, under the act of Congress approved August fifth, eighteen hundred and sixty-one, and the amendatory acts thereto." An appropriation is also made of such a sum as may be necessary to reimburse each State, Territory, and the District of Columbia for all money found due to it under the provisions of the bill, and it is provided that all money, still due to the United States on said direct tax, shall be remitted and relinquished.

The conceded effect of this bill is to take from the money now in the Treasury the sum of more than seventeen millions of dollars, or if the percentage allowed is not included, more than fifteen millions of dollars, and pay back to the respective States and Territories the sums they or their citizens paid more than twenty-five years ago upon a direct tax levied by the government of the United States for its defense and safety.

It is my belief that this appropriation of the public funds is not within the constitutional power of the Congress. Under the limited and delegated authority, conferred by the Constitution upon the general government, the statement of the purposes for which money may be lawfully raised, by taxation in any form, declares also the limit of the objects for which it may be expended.

All must agree that the direct tax was lawfully and constitutionally laid, and that it was rightfully and correctly collected. It cannot be claimed, therefore, nor is it pretended, that any debt arose against the government and in favor of any State or individual by the exaction of this tax. Surely, then, the appropriation directed by this bill cannot be justified as a payment of a debt of the United States.

The disbursement of this money clearly has no relation to the common defense. On the contrary, it is the repayment of money raised and long ago expended by the government to provide for the common defense.

The expenditure can not properly be advocated on the ground that the general welfare of the United States is thereby provided for or promoted. This "general welfare of the United States," as used in the Constitution, can only justify appropriations for national objects and for purposes which have to do with the prosperity, the growth, the honor, or the peace and dignity of the nation.

A sheer, bald gratuity bestowed either upon States or individuals, based upon no better reason than supports the gift proposed in this bill, has never been claimed to be a provision for the general welfare. More than fifty years ago a surplus of public money in the Treasury was distributed among the States ; but the unconstitutionality of such distribution, considered as a gift of money, appears to have been conceded, for it was put into the State treasuries under the guise of a deposit or loan, subject to the demand of the government.

If it was proposed to raise by assessment upon the people the sum necessary to refund the money collected upon this direct tax, I am sure many who are now silent would insist upon the limitations of the Constitution in opposition to such a scheme. A large surplus in the Treasury is the parent of many ills, and among them is found a tendency to an extremely liberal, if not loose, construction of the Constitution. It also attracts the gaze of States and individuals with a kind of fascination, and gives rise to plans and pretensions that an uncongested Treasury never could excite.

But, if the constitutional question involved in the consideration of this bill should be determined in its favor, there are other objections remaining which prevent my assent to its provisions.

There should be a certainty and stability about the enforcement of taxation which should teach the citizen that the government will only use the power to tax in cases where its necessity and justice are not doubtful, and which should also discourage the disturbing idea that the exercise of this power may be revoked by reimbursement of taxes once collected. Any other theory cheapens and in a measure discredits a process which more than any other is a manifestation of sovereign authority.

A government is not only kind, but performs its highest duty, when it restores to the citizen taxes unlawfully collected or which have been erroneously or oppressively extorted by its agents or officers ; but aside from these incidents, the people should not be familiarized with the spectacle of their government repenting the collection of taxes and restoring them.

The direct tax levied in 1861 is not even suspected of invalidity ; there never was a tax levied which was more needed, and its justice cannot be questioned. Why, then, should it be returned ?

The fact that the entire tax was not paid furnishes no reason that would not apply to nearly every case where taxes are laid. There are always delinquents, and while the more thorough and complete collection of taxes is a troublesome problem of government, the failure to solve the problem has never been held to call for the return of taxes actually collected.

The deficiency in the collection of this tax is found almost entirely in the insurrectionary States, while the quotas apportioned to the other States were, as a general rule, fully paid ; and three-fourths or four-fifths of the money which it is proposed in this bill to return would be paid into the treasuries of the loyal States. But no valid reason for such payment is found in the fact that the government at first could not, and afterward, for reasons probably perfectly valid, did not, enforce collection in the other States.

There were many Federal taxes which were not paid by the people in the rebellious States ; and if the non-payment by them of this direct tax entitles the other States to a donation of the share of said taxes paid by their citizens, why should not the income tax and many other internal taxes paid entirely by the citizens of loyal States be also paid into the treasuries of these States ? Considerations which recognize sectional divisions, or the loyalty of the different States at the time this tax was laid, should not enter into the discussion of the merits of this measure.

The loyal States should not be paid the large sums of money promised them by this bill because they were loyal and other States were not, nor should the States which rebelled against the government be paid the smaller sum promised them because they were in rebellion and thus prevented the collection of their entire quotas, nor because this concession to them is necessary to justify the proposed larger gifts to the other States.

The people of the loyal States paid this direct tax as they bore other burdens in support of the government ; and I believe the tax-payers themselves are content. In the light of these considerations I am opposed to the payment of money from the Federal Treasury to enrich the treasuries of the States. Their funds should be furnished by their own citizens, and thus should be fostered the tax-payers' watchfulness of State expenditures and the tax-payers' jealous insistence upon the strict accountability of State officials. These elements of purity and strength in a State are not safely exchanged for the threatened demoralization and carelessness attending the custody and management of large gifts from the Federal Treasury.

The baneful effect of a surplus, in the Treasury of the general government, is daily seen and felt. I do not think, however, that this surplus should be reduced or its contagion spread throughout the States by methods such as are provided in this bill.

There is still another objection to the bill, arising from what seems to me its unfairness and unjust discrimination.

In the case of proposed legislation, of at least doubtful constitutionality and based upon no legal right, the equities which recommend it should always be definite and clear.

The money appropriated by this bill is to be paid to the Governors of the respective States and Territories in which it was collected, whether the same was derived through said States and Territories or directly "from any of the citizens or inhabitants thereof or other persons"; and it is further provided that such sums as were collected in payment of this Federal tax through the instrumentality of the State or Territorial officials, and accounted for to the general government by such States and Territories, are to be paid unconditionally to their Governors, while the same collected in payment of said tax by the United States, or, in other words, by the Federal machinery created for that purpose, are to be held in trust by said States or Territories for the benefit of those paying the same.

I am unable to understand how this discrimination in favor of those who have made payment of this tax directly to the officers of the Federal Government, and against those who made such payments through State or Territorial agencies, can be defended upon fair and equitable principles. It was the general government in every case which exacted this tax from its citizens and people in the different States and Territories ; and to provide for reimbursement to a part of its citizens by the creation of a trust for their benefit, while the money exacted in payment of this tax from a far greater number is paid unconditionally into the State and Territorial treasuries, is an unjust and unfair proceeding, in which the government should not be implicated.

It will hardly do to say that the States and Territories who are the recipients of these large gifts may be trusted to do justice to its citizens who originally paid the money. This cannot be relied upon, nor should the government lose sight of the equality of which it boasts, and, having entered upon the plan of reimbursement, abandon to other agencies the duty of just distribution, and thus incur the risk of becoming accessory to actual inequality and injustice.

If, in defense of the plan proposed, it is claimed that exact equality cannot be reached in the premises, this may be readily conceded. The money raised by this direct tax was collected and expended twenty-seven years ago. Nearly a generation has passed away since that time. Even if distribution should be attempted by the States and Territories, as well as by the government, the taxpayers in many cases are neither alive nor represented, and in many other cases, if alive, they cannot be found. Fraudulent claims would often outrun honest applications, and innumerable and bitter contests would arise between claimants.

Another difficulty in the way of doing perfect justice in the operation of this plan of reimbursement is found in the fact that the money to be appropriated therefor was contributed to the Federal Treasury for entirely different purposes, by a generation many of whom were not born when the direct tax was levied and paid, who have no relation to said tax, and cannot share in its distribution. While they stand by and see the money they have been obliged to pay into the public Treasury, professedly to meet present necessities, expended to reimburse taxation long ago fairly, legally, and justly collected from others, they cannot fail to see the unfairness of the transaction.

The existence of a surplus in the Treasury is no answer to these objections. It is still the people's money, and better use can be found for it than the distribution of it upon the plea of the reimbursement of ancient taxation. A more desirable plan to reduce and prevent the recurrence of a large surplus can easily be adopted—one that, instead of creating injustice and inequality, promotes justice and equality by leaving in the hands of the people and for their use the money not needed by the government "to pay the debts and provide for the common defense and general welfare of the United States."

The difficulties in the way of making a just reimbursement of this direct tax, instead of excusing the imperfections of the bill under consideration, furnish reasons why the scheme it proposes should not be entered upon.

I am constrained, upon the considerations herein presented, to withhold my assent from the bill herewith returned, because I believe it to be without constitutional warrant, because I am of the opinion that there exist no adequate reasons either in right or equity for the return of the tax in said bill mentioned, and because I believe its execution would cause actual injustice and unfairness.

GROVER CLEVELAND.

CHAPTER XX.

I.

Concerning the Immigration Commissioner.

ALBANY, May 4, 1883.

TO THE SENATE:

I DEEM it my duty to remind you of the importance of giving effect to the law lately passed by the legislature "to amend the law relating to alien immigrants, and to secure an improved administration of alien immigration."

This statute was the result of investigation which demonstrated that the present management of this very important department is a scandal and a reproach to civilization. The money of the State is apparently expended with no regard to economy, the most disgraceful dissensions prevail among those having the matter in charge, barefaced jobbery has been permitted, and the poor immigrant who looks to the institution for protection, finds that his helplessness and forlorn condition afford the readily seized opportunity for imposition and swindling.

These facts lift the efforts to reform the management above partisan considerations, and make the cause one in which every right-minded man should be enlisted, and one in which those chosen to protect the rights and the honor of the people of the State should gladly co-operate.

The law lately passed, it is admitted, seeks in a practical way to remedy the evils referred to.

In the enforcement of this law, it became my duty to send to the Senate, for its confirmation, the name of a person who should act as commissioner, and who should have charge of the important matters provided for.

This I have done. In the discharge of this duty I was fortunate enough to be able to present the name of a citizen of the State, of conceded integrity, ability, and administrative capacity, who enjoys the respect and esteem of all who know him, and whose benevolent nature would insure the protection and kind care of the destitute and friendless strangers who should be put in his charge.

But the unmistakable indications are that, in its closing hours, the Senate will refuse to confirm his appointment, and thus continue the present scandal and abuses.

Some of those now in charge of this department and their beneficiaries are on the ground and about the halls of legislation, seeking to retain their control and their abused advantages.

The refusal to confirm the appointee is not based upon any allegation of unfitness, nor has such a thing been suggested. It has its rise, as I understand the situation, concededly and openly, in an overweening greed for the patronage which may attach to the place, and which will not be promised in advance, and in questionable partisanship, which is insisted on, at the expense of important interests.

There has not been a reason suggested why the name of the appointee should be withdrawn, and I should be unjust and derelict in my duty if I should pursue that course. The Senate is reminded, too, that the present situation of affairs precludes my submitting another name if I desired.

I am profoundly sensible of the absolute power and right of the Senate in the premises, and do not seek to question it even in this case. Every member knows the motives for his conduct, and must justify them to his constituents.

The fact remains, however, that a captious opposition to the execution of the best remedial law of the present session of the legislature perpetuates the oppression of the immigrant and the practice of unblushing peculation. I have endeavored to co-operate with the Senate in supplementing the passage of the law, by putting the machinery in motion for its execution; and I may, perhaps, be allowed to express the hope that its operation may not be defeated. If it is, the responsibility must rest where it belongs.

GROVER CLEVELAND.

————

II.

On Giving Reasons for Removals from Office.

EXECUTIVE MANSION,
WASHINGTON, March 1, 1886.

TO THE SENATE:

Ever since the beginning of the present session of the Senate, the different heads of the Departments attached to the executive branch of the government have been plied with various requests and demands from committees of the Senate, from members of such committees, and at last from the Senate itself, requiring the transmission of reason for the suspension of certain officials during the recess of that body, or for the papers touching the conduct of such officials, or for all papers and documents relating to such suspensions, or for all documents and papers filed in such Departments in relation to the management and conduct of the offices held by such suspended officials.

The different terms from time to time adopted in making these requests and demands, the order in which they succeeded each other, and the fact that when made by the Senate the resolution for that purpose was passed in executive session, have led to a presumption, the correctness of which will, I suppose, be candidly admitted, that, from first to last, the information thus sought and the papers thus demanded were desired for use by the Senate and its committees in considering the propriety of the suspensions referred to.

Though these suspensions are my executive acts, based upon considerations addressed to me alone, and for which I am wholly responsible, I have had no invitation from the Senate to state the position which I have felt constrained to assume in relation to the same, or to interpret for myself my acts and motives in the premises.

In this condition of affairs, I have forborne addressing the Senate upon the subject, lest I might be accused of thrusting myself unbidden upon the attention of that body.

But the report of the Committee on the Judiciary of the Senate, lately presented and published, which censures the Attorney-General of the United States for his refusal to transmit certain papers relating to a suspension from office, and which also, if I correctly interpret it, evinces a misapprehension of the position of the Executive upon the question of such suspensions, will, I hope, justify this communication.

This report is predicated upon a resolution of the Senate directed to the Attorney-General and his reply to the same. This resolution was adopted in executive session devoted entirely to business connected with the consideration of nominations for office. It required the Attorney-General "to transmit to the Senate copies of all documents and papers that have been filed in the Department of Justice since the 1st day of January, 1885, in relation to the management and conduct of the office of district attorney of the United States of the southern district of Alabama."

The incumbent of this office on the 1st day of January, 1885, and until the 17th day of July ensuing, was George M. Duskin, who, on the day last mentioned, was suspended by an Executive order, and John D. Burnett designated to perform the duties of said office. At the time of the passage of the resolution above referred to, the nomination of Burnett for said office was pending before the Senate, and all the papers relating to said nomination were before that body for its inspection and information.

In reply to this resolution, the Attorney-General, after referring to the fact that the papers relating to the nomination of Burnett had already been sent to the Senate, stated that he was directed by the President to say that "the papers and documents which are mentioned in said resolution and still remaining in the custody of this Department, having exclusive reference to the suspension by the President of George M. Duskin, the late incumbent of the office of district attorney for the southern district of Alabama, it is not considered that the public interests will be promoted by a compliance with said resolution and the transmission of the papers and documents therein mentioned to the Senate in executive session."

Upon this resolution and the answer thereto the issue is thus stated by the Committee on the Judiciary at the outset of the report:

The important question, then, is whether it is within the constitutional competence of either house of Congress to have access to the official papers and documents in the various public offices of the United States created by laws enacted by themselves.

I do not suppose that "the public offices of the United States" are regulated or controlled in their relations to either house of Congress by the fact that they were "created by laws enacted by themselves." It must be that these instrumentalities were created for the benefit of the people and to answer the general purposes of government under the Constitution and the laws, and that they are unincumbered by any lien in favor of either branch of Congress growing out of their construction, and unembarrassed by any obligation to the Senate as the price of their creation.

The complaint of the committee, that access to official papers in the public offices is denied the Senate, is met by the statement that at no time has it been the disposition or the intention of the President or any Department of the executive branch of the government to withhold from the Senate official documents or papers filed in any of the public offices. While it is by no means conceded that the Senate has the right, in any case, to review the act of the Executive in removing or suspending a public officer upon official documents or otherwise, it is considered that documents and papers of that nature should, because they are official, be freely transmitted to the

Senate upon its demand, trusting the use of the same for proper and legitimate purposes to the good faith of that body. And though no such paper or document has been specifically demanded· in any of the numerous requests and demands made upon the Departments, yet, as often as they were found in the public offices, they have been furnished in answer to such applications.

The letter of the Attorney-General in response to the resolution of the Senate, in the particular case mentioned in the committee's report, was written at my suggestion and by my direction. There had been no official papers or documents filed in this Department relating to the case, within the period specified in the resolution. The letter was intended, by its description of the papers and documents remaining in the custody of the Department, to convey the idea that they were not official; and it was assumed that the resolution called for information, papers, and documents of the same character as were required by the requests and demands which preceded it.

Everything that had been written or done on behalf of the Senate, from the beginning, pointed to all letters and papers of a private and unofficial nature as the objects of search, if they were to be found in the Departments, and provided that they had been presented to the Executive with a view to their consideration upon the question of suspension from office.

Against the transmission of such papers and documents I have interposed my advice and direction. This has not been done, as is suggested in the committee's report, upon the assumption on my part that the Attorney-General or any other head of a Department "is the servant of the President, and is to give or withhold copies of documents in his office according to the will of the Executive and not otherwise," but because I regard the papers and documents withheld and addressed to me, or intended for my use and action, purely unofficial and private, not infrequently confidential, and having reference to the performance of a duty exclusively mine. I consider them in no proper sense as upon the files of the

Department, but as deposited there for my convenience, remaining still completely under my control. I suppose if I desired to take them into my custody I might do so with entire propriety, and if I saw fit to destroy them no one could complain.

Even the committee in its report appears to concede that there may be, with the President or in the Departments, papers and documents which, on account of their unofficial character, are not subject to the inspection of the Congress. A reference in the report to instances where the House of Representatives ought not to succeed in a call for the production of papers is immediately followed by this statement:

> The committee feels authorized to state, after a somewhat careful research, that within the foregoing limits there is scarcely in the history of this government, until now, any instance of a refusal by a head of a Department, or even of the President himself, to communicate official facts and information as distinguished from private and unofficial papers, motions, views, reasons, and opinions, to either house of Congress when unconditionally demanded.

To which of the classes thus recognized do the papers and documents belong that are now the objects of the Senate's quest?

They consist of letters and representations addressed to the Executive or intended for his inspection; they are voluntarily written and presented by private citizens who are not in the least instigated thereto by any official invitation or at all subject to official control. While some of them are entitled to Executive consideration, many of them are so irrelevant, or in the light of other facts so worthless, that they have not been given the least weight in determining the question to which they are supposed to relate.

Are all these, simply because they are preserved, to be considered official documents and subject to the inspection of the Senate? If not, who is to determine which belong to this class? Are the motives and purposes of the Senate, as they are day by day developed, such as would be satisfied with my selection? Am I to submit to theirs at the risk of being charged with making a suspension from office upon evidence which was not even considered?

Are these papers to be regarded official because they have not only been presented but preserved in the public offices?

Their nature and character remain the same, whether they are kept in the Executive Mansion or deposited in the Departments. There is no mysterious power of transmutation in departmental custody, nor is there magic in the undefined and sacred solemnity of Department files. If the presence of these papers in the public offices is a stumbling-block in the way of the performance of senatorial duty, it can be easily removed.

The papers and documents which have been described derive no official character from any constitutional, statutory, or other requirement making them necessary to the performance of the official duty of the Executive.

It will not be denied, I suppose, that the President may suspend a public officer in the entire absence of any papers or documents to aid his official judgment and discretion. And I am quite prepared to avow that the cases are not few in which suspensions from office have depended more upon oral representations made to me by citizens of known good repute, and by members of the House of Representatives and Senators of the United States, than upon any letters and documents presented for my examination. I have not felt justified in suspecting the veracity, integrity, and patriotism of Senators, or ignoring their representations, because they were not in party affiliation with the majority of their associates; and I recall a few suspensions which bear the approval of individual members identified politically with the majority in the Senate.

While, therefore, I am constrained to deny the right of the Senate to the papers and documents described, so far as the right to the same is based upon the claim that they are in any view of the subject official, I am also led unequivocally to dispute the right of the Senate, by the aid of any documents whatever, or in any way save through the judicial process of trial on impeachment, to review or reverse the acts of the Executive in the suspension, during the recess of the Senate, of Federal officials.

I believe the power to remove or suspend such officials is vested in the President alone by the Constitution, which in express terms provides that "the executive power shall be vested in a President of the United States of America," and that "he shall take care that the laws be faithfully executed."

The Senate belongs to the legislative branch of the government. When the Constitution, by express provision, super-added to its legislative duties the right to advise and consent to appointments to office and to sit as a court of impeachment, it conferred upon that body all the control and regulation of Executive action supposed to be necessary for the safety of the people; and this express and special grant of such extraordinary powers, not in any way related to or growing out of general senatorial duty, and in itself a departure from the general plan of our government, should be held, under a familiar maxim of construction, to exclude every other right of interference with Executive functions.

In the first Congress which assembled after the adoption of the Constitution, comprising many who aided in its preparation, a legislative construction was given to that instrument in which the independence of the Executive in the matter of removals from office was fully sustained.

I think it will be found that in the subsequent discussions of this question there was generally, if not at all times, a proposition pending in some way to curtail this power of the President by legislation, which furnishes evidence that to limit such power it was supposed to be necessary to supplement the Constitution by such legislation.

The first enactment of this description was passed under a stress of partisanship and political bitterness which culminated in the President's impeachment.

This law provided that the Federal officers to which it

applied could only be suspended during the recess of the Senate when shown by evidence satisfactory to the President to be guilty of misconduct in office, or crime, or when incapable or disqualified to perform their duties, and that within twenty days after the next meeting of the Senate it should be the duty of the President "to report to the Senate such suspension, with the evidence and reasons for his action in the case."

This statute, passed in 1867, when Congress was overwhelmingly and bitterly opposed politically to the President, may be regarded as an indication that even then it was thought necessary by a Congress, determined upon the subjugation of the Executive to legislative will, to furnish itself a law for that purpose, instead of attempting to reach the object intended by an invocation of any pretended constitutional right.

The law which thus found its way to our statute book was plain in its terms, and its intent needed no avowal. If valid, and now in operation, it would justify the present course of the Senate and command the obedience of the Executive to its demands. It may, however, be remarked in passing, that, under this law, the President had the privilege of presenting to the body which assumed to review his executive acts his reasons therefor, instead of being excluded from explanation or judged by papers found in the Departments.

Two years after the law of 1867 was passed, and within less than five weeks after the inauguration of a President in political accord with both branches of Congress, the sections of the act regulating suspensions from office during the recess of the Senate were entirely repealed and in their place were substituted provisions which, instead of limiting the causes of suspension to misconduct, crime, disability, or disqualification, expressly permitted such suspension by the President "in his discretion," and completely abandoned the requirement obliging him to report to the Senate "the evidence and reasons" for his action.

With these modifications, and with all branches of the government in political harmony, and in the absence of partisan incentive to captious obstruction, the law, as it was left by the amendment of 1869, was much less destructive of Executive discretion.   And yet the great general and patriotic citizen who, on the 4th day of March, 1869, assumed the duties of Chief Executive, and for whose freer administration of his high office the most hateful restraints of the law of 1867 were, on the 5th day of April, 1869, removed, mindful of his obligation to defend and protect every prerogative of his great trust, and apprehensive of the injury threatened the public service in the continued operation of these statutes even in their modified form, in his first message to Congress advised their repeal and set forth their unconstitutional character and hurtful tendency in the following language:

It may be well to mention here the embarrassment possible to arise from leaving on the statute books the so-called " tenure-of-office acts" and to recommend earnestly their total repeal.   It could not have been the intention of the framers of the Constitution, when providing that appointments made by the President should receive the consent of the Senate, that the latter should have the power to retain in office persons placed there by Federal appointment against the will of the President.   The law is inconsistent with a faithful and efficient administration of the government.   What faith can an Executive put in officials forced upon him, and those, too, whom he has suspended for reason ?   How will such officials be likely to serve an administration which they know does not trust them ?

I am unable to state whether or not this recommendation for a repeal of these laws has been since repeated.   If it has not, the reason can probably be found in the experience which demonstrated the fact that the necessities of the political situation but rarely developed their vicious character.

And so it happens that, after an existence of nearly twenty years of almost innocuous desuetude, these laws are brought forth—apparently the repealed as well as the unrepealed—and put in the way of an Executive who is willing, if permitted, to attempt an improvement in the methods of administration.

The constitutionality of these laws is by no means admitted. But why should the provisions of the repealed law, which required specific cause for suspension and a report to the Senate of "evidence and reasons," be now, in effect, applied to the present Executive instead of the law, afterward passed, and unrepealed, which distinctly permits suspensions by the President "in his discretion," and carefully omits the requirement that "evidence and reasons for his actions in the case" shall be reported to the Senate?

The requests and demands which, by the score, have, for nearly three months, been presented to the different Departments of the government, whatever may be their form, have but one complexion. They assume the right of the Senate to sit in judgment upon the exercise of my exclusive discretion and executive function, for which I am solely responsible to the people from whom I have so lately received the sacred trust of office. My oath to support and defend the Constitution, my duty to the people, who have chosen me to execute the powers of their great office and not to relinquish them, and my duty to the Chief Magistracy, which I must preserve unimpaired in all its dignity and vigor, compel me to refuse compliance with these demands.

To the end that the service may be improved, the Senate is invited to the fullest scrutiny of the persons submitted to them for public office, in recognition of the constitutional power of that body to advise and consent to their appointment. I shall continue, as I have thus far done, to furnish, at the request of the confirming body, all the information I possess touching the fitness of the nominees placed before them for their action, both when they are proposed to fill vacancies and to take the place of suspended officials. Upon a refusal to confirm I shall not assume the right to ask the reasons for the action of the Senate nor question its determination. I cannot think that anything more is required to secure worthy incumbents in public office than a careful and independent discharge of our respective duties within their well-defined limits.

Though the propriety of suspensions might be better assured if the action of the President was subject to review by the

Senate, yet if the Constitution and the laws have placed this responsibility upon the executive branch of the government, it should not be divided nor the discretion which it involves relinquished.

It has been claimed that the present Executive having pledged himself not to remove officials except for cause, the fact of their suspension implies such misconduct on the part of a suspended official as injures his character and reputation, and therefore the Senate should review the case for his vindication.

I have said that certain officials should not, in my opinion, be removed during the continuance of the term for which they were appointed solely for the purpose of putting in their place those in political affiliation with the appointing power; and this declaration was immediately followed by a description of offensive partisanship which ought not to entitle those in whom it was exhibited to consideration. It is not apparent how an adherence to the course thus announced carries with it the consequences described. If in any degree the suggestion is worthy of consideration, it is to be hoped that there may be a defense against unjust suspension in the justice of the Executive.

Every pledge which I have made, by which I have placed a limitation upon my exercise of executive power, has been faithfully redeemed. Of course the pretense is not put forth that no mistakes have been committed; but not a suspension has been made except it appeared to my satisfaction that the public welfare would be improved thereby. Many applications for suspension have been denied, and the adherence to the rule laid down to govern my action as to such suspensions has caused much irritation and impatience on the part of those who have insisted upon more changes in the offices.

The pledges I have made were made to the people, and to them I am responsible for the manner in which they have been redeemed. I am not responsible to the Senate, and I am unwilling to submit my actions and official conduct to them for judgment.

There are no grounds for an allegation that the fear of being found false to my professions influences me in declining to submit to the demands of the Senate. I have not constantly refused to suspend officials, and thus incurred the displeasure of political friends, and yet willfully broken faith with the people for the sake of being false to them.

Neither the discontent of party friends nor the allurements constantly offered of confirmations of appointees conditioned upon the avowal that suspensions have been made on party grounds alone, nor the threat proposed in the resolutions now before the Senate that no confirmation will be made unless the demands of that body be complied with, are sufficient to discourage or deter me from following in the way which I am convinced leads to better government for the people.

GROVER CLEVELAND.

III.

Suggesting Certain Amendments to the Oleomargarine Act.

EXECUTIVE MANSION,
WASHINGTON, August 2, 1886.

TO THE CONGRESS:

I have this day approved a bill originating in the House of Representatives, entitled, "An Act defining butter, also imposing a tax upon and regulating the manufacture, sale, importation, and exportation of oleomargarine."

This legislation has awakened much interest among the people of the country, and earnest argument has been addressed to the Executive for the purpose of influencing his action thereupon. Many, in opposition, have urged its dangerous character as tending to break down the boundaries between the proper exercise of legislative power by Federal and State authority; many, in favor of the enactment, have represented that it promised great advantages to a large portion of our population who sadly need relief; and those, on both sides of the question, whose advocacy or opposition is based upon no broader foundation than local or personal interest, have outnumbered all the others.

This, upon its face and in its main features, is a revenue bill, and was first introduced in the House of Representatives, wherein the Constitution declares that all bills for raising revenue shall originate.

The Constitution has invested Congress with a very wide legislative discretion both as to the necessity of taxation and the selection of the objects of its burdens. And though, if the question was presented to me as an original proposition, I might doubt the present need of increased taxation, I deem it my duty in this instance to defer to the judgment of the legislative branch of the government, which has been so emphatically announced in both Houses of Congress upon the passage of this bill.

Moreover, those who desire to see removed the weight of taxation, now pressing upon the people from other directions, may well be justified in the hope and expectation that the selection of an additional subject of internal taxation, so well able to bear it, will in consistency be followed by legislation relieving our citizens from other revenue burdens, rendered by the passage of this bill even more than heretofore unnecessary and needlessly oppressive.

It has been urged as an objection to this measure that, while purporting to be legislation for revenue, its real purpose is to destroy, by the use of the taxing power, one industry of our people for the protection and benefit of another.

If entitled to indulge in such a suspicion, as a basis of official action in this case, and if entirely satisfied that the consequences indicated would ensue, I should doubtless feel constrained to interpose Executive dissent.

But I do not feel called upon to interpret the motives of Congress otherwise than by the apparent character of the bill which has been presented to me, and I am convinced that the taxes which it creates cannot possibly destroy the open and legitimate manufacture and sale of the thing upon which it is levied. If this article has the merit which its friends claim for it, and if the people of the land, with full knowledge of its real character, desire to purchase and use it, the taxes exacted by this bill will permit a fair profit to both manufacturer and dealer. If the existence of the commodity taxed, and the profits of its manufacture and sale, depend upon disposing of it to the people for something else which it deceitfully imitates, the entire enterprise is a fraud and not an industry; and if it cannot endure the exhibition of its real character which will be effected by the inspection, supervision, and stamping which this bill directs, the sooner it is destroyed the better, in the interest of fair dealing.

Such a result would not furnish the first instance in the history of legislation in which a revenue bill produced a benefit which was merely incidental to its main purpose.

There is certainly no industry better entitled to the incidental advantages which may follow this legislation than our farming and dairy interests; and to none of our people should they be less begrudged than our farmers and dairymen. The present depression of their occupations, the hard, steady, and often unremunerative toil which such occupations exact, and the burdens of taxation which our agriculturists necessarily bear, entitle them to every legitimate consideration.

Nor should there be opposition to the incidental effect of this legislation on the part of those who profess to be engaged honestly and fairly in the manufacture and sale of a wholesome and valuable article of food, which by its provisions may be subject to taxation. As long as their business is carried on under cover and by false pretenses, such men have bad companions in those whose manufactures, however vile and harmful, take their place without challenge with the better sort, in a common crusade of deceit against the public. But if this occupation and its methods are forced into the light,—and all these manufactures must thus either stand upon their merits or fall—the good and bad must soon part company, and the fittest only will survive.

Not the least important incident related to this legislation is the defense afforded to the consumer against the fraudulent substitution and sale of an imitation for a genuine article of food, of very general household use. Notwithstanding the immense quantity of the article described in this bill which is sold to the people for their consumption as food, and notwithstanding the claim made that its manufacture supplies a cheap substitute for butter, I venture to say that hardly a pound ever entered a poor man's house under its real name and in its true character.

While, in its relation to an article of this description, there should be no governmental regulation of what the citizen shall eat, it is certainly not a cause of regret if, by legislation of this character, he is afforded a means by which he may better protect himself against imposition in meeting the needs and wants of his daily life.

Having entered upon this legislation, it is manifestly a duty to render it as effective as possible in the accomplishment of all the good which should legitimately follow in its train.

This leads to the suggestion that the article proposed to be taxed, and the circumstances which subject it thereto, should be clearly and with great distinctness defined in the statute. It seems to me that this object has not been completely attained in the phraseology of the second section of the bill, and that question may well arise as to the precise condition the article to be taxed must assume in order to be regarded as "made in imitation or semblance of butter, or, when so made, calculated or intended to be sold as butter or for butter."

The fourteenth and fifteenth sections of the bill in my opinion are in danger of being construed as an interference with the police power of the States. Not being entirely satisfied of the unconstitutionality of these provisions, and regarding them as not being so connected and interwoven with the other sections as, if found invalid, to vitiate the entire measure, I have determined to commend them to the attention of the House with a view to an immediate amendment of the bill if it should be deemed necessary, and if it is practicable at this late day in the session of Congress.

The fact, too, that the bill does not take effect by its terms until ninety days have elapsed after its approval, thus leaving it but one month in operation before the next session of Congress, when, if time does not now permit, the safety and efficiency of the measure may be abundantly protected by remedial legislative action, and the desire to see realized the beneficial results which it is expected will immediately follow the inauguration of this legislation have had their influence in determining my official action.

The considerations which have been referred to will, I hope, justify this communication and the suggestions which it contains.

GROVER CLEVELAND.

CHAPTER XXI.

ESTIMATES OF PUBLIC MEN.

I.

THE PRINCIPLES OF THOMAS JEFFERSON.

1.

(Letter to John P. Adams, Brooklyn, N. Y., September 12, 1890.)

IT SEEMS but a very short time ago that I participated in the laying of the corner stone of the building now ready for occupancy, and I recognize in the vigor with which it has been pushed to completion the most gratifying evidence of the zeal and sturdiness of your Democratic organization.

The Kings County Democracy should certainly be congratulated upon the possession of such beautiful headquarters in a building whose name suggests the true Democratic faith. In the Thomas Jefferson there should be found no room for counsels in the least regardless of the value of pure and honest government, or lacking in sympathy with the highest and greatest good of the people.

I feel that I can wish nothing better for your association than that their new home may be long continued to them, and that they may take with them there and always maintain those principles of Jeffersonian Democracy, as old as the Nation, which, if steadfastly upheld and honestly applied, are certain to insure the felicity and prosperity of our country.

2.

(Letter to William E. Burnett, Springfield, O., February 3, 1891.)

The Democracy of Ohio is deserving of the utmost regard of its party friends everywhere on account of its steadfastness to a party creed and loyalty. This reflection but adds to my perplexity, as I see insurmountable obstacles in the way of my meeting those who will gather at your contemplated banquet.

These are days above all others in our generation when the memory of Jefferson's patriotism, conservatism, wisdom, and devotion to everything American should be kept warm in the hearts and minds of his countrymen, and especially of his political followers. The contemplation of these things should serve to check every tendency to follow false and delusive lights, and to tread untried and unsafe paths.

It is most fitting and useful, therefore, that your club, which bears the name of this illustrious man, should properly celebrate every anniversary of his birth.

3.

(Letter to Dethlef C. Hansen, Tacoma, Wash., March 26, 1891.)

It would afford me great satisfaction if I could accept your invitation to join the Democracy of the State of Washington in their celebration of the birthday of Thomas Jefferson, on the 13th day of April next.

It seems to me that there never was a time in our history when the American people could with so much profit recall the character and teachings of this illustrious man. The peril of our day lies in an inclination to disregard the virtue of patriotism—absolutely necessary to the success of free institutions— and the acceptance of the vicious lessons of selfishness, and in an ignoble toleration of the idea that the operations of our government may be used as aids in the advancement of special interests.

Jefferson has warned us that these things are all opposed to the principles upon which our scheme of popular rule is founded. He has admonished us that the requisites of success in the plan of government which we exhibit to the world are our united determination to reach the national destiny our institutions promise, a patriotic, unselfish care of every interest affecting the general prosperity of our people, and the scrupulous cultivation and preservation of that genuine Americanism which is considerate of all our conditions, tolerant of all our varied interests, and free from unworthy suspicion or jealousy.

It follows that, if there are dangerous political tendencies abroad in the land, they should not be found among those who profess the faith of true Democracy. We, who acknowledge Jefferson as the founder of our party, should never for a moment discredit the wisdom or devotion to principle of our great leader, who knew so well the essentials of our country's perpetuation and welfare, nor should we ever doubt that he has left to us a safe guide to the way of political duty.

———

4.

(Letter to E. O. Graves, Seattle, Wash., April 2, 1891.)

I very much regret that I am unable to accept the invitation thus courteously extended to me, for I believe that those who profess the political faith of Thomas Jefferson cannot too often contemplate his life and services, and all that he has done for our country and for the American name.

Every Democrat should be proud to claim that the services he rendered in the cause of freedom and humanity were rendered under the sanction of Democratic principles. Nor should we forget that the honest and fearless application of these principles is of no less importance now than when our great leader announced them.

The occasion which you contemplate should not, therefore, be allowed to pass without leaving, on the minds of those who participate, the conviction that, as followers of Thomas Jefferson, they assume a responsibility to their fellow-countrymen which exacts not only loyalty to party organization, but the intelligent and sturdy advocacy of Democratic doctrines in their purity and integrity.

If these doctrines are fairly and frankly taught, we need have no apprehension that the absolute reliance upon the deliberate thought of the American people, which Jefferson insisted upon, will disappoint us—either as members of the Democratic party or as patriotic American citizens.

———

5.

(Letter to Iroquois Club, Chicago, March 25, 1892.)

I am in receipt of the courteous invitation tendered me by the Iroquois Club, of Chicago, to attend its annual banquet in commemoration of the birthday of Thomas Jefferson on the 2d day of April. The fact that I have been obliged to decline other invitations of the club to meet its members and guests on similar occasions causes me especially to regret that I cannot accept this, but the work I have to do and the engagements I have made enforce another declination.

A contemplation of Jefferson's life and services, and a review of his political expressions, cannot fail to be improving and profitable to the Democracy of the present day. If entered upon in a proper spirit, Jefferson's teachings ought to increase the tenacity of our hold upon the simple truths which made up his political faith, and should satisfy us with the standards of Democracy which he established. In these days, when the Democratic party is beset with temptation, and when on every side false lights are set up for its destruction, its safety will be found in steadfastly and trustingly following the way which principle points out and shunning the allurements of temporary expedients, and resisting the seductions of popular misconceptions.

II.

THE CHARACTER OF ANDREW JACKSON.

1.

(Letter to Allen G. Thurman, January 4, 1886.)

I acknowledge with thanks the receipt of an invitation to be present at the annual reunion of the Jackson Club, of the city of Columbus, on the evening of the 8th inst.

My official duties here will prevent my acceptance of the invitation so kindly tendered, and I beg to assure the Club that the objects and purposes of the reunion, which are expressed in the note of the committee, meet with my cordial and sincere approval.

I should be most pleased to be one of those who, on that occasion, will congratulate the friends of good government on the success of the Democratic party, for I believe that the application of the true and pure principles of that political faith must result in the welfare of the country.

It is also proposed, I learn, to consult together as to the manner in which the accomplishment of "the greatest good to our people" can best be aided and assisted. No higher or more sacred mission was ever intrusted to a party organization, and I am convinced that it will be honestly and faithfully performed by a close sympathy with the people in their wants and needs, by a patriotic endeavor to quicken their love and devotion for American institutions, and by an earnest effort to enlarge their apprehensions and realizations of the benefits which the wise and unselfish administration of a free government will secure to them.

2.

(Letter to C. Kinney Smith, New York, December 26, 1890.)

It is with much disappointment and regret that I feel obliged to forego, on account of another engagement, the pleasure of meeting the Business Men's Association at its celebration of the battle of New Orleans, on the evening of the 8th of January next.

I hope the time will never come when the day your club proposes to celebrate will be neglected by the Democracy of our land. It seems to me that you appropriately call it " Jackson's Day," and I wish that designation might become universal among those who love the Democratic faith and believe in its fearless advocacy.

Especially at this particular time ought the celebration of this day to be enthusiastic. The fact that our party is united in its devotion to the professions and doctrines which have made it great, for which Jackson stood, and in the inspiration of which he led the Democracy of his time to victory, is enough to furnish abundant cause for congratulation. When we add to this the fact that we are permitted to celebrate on the " Jackson's Day " now at hand a recent sweeping triumph of Democratic principle, we are justified in the indulgence of unrestrained and hearty rejoicing.

3.

(Letter to Samuel Gustine Thompson, Philadelphia, January 3, 1892.)

I hope the Democracy of the country will generally observe this day, and that their observance will serve to stimulate a real genuine Democratic sentiment, which recognizes the responsibility of our party to the people, and the duty we owe to those who have reposed confidence in our professions. We will thus be constrained to a steady and persistent advocacy of the principles which are concededly Democratic, and will be prepared to resist the temptation to attempt to win party supremacy by the support of theories challenged as to their Democratic character, and certainly dangerous and distracting to the harmony of our party.

Temporary shifts and reckless expedients do not accord with the nature and policy of true Democracy. Its best hope and reliance have always been and must continue to be in a constant adherence to its acknowledged principles, and a plain and persistent presentation of those principles to the intelligence and thoughtfulness of the American people.

III.

TRIBUTES TO SAMUEL J. TILDEN.

I.

EXECUTIVE MANSION,
WASHINGTON, D. C., February 2, 1888.

WILLIAM A. FUREY, ESQ., *Chairman, etc.*

MY DEAR SIR : I acknowledge with sincere thanks the invitation extended to me, on behalf of the Kings County Democratic Club, to attend a banquet to be given in the City of Brooklyn on the 9th instant, in commemoration of the birthday of Samuel J. Tilden.

I indulge, with the utmost pleasure and satisfaction, the belief that this invitation is not a mere formal compliment tendered to me in fulfillment of customary propriety, but that it is an additional evidence of the genuine kindness of the people and my political friends of Brooklyn and Kings County, which has more than once during my public life been heartily manifested.

Entertaining this belief, I know that its expression will make it unnecessary for me to assure you that I would gladly accept your invitation if it were possible. I am not only certain that at your banquet I should be among true and steadfast friends, but that the occasion and its prevailing spirit cannot fail to inspire every participant with new strength and increased patriotism and courage.

The birthday of Samuel J. Tilden is fittingly celebrated by the Democracy of Kings County, for he found there in all his efforts to reform the public service and to reinstate his party in the confidence of the American people firm and stanch friends, never wavering in their willing and effective support. Let these friends now remind all their fellow-citizens of the patriotic and useful career of their honored and trusted leader, and let everyone professing his political faith proclaim the value of his teachings. He taught the limitation of Federal power under the Constitution, the absolute necessity of public economy, the safety of a sound currency, honesty in public place, the responsibility of public servants to the people, care for those who toil with their hands, a proper limitation of corpo rate privileges and a reform in the Civil Service.

His was true Democracy. It led him to meet boldly every public issue as it rose. With his conception of political duty, he thought it never too early and never too late to give battle to vicious doctrines and corrupt practices. He believed that pure and sound Democracy flourished and grew in open, bold, and honest championship of the interests of the people, and that it but feebly lived upon deceit, false pretenses, and fear.

And he was right. His success proved him right, and proved, too, that the American people appreciate a courageous struggle in their defense.

I should certainly join you in recalling the virtues and achievements of this illustrious Democrat, on the anniversary of his birth, if, in the arrangement of the social events connected with my official life, an important one had not been appointed to take place on the evening of your banquet. This necessarily detains me here.

Hoping that your celebration will be very successful and full of profitable enjoyment,

I am,

Yours very truly,
GROVER CLEVELAND.

————

2.

(Letter to the Greystone Club, February, 1890.)

It seems to me that the celebration of that day should give rise to inspiring thoughts in the minds of all true Democrats and stimulate them in their efforts for reform and their insistence upon better care for the interests of the people. The faith of Mr. Tilden in the Democratic party is vindicated by the manner in which it has rushed to the front in the struggle for the accomplishment of more valuable, practical results than the loaves and fishes of party. It ought to delight every member of the party to see how readily and how eagerly it seized upon a political principle when it was presented, and how naturally and easily it espoused, in discussing it, the cause of the people, instead of the selfish and sordid side of the question.

After all, this is but being true to the Democratic faith and profession. No member of the party who appreciates the advantage of honesty and consistency, and who fairly values the constantly growing acceptance of our principles, can fail to congratulate himself upon his right to a place in the brotherhood to which Jefferson and Jackson and Tilden belonged.

3.

(Letter to A. B. McKinley, Denver, Col., February 5, 1892.)

This is a most excellent and appropriate time to recall the virtues and attributes of Samuel J. Tilden, the late great leader of the Democracy of the land. In these days our party may remember with extreme profit his pure patriotism, his ambition permeated with a desire for the welfare of his fellow-countrymen, his splendid organizing ability, stimulated by his love of country and untainted with ignoble motives, his unyielding resistance to all that was undemocratic and unsafe, and his stubborn insistence upon everything which had the clear sanction of party principles. These characteristics, combined with his love for the people and his unfaltering trust in their intelligence and fair-mindedness, made him a great Democrat, and we cannot go amiss if we accept him as our political example.

I hope the banquet contemplated by your club will be an occasion full of invigoration to those who, in the celebration of the 9th of February, demonstrate their devotion to the political honesty and sincerity which characterized Samuel J. Tilden, and that those who are fortunate enough to participate will see plainer than ever their duty and mission in resistance within their party to all that is not safely and surely in accord with Democratic doctrine and in the bold advocacy, at all times and in all places, of the saving qualities of the true Democratic faith.

IV.

DEATH OF GENERAL U. S. GRANT.

(Presidential Proclamation, July 23, 1885.)

The President of the United States has just received the sad tidings of the death of that illustrious citizen and ex-President of the United States, General Ulysses S. Grant, at Mount McGregor, in the State of New York, to which place he had lately been removed in the endeavor to prolong his life.

In making this announcement to the people of the United States, the President is impressed with the magnitude of the public loss of a great military leader, who was, in the hour of victory, magnanimous ; amid disaster, serene and self-sustained; who, in every station, whether as a soldier, or as a Chief Magistrate, twice called to power by his fellow-countrymen, trod unswervingly the pathway of duty, undeterred by doubts, single-minded, and straightforward.

The entire country has witnessed with deep emotion his prolonged and patient struggle with painful disease, and has watched by his couch of suffering with tearful sympathy.

The destined end has come at last, and his spirit has returned to the Creator who sent it forth.

The great heart of the nation, that followed him when living with love and pride, bows now in sorrow above him dead, tenderly mindful of his virtues, his great patriotic services, and of the loss occasioned by his death.

V.

VICE-PRESIDENT THOMAS A. HENDRICKS.

I.

(Opening Sentence of First Annual Message, December, 1885.)

Your assembling is clouded by a sense of public bereavement caused by the recent and sudden death of Thomas A. Hendricks, Vice President of the United States. His distinguished public services, his complete integrity and devotion to every duty, and his personal virtues will find honorable record in his country's history.

Ample and repeated proofs of the esteem and confidence in which he was held by his fellow-countrymen were manifested by his election to offices of the most important trust and highest dignity; and at length, full of years and honors, he has been laid at rest amid universal sorrow and benediction.

2.

(To John A. Holman, Indianapolis, Secretary of the Monument Committee.)

MARION, MASS., June 18, 1890.

DEAR SIR :

I acknowledge with thanks the invitation I have just received to be present at the unveiling of the monument to the memory of the late Thomas A. Hendricks, on the 1st day of July next.

It is useless, I hope, to assure you of the satisfaction it would afford me to testify my respect and affection for your distinguished fellow-townsman by joining those who will gather to honor his memory on the occasion you contemplate. His eminent public service, and his faithful discharge of many and important official duties, render the commemoration of his public and private virtues most fitting and proper. I sincerely regret that a positive engagement, for the day appointed for the unveiling of the monument erected to his memory, makes it impossible for me to accept your invitation.

Yours very truly,

GROVER CLEVELAND.

VI.

THE DEATH OF GENERAL HANCOCK.

(Executive Order, February 9, 1886.)

Tidings of the death of Winfield Scott Hancock, the senior Major-General of the Army of the United States, have just been received.

A patriotic and valiant defender of his country ; an able and heroic soldier ; a spotless and accomplished gentleman— crowned alike with the laurels of military renown and the highest tribute of his fellow-countrymen to his worth as a citizen—he has gone to his reward.

It is fitting that every mark of public respect should be paid to his memory. Therefore it is now ordered by the President that the national flag be displayed at half-mast upon all the buildings of the Executive Departments in this city until after his funeral shall have taken place.

VII.

EX-PRESIDENT CHESTER A. ARTHUR.

(Executive Proclamation, November 18, 1886.)

It is my painful duty to announce the death of Chester Alan Arthur, lately the President of the United States, which oc- curred after an illness of long duration, at an early hour this morning, at his residence in the city of New York.

Mr. Arthur was called to the chair of Chief Magistrate of the nation by a tragedy which cast its shadow over the entire government.

His assumption of the grave duties was marked by an evident and conscientious sense of his responsibilities, and an earnest desire to meet them in a patriotic and benevolent spirit.

With dignity and ability he sustained the important duties of his station, and the reputation of his personal worth, con- spicuous graciousness, and patriotic fidelity will long be cherished by his fellow-countrymen.

VIII.

THE CAREER OF HENRY WARD BEECHER.

EXECUTIVE MANSION,
WASHINGTON, D. C., May 22, 1888.

MY DEAR MRS. BEECHER :

I have been asked to furnish a contribution to a proposed memorial of your late husband.

While I am by no means certain that anything I might prepare would be worthy of a place among the eloquent and beautiful tributes which are sure to be presented, this request spurs to action my desire and intention to express to you, more fully than I have yet done, my sympathy in your affliction and my appreciation of my own and the country's loss in the death of Mr. Beecher.

More than thirty years ago I repeatedly enjoyed the opportunity of hearing him in his own pulpit. His warm utterances, and the earnest interest he displayed in the practical things related to useful living, the hopes he inspired, and the manner in which he relieved the precepts of Christianity from gloom and cheerlessness, made me feel that, though a stranger, he was my friend. Many years afterward we came to know each other ; and since that time my belief in his friendship, based upon acquaintance and personal contact, has been to me a source of the greatest satisfaction.

His goodness and kindness of heart, so far as they were manifested in his personal life and in his home, are sacred to you and to your grief ; but, so far as they gave color and direction to his teachings and opinions, they are proper subjects for gratitude and congratulation on the part of every American citizen. They caused him to take the side of the common people in every discussion. He loved his fellows in their homes ; he rejoiced in their contentment and comfort, and sympathized with them in their daily hardships and trials. As their champion he advocated in all things the utmost regulated and wholesome liberty and freedom. His sublime faith

in the success of popular government led him to trust the
people, and to treat their errors and misconceptions with generous toleration.   An honorable pride in American citizenship,
when guided by the teachings of religion, he believed to be a
sure guarantee of a splendid national destiny.   I never met
him without gaining something from his broad views and wise
reflections.

Your personal affliction in his death stands alone, in its magnitude and depth.   But thousands wish that their sense of loss
might temper your grief, and that they, by sharing your sorrow, might lighten it.

Such kindly assurances, and your realization of the high and
sacred mission accomplished in your husband's useful life, furnish all this world can supply of comfort ; but your faith and
piety will not fail to lead you to a higher and better source of
consolation.

Yours very sincerely,
Grover Cleveland.

IX.

DEATH OF GENERAL P. H. SHERIDAN.

I.

(Special Message to Congress, August 6, 1888.)

It becomes my painful duty to announce to the Congress and
to the people of the United States the death of Philip H.
Sheridan, General of the Army, which occurred at a late hour
last night at his summer home, in the State of Massachusetts.
The death of this valiant soldier and patriotic son of the republic, though his long illness has been regarded with anxiety, has
nevertheless shocked the country and caused universal grief.

He had established for himself a stronghold in the hearts of
his fellow-countrymen, who soon caught the true meaning and
purpose of his soldierly devotion and heroic temper.   His intrepid courage, his steadfast patriotism, and the generosity of

his nature inspired with peculiar warmth the admiration of all the people. Above his grave affection for the man and pride in his achievements will struggle for mastery, and too much honor cannot be accorded to one who was so richly endowed with all the qualities which make his death a national loss.

2.

(Paragraph in the Fourth Annual Message, December, 1888.)

The death of General Sheridan in August last was a national affliction. The Army then lost the grandest of its chiefs. The country lost a brave and experienced soldier, a wise and discreet counselor, and a modest and sensible man. Those who, in any manner, came within the range of his personal association will never fail to pay deserved and willing homage to his greatness and the glory of his career ; but they will cherish with more tender sensibility the loving memory of his simple, generous, and considerate nature.

X.

THE CHARACTER OF SAMUEL S. COX.

(Speech as Presiding Officer Over Memorial Meeting in the Cooper Union, October 9, 1889.)

It is peculiarly fit and proper that among the tributes paid to the worth and usefulness of Samuel S. Cox the most hearty and sincere should flow from the hearts of his Congressional constituents. These he served faithfully and well ; and they were honored by the honor of his life. It was as their chosen public servant that he gathered fame, and exhibited to the entire country the strength and the brightness of true American statesmanship. It was while he still served them that he died. All his fellow-citizens mourn his death, and speak in praise of his character and his achievements in public life ; but his constituents may well feel that the affliction of his death is nearer to them than to others, by so much that they are entitled to a greater share of pride in all that he wrought.

I should not suit the part allotted to me on this occasion if I were to speak at length of the many traits of character within my personal knowledge that made your friend and mine the wise and efficient legislator, the useful and patriotic citizen, and the kind and generous man. These things constitute a theme upon which his fellow-countrymen love to dwell, and they will be presented to you to-night in more eloquent terms than I can command.

I shall not, however, forbear mentioning the fact that your representative, in all his public career, and in his relations to legislation, was never actuated by a corrupt or selfish interest. His zeal was born of public spirit, and the motive of his labor was the public good. He was never found among those who cloak their efforts for personal gain and advantage beneath the disguise of disinterested activity for the welfare of the people.

These are pleasant things for his friends to remember to-night, and they are without doubt the things upon which rest the greatest share of the honor and respect which his memory exacts from his fellow-citizens.

But while we thus contemplate the value of unselfish public usefulness, we cannot restrain a reflection which has a somber coloring. What is the condition of the times when we may justly and fairly exalt the memory of a deceased public servant because he was true and honest and faithful to his trust? Are we maintaining a safe standard of public duty when the existence of these virtues, instead of being general, are exceptional enough to cause congratulation? All public servants should be as true and honest and faithful as the man whom we mourn to-night.

I beg you to take home with you among the reflections which this occasion shall awaken, an appreciation of the truth that if we are to secure for ourselves all the blessings of our free institutions we must better apprehend the interest we have at stake in their scrupulous maintenance, and must exact of those whom we trust in public office a more rigid adherence to the demands of public duty.

I congratulate you and myself upon the fact that we are to be addressed to-night by one whose eloquence and ability, as well as his warm friendship for Mr. Cox, eminently fit him to be the orator of the occasion.

XI.

A TRIBUTE TO WILLIAM L. SCOTT.

(Written for the Erie [Pa.] *Herald*, of September 26, 1891.)

My acquaintance with Mr. Scott dates no further back than his prominence in public life. That acquaintance, however, rapidly grew to a close intimacy, which was only interrupted by his death. I learned to love him for his sincerity and for his steadfastness in his relations to his friends. His preference for people was based upon something he saw in them of sturdy usefulness, and upon qualities of independent strength that commanded his respect; and, having once selected a friend, he remained a friend in all circumstances and without a shadow of turning.

But there was another phase of his character which should endear his memory not only to his personal friends but to every true American. As a public servant he was patriotic, disinterested, honest, and sincere. As a member of Congress he spent his efforts and his thought in advancing those measures and objects which he deemed for the good of the entire country, and he never belittled his position, nor diminished his usefulness by seeking to accomplish legislation which had relation to his own benefits or to interests merely local and circumscribed. It was certainly true of him that, having determined that a certain course of conduct led to the promotion of the public good, his private interests and all personal considerations were set aside as he followed in the way of public duty.

If his life had only been valuable for the example he set for the faithful performance of the trust the people repose in their public servants, he should be remembered with gratitude and affection, and, when we recall his other traits of mind and heart, those who loved him cannot fail to be comforted by the precious memories he has left to them.

XII.

THE CHARACTER OF CHARLES STEWART PARNELL.

> No. 816 Madison Avenue,
> November 11, 1891.

John McConvill, Esq., *Chairman, etc.*

Dear Sir : I am a stanch believer in the doctrine of home rule, and have not failed to appreciate the labors in the cause, of the man whose services you propose to commemorate.

For what he accomplished and sought to accomplish for home rule, he deserves to be honored by all those who love a free and representative government, but his aim and purposes had their rise so completely in patriotism, and his unselfish love for his countrymen was so conspicuous and disinterested, that the reverence and devotion due to the memory of a patriot must always be associated with his name.

The influence of his example surely ought not to be lost upon those who take up his work, to which he so thoroughly consecrated all his efforts and aspirations.

> Yours very truly,
> Grover Cleveland.

CHAPTER XXII.

THE MAINTENANCE OF NATIONAL HONOR.

I.

To the President of the American Fishery Union.

EXECUTIVE MANSION,
WASHINGTON, April 7, 1887.

GEORGE STEELE, ESQ., *President American Fishery Union, and others, Gloucester, Mass.*

GENTLEMEN : I have received your letter lately addressed to me, and have given full consideration to the expression of the views and wishes therein contained, in relation to the existing differences between the governments of Great Britain and the United States, growing out of the refusal to award to our citizens, engaged in fishing enterprises, the privileges to which they are entitled, either under treaty stipulations or the guarantees of international comity and neighborly concession.

I sincerely trust the apprehension you express, of unjust and unfriendly treatment of American fishermen lawfully found in Canadian waters, will not be realized. But if such apprehension should prove to be well founded, I earnestly hope that no fault or inconsiderate action of any of our citizens will in the least weaken the just position of our government, or deprive us of the universal sympathy and support to which we should be entitled.

The action of this administration since June, 1885, when the fishing articles of the treaty of 1871 were terminated, under the notification which had two years before been given to our government, has been fully disclosed by the correspondence between the representatives and the appropriate departments of the respective governments, with which I am apprised by your letter you are entirely familiar. An examination of this correspondence has doubtless satisfied you that in no case have the rights or privileges of American fishermen been overlooked or neglected, but that, on the contrary they have been sedulously insisted upon and cared for by every means within the control of the Executive branch of the government.

The Act of Congress approved March 3, 1887, authorizing a course of retaliation through Executive action, in the event of a continuance on the part of the British American authorities of unfriendly conduct and treaty violations affecting American fishermen, has devolved upon the President of the United States exceedingly grave and solemn responsibilities, comprehending highly important consequences to our national character and dignity, and involving extremely valuable commercial intercourse between the British Possessions in North America and the people of the United States.

I understand the main purpose of your letter is to suggest that, in case recourse to the retaliatory measures authorized by this Act should be invited by unjust treatment of our fishermen in the future, the object of such retaliation might be fully accomplished by " prohibiting Canadian-caught fish from entry into the ports of the United States."

The existing controversy is one in which two nations are the parties concerned. The retaliation contemplated by the Act of Congress is to be enforced, not to protect solely any particular interest, however meritorious or valuable, but to maintain the national honor, and thus protect all our people. In this view, the violation of American fishery rights, and unjust or unfriendly acts toward a portion of our citizens engaged in this business, are but the occasion for action, and constitute a national affront which gives birth to or may justify retaliation. This measure, once resorted to, its effectiveness and value may well depend upon the thoroughness and extent of its application ; and in the performance of international duties, the enforcement of international rights, and the protection of our citizens, this government and the people of the United States must act as a unit—all intent upon attaining the best result of retaliation upon the basis of a maintenance of national honor and dignity.

A nation seeking by any means to maintain its honor, dignity, and integrity is engaged in protecting the rights of its people ; and if in such efforts particular interests are injured and special advantages forfeited, these things should be patriotically borne for the public good.

An immense volume of population, manufactures, and agricultural productions, and the marine tonnage and railways to which these have given activity, all largely the result of intercourse between the United States and British America, and the natural growth of a full half century of good neighborhood and friendly communication, form an aggregate of material wealth and incidental relations of most impressive magnitude. I fully appreciate these things, and am not unmindful of the great number of our people who are concerned in such vast and diversified interests.

In the performance of the serious duty which the Congress has imposed upon me, and in the exercise upon just occasion of the power conferred under the Act referred to, I shall deem myself bound to inflict no unnecessary damage or injury upon any portion of our people ; but I shall, nevertheless, be unflinchingly guided by a sense of what the self-respect and dignity of the nation demand. In the maintenance of these, and in the support of the honor of the government, beneath which every citizen may repose in safety, no sacrifice of personal or private interests shall be considered as against the general welfare.

Yours very truly,
GROVER CLEVELAND.

II.

Concerning Retaliation on Canada.

TO THE CONGRESS :

The rejection by the Senate of the treaty lately negotiated for the settlement and adjustment of the differences existing between the United States and Great Britain concerning the rights and privileges of American fishermen in the ports and waters of British North America, seems to justify a survey of the condition to which the pending question is thus remitted.

The treaty upon this subject concluded in 1818, through disagreements as to the meaning of its terms, has been a fruitful source of irritation and trouble. Our citizens engaged in fishing enterprises in waters adjacent to Canada have been subjected to numerous vexatious interferences and annoyances, their vessels have been seized upon pretexts which appeared to be entirely inadmissible, and they have been otherwise treated by the Canadian authorities and officials in a manner inexcusably harsh and oppressive.

This conduct has been justified by Great Britain and Canada, by the claim that the treaty of 1818 permitted it, and upon the ground that it was necessary to the proper protection of Canadian interests. We deny that treaty agreements justify these acts, and we further maintain that, aside from any treaty restraints of disputed interpretation, the relative positions of the United States and Canada as near neighbors, the growth of our joint commerce, the development and prosperity of both countries, which amicable relations surely guarantee, and above all, the liberality always extended by the United States to the people of Canada, furnished motives for kindness and consideration higher and better than treaty covenants.

While keenly sensitive to all that was exasperating in the condition, and by no means indisposed to support the just complaints of our injured citizens, I still deemed it my duty, for the preservation of important American interests which were directly involved. and in view of all the details of the situation, to attempt by negotiation to remedy existing wrongs and to terminate, finally, by a fair and just treaty, these ever-recurring causes of difficulty.

I fully believe that the treaty just rejected by the Senate was well suited to the exigency, and that its provisions were adequate for our security, in the future, from vexatious incidents and for the promotion of friendly neighborhood and intimacy, without sacrificing in the least our national pride or dignity.

I am quite conscious that neither my opinion of the value of the rejected treaty nor the motives which prompted its negotiation are of importance in the light of the judgment of the Senate thereupon. But it is of importance to note that this treaty has been rejected without any apparent disposition on the part of the Senate to alter or amend its provisions, and with the evident intention, not wanting expression, that no negotiation should at present be concluded touching the matter at issue.

The co-operation necessary for the adjustment of the long-standing national differences with which we have to deal, by methods of conference and agreement, having thus been declined, I am by no means disposed to abandon the interests and the rights of our people in the premises, or to neglect their grievances ; and I therefore turn to the contemplation of a plan of retaliation as a mode, which still remains, of treating the situation.

I am not unmindful of the gravity of the responsibility assumed in adopting this line of conduct, nor do I fail in the least to appreciate its serious consequences. It will be impossible to injure our Canadian neighbors by retaliatory measures without inflicting some damage upon our own citizens. This results from our proximity, our community of interests, and the inevitable commingling of the business enterprises which have been developed by mutual activity.

Plainly stated, the policy of national retaliation manifestly embraces the infliction of the greatest harm upon those who have injured us, with the least possible damage to ourselves. There is also an evident propriety as well as an invitation to moral support, found in visiting upon the offending party the same measure or kind of treatment of which we complain, and as far as possible within the same limes. And above all things the plan of retaliation, if entered upon, should be thorough and vigorous.

These considerations lead me at this time to invoke the aid and counsel of the Congress and its support in such a further grant of power as seems to me necessary and desirable to render effective the policy I have indicated.

The Congress has already passed a law, which received Executive assent on the 3d day of March, 1887, providing that in case American fishing vessels being or visiting in the waters, or at any of the ports of the British dominions of North America, should be, or lately had been, deprived of the rights to which they were entitled by treaty or law, or if they were denied certain other privileges therein specified, or vexed and harassed in the enjoyment of the same, the President might deny to vessels and their masters and crews of the British dominions of North America any entrance into the waters, ports, or harbors of the United States, and also deny entry into any port or place of the United States of any product of said dominions, or other goods coming from said dominions to the United States.

While I shall not hesitate upon proper occasion to enforce this Act, it would seem to be unnecessary to suggest that if such enforcement is limited in such a manner as shall result in the least possible injury to our own people the effect would probably be entirely inadequate to the accomplishment of the purpose desired.

I deem it my duty, therefore, to call the attention of the Congress to certain particulars in the action of the authorities of the Dominion of Canada, in addition to the general allegations already made, which appear to be in such marked contrast to the liberal and friendly disposition of our country as in my opinion to call for such legislation as will, upon the principles already stated, properly supplement the power to inaugurate retaliation, already vested in the Executive.

Actuated by the generous and neighborly spirit which has characterized our legislation, our tariff laws have, since 1866, been so far waived in favor of Canada as to allow free of duty the transit across the territory of the United States of property arriving at our ports and destined to Canada, or exported from Canada to other foreign countries.

When the treaty of Washington was negotiated in 1871, between the United States and Great Britain, having for its object very largely the modification of the treaty of 1818, the privileges above referred to were made reciprocal and given in return by Canada to the United States in the following language, contained in the twenty-ninth article of said treaty :

It is agreed that, for the term of years mentioned in article thirty-three of this treaty, goods, wares, or merchandise arriving at the ports of New York, Boston, and Portland, and any other ports in the United States which have been or may, from time to time, be specially designated by the President of the United States, and destined for Her Britannic Majesty's possessions in North America, may be entered at the proper customhouse and conveyed in transit, without the payment of duties, through the territory of the United States, under such rules, regulations, and conditions for the protection of the revenue as the Government of the United States may from time to time prescribe ; and, under like rules, regulations, and conditions, goods, wares, or merchandise may be conveyed in transit, without the payment of duties, from such possessions through the territory of the United States, for export from the said ports of the United States.

It is further agreed that, for the like period, goods, wares, or merchandise arriving at any of the ports of Her Britannic Majesty's possessions in North America, and destined for the United States, may be entered at the proper customhouse and conveyed in transit, without the payment of duties, through the said possessions, under such rules and regulations and conditions for the protection of the revenue, as the governments of the said possessions may from time to time prescribe ; and, under like rules, and regulations, and conditions, goods, wares, or merchandise may be conveyed, in transit, without payment of duties, from the United States through the said possessions to other places in the United States, or for export from ports in the said possessions.

In the year 1886 notice was received by the representatives of our government that our fishermen would no longer be allowed to ship their fish in bond and free of duty through Canadian territory to this country ; and ever since that time such shipment has been denied.

The privilege of such shipment, which had been extended to our fishermen, was a most important one, allowing them to spend the time upon the fishing-grounds, which would otherwise be devoted to a voyage home with their catch, and doubling their opportunities for profitably prosecuting their avocation.

In forbidding the transit of the catch of our fishermen over their territory, in bond and free of duty, the Canadian authorities deprived us of the only facility dependent upon their concession, and for which we could supply no substitute.

The value to the Dominion of Canada of the privilege of transit for their exports and imports, across our territory, to and from our ports, though great in every respect, will be better appreciated when it is remembered that, for a considerable portion of each year, the St. Lawrence River, which constitutes the direct avenue of foreign commerce leading to Canada, is closed by ice.

During the last six years the imports and exports of British Canadian provinces, carried across our territory under the privileges granted by our laws, amounted in value to about two hundred and seventy-five millions of dollars, nearly all of which were goods dutiable under our tariff laws, by far the larger part of this traffic consisting of exchanges of goods between Great Britain and her American provinces, brought to and carried from our ports in their own vessels.

The treaty stipulation entered into by our government was in harmony with laws which were then on our statute book and are still in force.

I recommend immediate legislative action conferring upon the Executive the power to suspend by proclamation the operation of all laws and regulations permitting the transit of goods, wares, and merchandise in bond across or over the territory of the United States to or from Canada.

There need be no hesitation in suspending these laws, arising from the supposition that their continuation is secured by treaty obligations, for it seems quite plain that article twenty-nine of the treaty of 1871, which was the only article incorporating such laws, terminated the 1st day of July, 1885.

The article itself declares that its provisions shall be in force "for the term of years mentioned in article thirty-three of this treaty." Turning to article thirty-three, we find no mention of the twenty-ninth article, but only a provision that articles eighteen to twenty-five, inclusive, and article thirty shall take effect as soon as the laws required to carry them into operation shall be passed by the legislative bodies of the different countries concerned, and that " they shall remain in force for the period of ten years from the date at which they may come into operation, and further until the expiration of two years after either of the high contracting parties shall have given notice to the other of its wish to terminate the same."

I am of the opinion that the "term of years mentioned in article thirty-three," referred to in article twenty-nine as the limit of its duration, means the period during which articles eighteen to twenty-five inclusive, and article thirty, commonly called the "fishery articles," should continue in force under the language of said article thirty-three.

That the Joint High Commissioners who negotiated the treaty so understood and intended the phrase is certain ; for in a statement containing an account of their negotiations, prepared under their supervision and approved by them, we find the following entry on the subject :

> The transit question was discussed, and it was agreed that any settlement that might be made should include a reciprocal arrangement in that respect for the period for which the fishery articles should be in force.

In addition to this very satisfactory evidence, supporting this construction of the language of article twenty-nine, it will be found that the law passed by Congress to carry the treaty into effect furnishes conclusive proof of the correctness of such construction.

This law was passed March 1, 1873, and is entitled " An Act to carry into effect the provisions of the treaty between the United States and Great Britain, signed in the city of Washington the eighth day of May, eighteen hundred and seventy-one, relating to the fisheries." After providing in its first and second sections for putting in operation articles eighteen to twenty-five, inclusive, and article thirty of the treaty, the third section is devoted to article twenty-nine as follows :

SECTION 3. That from the date of the President's proclamation authorized by the first section of this Act, and so long as the articles eighteenth to twenty-fifth, inclusive, and article thirtieth of said treaty shall remain in force according to the terms and conditions of article thirty-third of said treaty, all goods, wares, and merchandise arriving, etc., etc.

following in the remainder of the section the precise words of the stipulation on the part of the United States as contained in article twenty-nine which I have already fully quoted.

Here, then, is a distinct enactment of the Congress limiting the duration of this article of the treaty to the time that articles eighteen to twenty-five inclusive, and article thirty, should continue in force. That in fixing such limitation it but gave the meaning of the treaty itself, is indicated by the fact that its purpose is declared to be to carry into effect the provisions of the treaty, and by the further fact that this law appears to have been submitted before the promulgation of the treaty to certain members of the Joint High Commission representing both countries, and met with no objection or dissent.

There appearing to be no conflict or inconsistency between the treaty and the Act of Congress last cited, it is not necessary to invoke the well-settled principle that in case of such conflict the statute governs the question.

In any event, and whether the law of 1873 construes the treaty or governs it, section twenty-nine of such treaty, I have no doubt, terminated with the proceedings taken by our government to terminate articles eighteen to twenty-five, inclusive and article thirty of the treaty. These proceedings had their inception in a joint resolution of Congress passed May 3, 1883, declaring that, in the judgment of Congress, these articles ought to be terminated, and directing the President to give the notice to the government of Great Britain provided for in article thirty-three of the treaty. Such notice having been given two years prior to the 1st day of July, 1885, the articles mentioned were absolutely terminated on the last-named day, and with them article twenty-nine was also terminated.

If by any language used in the joint resolution it was intended to relieve section three of the Act of 1873, embodying article twenty-nine of the treaty, from its own limitations, or to save the article itself, I am entirely satisfied that the intention miscarried.

But statutes granting to the people of Canada the valuable privileges of transit for their goods from our ports and over our soil, which had been passed prior to the making of the treaty of 1871, and independently of it, remained in force ; and ever since the abrogation of the treaty, and notwithstanding the refusal of Canada to permit our fishermen to send their fish to their home market through her territory in bond, the people of that Dominion have enjoyed without diminution the advantages of our liberal and generous laws.

Without basing our complaint upon a violation of treaty obligations, it is nevertheless true that such refusal of transit, and the other injurious acts which have been recited, constitute a provoking insistence upon rights neither mitigated by the amenities of national intercourse nor modified by the recognition of our liberality and generous consideration.

The history of events connected with this subject makes it manifest that the Canadian Government can, if so disposed, administer its laws and protect the interest of its people without manifestation of unfriendliness, and without the unneighborly treatment of our fishing-vessels of which we have justly complained ; and whatever is done on our part should be done in the hope that the disposition of the Canadian Government may remove the occasion of a resort to the additional executive power now sought through legislative action.

I am satisfied that, upon the principles which should govern retaliation, our intercourse and relations with the Dominion of Canada furnish no better opportunity for its application than are suggested by the conditions herein presented ; and that it could not be more effectively inaugurated than under the power of suspension recommended.

While I have expressed my clear conviction upon the question of the continuance of section twenty-nine of the treaty of 1871, I, of course, fully concede the power and the duty of the Congress, in contemplating legislative action, to construe the terms of any treaty stipulation which might, upon any possible consideration of good faith, limit such action ; and likewise, the peculiar propriety, in the case here presented of its interpretation of its own language as contained in the laws of 1873 putting in operation said treaty, and of 1883 directing the termination thereof ; and if, in the deliberate judgment of Congress, any restraint to the proposed legislation exists, it is to be hoped that the expediency of its early removal will be recognized.

I desire, also, to call the attention of the Congress to another subject involving such wrongs and unfair treatment to our citizens as, in my opinion, require prompt action.

The navigation of the Great Lakes, and the immense business and carrying trade growing out of the same, have been treated broadly and liberally by the United States Government, and made free to all mankind, while Canadian railroads and navigation companies share in our country's transportation upon terms as favorable as are accorded to our own citizens.

The canals and other public works built and maintained by the government along the line of the Lakes are made free to all.

In contrast to this condition, and evincing a narrow and ungenerous commercial spirit, every lock and canal which is a public work of the Dominion of Canada is subject to tolls and charges.

By article twenty-seven of the treaty of 1871 provision was made to secure to the citizens of the United States the use of the Welland, St. Lawrence, and other canals in the Dominion of Canada, on terms of equality with the inhabitants of the Dominion, and also to secure to the subjects of Great Britain the use of the St. Clair Flats Canal on terms of equality with the inhabitants of the United States.

The equality with the inhabitants of the Dominion, which we were promised in the use of the canals of Canada, did not secure to us freedom from tolls in their navigation, but we had a right to expect that we, being Americans and interested in American commerce, would be no more burdened in regard to the same than Canadians engaged in their own trade ; and the whole spirit of the concession made was, or should have been, that merchandise and property transported to an American market through these canals should not be enhanced in its cost by tolls many times higher than such as were carried to an ad-joining Canadian market. All our citizens, producers and consumers as well as vessel-owners, were to enjoy the equality promised.

And yet evidence has for some time been before the Congress, furnished by the Secretary of the Treasury, showing that while the tolls charged in the first instance are the same to all, such vessels and cargoes as are destined to certain Canadian ports are allowed a refund of nearly the entire tolls, while those bound for American ports are not allowed any such advantage.

To promise equality, and then in practice make it conditional upon our vessels doing Canadian business instead of their own, is to fulfill a promise with a shadow of performance.

I recommend that such legislative action be taken as will give Canadian vessels navigating our canals, and their cargoes, precisely the advantages granted to our vessels and cargoes upon Canadian canals, and that the same be measured by exactly the same rule of discrimination.

The course which I have outlined, and the recommendations made, relate to the honor and dignity of our country, and the protection and preservation of the rights and interests of all our people. A government does but half its duty when it protects its citizens at home and permits them to be imposed upon and humiliated by the unfair and over-reaching disposition of other nations. If we invite our people to rely upon arrangements made for their benefit abroad, we should see to it that they are not deceived ; and if we are generous and liberal to a neighboring country our people should reap the advantage of it by a return of liberality and generosity.

These are subjects which partisanship should not disturb or confuse. Let us survey the ground calmly and moderately, and having put aside other means of settlement, if we enter upon the policy of retaliation let us pursue it firmly, with a determination only to subserve the interests of our people and maintain the high standard and the becoming pride of American citizenship.

GROVER CLEVELAND.

EXECUTIVE MANSION,
WASHINGTON, August 23, 1888.

CHAPTER XXIII.

MISCELLANEOUS RECOMMENDATIONS.

I.

THE REBUILDING OF THE NAVY.

(From the First Annual Message, December, 1885.)

ALL must admit the importance of an effective Navy to a nation like ours, having such an extended seacoast to protect. And yet we have not a single vessel of war that could keep the seas against a first-class vessel of any important power. Such a condition ought no longer to continue. The nation that cannot resist aggression is constantly exposed to it. Its foreign policy is of necessity weak, and its negotiations are conducted with disadvantage, because it is not in condition to enforce the terms dictated by its sense of right and justice.

Inspired, as I am, by the hope, shared by all patriotic citizens, that the day is not very far distant when our Navy will be such as befits our standing among the nations of the earth, and rejoiced at every step that leads in the direction of such a consummation, I deem it my duty especially to direct the attention of Congress to the close of the report of the Secretary of the Navy, in which the humiliating weakness of the present organization of his Department is exhibited, and the startling abuses and waste of its present methods are exposed. The conviction is forced upon us, with the certainty of mathematical demonstrations, that before we proceed further in the restoration of a Navy we need a thoroughly reorganized Navy Department.

The fact that within seventeen years more than seventy-five millions of dollars have been spent in the construction, repair, equipment, and armament of vessels, and the further fact that, instead of an effective and creditable fleet, we have only the discontent and apprehension of a nation undefended by war vessels, added to the disclosures now made, do not permit us to doubt that every attempt to revive our Navy has thus far, for the most part, been misdirected, and all our efforts in that direction have been little better than blind gropings, and expensive, aimless follies.

Unquestionably if we are content with the maintenance of a Navy Department simply as a shabby ornament to the government, a constant watchfulness may prevent some of the scandal and abuse which have found their way into our present organization, and its incurable waste may be reduced to the minimum. But if we desire to build ships for present usefulness, instead of naval reminders of the days that are past, we must have a Department organized for the work, supplied with all the talent and ingenuity our country affords, prepared to take advantage of the experience of other nations, systematized so that all efforts shall unite and lead in one direction, and fully imbued with the conviction that war vessels, though new, are useless unless they combine all that the ingenuity of man has up to this day brought forth relating to their construction.

I earnestly commend the portion of the Secretary's report devoted to this subject to the attention of Congress, in the hope that his suggestions touching the reorganization of his Department may be adopted as the first step toward the reconstruction of our Navy.

II.

THE AGRICULTURAL DEPARTMENT AND ITS WORK.

I.

(From the First Annual Message, December, 1885.)

The agricultural interest of the country demands just recognition and liberal encouragement. It sustains with certainty and unfailing strength our nation's prosperity by the products

of its steady toil, and bears its full share of the burden of taxation without complaints. Our agriculturists have but slight
personal representation in the councils of the nation, and are
generally content with the humbler duties of citizenship, and
willing to trust to the bounty of nature for a reward of their
labor.   But the magnitude and value of this industry are
appreciated, when the statement is made that of our total
annual exports more than three-fourths are the products of
agriculture, and of our total population nearly one-half are
exclusively engaged in that occupation.

The Department of Agriculture was created for the purpose
of acquiring and diffusing among the people useful information respecting the subjects it has in charge, and aiding in the
cause of intelligent and progressive farming, by the collection
of statistics, by testing the value and usefulness of new seeds
and plants, and distributing such as are found desirable
among agriculturists.   This and other powers and duties with
which this Department is invested are of the utmost importance, and, if wisely exercised, must be of great benefit to the
country.   The aim of our beneficent government is the improvement of the people in every station, and the amelioration of their condition.   Surely our agriculturists should not
be neglected.   The instrumentality established in aid of the
farmers of the land should not only be well equipped for the
accomplishment of its purpose, but those for whose benefit it
has been adopted should be encouraged to avail themselves
fully of its advantages.

The prohibition of the importation into several countries of
certain of our animals and their products, based upon the
suspicion that health is endangered in their use and consumption, suggests the importance of such precautions, for the protection of our stock of all kinds against disease, as will disarm
suspicion of danger and cause the removal of such an injurious
prohibition.

If the laws now in operation are insufficient to acomplish
this protection, I recommend their amendment to meet the

necessities of the situation, and I commend to the consideration of Congress the suggestions contained in the report of the Commissioner of Agriculture calculated to increase the value and efficiency of this Department.

————

2.

(From the Second Annual Message, December, 1886.)

The Department of Agriculture, representing the oldest and largest of our national industries, is subserving well the purposes of its organization. By the introduction of new subjects of farming enterprise, and by opening new sources of agricultural wealth, and the dissemination of early information concerning production and prices, it has contributed largely to the country's prosperity. Through this agency advanced thought and investigation, touching the subjects it has in charge, should, among other things, be practically applied to the home production at a low cost of articles of food which are now imported from abroad. Such an innovation will necessarily, of course, in the beginning, be within the domain of intelligent experiment; and the subject in every stage should receive all possible encouragement from the government.

The interests of millions of our citizens engaged in agriculture are involved in an enlargement and improvement of the results of their labor; and a zealous regard for their welfare should be a willing tribute to those whose productive returns are a main source of our progress and power.

The existence of pleuro-pneumonia among the cattle of various States has led to burdensome and in some cases disastrous restrictions in an important branch of our commerce, threatening to affect the quantity and quality of our food supply. This is a matter of such importance, and of such far-reaching consequences, that I hope it will engage the serious attention of the Congress, to the end that such a remedy may be applied as the limits of a constitutional delegation of power to the general government will permit.

III.

REFORMS IN THE DEPARTMENT OF JUSTICE.

(From the First Annual Message, December, 1885.)

The present mode of compensating United States marshals and district attorneys should in my opinion be changed. They are allowed to charge against the government certain fees for services, their income being measured by the amount of such fees within a fixed limit as to their annual aggregate. This is a direct inducement for them to make their fees in criminal cases as large as possible in an effort to reach the maximum sum permitted. As an entirely natural consequence, unscrupulous marshals are found encouraging frivolous prosecutions, arresting people on petty charges of crime and transporting them to distant places for examination and trial, for the purpose of earning mileage and other fees. And district attorneys uselessly attend criminal examinations far from their places of residence, for the express purpose of swelling their accounts against the government. The actual expenses incurred in these transactions are also charged against the government.

Thus the rights and freedom of our citizens are outraged and public expenditures increased, for the purpose of furnishing public officers pretexts for increasing the measure of their compensation.

I think marshals and district attorneys should be paid salaries, adjusted by a rule which will make them commensurate with services fairly rendered.

In connection with this subject I desire to suggest the advisability, if it be found not obnoxious to constitutional objection, of investing United States commissioners with the power to try and determine certain violations of law within the grade of misdemeanors. Such trials might be made to depend upon the option of the accused. The multiplication of small and technical offenses, especially under the provisions of our internal revenue law, renders some change in our present system very desirable, in the interests of humanity as well as economy. The district courts are now crowded with petty prosecutions, involving a punishment, in cases of conviction, of only a slight fine, while the parties accused are harassed by an enforced attendance upon courts held hundreds of miles from their homes. If poor and friendless they are obliged to remain in jail during months, perhaps, that elapse before a session·of the court is held, and are finally brought to trial surrounded by strangers and with but little real opportunity for defense. In the meantime, frequently, the marshal has charged against the government his fees for an arrest, the transportation of the accused and the expense of the same, and for summoning witnesses before a commissioner, a grand jury, and a court; the witnesses have been paid from the public funds large fees and traveling expenses; and the commissioner and district attorney have also made their charges against the government.

This abuse in the administration of our criminal law should be remedied; and if the plan above suggested is not practicable, some other should be devised.

IV.

LANDS GRANTED TO THE PACIFIC RAILROADS.

(From the First Annual Message to Congress, December, 1885.)

The nation has made princely grants and subsidies to a system of railroads projected as great national highways to connect the Pacific States with the East. It has been charged that these donations from the people have been diverted to private gain and corrupt uses, and thus public indignation has been aroused and suspicion engendered. Our great nation does not begrudge its generosity, but it abhors peculation and fraud; and the favorable regard of our people for the great corporations to which these grants were made, can only be revived by a restoration of confidence, to be secured by their constant, unequivocal, and clearly manifested integrity.

A faithful application of the undiminished proceeds of the grants to the construction and perfecting of their roads, an honest discharge of their obligations, and entire justice to all the people in the enjoyment of their rights on these highways of travel are all the public asks, and it will be content with no less. To secure these things should be the common purpose of the officers of the government, as well as of the corporations. With this accomplishment, prosperity would be permanently secured to the roads, and national pride would take the place of national complaint.

V.

VETOES OF PUBLIC BUILDING BILLS.

I.

(At Zanesville, O., June 19, 1886.)

So far as I am informed the patrons of the post office are fairly well accommodated in a building which is rented by the government at the rate of eight hundred dollars per annum; and though the postmaster naturally certifies that he and his fourteen employees require much more spacious surroundings, I have no doubt he and they can be induced to continue to serve the government in its present quarters.

The public buildings now in process of construction, numbering eighty, involving constant supervision, are all the building projects which the government ought to have on hand at one time, unless a very palpable necessity exists for an increase in the number. The multiplication of these structures involves not only the appropriations made for their completion, but great expense in their care and preservation thereafter.

While a fine government building is a desirable ornament to any town or city, and while the securing of an appropriation therefor is often considered as an illustration of zeal and activity in the interest of a constituency, I am of the opinion that the expenditure of public money for such a purpose should depend upon the necessity of such a building for public uses.

———

2.

(At Portsmouth, O., February 26, 1887.)

It is further stated, in a communication from the promoter of this bill, that "there is not a Federal public building in the State of Ohio east of the line drawn on the accompanying map from Cleveland through Columbus to Cincinnati; and when wealth and population and the needs of the public service are considered, the distribution of public buildings in the State is an unfair one."

Here is disclosed a theory of expenditure for public buildings which I can hardly think should be adopted. If an application for the erection of such a building is to be determined by the distance between its proposed location and another public building, or upon the allegation that a certain division of a State is without a government building, or that the distribution of these buildings in a particular State is unfair, we shall rapidly be led to an entire disregard of the considerations of necessity and public need which, it seems to me, should alone justify the expenditure of public funds for such a purpose.

The care and protection which the government owes to the people do not embrace the grant of public buildings to decorate thriving and prosperous cities and villages, nor should such buildings be erected upon any principle of fair distributions among localities. The government is not an almoner of gifts among the people, but an instrumentality by which the people's affairs should be conducted upon business principles, regulated by the public needs.

3.

(At Allentown, Pa., May 9, 1888.)

The usual statement is made in support of this bill, setting forth the growth of the city where it is proposed to locate the building and the amount and variety of the business which is there transacted. And the postmaster in stereotyped phrase represents the desirability of increased accommodation for the transaction of the business under his charge.

But I am thoroughly convinced that there is no present necessity for the expenditure of one hundred thousand dollars for any purpose connected with the public business at this place. The annual rent now paid for the post office is thirteen hundred dollars. The interest, at three per cent., upon the amount now asked for this new building is three thousand dollars. As soon as it is undertaken, the pay of a superintendent of its construction will begin, and after its completion the compensation of janitors and other expenses of its maintenance will follow.

The plan now pursued for the erection of public buildings is, in my opinion, very objectionable. They are often built where they are not needed, of dimensions and at a cost entirely disproportionate to any public use to which they can be applied, and, as a consequence, they frequently serve more to demonstrate the activity and pertinency of those who represent localities desiring this kind of decoration at public expense, than to meet any necessity of the government.

4.

(At Youngstown, O., May 28, 1888.)

I have listened to an unusual amount of personal representation in favor of this bill from parties whose desires I should be glad to meet on this or any other question. But none of them has insisted that there is any present governmental need of the proposed new building even for postal purposes. On the contrary, I am informed that the post office is at present well accommodated in quarters held under a lease which does not expire, I believe, until 1892. A letter addressed to the postmaster at Youngstown, containing certain questions bearing upon the necessity of a new building, failed to elicit a reply. This fact is very unusual and extraordinary, for the postmaster can almost always be relied upon to make an exhibit of the great necessity of larger quarters when a new public building is in prospect.

The fact was communicated to me, early in the present session of the Congress, that the aggregate sum of the appropriations, contained in bills for the erection and extension of public buildings which had up to that time been referred to the House Committee on Public Buildings and Grounds, was about thirty-seven millions of dollars. Of course this fact would have no particular relevancy if all the buildings asked for were necessary for the transaction of public business, as long as we have the money to pay for them. But inasmuch as a large number of the buildings proposed are unnecessary, and their erection would be wasteful and extravagant, besides furnishing precedents for further and more extended reckless expenditures of a like character, it seems to me that applications for new and expensive public buildings should be carefully scrutinized.

VI.

THE TEHUANTEPEC CANAL ROUTE.

(From First Annual Message, December, 1885.)

The interest of the United States in a practical transit for ships across the strip of land separating the Atlantic from the Pacific has been repeatedly manifested during the last half century.

My immediate predecessor caused to be negotiated with Nicaragua a treaty for the construction, by and at the sole cost of the United States, of a canal through Nicaraguan

territory, and laid it before the Senate. Pending the action
of that body thereon, I withdrew the treaty for re-examination.
Attentive consideration of its provisions leads me to withhold
it from resubmission to the Senate.

Maintaining, as I do, the tenets of a line of precedents from
Washington's day, which proscribe entangling alliances with
foreign states, I do not favor a policy of acquisition of new
and distant territory or the incorporation of remote interests
with our own.

The laws of progress are vital and organic, and we must be
conscious of that irresistible tide of commercial expansion
which, as the concomitant of our active civilization, day by day,
is being urged onward by those increasing facilities of production, transportation, and communication to which steam and
electricity have given birth ; but our duty in the present in-
structs us to address ourselves mainly to the development of
the vast resources of the great area committed to our charge,
and to the cultivation of the arts of peace within our own
borders, though jealously alert in preventing the American
hemisphere from being involved in the political problems and
complications of distant governments. Therefore I am unable to recommend propositions involving paramount privileges
of ownership or right outside of our own territory, when
coupled with absolute and unlimited engagements to defend
the territorial integrity of the state where such interests lie.
While the general project of connecting the two oceans by
means of a canal is to be encouraged, I am of opinion that any
scheme to that end, to be considered with favor, should be free
from the features alluded to.

The Tehuantepec route is declared by engineers of the
highest repute, and by competent scientists, to afford an entirely practicable transit for vessels and cargoes by means of
a ship railway from the Atlantic to the Pacific. The obvious
advantages of such a route, if feasible, over others more remote from the axial lines of traffic between Europe and the
Pacific, and particularly between the valley of the Mississippi

and the western coast of North and South America, are deserving of consideration.

Whatever highway may be constructed across the barrier dividing the two greatest maritime areas of the world must be for the world's benefit, a trust for mankind, to be removed from the chance of domination by any single power, nor become a point of invitation for hostilities or a prize for warlike ambition. An engagement combining the construction, ownership, and operation of such a work by this government, with an offensive and defensive alliance for its protection, with the foreign state whose responsibilities and rights we would share, is, in my judgment, inconsistent with such dedication to universal and neutral use, and would moreover entail measures for its realization beyond the scope of our national polity or present means.

The lapse of years has abundantly confirmed the wisdom and foresight of those earlier administrations which, long before the conditions of maritime intercourse were changed and enlarged by the progress of the age, proclaimed the vital need of interoceanic transit across the American isthmus and consecrated it in advance to the common use of mankind by their positive declarations and through the formal obligation of treaties. Toward such realization the efforts of my administration will be applied, ever bearing in mind the principles on which it must rest, and which were declared in no uncertain tones by Mr. Cass, who, while Secretary of State, in 185?, announced that "What the United States want in Central America, next to the happiness of its people, is the security and neutrality of the interoceanic routes which lead through it."

The construction of three transcontinental lines of railway, all in successful operation, wholly within our territory and uniting the Atlantic and the Pacific Oceans, has been accompanied by results of a most interesting and impressive nature, and has created new conditions, not in the routes of commerce only, but in political geography, which powerfully affect our relations toward and necessarily increase our interests in any transisthmian route which may be opened and employed for the ends of peace and traffic, or, in other contingencies, for uses inimical to both.

Transportation is a factor in the cost of commodities scarcely second to that of their production, and weighs as heavily upon the consumer.

Our experience already has proved the great importance of having the competition between land carriage and water carriage fully developed, each acting as a protection to the public against the tendencies to monopoly which are inherent in the consolidation of wealth and power in the hands of vast corporations.

These suggestions may serve to emphasize what I have already said on the score of the necessity of a neutralization of any interoceanic transit; and this can only be accomplished by making the uses of the route open to all nations and subject to the ambitions and warlike necessities of none.

———

VII.

THE RIGHT OF EXPATRIATION.

(From the First Annual Message, December, 1885.)

While recognizing the right of expatriation, no statutory provision exists providing means for renouncing citizenship by an American citizen, native-born or naturalized, nor for terminating and vacating an improper acquisition of citizenship. Even a fraudulent decree of naturalization cannot now be canceled. The privilege and franchise of American citizenship should be granted with care, and extended to those only who intend in good faith to assume its duties and responsibilities when attaining its privileges and benefits; it should be withheld from those who merely go through the forms of naturalization with the intent of escaping the duties of their original allegiance without taking upon themselves those of their new status, or who may acquire the rights of American citizenship for no other than a hostile purpose toward their original governments. These evils have had many flagrant illustrations.

I regard with favor the suggestion, put forth by one of my predecessors, that provision be made for a central bureau of record of the decrees of naturalization granted by the various courts throughout the United States now invested with that power.

The rights which spring from domicile in the United States, especially when coupled with a declaration of intention to become a citizen, are worthy of definition by statute. The stranger coming hither with intent to remain, establishing his residence in our midst, contributing to the general welfare, and, by his voluntary act, declaring his purpose to assume the responsibilities of citizenship, thereby gains an inchoate status which legislation may properly define. The laws of certain States and Territories admit a domiciled alien to the local franchise, conferring on him the rights of citizenship to a degree which places him in the anomalous position of being a citizen of a State and yet not of the United States within the purview of Federal and international law.

It is important, within the scope of national legislation, to define this right of alien domicile as distinguished from Federal naturalization.

CHAPTER XXIV.

THANKSGIVING PROCLAMATIONS.

I.

As Governor of New York, October 29, 1883.

THE people of our State should continually be mindful of their dependence upon the Supreme Ruler of the universe, and grateful for his goodness and mercy. Without his guidance, the efforts of man are in vain ; and from his forbearance and kindness comes every good gift.

And while they should thus hold in constant remembrance the debt of gratitude they owe, it is fit and proper, and in accordance with established custom, that a day should be annually set apart for their special and public acknowledgment of the goodness of God.

We cannot fail to recall, at this time, abundant cause for thankfulness. During the year just passed, we have been protected against pestilence and dire calamity; peace and quiet have reigned within our borders ; the supremacy of law and order has been complete ; plenteous crops have rewarded the toil of the husbandman ; the hum of busy manufacture has been uninterrupted ; industry in every department of labor has brought its just reward ; enterprises of great magnitude have been completed, adding wealth and greatness to the State ; and we have advanced in all that pertains to the material, social, and educational interests of our people.

I, therefore, hereby designate and set apart Thursday, the 29th day of November, 1883, to be observed by the people of this State as a day of Thanksgiving to God for all his mercies, and humble supplication to the Throne of Grace for a continuance of Divine favor.

On that day let all within the State put aside their business cares and ordinary employments, and assemble in their places of worship and join in prayer and praise.

And let us be prompted to deeds of charity, by the acknowledgment of the gifts of God ; and while we ask of him, let us not close our hearts to the appeals of poverty and distress.

II.

As Governor of New York, November 8, 1884.

The people of the State of New York should permit neither their ordinary occupations and cares, nor any unusual cause of excitement, to divert their minds from a sober and humble acknowledgment of their dependence upon Almighty God for all that contributes to their happiness and contentment, and for all that secures greatness and prosperity to our proud commonwealth.

In accordance with a long-continued custom, I hereby appoint and designate Thursday, the 27th day of November, 1884, to be specially observed as a day of thanksgiving and praise. Let all the people of the State, at that time, forego their usual business and employments, and in their several places of worship, give thanks to Almighty God for all that he has done for them. Let the cheer of family reunions be hallowed by a tender remembrance of the love and watchful care of our Heavenly Father ; and in the social gatherings of friends and neighbors, let hearty good will and fellowship be chastened by a confession of the kindness and mercy of God.

III.

As President of the United States, November 2, 1885.

The American people have always abundant cause to be thankful to Almighty God, whose watchful care and guiding hand have been manifested in every stage of their national life —guarding and protecting them in time of peril, and safely leading them in the hour of darkness and of danger.

It is fitting and proper that a nation thus favored should, on one day in every year, for that purpose especially appointed, publicly acknowledge the goodness of God, and return thanks to him for all his gracious gifts.

Therefore I, Grover Cleveland, President of the United States of America, do hereby designate and set apart Thursday, the twenty-sixth day of November instant, as a day of public Thanksgiving and Prayer ; and do invoke the observance of the same by all the people of the land.

On that day let all secular business be suspended ; and let the people assemble in their usual places of worship, and with prayer and songs of praise devoutly testify their gratitude to the Giver of every good and perfect gift for all that he has done for us in the year that has passed ; for our preservation as a nation and for our deliverance from the shock and danger of political convulsion ; for the blessings of peace and for our safety and quiet, while wars and rumors of wars have agitated and afflicted other nations of the earth ; for our security against the scourge of pestilence, which in other lands has claimed its dead by thousands and filled the streets with mourners ; for plenteous crops which reward the labor of the husbandman and increase our nation's wealth ; and for the contentment throughout our borders which follows in the train of prosperity and abundance.

And let there also be, on the day thus set apart, a reunion of families, sanctified and chastened by tender memories and associations ; and let the social intercourse of friends, with pleasant reminiscence, renew the ties of affection and strengthen the bonds of kindly feeling.

And let us by no means forget, while we give thanks and enjoy the comforts which have crowned our lives, that truly grateful hearts are inclined to deeds of charity ; and that a kind and thoughtful remembrance of the poor will double the pleasures of our condition, and render our praise and thanksgiving more acceptable in the sight of the Lord.

IV.

As President of the United States, November 1, 1886.

It has long been the custom of the people of the United States, on a day in each year especially set apart for that purpose by their Chief Executive, to acknowledge the goodness and mercy of God, and to invoke his continued care and protection.

In observance of such custom, I, Grover Cleveland, President of the United States, do hereby designate and set apart Thursday, the twenty-fifth day of November instant, to be observed and kept as a day of Thanksgiving and Prayer.

On that day let all our people forego their accustomed employments and assemble in their usual places of worship, to give thanks to the Ruler of the Universe for our continued enjoyment of the blessings of a free government, for a renewal of business prosperity throughout our land, for the return which has rewarded the labor of those who till the soil, and for our progress as a people in all that makes a nation great.

And while we contemplate the infinite power of God in earthquake, flood, and storm, let the grateful hearts of those who have been shielded from harm through his mercy, be turned in sympathy and kindness toward those who have suffered through his visitations.

Let us also in the midst of our thanksgiving remember the

poor and needy with cheerful gifts and alms, so that our service may, by deeds of charity, be made acceptable in the sight of the Lord.

_____

V.

As President of the United States, October 25, 1887.

The goodness and the mercy of God which have followed the American people during all the days of the past year claim their grateful recognition and humble acknowledgment. By his omnipotent power he has protected us from war and pestilence, and from every national calamity; by his gracious favor the earth has yielded a generous return to the labor of the husbandman, and every path of honest toil has led to comfort and contentment; by his loving-kindness the hearts of our people have been replenished with fraternal sentiment and patriotic endeavor, and by his unerring guidance we have been directed in the way of national prosperity.

To the end that we may, with one accord, testify our gratitude for all these blessings, I, Grover Cleveland, President of the United States, do hereby designate and set apart Thursday, the twenty-fourth day of November next, as a day of thanksgiving and prayer, to be observed by all the people of the land.

On that day let all secular work and employment be suspended, and let our people assemble in their accustomed places of worship and, with prayer and songs of praise, give thanks to our heavenly Father for all that he has done for us, while we humbly implore the forgiveness of our sins and a continuance of his mercy.

Let families and kindred be reunited on that day, and let their hearts, filled with kindly cheer and affectionate reminiscence, be turned in thankfulness to the Source of all their pleasures and the Giver of all that makes the day glad and joyous.

And in the midst of our worship and our happiness, let us remember the poor, the needy, and the unfortunate, and by our gifts of charity and ready benevolence let us increase the number of those who with grateful hearts shall join in our thanksgiving.

VI.

As President of the United States, November 1, 1888.

Constant thanksgiving and gratitude are due from the American people to Almighty God for his goodness and mercy which have followed them since the day he made them a nation and vouchsafed to them a free government. With loving-kindness he has constantly led us in the way of prosperity and greatness. He has not visited with swift punishment our short-comings, but with gracious care he has warned us of our dependence upon his forbearance, and has taught us that obedience to his holy law is the price of a continuance of his precious gifts.

In acknowledgment of all that God has done for us as a nation, and to the end that on an appointed day, the united prayers and praise of a grateful country may reach the Throne of Grace, I, Grover Cleveland, President of the United States, do hereby designate and set apart Thursday, the twenty-ninth day of November instant, as a day of thanksgiving and prayer, to be kept and observed throughout the land.

On that day let all our people suspend their ordinary work and occupations, and, in their accustomed places of worship, with prayer and songs of praise, render thanks to God for all his mercies, for the abundant harvests which have rewarded the toil of the husbandman during the year that has passed, and for the rich rewards that have followed the labors of our people in their shops and their marts of trade and traffic. Let us give thanks for peace and for social order and contentment within our borders, and for our advancement in all that adds to national greatness.

And, mindful of the afflictive dispensation with which a portion of our land has been visited, let us, while we humble ourselves before the power of God, acknowledge his mercy in setting bounds to the deadly march of pestilence, and let our hearts be chastened by sympathy with our fellow-countrymen who have suffered and who mourn.

And as we return thanks for all the blessings which we have received from the hands of our heavenly Father, let us not forget that he has enjoined upon us charity; and on this day of thanksgiving let us generously remember the poor and needy, so that our tribute of praise and gratitude may be acceptable in the sight of the Lord.

CHAPTER XXV.

LETTERS AND SPEECHES OF A PERSONAL NATURE.

I.

Upon his Election as Governor of New York.

MAYOR'S OFFICE,
BUFFALO, N. Y., November 7, 1882.

MY DEAR BROTHER :

I have just voted. I sit here in the mayor's office alone, with the exception of an artist from *Frank Leslie's Newspaper,* who is sketching the office. If mother was here I should be writing to her, and I feel as if it were time for me to write to someone who will believe what I write.

I have been for some time in the atmosphere of certain success, so that I have been sure that I should assume the duties of the high office for which I have been named. I have tried hard, in the light of this fact, to appreciate properly the responsibilities that will rest upon me, and they are much, too much underestimated. But the thought that has troubled me is, can I well perform my duties, and in such a manner as to do some good to the people of the State? I know there is room for it, and I know that I am honest and sincere in my desire to do well ; but the question is whether I *know enough* to accomplish what I desire.

The social life which seems to await me has also been a subject of much anxious thought. I have a notion that I can regulate that very much as I desire ; and, if I can, I shall spend very little time in the purely ornamental part of the office. In point of fact, I will tell you, first of all others, the policy I intend to adopt, and that is, to make the matter a business engagement between the people of the State and myself, in which the obligation on my side is to perform the duties assigned me with an eye single to the interest of my employers. I shall have no idea of re-election, or any higher political preferment in my head, but be very thankful and happy if I can well serve one term as the people's Governor. Do you know that if mother were alive, I should feel so much safer? I have always thought that her prayers had much to do with my success. I shall expect you all to help me in that way. Give my love to ———— and to —:——, if she is with you, and believe me,

Your affectionate brother,

GROVER CLEVELAND.

Rev. William N. Cleveland.

———

II.

On a Visit to Buffalo, October 2, 1884.

I can hardly tell the people of Buffalo how I rejoice to-night, and how grateful I am for this demonstration of the confidence and esteem of my friends and fellow-citizens. I have resided among you, and in the city where all my success in private life has been achieved, for nearly thirty years. To-night I come to you, after the longest absence that has occurred in all that time, and yet within the few weeks that have passed since I saw you last, an event has happened of supreme importance to me, and that places me within the nation's gaze.

The honor it has brought me I ask my fellow-townsmen to share, while I acknowledge with grateful heart all that they have in the past done for me. But two short years ago you stood steadily by my side in every effort of mine, as the Chief Executive of our city, to advance its interests and welfare. Whatever I was able to accomplish of value to this community was largely due to your strong and intelligent support, nor can I ever forget the generous indorsement you gave my candidacy for the high office I now hold in the State, and I assure you that in its administration I have received no greater encouragement than the approval of friends at home.

What I have seen and heard to-night has touched me deeply. It tells me that my neighbors are still my friends, and assures me that I have not been altogether unsuccessful in my efforts to deserve their confidence and attachment. In years to come I shall deem myself not far wrong if I still retain their good opinion; and if surrounding cares and perplexities bring anxiety and vexation, I shall find solace and comfort in the memory of the days spent here and in recalling the kindness of my Buffalo friends.

But other friends are here to-night, and to all who tender me their kindly welcome I extend a heartfelt greeting as citizens with me of the greatest commonwealth in the sisterhood of States, and one immensely interested in the general weal. Because I love my State and her people, I cannot refrain from reminding you that she should be in the van of every movement which promises a safer and better administration of the general government, so closely related to her prosperity and greatness. And let me leave you with the thought that your safety lies in impressing upon the endeavor of those intrusted with the guardianship of your rights and interests, a pure, patriotic, and exacting popular sentiment. The character of the government can hardly rise higher than the source from which it springs, and the integrity and faithfulness of public servants are not apt to be greater than the public demand.

III.

*To a Politician who had Deceived Him.**

EXECUTIVE MANSION,
WASHINGTON, August 1, 1885.

DEAR SIR :

I have read your letter with amazement and indignation. There is one—but one—mitigation to the perfidy which your letter discloses, and that is found in the fact you confess your share in it. I don't know whether you are a Democrat or not, but if you are the crime which you confess is the more unpardonable.

The idea that this administration, pledged to give the people better officers and engaged in a hand-to-hand fight with the bad elements of both parties, should be betrayed by those who ought to be worthy of implicit trust, is atrocious, and such treason to the people and to the party ought to be punished by imprisonment.

Your confession comes too late to be of immediate use to the public service, and I can only say that, while this is not the first time I have been deceived and misled by lying and treacherous representations, you are the first one that has so frankly

---

* The indignant letter of Mr. Cleveland's here given was written in answer to one sent him by a prominent politician in one of the States of the Pacific Coast. In order to make clearer his cause of indignation the letter to which the above is an answer is given herewith, only concealing the names of persons still living.

To THE PRESIDENT, WASHINGTON, D. C.

DEAR SIR :

This community read the announcement of —— to the ———— judgeship with astonishment and regret, if not pain ; and none were more astonished than those who had signed his petition, and I regret to say that my name is to be found upon it. I have refused several whom I knew to be unfit, but I signed this one, thinking it would never be considered, and not for one moment believing the appointment was possible. When first presented to me I put him off and hoped to escape, but he came again with it ; and, with others, I signed it, thinking there was no chance of its reaching even a consideration. It was signed by many prominent men, who hated to refuse, and hoped and thought it would result in nothing.

Yours very respectfully,

———— ————

owned his grievous fault. If any comfort is to be extracted from this assurance you are welcome to it.

GROVER CLEVELAND.

————

IV.

At his Boyhood Home, Clinton, N. Y., July 13, 1887.

I am by no means certain of my standing here among those who celebrate the centennial of Clinton's existence as a village. My recollections of the place reach backward but about thirty-six years, and my residence here covered a very brief period. But these recollections are fresh and distinct to-day, and pleasant too, though not entirely free from somber coloring.

It was here, in the school at the foot of College Hill, that I began my preparation for college life and enjoyed the anticipation of a collegiate education. We had two teachers in our school. One became afterward a judge in Chicago, and the other passed through the legal profession to the ministry, and within the last two years was living farther West. I read a little Latin with two other boys in the class. I think I floundered through four books of the Æneid. The other boys had nice large modern editions of Virgil, with big print and plenty of notes to help one over the hard places. Mine was a little old-fashioned copy which my father used before me, with no notes, and which was only translated by hard knocks. I believe I have forgiven those other boys for their persistent refusal to allow me the use of the notes in their books. At any rate, they do not seem to have been overtaken by any dire retribution, for one of them is now a rich and prosperous lawyer in Buffalo, and the other is a professor in your college and the orator of to-day's celebration. The struggles with ten lines of Virgil, which at first made up my daily task, are amusing as remembered now ; but with them I am also forced to remember that, instead of being the beginning of the higher education for which I honestly longed, they occurred near the end of my school advantages. This suggests a disappointment which no lapse of time can alleviate, and a deprivation I have sadly felt with every passing year.

I remember Benoni Butler and his store. I don't know whether he was an habitual poet or not, but I heard him recite one poem of his own manufacture which embodied an account of a travel to or from Clinton in the early days. I can recall but two lines of this poem, as follows :

> Paris Hill next came in sight ;
> And there we tarried overnight.

I remember the next-door neighbors, Doctors Bissell and Scollard—and good, kind neighbors they were, too—not your cross, crabbed kind who could not bear to see a boy about. It always seemed to me that they drove very fine horses ; and for that reason I thought they must be extremely rich.

I don't know that I should indulge further recollections that must seem very little like centennial history ; but I want to establish as well as I can my right to be here. I might speak of the college faculty, who cast such a pleasing though sober shade of dignity over the place, and who, with other educated and substantial citizens, made up the best of social life. I was a boy then, and slightly felt the atmosphere of this condition ; but, notwithstanding, I believe I absorbed a lasting appreciation of the intelligence and refinement which made this a delightful home.

I know that you will bear with me, my friends, if I yield to the impulse which the mention of home creates, and speak of my own home here, and how through the memories which cluster about it I may claim a tender relationship to your village. Here it was that our family circle entire, parents and children, lived day after day in loving and affectionate converse ; and here, for the last time, we met around the family altar and thanked God that our household was unbroken by death or separation. We never met together in any other home after leaving this, and Death followed closely our de-parture. And thus it is that, as with advancing years I survey the havoc Death has made, and as the thoughts of my early home become more sacred, the remembrance of this pleasant spot, so related, is revived and chastened.

I can only add my thanks for the privilege of being with you to-day, and wish for the village of Clinton in the future a continuation and increase of the blessing of the past.

———

V.

At a Reception given by Early Friends and Associates at Buffalo, N. Y., May 11, 1892.

MY FRIENDS:

I have been striving for several years to believe that I am still on the bright and sunny side of the time which separates middle age from the last declivity of life; but now and here, amid the memories of early manhood, and recalling the scenes of thirty-five years ago, I yield the struggle and enroll myself among those who are no longer young.

You need have no fear from this introduction, that I intend to indulge in the tedious garrulity which is sometimes kindly tolerated on account of the privileges and immunities which are accorded to old age. I do, however, intend to hint that I have reached the time in life when I begin to enjoy the compensation of advancing years which is born of retrospection; when it dis-cards all past irritations, and dwells only upon the things in memory's keeping that are pleasant and consoling.

My mind at this moment is full of the recollection of experi-ences connected with my early life in Buffalo. Some of these experiences were rugged, but they were healthful; and they appear to me now robbed of everything save the features that make them welcome memories. I recall, too, hosts of the good friends who were about me in those days. The living attach-ments of many of them I still cherish as priceless possessions;

and many others I loved until inexorable death decreed our separations. I often look at a picture, among my keepsakes, now more than thirty years old, which represents a group composed of seven of Buffalo's young men—all close companions, all full of the hopes and ambitions of manhood's early days, and all having in full sight the high aims and purposes that beckon to success. Of this group of friends five are dead—only one of them survives with me. I shall not trust myself to speak of these dead friends, nor will I attempt to express all that their friendship meant to me ; but you will not wonder that this picture makes me feel that I have lived a long time.

As I turn from these saddening reflections and glance over this company, I am still further and more cheerfully reminded of the years which have passed since my life in Buffalo began.

I see here Mr. Bissell. I remember well the day he called at the law office where I was a partner, and in which he expected to begin the study of his profession, and modestly said he had called to learn something of the work expected of him as a clerk and student. He wrote a good hand, and was a very obedient, industrious young man. I am glad to know that he has grown to be a very fair lawyer, and is a respectable citizen. I understand he has lately married, which is something that for the last five or six years I have thought was a very proper thing for a man of his age—or even my age—to do.

When I look at Mr. Locke and think of the position he now occupies in your community, I am reminded of his terrible disappointment when he failed to secure the place of assistant district attorney of this county. I am pleased to know that he has done fairly well without it, and I believe he is entirely cured of his thirst for political office.

I remember when Mr. Milburn, the gentleman who so gracefully presides on this occasion, was admitted to practice as a lawyer. He was a handsome young man, and I observe he has not altogether outgrown it. He usually had a law book under his arm in the street, and I used to wonder if he was trying to absorb law through his armpits. It is quite clear that he has managed to get a good deal of it into his head through some channel.

Just at this point it occurs to me that I have allowed myself to get on a wrong tack, and that I should have presented these latter recollections as illustrating how rapidly Buffalo's soil and atmosphere develop its young men, instead of referring to them as proofs of my own longevity. I am almost sorry that I have assumed to speak as though I was entitled to be regarded as an old citizen of Buffalo ; for, to be frank with you, I do not remember Joseph Ellicott nor the first Mayor of the city, who held that office in 1832. I recall distinctly, however, the celebration of the city's semi-centennial fifty years afterward, and the work George Hayward did to make it a success ought to make him remember it, too. I was very well acquainted with the man who was Mayor at that time. I believe he dabbled a little afterward in State and National politics. At any rate, I know he had a job for four years in government employ, and then, like many others in public position, when there came a change of Administration he lost his place. He was accused, I am told, of talking too much about the tariff, and was charged with attempting to ruin the country in sundry and divers ways. In point of fact, however, I am convinced that, notwithstanding all we hear of civil service reform, he was discharged for purely partisan reasons, and because someone else wanted his place. He did a great deal of hard work and was much perplexed and troubled ; but I know that his greatest trial was his alienation of many personal and political friends in making appointments to office. It was impossible to avoid this, and it will continue to be impossible in all like cases so long as the applicant for office and the man who is charged with the responsibility of appointment occupy such entirely different points of observation—and just so long as public duty may sometimes stand in the way of personal friendship.

I cannot forbear saying to you before I conclude that I have never forgotten the assurance I gave in the presence of thousands of my Buffalo friends, during the Presidential campaign of 1884, to the effect that, whatever the future might have in store for me, I should endeavor so to perform my duty as to merit their approval and friendship.   As I visit these friends again, self-examination brings home to me no reproaches. I know that I have done no violence to the sentiments and resolutions which, when I lived among you, received your approval and indorsement.

I feel that I can but feebly express my appreciation of the courtesy of this occasion—because language is weak. You must know how I have enjoyed the kindly greeting of my old friends ; and I hope I need not tell you how it delights me to witness the growth and increased beauty of my old home. I assure you that from the fullness of a grateful heart, I wish for the City of Buffalo boundless prosperity and advancement, and, for the people of Buffalo, Heaven's choicest blessings and the happiness and contentment which find their abiding-place in generous and unselfish hearts.

VI.

On being Received into Fellowship by his Neighbors, at Sandwich, Mass., July 25, 1891.

MR. CHAIRMAN AND LADIES AND GENTLEMEN:

More than eighteen hundred years ago a lawyer pertly asked the Divine Teacher, "And who is my neighbor?" The answer given to this question is quite familiar to us, and is embodied in the parable of the Good Samaritan. I hasten to assure you that this parable is here introduced for the lesson it teaches rather than for the purpose of suggesting that its incidents have any appropriateness to this occasion or its surroundings. I see no similarity between my situation and that of the man who went down from Jerusalem to Jericho and fell among thieves.

Whatever unfavorable impression may be prevalent concerning dog-day politics and politicians, which I left behind me, I am convinced that if there were a chapter written about the thieves of Cape Cod, it would be as short and as much to the point as the chapter on the snakes of Ireland, which began and ended in the single sentence, "There are no snakes in Ireland." I confess I have occasionally in my journeying seen a Levite pass by on the other side, but that was before I reached Barnstable County, and at a time when I cared but little whether he came on my side of the road or the other. But in the parable only one Good Samaritan is mentioned as having compassion on the man who went down from Jerusalem to Jericho, while the man who came down from New York to Cape Cod and Barnstable County has been surrounded by them ever since he started.

I suppose that when you greet me as your neighbor, to-day, you have in mind the fact that I have come among you to spend at least a large part of each year, and that I intend to maintain this sort of residence here as long as the expense of farming and fishing enables me, from a slender purse, to meet your rate of taxation and the cost of provisions. In the meantime I declare my intention to be a good neighbor. No quarrels can arise over my line fences, for I have none. I keep no chickens, and my cattle do not run at large. I suppose I have pretty decided political opinions, and I judge from the election returns of this county that they are not such as have heretofore received the utmost sympathy and encouragement in this particular locality. Notwithstanding, however, my positive knowledge that the large majority of my new neighbors are in a sad state of delusion politically, I shall not quarrel with them on this subject, nor permit myself to become a political scold. I must be peaceful and neighborly, even if I see my neighbors go to political destruction before my eyes. Besides, I think there are prudential reasons why I should, in present circumstances, be politically docile. To be sure I have not, like the man who started for Jericho, fallen among thieves; but I know perfectly well that I have politically fallen among those who are too many for me, and that only my own peacefulness or many conversions to my side in Barnstable County can secure my immunity from being stripped of my political raiment and wounded and left half dead, as was the case with the man from Jerusalem. While I do not want to tempt such a fate, I confess that my political convictions are so fixed that I can hardly avoid dwelling upon them even here. Some things we can certainly do safely and properly. We can be tolerant of one another. We can constantly test our political beliefs by the light of patriotism, good citizenship, and true Americanism, and we can be brave enough and honest enough to follow where they lead. We shall thus elevate our political efforts and find incentives to activity in a determination to aid in making our country as great as it ought to be, and in securing to ourselves and our fellow-countrymen the happiness and prosperity due to all of us under a free government by the people. If our political endeavor is thus directed, we shall rid ourselves of the blindness and bigotry which accept unreasoning party association as a sufficient guide to political action, and which count the spoils of partisan success the sole object of political struggle. So, though we may differ in party affiliation, if we thoughtfully and sincerely believe and act, we may still be the best of neighbors, bound together by an unselfish willingness to forego special advantages which can only be gained at the expense of our fellows, and all engage, with hearty co-operation, in the achievement of our country's high destiny.

I am inclined at this point to suggest to you the lesson of the parable with which I began. It teaches that a neighbor is not necessarily one whose residence is near, and that kindness and consideration make men neighbors. The Samaritan was the neighbor of his robbed and wounded fellow-man, not because he lived near him, but because in his need he had compassion on him and bound up his wounds and cared for him. Indeed, we all know that the worst quarrels often arise and the most bitter malice and resentment often rage, among those whose homes are adjoining. These are sometimes called bad neighbors; but in my opinion they ought not to be called neighbors at all.

You are by no means to suppose, from what has been said, that I in the least fail to appreciate my good fortune in being an almost fully fledged resident of Cape Cod and Barnstable County. I prize my home here so much that I actually look forward, with trepidation, to the time when I shall temporarily leave it, fearing that in my absence some envious mortal from a distant and benighted quarter may, in some manner, rob me of it. The wonder is that the entire American people do not flock hither and attempt to take possession of all our domain in true Oklahoma style. Let us look for a moment at some of our suburbs and surroundings. We have located Boston just far enough away to be a convenient trading-place, and yet not near enough to annoy us with its noise and dirt, nor to permit its children to damage our cranberry bogs. Though we know that the Pilgrims landed in Barnstable County, we see fit to maintain Plymouth Rock just far enough outside to serve as a stimulus to our patriotism without being bothered by the strangers who visit the spot. We keep the waters of Buzzard's Bay clean and pure for fishing purposes, and do not propose to have our preserve stirred up and contaminated by the inflow of other waters through the Cape Cod Canal.

We pity the deluded men and women who know nothing of Barnstable County, and who have doubts regarding the fertility and productiveness of our soil. Cape Cod never fails to respond to intelligent husbandry, though we do not expect immunity from the depression in farming occupations which afflicts our agricultural brethren in other localities. We make no complaint at such times, for it is easy to beat our plowshares into fishing-hooks, and we know that when farming does not pay, neither drouth nor destructive insects will prevent the fish from biting. The delightful healthfulness of our climate is so perfect that the practice of medicine is the one occupation which never thrives. Recreation in every sensible and wholesome variety crowds upon us, and, free from vain and distracting care, we enjoy with thankfulness the peace and quietude which here have their abiding-place.

With a heart full of gratitude for the cordiality and consideration which you have at all times extended to me, I have, with the utmost sincerity, attempted to demonstrate my appreciation of all I enjoy among you, and to approve myself in your sight as worthy to be admitted to free fellowship in the Cape Cod community. If more is needed to prove my complete devotion to the guild, let me remind you of the saying, "A man is known by the company he keeps." If he is born and reared amid certain conditions he may, from habit and association and without severe condemnation, be content with them and the companionship which they impose, though such companionship be undesirable. But when, after mature deliberation and in full view of the importance and significance of his choice of neighbors, he chooses an abode with complete knowledge of those by whom he is to be surrounded, the adage I have quoted should be applied to him with the utmost strictness. I have only to add that so far as my case is related to the people of Barnstable County, I am entirely content to be thus judged.

I must remember that you have not only kindly spoken of me as your neighbor, but have also referred to me as an ex-President. I have never failed to be profoundly sensible of the generosity and confidence of my countrymen in making me the recipient of the greatest honor that can be bestowed upon any man; but what I remember most vividly in connection with the great office of President is its responsibilities and the labor and anxiety attending an attempt to do the work which the people had intrusted to me. The impress made upon the mind and heart of one who stands daily face to face with the American people, charged with the protection of their rights and the advancement of their varied interests, can never be effaced, and scarcely gives room for the gratification naturally supposed to attach to high and exalted place. I am led to mention in this connection, as a spur to official labor and as a sign of political health, the watchfulness of the people and their exactions from their chosen representative to whom they have confided their highest trust. If they are exacting and critical, sometimes almost to the point of injustice, this is better than popular heedlessness and indifference concerning the conduct of public servants.

It has always seemed to me that, beyond the greatness of the office and the supreme importance of its duties and responsibilities, the most impressive thing connected with the Presidency is the fact that after its honor has been relinquished, and after its labor and responsibility are past, we simply see that a citizen whom the people had selected from their ranks to do their bidding for a time and to be their agent in the discharge of public duty, has laid aside the honor and the work of the highest office in the world and has returned again to the people, to resume at their side the ordinary duties which pertain to everyday citizenship. Here, he is, or should be, subject to the same rules of behavior which apply to his fellow-countrymen, and should be accorded the same fair and decent treatment, unless he has in some way forfeited it.

But it must be admitted that our people are by no means united in their ideas concerning the place which our ex-Presidents ought to occupy, or the disposition which should be made of them. Of course the subject would be relieved of all uncertainty and embarrassment if every President would die at the end of his term. This does not seem, however, to meet the views of those who under such an arrangement would be called on to do the dying; and so some of them continue to live, and thus perpetuate the perplexity of those who burden themselves with plans for their utilization or disposition.

A very amusing class among these anxious souls make us useful by laying upon our shoulders all sorts of political conspiracies. If they are to be believed, we are constantly engaged in plotting for our own benefit and advancement, and are quite willing, for the sake of reaching our ends, not only to destroy the party to which we belong, but to subvert popular liberty and utterly uproot our free American institutions. Others seem of the opinion that we should be utilized as orators at county fairs and other occasions of all sorts and at all sorts of places. Some think we should interfere in every political contest, and should be constantly in readiness to express an opinion on every subject of a political character that anybody has the ingenuity to suggest. Others still regard it as simply dreadful for us to do these things, and are greatly disturbed every time an ex-President ventures to express an opinion on any subject. Not a few appear to think we should simply exist and be blind, deaf, and dumb the remainder of our days.

In the midst of all this a vast majority of the plain American people are, as usual, sound and sensible. They are self-respecting enough and have dignity enough to appreciate the fact that their respect and confidence as neighbors is something which an ex-President may well covet, and which, like any other man, he ought to earn. They will measure the regard and consideration due to him by his usefulness and worth as a private citizen. They will not agree that the fact of his having been President gives him any license for bad behavior, nor that it burdens him with an unfavorable presumption. These are sentiments which we, on the side of the ex-Presidents, will gladly adopt, and these conditions we can well afford to accept. In conclusion I desire to express the confident opinion, based upon a short experience, and supplemented by the kindness which characterizes this occasion, that no better place can be found as a retreat for ex-Presidents than Barnstable County. They are sure to receive here all the Cape Cod hospitality and friendly treatment they deserve, with a great many other things thrown in.

From the bottom of my heart I say to you, that while I do not mean in the least to detract from the honor arising from the incumbency of high official place, nor undervalue the designation of ex-President, the pleasure which this occasion affords me chiefly consists in the cordiality with which you have greeted me as your neighbor.

VII.

Concerning a Renomination for President.

LAKEWOOD, N. J., March 9, 1892.

THE HON. EDWARD S. BRAGG:

MY DEAR SIR: Your letter of the 5th inst. is received. I have thought until now that I might continue silent on the subject which, under the high sanction of your position as my "fellow-Democrat and fellow-citizen," and in your relation as a true and trusted friend, you present to me. If, in answering your questions, I might only consider my personal desires and my individual ease and comfort, my response would be promptly made, and without the least reservation or difficulty.

But if you are right in supposing that the subject is related to a duty I owe to the country and to my party, a condition exists which makes such private and personal considerations entirely irrelevant. I cannot, however, refrain from declaring to you that my experience in the great office of President of the United States has so impressed me with the solemnity of the trust, and its awful responsibilities, that I cannot bring myself to regard a candidacy for the place as something to be won by personal strife and active self-assertion.

I have also an idea that the Presidency is pre-eminently the people's office, and I have been sincere in my constant advocacy of the effective participation in political affairs on the part of all our citizens. Consequently, I believe the people should be heard in the choice of their party candidates, and that they themselves should make nominations as directly as is consistent with open, fair, and full party organizations and methods.

I speak of these things solely for the purpose of advising you that my conception of the nature of the Presidential office, and my conviction that the voters of our party should be free in the selection of their candidates, preclude the possibility of my leading and pushing a self-seeking canvass for the Presidential nomination, even if I had a desire to be again a candidate.

Believing that the complete supremacy of Democratic principles means increased national prosperity and the increased
happiness of our people, I am earnestly anxious for the success
of the party. I am confident success is still within our reach,
but I believe this is a time for Democratic thoughtfulness and
deliberation, not only as to candidates, but concerning party
action upon questions of immense interest to the patriotic and
intelligent voters of the land, who watch for an assurance of
safety as the price of their confidence and support.

Yours very truly,

GROVER CLEVELAND.

VIII.

To James H. Bible, Chattanooga, Tenn.

LAKEWOOD, N. J., April 8, 1892.

MY DEAR SIR:

I desire to thank you for the report of the meeting at Chattanooga, which you so kindly sent me, and for the friendly
words you spoke of me on that occasion.

I am exceedingly anxious to have our party do exactly the
right thing at the Chicago Convention, and I hope that the
delegates will be guarded by judgment and actuated by true
Democratic spirit and the single desire to succeed on principle.

I should not be frank if I did not say to you that I often
fear I do not deserve all the kind things such friends as you
say of me, and I have frequent misgivings as to the wisdom of
again putting me in nomination.

I, therefore, am anxious that sentiment and too unmeasured
personal devotion should be checked when the delegates to
the convention reach the period of deliberation. In any event
there will be no disappointment for me in the result.

Yours very truly,

GROVER CLEVELAND.

INDEX.